WASHINGTON'S END

WASHINGTON'S END

THE FINAL YEARS AND FORGOTTEN STRUGGLE

JONATHAN HORN

THORNDIKE PRESS
A part of Gale, a Cengage Company

LIBRARY OF CONGRESS CIP DATA ON FILE.
CATALOGUING IN PUBLICATION FOR THIS BOOK
IS AVAILABLE FROM THE LIBRARY OF CONGRESS

ISBN-13: 978-1-4328-7915-0 (hardcover alk. paper)

Published in 2020 by arrangement with Scribner, an imprint of Simon & Schuster, Inc.

Printed in Mexico
Print Number: 01   Print Year: 2020

To my parents for a beginning
To Caroline and Laura for
believing in the end

We know little of ourselves & much less
the designs of Providence.

— George Washington

CONTENTS

LIST OF MAPS

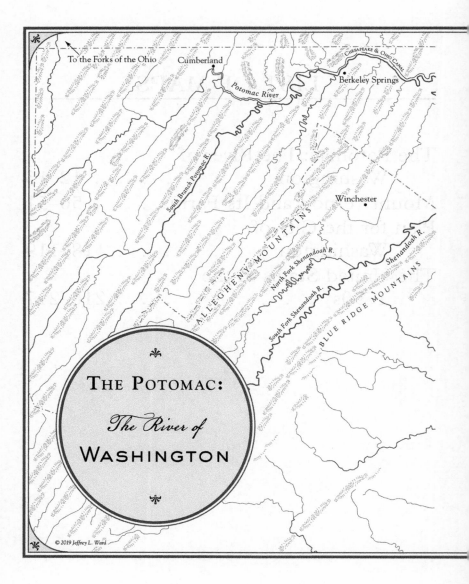

To the Forks of the Ohio · Cumberland

CHESAPEAKE & OHIO CANAL

Potomac River

· Berkeley Springs

South Branch Potomac R.

Winchester ·

ALLEGHENY MOUNTAINS

North Fork Shenandoah R.

Shenandoah R.

South Fork Shenandoah R.

BLUE RIDGE MOUNTAINS

THE POTOMAC:

The River of

WASHINGTON

© 2019 Jeffrey L. Ward

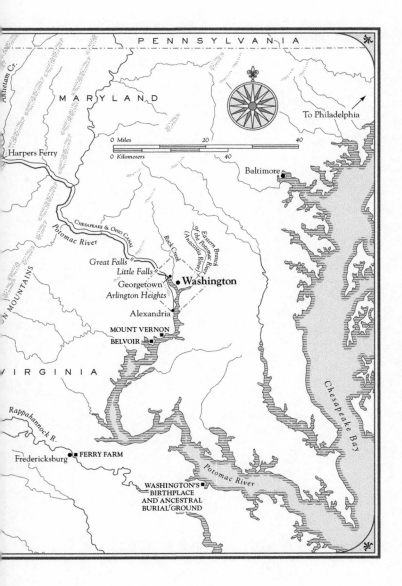

PENNSYLVANIA

MARYLAND

To Philadelphia

Antietam Cr.

Harpers Ferry

0 Miles   20   40

0 Kilometers   40

Baltimore

CHESAPEAKE & OHIO CANAL

Potomac River

Rock Creek

Eastern Branch
of the Potomac River
(Anacostia River)

Great Falls

Little Falls

Georgetown

Arlington Heights

• Washington

Alexandria

MOUNT VERNON

BELVOIR

VIRGINIA

Chesapeake Bay

Rappahannock R.

Fredericksburg • ■ FERRY FARM

WASHINGTON'S
BIRTHPLACE
AND ANCESTRAL
BURIAL GROUND

Potomac River

MOUNTAINS

PROLOGUE:
HISTORY'S CURRENT

Peering through the doorway into the chamber minutes before noon on March 4, 1797, John Adams hears whispers and sees the backside of the hero receding down the aisle: his long hair powdered and pulled back into a queue that is tied and tucked into a bag below the nape of the neck, in a style common among the now old men who wrote the first chapter of their country's history. The back of the head would look much like Adams's own if not standing a half foot taller. The whispers in the chamber rise to a roar as the great man nears the halfway point between the door to the east and the dais to the west. "Washington! Washington!" the people packing the gallery on the north side cry. Soon they will see what no one alive ever has: the title of head of state peacefully passing from one breathing man to another. The thought leaves Adams light-headed.

Outside the chamber, the wind blows from the southwest, the direction George Washington will soon ride to his Virginia home, as if nature itself resists his leaving Philadelphia, the country's interim capital. Adams waits under the cover of the portico connecting the lower chamber of Congress Hall to the old state house now shorn of the rotting steeple that watched over the Continental Congress in 1775, at the beginning of the Revolutionary War, when he nominated Washington for commander in chief of the Continental Army. The old stories of Washington's courage during the French and Indian War had impressed everyone. How "handsome" he looked in the uniform he wore to the Congress! Even then, Adams envied Washington. "[His] excellent universal character would command the approbation of all America and unite the cordial exertions of all the colonies better than any other person in the Union," Adams remembers having told the delegates, while worrying that the people might turn the general into an idol.

In a sense, the people have. They bestow Washington's name on their children and towns, hang his portrait in their homes, and celebrate his birthday with balls, like the "splendid but tedious" one Adams attended ten days ago when Washington turned sixty-five. The Philadelphia socialites have hinted at the advice they would give: rent the house Washington will vacate; dress and act as he would. Disappointment, Adams knows, awaits. The people must adjust to a new kind of president, one who cannot afford to entertain in the same style. No more formal dinner parties with carefully curated guest lists; the company of "a few select friends" must do. No more driving through Philadelphia's streets behind six horses; two must suffice. No more congressmen pausing to pay tribute on the president's birthday, if for no other reason than the calendar: Adams's upcoming sixty-second will occur during a recess (he has already checked).

Adams has not slept in more than a day. The stress has built ever since he heard Washington promise to attend the inauguration. Adams misses Abigail, the wife he left back home in Massachusetts, though even she doubts whether he can "fill" Washington's "place." It is not because of a superior education, for Adams knows Washington's schooling ceased around his fifteenth birthday, before he ever attended a college like Adams's alma mater, Harvard. Nor does Adams think it is because of Washington's superior character, for "there are thousands of others who have in them all the essential qualities — moral & intellectual — which compose it." Washington's willingness to surrender power merely conforms to a culture obsessed with Cincinnatus, the ancient Roman general who saved the republic only to surrender power and return to his farm. Had Washington lived in another culture or at another time, he might have instead copied Caesar. Where the people applauding in the chamber see selflessness, Adams sees ambition for the same fame he detests himself for coveting.

What, then, accounts for Washington's "immense elevation above his fellows"? The answers, Adams believes, are so obvious as to be overlooked: for example, Washington's standing six feet tall and looking even taller thanks to the king-sized hands and feet crowning those long, "elegant" limbs. There has never been a choice but to look up to Washington. Hailing from Virginia, the oldest colony and largest state, has magnified his advantage because "Virginian geese are all swans," or so they tell themselves in the Old Dominion. Wedding the wealthy widow Martha Dandridge Custis thirty-eight years ago has given Washington control over an immense fortune and an unsurpassed reputation for "disinterestedness," all because he could afford to serve without salary during the war. Having no biological children — the two Custis grandchildren who have lived with him during the presidency are the fruit of Mrs. Washington's first marriage — has reassured a people paranoid about hereditary succession and has mostly spared Washington from irritating rumors like the one dogging Adams about positioning his oldest son, John Quincy, as heir apparent. Possessing unusual "self-command" allows Washington to conceal his fierce temper, even though he often loses control of it behind closed doors. In public, he has "the gift of silence," a rare talent for pursing his lips and clenching his jaw so as to hide those ugly blackish-looking false teeth and let people imagine instead the wondrous depths of "rivers whose bottoms we cannot see."

Washington knows how to leave people wanting more. For their eyes, he has always staged his entrances and exits with "a strain of Shakespearean . . . excellence": the moment in 1775 when he "darted" out of the room rather than ("modesty" forbid!) hear his name nominated for commander of the Continental Army; the "solemn" scene eight years later when he resigned his commission after securing America's independence; the reluctance he manifested before emerging from retirement to chair the Constitutional Convention in 1787 and to accept the newly created office of president in 1789; the prophetic-sounding farewell address he published this past September, weeks before the election so as to deter the electors from giving him the third term he would otherwise have received.

An encore now ensues. As the cheers in the chamber grow louder, Washington walks faster so as to signal how desperate he is to break free of the trappings of power that have detained him for two terms from Mount Vernon, his beloved Virginia estate overlooking the Potomac River. This time, Adams believes, it is more than an act. Washington staying in office a single day more would endanger his health. "He must plunge into agriculture and ride away his reflections," the memories of the controversies and calumnies that he fears have tarnished his reputation.

The country has divided into the parties Washington hoped never to see but can no longer transcend. Federalists have supported his administration; Republicans have opposed it. Both parties have their bases: the Federalists in the North, the Republicans in the South. Both parties have their own presses. Off the Republican ones come stories accusing Washington of betraying the legacy of the American Revolution and of craving a crown. Not being accustomed to criticism makes it harder to bear. The words wound Washington deeper than the public imagines. "His skin is thinner than mine," Adams realizes. Some say Washington refused to stand for a third term, in part, because he knew he could no longer carry every electoral vote as he did in his first two elections.

So it is Adams who has suffered the indignity of defeating the Republican candidate, Thomas Jefferson of Virginia, by only three votes. Finishing second has given Jefferson what the past eight years of personal experience have revealed to Adams as "the most insignificant office that ever the invention of man contrived": the vice presidency. Not far from where Washington now sits waits Jefferson, looking about the same height as his fellow Virginian but powdering his hair only a little and letting the queue hang free over his back. Not since resigning as secretary of state at the end of 1793, after feuding with Washington's other cabinet members over foreign policy, has Jefferson appeared in Philadelphia. He "is as he was," Adams notes, as romantic as ever about the bloodlettings and beheadings known as the

French Revolution.

Nothing, it seems, will "awake" Jefferson from his "golden dreams" and show him that the French Revolution has replaced monarchy not with the liberty he hoped but with the mobocracy Adams dreaded from the start. Four years have passed since Louis XVI, the French king who sent ships and soldiers to support the American Revolution, went to the guillotine and his country, now a republic, went back to war against the United States' old colonial overlord. Britain has fought on even as Europe's other royal powers have fallen to the French forces fanning out across the Continent. With Republicans favoring France and with Federalists favoring Britain, the war has accelerated the forces pulling Americans to opposite sides, even as Washington has said the country will take no sides. He has labored to keep America at peace. Maintaining it has required him to ratify with George III of Britain the so-called Jay Treaty, a controversial accord that Republicans denounce as a betrayal of France. To undermine the deal, they have gone so far as to urge the French to meddle in the recent election on Jefferson's behalf. Franco-American relations have all but collapsed. There are whispers of war. Already French privateers have declared open season on American shipping.

If war comes, the American people will long for Washington. They will want a general at the helm. Instead, they will have Adams. The years chairing committees at the Continental Congress and conducting diplomacy abroad have brought him to this moment. Down the aisle that Washington has walked — and up the dais where he sits — now goes John Adams. The sword he wears across the waist of a light-colored suit cannot change how he sees himself: a "short, thick, fat" man insecure over having never worn a sword in battle. "Adams!" the people cheer, but not as loudly as they cheered for Washington, as if having engaged in the ritual before has dulled their enthusiasm. "I have been so strangely used in this Country, so belied and so undefended," Adams thinks. Republicans think him too much a Federalist. Federalists know him to be too much an independent. Even those who have supported his election do not love him. They "seem to be afraid to approve anybody but Washington." Only thanks to Mrs. Washington does Adams know he had the support of her husband in the election.

The faint feeling lingers. Perhaps Adams should say little more than the oath required for office. The address Washington gave at his second inaugural totaled just 135 words. But silence has never been among Adams's gifts. Even if it leaves him "open to scoffs and sarcasms," Adams must speak his mind. He worries he will not "get through" it all. On he goes praising the Constitution, insisting that he has no desire to turn the Senate into a House of Lords or the presidency into a monarchy, and warning about the danger of political parties and foreign attachments. Toward the end comes the tribute he has prepared to Washington. "In that retirement, which is his voluntary choice, may he long live to enjoy the delicious recollection of his services, the gratitude of mankind, the happy fruits of them to himself and the world, which are daily increasing, and that splendid prospect of the future fortunes of his country, which is opening from year to year." Knowing that people worry how the country will endure without Washington makes it necessary to add this: "His name may be still a rampart, and the knowledge that he lives a bulwark, against all open or secret enemies of his country's peace."

The worries for Washington's health vanish. The old man suddenly looks "as serene and unclouded as the day." Washington needs to say nothing in response, for the expression says everything. "Ay!" Adams imagines his predecessor saying. "I am fairly out and you fairly in! See which of us will be happiest." The chief justice administers the oath. To the people watching, Adams bows. There is "more weeping than there has ever been at the representation of any tragedy." He looks for a "dry eye" in the room but can find "scarcely" one other than Washington's. The number of "ladies" in attendance astonishes Adams. Then the realization strikes: The audience has not come to see Adams's reign begin. The people have come to witness Washington's end.

Into the freezing air on the morning of March 9, down the paved streets splitting the brick sidewalks, past the mansions belonging to the wealthiest of the forty thousand or so people who call Philadelphia home, away from the market and circus and theater, beyond the reach of the tidy grid, down the banks of the Delaware River to the southwest, toward the head of the Chesapeake Bay, and onward to the Potomac River, the carriage rolls. Only "a child within view of the holidays" can appreciate the "happiness" spurring George Washington. He has tried to hide it. "My countenance never yet betrayed my feelings," he insists. But for months, he has "counted" the weeks and days until this moment: his "release" from the high walls running to the right and left of the three-story house he has rented in Philadelphia. Mount Vernon lies ahead. The journey, he expects, will take about a week. The luggage-laden wagon accompanying the carriage will undoubtedly slow the pace. So will the women sitting on either side of him.

On one side sits sixty-five-year-old Martha. She is "dear Patcy" when they are alone, "Mrs. Washington" when in company. With a double chin and dentures she did not have when they wed thirty-eight years ago, she will not miss needing to have her white hair dressed every day. For many years, "the first and dearest wish" of her "heart," he recognizes, has been for the two of them "to grow old in solitude and tranquility together." Unless she dies before him — and he remarries a much younger woman, which he has vowed never to do so long as he retains "the faculty of reasoning" — he knows he will never reproduce. The problem, he tells himself, lay with her, never mind the two children she brought to Mount Vernon from an earlier marriage. Having lost them both to disease has made her all the more protective of her grandchildren and all the more worried she will lose those she loves. Between coughs caused by a "violent cold," she begs Washington to "remember" the pet parrot they left behind in Philadelphia.

On the other side come worries for a dog named Frisk from one of the two Custis grandchildren who have grown up with the Washingtons. Nelly Custis, an endearing doe-eyed girl approaching her eighteenth birthday, misses her "poor little" canine companion. Alas, the carriage could not accommodate the unruly animal. Along with the parrot and many other belongings, Frisk will come to Mount Vernon later by boat, Washington promises, though he personally "should not pine much if both [pets] were forgot." At least, he will not have to deal with the other adopted grandchild, Nelly's brother, fifteen-year-old George Washington Parke Custis (Wash for short), getting carriage sick again. Allegedly to study, the boy has gone to the College of New Jersey in Princeton.

In his place travels another namesake: seventeen-year-old Georges Washington Lafayette, a refugee of the French Revolution. Ever since arriving in America in 1795, the tall and thin teenager known as Georges has brought out emotions Washington has struggled to "reconcile." First is pleasure because Georges's upright character conjures memories of his father, the Marquis de Lafayette, who was just a few years older when he sailed from France, risked his noble blood and riches in America's fight for freedom, and won a place in Washington's military family and in his heart as "the man I love." Second is sadness because the gloomy look creeping across the boy's face reminds how the seeds of revolution that the older Lafayette brought back to his native soil yielded a bloody harvest that spread beyond his control, forced him to flee the radicals taking power in France, and landed him in the custody of royalist forces who liked him just as little and eventually banished him to the Austrian prison where he has suffered since. Finally, there is lingering embarrassment for the months Washington waited before welcoming Georges into the president's house for fear of being criticized by pro-French Republicans.

Never did Washington imagine the newspapers would take their attacks so far. "Every act" of his life, he believes, has been "misrepresented and tortured with a view to make it appear odious." For eight years, he fought the British in the field. Now, because he recently signed a treaty with them, "infamous scribblers" hiding behind pseudonyms dare to suggest that he supported the redcoats all along. To prove the preposterous, Benjamin Franklin Bache, the editor of the Philadelphia-based *Aurora,* has reprinted old forged letters that first appeared during the Revolutionary War and that, if real, would have unmasked Washington as a halfhearted patriot. Long as he resisted responding to these obvious lies — much as he wanted to trust the people to find truth for themselves — the "pains" Bache "has taken . . . to impose [the letters] on the public as genuine productions" have required a response. Part of Washington's last full day in office went to finishing a letter exposing the falsehoods for the public and "posterity."

Riding away from Philadelphia has not made the anger over these libels go away. "To the wearied traveler who sees a resting place and is bending his body to lean thereon, I now compare myself," he says. "But to be suffered to do *this* in peace is, I perceive, too much to be endured by *some.*" He recalls the discontent that infected his camp in Newburgh, New York, during the final months of the Revolutionary War. If only the critics now accusing him of having "cankered the principles of republicanism" could have heard him then, as he persuaded his underpaid officers not to challenge civilian authority, "just" and "honorable" as their grievances were. If only the critics now accusing him of acting like a king could see him presently riding home to his farm. "To some whose minds are differently formed from mine," he thinks, the parades that people along the way wish to give "would have been highly relished, but I avoided in every instance where I had any previous knowledge of the intention."

At times, he cannot elude the militiamen on horseback desperate to escort him. One troop accompanies the caravan through Delaware; another meets it in Maryland. The ruts in the road increase as the wheels roll south; the number of "buildings and other improvements" that one can see decreases. It is always this way when crossing from the North into the South. The chasm between the sections has only grown as states such as Pennsylvania break free of the slave labor system entrenched in the South. Only by rotating slaves in and out of Pennsylvania can one skirt the state's "gradual abolition" law giving freedom to any person residing in Pennsylvania for six straight months. Word from Mount Vernon is that Washington's prized chef Hercules, who left Philadelphia earlier, has dis-appeared despite his having promised never to run off and despite there being orders to watch him carefully even so. From the road, Washington sends a letter asking if Hercules has shown his face back in Philadelphia. Perhaps he grew too fond of the freedoms he found there. "If he can be discovered & apprehended," Washington writes, "send him round in the vessel" that will carry the other belongings to Mount Vernon.

On March 12, the caravan reaches Balti-more. "Met & escorted into town by a great concourse of people," Washington notes in his diary, before setting off again the next morning and the morning after that over dirt roads cut through thick woods. The trees have stood for centuries, long before any of Washington's ancestors sailed from England for America in the mid-1600s and long before any of his countrymen pushed west over the mountains into the Ohio Country, the wilderness where rivers drain not east back to the Atlantic Ocean but west to the Mississippi, the river marking the United States' western boundary. Can a divided republic of several million people dispersed across an undeveloped country of vast distances hold together? Only "experi-ence," Washington thinks, will reveal the answer. Hope, however, lies ahead.

Almost seven years have passed since Congress voted to create a permanent seat for the federal government on the Potomac, the river that rises over the mountains not far from the Ohio Country and flows east between Maryland and Virginia toward the Chesapeake Bay and the Atlantic Ocean, the river that Adams won sixty-nine of his electoral votes above but only two below. The selection of the Potomac emerged as part of a compromise between representatives from different sections of the country. Where exactly the new capital should go on the river was entrusted solely to Washington's discretion as president. He settled on a spot just up the Potomac from his Mount Vernon home but just below the falls, the line of rocks and rapids that have thwarted generations of English-speaking sailors seeking to ascend the river.

The four ten-mile boundary lines he plotted compose a perfect diamond-square federal district incorporating land from both sides of the river. The town of Alexandria, formerly of Virginia, anchors the bottom corner of the district nearest to Mount Vernon. On the western end of what was the Maryland side stands the village of Georgetown. Just east of it, out of the V formed by the confluence of the Potomac and its so-called Eastern Branch, rises a new capital city, whose construction Washington has personally directed but whose destiny nature itself, he believes, dictates. The city will be the Union's core, the heart to which every limb of the country connects. Once the canals being constructed open navigation of the river beyond the falls, the city will draw the West into trade with the East. Once the national university he imagines opens its doors, the city will draw into friendship the finest students of the country, its future leaders from the North and the South.

The sound of artillery echoes through the woods as the carriage climbs a final hill and enters a clearing where other roads converge upon what, if finished, would be the largest building he has ever seen: the future Capitol of the United States. The outlines of second-story windows have begun emerging in the sandstone walls rising beneath the scaffolding of the north wing, while only an imperfectly laid foundation reveals the location of the south wing. Between the two wings lie empty trenches, out of which a dome and portico must one day grow. The delays and disappointments have detained Washington at his desk deep into the night and have dis-

33

seminated "doubt" and "despair" in the "public mind" about the future of the project. "The year 1800," he has repeatedly warned, "is approaching by hasty strides." By the end of that year, the sandstone walls must be ready to house the Congress and the wilderness around them ready to replace Philadelphia as the capital of the United States.

Only the broad avenues radiating out from the clearing around the Capitol hint at the possibility of a city beyond the ring of trees, at the master plan that the French "genius" Pierre Charles L'Enfant conceived. Progress would have come so much quicker if only L'Enfant would have subordinated himself to the commissioners appointed to oversee the project. But without their permission, he tore down a private home obstructing one of his precious avenues, as if "every person and thing was *obliged* to yield" to his plan. Such eccentricity left no choice but to dispense with the indispensable planner, even though no one knew how to replace him. "It is much to be regretted," Washington thinks, "that men who possess talents which fit them for peculiar purposes should almost invariably be under the influence of untoward dispositions."

Fording a little creek called the Tiber and

following the tree stumps and brush known as Pennsylvania Avenue for more than a mile to the northwest take the carriage into another clearing. As before, artillery welcomes Washington. So, this time, do "huzzas" from the crowd gathered beside the almost finished off-white-colored stone walls forming the president's future house. Some have said the amount of land set aside for the house suits a king better than a president. He disagrees. The office needs room to expand. "A house which would be very proper for a President of the United States for some years to come might not be considered as corresponding with other circumstances at a more distant period," when the United States has fulfilled the future he sees for it as a continental empire with this capital city as its center. Only recently has he grown comfortable using the name his appointees have given the city: Washington.

The honor would have fulfilled the ambitions of the younger self who dreamed of making a name for himself on the Potomac. In search of fame, he went up the river, over the mountains, and into the Ohio Country, where he heard the first shots of the French and Indian War "whistle" past him in 1754 ("there was something charming in the sound"), miraculously survived Indians surprising and slaughtering the British regulars whom he accompanied the following year (he can still hear the screams), and glimpsed a future for his country apart from the empires of Europe. This future, he believes, still awaits his country upriver. But it is no longer the future he sees for himself.

That future is downriver. The men who have borne his surname through the centuries have not lived long lives. "I will move gently down the stream of life, until I sleep with my fathers," he says. Their bodies lie near his birthplace, on the lower stretch of the river, where the water widens before meeting the bay. He feels his age every time his dentures push out his lips as if the gold coils wiring the upper and lower ivory bases will spring out of his mouth if he dares unclench his jaw. His last real tooth — the one that fit into a hole in the apparatus and, thus, held it in place — has recently come out. His replacements — actual human teeth affixed to the ivory — wiggle, wobble, and wear away. His face looks distorted, he thinks. His hands are not as steady as they once were. His back stoops. His hearing has weakened but not so much that he does not hear the whispers about his senility. "His memory, always bad," has become "worse."

His vision has declined. Objects that look clear in the distance blur as they near.

From the president's house, he can see miles down the Potomac as the river flowing east bends rightward to the south and then disappears after Alexandria. Though he cannot see the rest of the road, he has never doubted the destination. "The remainder of my life (which in the course of nature cannot be long) will be occupied in rural amusements . . . at Mount Vernon, more than 20 miles from which, after I arrive there, it is not likely I ever shall be."

The traveler on the road to Mount Vernon today discovers that the Potomac delivers one last surprising twist just before the mansion house. The usually eastbound river traveling south for a stretch past Alexandria makes another and far more dramatic right turn, as if intent on completing a sweeping U. Suddenly downriver is west; upriver is east. The reversal cannot last long, but it persists just long enough, perhaps, to fool a farsighted old man nearing the end of his journey. He might confuse upriver with down; his country's future with his own; the virgin water coming from the mountains with the water that has already borne his sparkling image toward the bay.

A little more than a year after returning to private life, George Washington will return to public service. The soldier and statesman famous for surrendering power will reclaim the republic's most awesome title: commander in chief. The man committed to concealing his emotions will feud with his immediate and future successors and will release his fury. The American Cincinnatus, who has played the leading role in what he calls the "public theatre," will struggle to read his lines in the twilight. To be fair, there is no obvious script for an ex-president to follow, no modern precedent. The kings of Europe do not surrender their crowns without bloodshed. Louis XVI of France lost his head. In a different sense, Washington will lose his, too.

For too long, the story of Washington's last years has been squeezed into the margins of manuscripts, if included at all. Writers nearing the end of the greatest American life have already exceeded their word counts, deadlines, and sometimes even the hours allotted to them on earth, as in the case of the man who aspired to be Washington's most comprehensive biographer, the Pulitzer Prize–winning historian Douglas Southall Freeman. The final sentence to flow from Freeman's pen on the day of his death in 1953 appears at the end of the sixth volume of his biography, which takes Washington only to the end of his first term as president.

The present author, while in no way aspiring to finish Freeman's work as others have attempted, does dust off the largely forgotten rule that the finest of Freeman's writings follow: that the biographer should supply readers with "no information beyond" what his subjects "possessed at a particular moment" so as to present the past with all its uncertainties. This "fog-of-war" style lets the reader view history through the eyes of those who made it rather than through the hindsight of historians convinced of the omniscience of their own narratives. "A biographer," one learns from reading Freeman, "has no place on the stage. When he has made his bow to his audience and has spoken his prologue, telling what he will try to exhibit, it is his duty to retire to the wings, to raise the curtain and to leave the play to the actors."

To whom, then, should the chronicler of Washington's last years cede the stage? Not to the title character alone, for no longer can he control the script the way he once did. No longer can he alone even speak for Washington. The name is no longer his own.

It belongs to a rising capital city that must somehow contain the personalities and parties he no longer can. This is Washington's end. This is Washington's beginning.

■ ■ ■ ■

PART I
CITIZEN

■ ■ ■ ■

PART 1

CITIZEN

CHAPTER ONE:
PRIVATE LIFE

Like everyone else she knew, Eliza Willing
Powel immediately reverted to referring to
the now ex-president as General Washington. He was her friend. Upon leaving Philadelphia, he had sold her the writing desk he
had used in office. Only after moving it a
few blocks to the ornate house where she
and her late husband had once entertained
at the center of the city's most exclusive
social circle did she discover a surprise: in
his rush to return to Mount Vernon, the
general had not left a clean desk. Inside one
of the drawers lay "a large bundle of letters."

The general needed to know about these
letters. They bore the signature of a woman.
"Suppose I should prove incontestably that
you have without design put into my possession the love letters of a lady addressed
to you under the most solemn sanction, and
a large packet too," Eliza wrote. "What will

the Goddess of Prudence and Circumspection say to her favorite son and votary for his dereliction of principles to which he has hitherto made such serious sacrifices? Was the taste of your sex predominant in your breast? And did the love of variety so preponderate that because you had never blundered as President . . . , you [were] determined to try its delights as a private gentleman?" The joke, she decided at this point, had gone far enough. "I will with the generosity of my sex relieve you." The letters she had found did not come from the pen of a paramour. They were from Mrs. Washington.

Not many people felt comfortable teasing the general. Eliza did. At age fifty-four, she had eyes that could look "radiant," a "gaze" that could "entrance," and shapely shoulders that, though usually not shown, could hold up a dress dipping deep between her "fair breasts." It was not her fault she had a "well cultivated" mind that few men could match and a playful writing style that other women could not imitate. At a time when men did not always welcome political opinions from the "softer sex," the general welcomed Eliza's. In 1793, during the Philadelphia yellow fever epidemic, he had asked her to flee with him and Martha to

Mount Vernon. Mr. Powel could have come, too. Eliza had wanted to say yes. Only her husband seeing "no propriety" in the trip had forced her to say no. He had insisted on staying, and died as a result. Some said she had not mourned Mr. Powel enough, even though she had worn black as recently as the ball a few weeks ago in honor of Washington's final birthday in Philadelphia.

Eliza would miss the general. There he was, as he had looked at the end of the Revolutionary War, in the portrait she and her late husband had hung in the house: the hips jutting out, the large hand wrapped around a sword, the surprisingly slender shoulders capped in epaulettes, the chin cleft, the pursed lips giving the blockish-looking face a muscular tone, the nose broadening near the brows, the muted blue eyes buried into the skull. The general himself deemed it a "good likeness but not flattering."

He needed no "flattery," Eliza thought. It was, she found, "offensive to his virtue." Already "his countrymen gaze[d] on him like a God. The fairer sex was charmed with his agreeable person and manners." He had always insisted that other men had the "abilities and virtues" necessary to succeed him in office. So close, in fact, had he come to retiring after his first term that he had required Eliza's coaxing before agreeing to serve a second. "I will venture to assert that . . . you are the only man in America that dares to do right on all public occasions," she had told him. It had not just been the country's future that had concerned her. It had been Washington's own future. Retirement might not bring the bliss he thought he would find, she had warned. "Have you not often experienced that your judgement was fallible with respect to the means of happiness? Have you not, on some occasions, found the consummation of your wishes the source of the keenest of your sufferings?" All these years later, those questions remained unanswered.

The first fleeting glimpse had come a mile away through the trees toward the Potomac: the cupola crowning the center, the pediment and dormer windows poking through the red wooden shingles of the sloping trapezoidal-shaped roof, the new green shutters framing the windows on the two main stories, the white walls looking as if constructed with stone instead of wood cut and colored to fool the eye from a distance. The view had receded into the trees only to reappear intermittently as the carriage had driven up the serpentine path until pulling up at the front of the house. For years, George Washington had longed to say the words. Upon the afternoon of March 15, 1797, he finally could: "I am once more seated under my own vine and fig tree."

It was good to be back at Mount Vernon. "No estate in United America is more pleasantly situated than this," he thought. "It lies in a high, dry & healthy country . . . [and] on one of the finest rivers in the world." For "more than ten miles" on the Virginia side, the tidal Potomac and its tributaries lapped up against lands belonging to him, an empire totaling eight thousand acres. On the outskirts of the estate beyond its extensive "woodland" lay four separate farms ranging in size from more than twelve hundred acres of "plowable" land to just under five hundred acres and each including fields, barns, "comfortable" housing for an overseer, and quarters for "warmly lodged" slaves. At the center of the estate lay a fifth farm, the one around the mansion house that was "going fast to ruin": fireplaces and steps crumbling, paint cracking, wallpaper wearing away.

The repairs began at once. "I am already surrounded by joiners, masons, [and] painters," Washington wrote, "and such is my

47

anxiety to get out of their hands that I have scarcely a room to put a friend into, or to set in myself, without the music of hammers or the odoriferous smell of paint." The chaos turned his memory back four decades to the final days of his involvement in the French and Indian War, when he had begun to expand the small house where he had lived for a few years during boyhood. The addition of a full second floor had elevated the garret and the roof just in time to accommodate Martha and the two children she brought from her first marriage. Construction of wings extending the house on either side and of a piazza spanning the back, where the lawn sloped toward the river, had continued during the Revolutionary War, even though being away had prevented him from managing the workers in person as he would have preferred and as he now finally could. "At no period," he said shortly after returning, "have I been more engaged than in the . . . [time since] I have been at home."

The days started before dawn, when he crept out of "Mrs. Washington's bedchamber," as he called the room they shared, and down the private staircase leading to his study, where he dressed. By sunrise, he was out about the house. "If my hirelings are not in their places at that time, I send them messages expressive of my sorrow for their indisposition. Then having put these wheels in motion, I examine the state of things farther; and the more they are probed, the deeper I find the wounds are, which my buildings have sustained by an absence and neglect of eight years. By the time I have accomplished these matters, breakfast (a little after seven o'clock) . . . is ready." No one need ask what he wanted. It was always three hoecakes soaked in honey, slathered with butter, and washed down with tea. The mushier the cakes, the better for his dentures. "This over, I mount my horse."

The daily ride around the estate could range as far as the twenty miles required to complete an inspection loop encompassing the mansion house farm as well as each of the four surrounding ones. A "broad-brimmed white hat" and, when necessary, an umbrella protected his fair-colored face, which had recently undergone an operation to remove a cancerous spot. Never did he

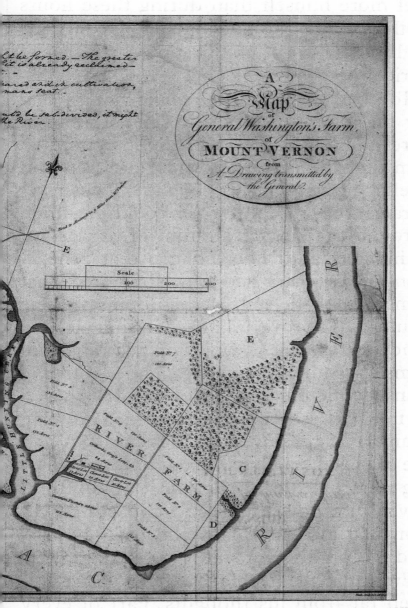

feel more himself than during these hours in the saddle. "No pursuit is more congenial with my nature & gratifications than that of agriculture," he said.

Too bad that the same could not be said for the nature of Mount Vernon. The "eyesore gullies" he saw all around reminded him that the earth he owned did not lend itself to agriculture. Topsoil ran off whenever it rained because the water could not drain through the "under stratum of hard clay" lining the land. The tobacco that generations of Virginians had grown had tired what remained of the soil. He had done what he could to improve it. The decision he had made before the Revolution to transform himself from a planter dependent on the transatlantic tobacco trade with Britain to a farmer diversifying into healthier-growing grains had improved his fortunes. So had the knowledge he had reaped through reading journals full of the latest agricultural advances from Britain and collecting data from the intricate plans and trials he carried out on his own lands.

Even in Philadelphia, the fields had never been far from his thoughts. Part of every Sunday in office had gone to reading the detailed weekly reports he required his estate manager to produce, and to writing lengthy responses full of instructions and inquiries. An absentee owner could devise no better system, but it had never sufficed for him. "It is more than probable I often repeat things over & over again," he had admitted. "Consider it as a strong evidence that things *so repeated* are such as I am anxious about." He needed to see "things" for himself. He could not stand the "suspense."

The "suspense" of waiting to learn the results of the experimental crop rotations that he hoped would restore his fields. "I am really mortified," he had noted, "at not knowing the quantity of potatoes that grew in [field] number 4 . . . that I might have compared it with the yield of corn in the same field & thereby decided with more certainty & precision on cultivating of both in that manner."

The "suspense" of wondering why longstanding orders went undone. "In nothing have I discovered half so much anxiety as to reclaim meadow lands & to substitute live [hedges] in place of dead [wood-wasting] fences, and yet in nothing . . . have I met with greater disappointment & vexation . . . from the inattention given to these things."

The "suspense" of not knowing why Betty Davis, one of the three hundred or so slaves he kept at Mount Vernon, had accounted for no days of work on report after report. "What kind of sickness is Betty Davis's that it should have had a similar effect upon her? If pretended ailments, without apparent causes, or visible effects, will screen her from work, I shall get no service at all from her, for a more lazy, deceitful & impudent hussy is not to be found in the United States." If Betty proved really sick, of course, she should have received the same medical care he himself would have received. The thought that his overseers might not summon a doctor — that they might treat his slaves "in scarcely any other light than they do a draught horse or ox" — disturbed him. So did the possibility of slaves fabricating excuses. "Lost labor," he liked to say, "is never to be regained." Considering all he gave his slaves — clothes ("a jacket, breeches, 2 shirts, 1 [pair of] stockings, 1 [pair of] shoes"), blankets ("to the grown Negroes, the larger or better sort"), and food ("[not] an ounce of meal more, nor less, than is sufficient to feed them plentifully") — six days of dawn-to-dusk labor every week hardly seemed too much to ask in return. Sadly, the labor system left the slaves with "no ambition" to strive for what he most wanted for himself:

"a *good* name." Betty Davis was the rare slave with a surname he knew. Getting work out of "my people," as he called his slaves, required much of the "master's eye" and, sometimes, a little of the overseer's whip.

Getting work out of the slaves also required coming up with work for them to do. That was harder than it sounded at Mount Vernon. Transitioning away from tobacco to wheat and other less labor-intensive crops had decreased the demand for slaves in the fields even as their numbers continued to multiply. How to keep the surplus bodies occupied had become an obsession. While riding around that spring, he saw slave fishermen "hauling" in nets full of shad and herring that he would salt and sell; slave carpenters and coopers showing their skills with wood; slave "spinners, knitters, and sewers" manufacturing the clothes their own families would wear; and, of course, slave field hands plowing the fields that supplied the grain that would fetch eight or so dollars a barrel at market once turned into flour at the water-powered mill he operated.

There was a chain of command — slaves reporting to overseers, overseers reporting to the estate manager, the estate manager reporting to the owner — but that did not mean Washington himself could not stop his horse and stoop down to call out a slave by name. He often did. As he rode on, he also looked at his livestock. There were the mules he had introduced to the country after coaxing the late Royal Gift, the studly jackass the Spanish Crown had sent as a present, into putting aside old-world class distinctions and copulating with "plebeian" American mares. There were also the sheep whose fleeces now averaged less than half as much wool as they had on the eve of his first election to the presidency. Seeing how the flock had deteriorated saddened him.

Only when trying to make it back to the house before a quarter to three did he hurry his horse. He needed fifteen minutes to change clothes. Dinner started at three o'clock. He hated keeping the "servants" waiting, not to mention the uninvited guests. "I rarely miss seeing strange faces — come, as they say, out of respect to me. Pray, would not the word curiosity answer as well?" Mount Vernon, he thought, "may be compared to a well resorted tavern, as scarcely any strangers who are going from north to south, or from south to north, do not spend a day or two at it." To turn strangers away would not be the Virginia way. So they took a seat around a table stocked with meats and vegetables for dinner and pies, nuts, and fruits for dessert. Fish was his own favorite. He washed it down with Madeira, the wine that had dyed his dentures a darkish color.

As little as possible would he show his teeth to his guests. Prudence dictated keeping his mouth shut. Every so often some joke of Georges Washington Lafayette's or some comical expression of Nelly Custis's would force a chuckle. But far more often, Washington would let silence snuff out conversations either because he struggled to hear what his guests said or because he could not decide what to say back. He needed to choose his words carefully, especially among strangers bound to repeat them. A regrettable remark at the table could spread through the mail across the country and live on in diaries forever. Much as possible, he steered conversation away from old military battles and politics and toward comfortable subjects: advances in agriculture and the engineering projects enhancing navigation of the river flowing past his house. So his guests could see the Potomac for themselves, if weather permitted, he would lead them out to the piazza after raising his glass for a toast: "All our friends!"

The sun going down presented a chance to slip away to the study, where letters requiring responses waited by candlelight on the writing table. Not dispatching a courier to the Alexandria post office daily, as he had when at Mount Vernon during his presidency, became a point of pride. Letters to a president could not wait. Letters to a retiree could, at least, for a few days. Then again, he had no patience for receiving an incomplete response to a letter he had written. He could not understand why his correspondents did not adopt the systematic approach he had long used. It was simple: when reading a letter, note every item requiring a response on "a piece of waste paper" and then, if possessed with sufficient time (he often did not have it), group these items into "heads" that could serve as a primitive outline. "Having gone through the letter in this manner, you begin your own, and note after note, as the contents are inserted in your letter, is scratched out. By this means no part of a long letter can ever escape notice, by not carrying the whole in your memory, when you sit down to write."

Even in the solitude of his study, he did not feel alone. How could he while knowing that historians would one day pore over the pages he wrote? For decades, he had preserved records: the exercises he had copied as a boy learning geometry and memorizing the 110 *Rules of Civility* for navigating polite society; the letter books he had filled during the French and Indian War; the diaries in which he had recorded "where and how my time is spent" between the wars; the Revolutionary War papers that he had kept under guard and ordered clerks to start copying into bound volumes long before the fighting had ended; the presidential papers that he had not yet unpacked from Philadelphia; the weather logs, account books, and incoming and outgoing personal correspondence to which he added even now. People and papers — those were what he wanted saved from the house if disaster ever befell it. Most everything else could be reconstructed. The historical record could not be. It was his country's history. It was his legacy. If repairs to the existing buildings ever finished, construction would commence on the one new building he wished to erect: an archive for his "voluminous" papers.

Drooping eyelids usually brought his writing sessions to a close. Occasionally, as when responding to Eliza Powel's recent letter, only nearing the end of a page did. The ruse Eliza had put on about discovering love letters to a paramour would have caused "serious alarm," Washington wrote back, "had it not been for one circumstance, which by the bye is a pretty material one, viz., that I had no love letters to lose." If Eliza broke her promise not to read the Washingtons' marital letters, she would find the correspondence "more fraught with expressions of friendship, than of *enamored* love." Had Washington set his heart on finding "the warmth" of "the *romantic order*" in Martha's letters, he would have immediately committed them "to the flames."

Left unsaid was that there had been a time, long ago, when he had wanted nothing so much as a "romantic" letter: one answering whether Sally Cary Fairfax, the bewitching older woman who lived just down the Potomac from Mount Vernon, loved him as much as he loved her. It had been the "one thing above all things in this world . . . [he wished] to know." The question had courted scandal. She was married; he was soon to be. So he had encoded his message in double meanings. "The world has no business to know the object of my love, declared in this manner to you when I want to conceal it." An interloper reading the letter now or in the future — not that he intended a copy to survive — would assume he had Martha in mind. "Only one person of your acquaintance can . . . guess my meaning," he had written Sally. But even she had pretended to "misunderstand." Probably it had been for the best. He had vowed to "say no more."

Experience had taught him not to put stock in love letters. Only the young and innocent could believe in "the fine tales the poets & lovers of old have told us of the transports of mutual love, that heaven has taken its abode on earth." A successful marriage required firmer footing. "When . . . passion begins to subside, which it assuredly will do, and yield — oftentimes too late — to more sober reflections, it serves to evince that love is too dainty a food to live upon *alone*." He and Martha had found "friendship." While, so far as he could remember, they had not dined alone in two decades, always did they like to be near each other. That seemed enough. "More permanent & genuine happiness," he believed, "is to be found in the sequestered walks of connubial life than in the giddy rounds of promiscuous pleasure."

Most evenings, he noticed that he and Martha wanted nothing so much as to go to sleep. Leaving the letters in his study around suppertime, he would find her back with the guests and would join them for tea and a reading of the newspapers. At nine o'clock, "unless prevented by very particular company," he and she retired to bed.

The schedule rarely varied. "The history of a day," he explained to anyone curious to hear it, "will serve for a year." The routine left no time for reading the hundreds of books lining his shelves. "I have not looked into a book since I came home, nor shall be able to do it until I have discharged my workmen, probably not before the nights grow longer, when, possibly, I may be looking in doomsday book."

He had recently learned that Betty Lewis, his younger sister, had died. "The melancholy occasion of your writing has filled me with inexpressible concern," he wrote Betty's son. "The debt of nature, however, sooner or later must be paid by us all, and although the separation from our nearest relatives is a heart-rending circumstance, reason, religion & philosophy teach us to bear it with resignation." Speaking of decay, he transitioned, he had a question regarding his house: Did Betty's son "know of a good house joiner (white or black) that could be hired by the year or month & on what terms?"

For the most part, Nelly Custis marveled at the ease with which Grandpapa Washington adjusted to life back at Mount Vernon. "Since I left Philadelphia, everything has appeared to be a dream. I can hardly realize my being *here* & that Grandpapa is no longer in office. If it is a dream, I hope never to awaken from it," she wrote a friend. "Grandpapa is very well & has already turned farmer again."

Just occasionally would Grandpapa give a hint of struggle. It happened at the end of long days, when he rejoined the family for tea. Nelly would play the harpsichord that she had learned to love only through the hours of teary-eyed practice that Grandmama Washington enforced and that Grandpapa seemed to enjoy. Nelly would suddenly glance at Grandpapa and see "his lips moving, but no sound . . . perceptible," as if he were "perfectly abstracted" from the company around him and summoned back to the problems he had left in Philadelphia. Similar flashbacks had haunted him after he had returned from the Revolution in 1783. For months, he said, he had awoken in the morning as if still among his shivering soldiers instead of his loving family.

Nelly, then, had been just a four-year-old, possessing no memory of the father she had lost two years earlier. Her first recollection was of racing out to welcome Grandpapa as he had arrived home. Ever since, he had been "the most affectionate of fathers," even though he had refused to accept legal guardianship of her and her brother, Wash. Grandpapa had enough other responsibilities. Grandmama Washington had devoted herself to the child-rearing. "She has been ever more than a mother to me," Nelly thought. She did not envy her two older sisters, Betsey and Patty, who had continued living with their birth mother. The envy went the other way. During youthful visits to Mount Vernon, when the time to go had come, one of the older sisters had always cried out that she, too, loved Grandmama more than Mama and wanted to stay.

It was easy to see why all these years later, as Nelly looked around the mansion house. "Everything appears to be revived. The grass begins to look green. Some trees are in blossom, others budding. The flowers are coming out, and the numerous different birds keep up a constant serenading. . . . When I look at this noble river & all the beautiful prospects around, I pity all those who are in cities, for surely a country life is the most rational & the most happy of any, and all the refinements of art and luxury are nothing in comparison to the beauties of nature."

The spring brought brother Wash to Mount Vernon for a vacation from Princeton. "Grandmama [had] always spoiled" him when home because "he was 'the pride of her heart.' " No one had known how he would adjust to a rigorous academic schedule, especially given how he had struggled at his previous school. To everyone's delight — even Grandpapa's — Wash spoke of the strides he had made in history, French, and philosophy. The fair-headed boy Grandpapa had once called Tub had begun maturing into at least an average-sized young man. "My dearest brother," Nelly wrote, "is very grown." She herself had grown, too. No longer did she want family members calling her Nelly. They should call her "Eleanor." Her two older sisters had already married men living in the federal district and had begun raising children of their own.

When Nelly would follow suit aroused gossip. Some even went so far as to say that she would wed Georges Washington Lafayette. That would be like marrying one's French "adopted brother," she thought.

"Being *in love with him* . . . is entirely out of the question." People should mind their own affairs, she believed. Just because she attended balls did not mean she was in "danger of being captivated by anyone." She simply loved dancing. So had Grandpapa during his younger days. He had stopped dancing after the war. But Nelly knew he still liked receiving precise counts of how many young "ladies" and "gentlemen" ventured onto the floor.

Grandpapa also liked to caution against swearing off love. His return to Mount Vernon, he said, would bring many eligible men by the house. "Men and women," read a letter he had written Nelly, "feel the same inclinations towards each other *now* that they always have done and which they will continue to do until there is a new order of things. And *you,* as others have done, may find perhaps that the passions of your sex are easier roused than allayed. Do not therefore boast too soon, nor too strongly, of your insensibility to or resistance of its powers." Then he added this: "In the composition of the human frame, there is a good deal of inflammable matter; however dormant it may be for a while, . . . when the torch is put to it, that which is *within you* may burst into a blaze." The words read as if they reflected experience.

A man returning to private life could retain an interest in public affairs. Indeed, Washington did. He had subscriptions to ten or so gazettes and wondered if the number should be more. What about the new paper William Cobbett had begun editing in Philadelphia, the *Porcupine's Gazette*? The editor tended toward "strong and coarse expressions," but, at least, he had sworn to provide "a rallying point for the friends of government." That was the kind of bias a former president could support.

By late March, officials could confirm reports of the hostile greeting that Charles Cotesworth Pinckney, the new minister whom Washington had sent late in his presidency to France, had received upon arriving in the country. The French government under the control of the Directory, the five-man body that had seized executive power in the wake of the blood-soaked days known as the Reign of Terror, had "refused" to recognize Pinckney and expelled him. The audacity astonished Washington. The countries could not resolve the crisis between their ships at sea if their representatives could not meet on the same soil. "The conduct of the French government is so much beyond calculation and so unaccountable upon any principle of justice . . . that I shall not *now* puzzle my brains in attempting to develop their motives to it," he said. Unraveling that mystery was not his job any longer. It was John Adams's.

And so far as Washington could tell, Adams had badly botched the first important decision of his presidency: he had refused to purchase some of the furniture Washington had left behind at the president's house. "It was intimated to me that, if the President took the house in which I lived, that he would be glad (in case I was disposed to part with it) to take the furniture of the two largest rooms." Washington had offered the pieces at "reduced prices," as a courtesy that Adams had repaid with rudeness. Only "in the last moment [had] he declined" the bargain. By then, the window to sell some of the items had closed. The chandelier would have to be given away for free.

One thing Adams did keep — wisely, Washington thought — was the final cabinet that he had painstakingly pieced together in 1795 and 1796 out of "second-rate" men after narrowing the possibilities only to "friends" of the government (meaning not Republicans) and then seeing almost all of his first choices and many of his second and third ones say no. He had ended up with Timothy Pickering at the State Department, Oliver Wolcott Jr. at the Treasury, James McHenry at the War Department, and Charles Lee as attorney general. Although no longer working for Washington, these men could still do him an unofficial favor from time to time. "No apology" was needed, for example, for sending letters seeking Wolcott's help with a personal banking issue "in the course of business" at the Treasury or for asking McHenry to forward some confidential letters. Perhaps the secretaries could also send briefings on the news. "Let me pray you to have the goodness to communicate to me occasionally, such matters as are interesting, and not contrary to the rules of your official duty to disclose," Washington wrote. "We get so many details in the gazettes, and of such different complexions, that it is impossible to know what credence to give to any of them."

Adams had summoned Congress for a special session in May. Attention to the crisis with France could not wait. Nor could Washington. What would Adams announce? Whatever policy the president pursued would find support at Mount Vernon. "Every good citizen," Washington believed, "[ought to] conform to whatsoever the ruling powers shall decide." He just wanted to know what that was. He could not stand the suspense. He was far from the great city of Philadelphia, but it was not far from his thoughts.

CHAPTER TWO:
PLACE IN HISTORY

About three hundred since the previous summer. That was the number of American ships that had fallen prey to French privateers around the West Indies, if one counted the stories in the newspapers, as Secretary of State Timothy Pickering did. The outrages were there for all to see: the American ship captain "detained" for months, including "thirty-six hours without provisions"; sailors incapable of signing their names coerced into making "their marks at the bottom" of confessions they could not read; four Americans wounded when a French privateer "poured . . . several broadsides" into a ship out of Salem, Massachusetts, the town where Pickering had been born a deacon's son nearly fifty-two years earlier. Never in that time could he recall such a "scene of plunder and piracy." In his mind, only one remedy remained: war.

Nonetheless, the speech that President

Adams delivered to Congress on May 16, 1797, called for new negotiations with France. Charles Cotesworth Pinckney would return, this time as part of a three-man diplomatic mission, never mind that the French had only recently expelled him. Timothy Pickering would never have supported such a policy if not for two factors: first, much of the speech sounded the warlike tone he wished to hear (more than one line had come from his pen) and, second, he calculated that the peace mission stood little chance of success anyway.

Then came word of a ruinous idea wrecking all calculations. President Adams planned to include someone with Republican leanings on the mission. It was as if he had learned nothing from his predecessor's mistakes. George Washington had already tried sending a Republican to France. In 1794, James Monroe of Virginia had gone there under the theory that his Republican politics would please France's republican government. And they did. All too much! Hearing Monroe profess his love for all things French had convinced France's leaders that their interests lay not in accommodating the United States government but in supporting a rising opposition party claiming to represent the true sentiments of the American people. It was to replace Monroe that Pinckney had originally sailed for France during the final months of Washington's presidency. Washington, Pickering thought, had waited much too long before making the switch.

Little had frustrated Pickering so much as watching the "extremely slow" speed at which Washington processed information. "In cases requiring instant determination," he suffered from "indecision." His fellow citizens would have learned about the flaw long ago had not his subordinates during the Revolutionary War conspired to hide it. Only Pickering refused to keep up the lie. He, too, had served in the war, and through the glasses bisecting his long bald head, he had seen the general all too clearly. "So extremely illiterate! He could not write a sentence without misspelling some word, nor three paragraphs without false grammar." Those were the words Pickering had used to describe the general in a recent conversation with Adams. The new president needed to know the truth about the old one. How, Adams had responded, did Washington maintain his vast correspondence? It was true Washington's writing had improved as he had aged. More essential to his success, however, was his willingness to ask aides for help. They "saw that he was . . . [always] willing and desirous to receive advice," which was exactly what Adams needed to do now on the question of who should go to France.

Fortunately, around the same time as Adams's speech to Congress, there came a reminder of the dangers of appointing Republicans to powerful positions, thanks to the publication of the indiscreet letter that Washington's first secretary of state and the country's most influential Republican, Vice President Thomas Jefferson, had written the previous year to one Philip Mazzei, a friend living in Italy. Through mysterious channels, the Mazzei letter, as it became known, had made its way into a Parisian newspaper after being translated into French and then into the hands of Noah Webster, who published it in his New York newspaper after having it translated back into English. "An Anglo-Monarchico-Aristocratic party has arisen. Their avowed object is to impose on us the *substance,* as they have already given us the *form,* of the British government," read the translation of the translation. "I should give you a fever, if I should name the apostates who have embraced these heresies; men who were Solomons in council, and Samsons in com-

74

bat, but whose hair has been cut off by the whore England."

To whom did that lewd last line allude? One man, above all others, had achieved fame as both a Samson and a Solomon. "There is no room to doubt," Pickering thought. Jefferson had defamed George Washington. That Pickering himself often criticized Washington mattered not. They were on the same side. Besides, Pickering never doubted Washington's "patriotism" and "integrity," as Jefferson had. How would he explain himself? "I am told that Mr. Jefferson complains that his letter to Mazzei has been ill translated," Pickering wrote Noah Webster on May 19. If Webster would send a copy of the French text that had served as his source, Pickering would have it published in the Philadelphia newspapers. Educated readers, then, could judge the translation for themselves. They would see Jefferson for what he really was: an enemy of Washington.

Never had politics so divided the people of Philadelphia. Not many years ago, Thomas Jefferson recalled, differences of opinion had not stopped Republicans and Federalists from socializing. "It is not so now. Men who have been intimate all their lives cross the streets to avoid meeting and turn their heads another way, lest they should be obliged to touch their hat. This may do for young men, with whom passion is enjoyment. But it is afflicting to peaceable minds." Even his own relationship with Adams, who had served on the Continental Congress committee that had tapped Jefferson to write the Declaration of Independence, had suffered.

The belligerence of Adams's recent address came as a shock to Jefferson. The language would insult France. Why would the French agree to negotiate with an insolent country across the Atlantic Ocean at a time when their armies were ascendant in Europe? French troops fighting under a general named Bonaparte had repeatedly humiliated the armies of Austria, the only other major royal power still fighting beside Britain. Had anyone consulted Jefferson, he would have advised against the "military preparations" that Adams had called for not only at sea but also on land.

Then again, Jefferson could not complain about being left out of cabinet deliberations. It was what he wanted as vice president. Almost immediately after the inauguration, he had retreated to Monticello, the house he kept in constant renovation on a little mountaintop just east of Virginia's Blue Ridge. The fruit trees had just blossomed, as if to remind of the purity of rural life beyond the stench of corrupting cities. Only Adams convening Congress could have forced Jefferson to return to the capital so soon.

The road back to Philadelphia had taken Jefferson by Mount Vernon, but he had not stopped at the house. It had been just a little past that point that he received word of the publication of the Mazzei letter. Once back in Philadelphia, Jefferson found everyone waiting to learn whether he would confirm or deny authorship. The question defied a simple answer. He could not "disavow" the letter "wholly," because much of the newspaper copy accurately conveyed what he had written his old friend Mazzei. Neither could Jefferson "avow" the letter "as it stood," because minor textual changes resulting from the translation and retranslation had produced major changes in meaning. For starters, he had not called England a "whore." He had called her a "harlot." More important, he had not written that Federalists had "already given us the *form,* of the British government," that is, a monarchy, though he did not doubt they would if they could. He had written only that the Federalists had given "[us] the *forms* of the British government," by which he meant the trappings of a monarchy: inaugurations resembling coronations, presidential birthday celebrations befitting a king.

Explaining such nuances would require a detailed written response. At first, Jefferson saw no choice but to provide it. "I must take the field of the public papers." Publishing a faithful copy of the Mazzei letter alone would not suffice. A complete reckoning would require more: "a publication of all (even the secret) transactions of the [Washington] administration while I was of it." Jefferson was better prepared to furnish such a history than most would have imagined, because he had documented his frustrations as secretary of state. Some of the notes he had made contemporaneously. Others he had drafted only years after the events described. Many would require editing for accuracy and context. But here lay the makings of the "secret" history that would explain the letter he had written and exonerate his reputation.

Readers would see the past eight years as Jefferson had experienced them: the hope with which he had returned to America in late 1789 after having served as American minister to France and having seen the

78

French Revolution commence with a "fervor" for "natural rights"; the disappointment of discovering that the revolutionary spirit had cooled in his own country upon arriving in the then-temporary capital of New York in March 1790 and taking office as America's first secretary of state. At that point, Washington had already been president for nearly a year, and a collection of courtiers had already coalesced around him. "The courtesies of dinner parties given me as a stranger newly arrived among them, placed me at once in their familiar society," Jefferson remembered. "But I cannot describe the wonder and mortification with which the table conversations filled me. Politics were the chief topic, and a preference of kingly, over republican, government was evidently the favorite sentiment."

It had not just been idle talk. People had begun treating Washington like a monarch. According to gossip, the organizers of a ball during the early days of the presidency had propped up a sofa on a platform so that President and Mrs. Washington could reign above the "gentlemen" wearing their dress swords on the dance floor. "Each one when going to dance was to lead his partner to the foot of the sofa; make a low obeisance to the President and his lady; then go and dance; and when done, bring his partner again to the foot of the sofa for new obeisances." The protocol had come from the royal courts of Europe. Ditto for the so-called levees, the stuffy weekly visiting hour when the doors to the president's house had opened to callers who had found Washington wearing a black suit and dress sword and willing to exchange bows but never handshakes. At the first such levee, an aide preceding Washington into a room full of sycophants shouted, "The President of the United States." To his credit, Washington had rebuked the aide afterward. As far as Jefferson could see, Washington had no love for the levees. "He had been led into them by the persons he consulted at New York."

As to who had led Washington to the levees, there could be little doubt: Treasury Secretary Alexander Hamilton, the Caribbean immigrant who had come to New York on the eve of the Revolution, who had served as one of Washington's aides during the war, and who had given a hopeless speech in favor of what could be described only as a monarchial government at the Constitutional Convention. That Hamilton looked to a day when the United States would adopt the British form of government — that his followers had a plan to bring about the transformation — had dawned on Jefferson only after the two had arranged a dinner in June 1790. Out of that meal had come a compromise that allowed for passage of the cornerstone of Hamilton's financial plan: federal assumption of state debts racked up during the Revolution. At the time, Jefferson had understood little more about "assumption" than how it divided the Union along sectional lines with almost all the southern states (especially Virginia) strongly opposing it as a handout to northern states that had not paid down their debts and to the northern speculators snatching up previously worthless securities sure to rise in value. "It was observed [at the dinner]," Jefferson remembered, "that as the pill would be a bitter one to the Southern states, something should be done to soothe them." That something was moving the federal capital. In the short run, it would go to Philadelphia. In the long run, it would go south, to a site of Washington's choosing on the river flowing past his Virginia home.

Only after the capital had moved to Philadelphia had Jefferson realized what a disastrous deal he had struck. For a city, it seemed, he had traded away a country. "I was duped . . . by the Secretary of the

Treasury and made a tool for forwarding his schemes, not then sufficiently understood by me." Assumption of state debts had represented only one part of Hamilton's master plan. A commitment to fully funding the enormous national debt had represented another. A dangerous and growing dependence on the British imports so crucial for generating tariff revenue had followed. So had an unpopular whiskey excise tax that had caused serious unrest in the west. So had the creation of a national bank that had stretched to the breaking point the constitutional limits placed on the federal government's powers. So had a culture of speculating that had led people away from "commerce & agriculture" and into "vice & idleness," no better than one would find at "a gaming table." So had the "corruption" of congressmen who had tied, first, their fortunes — and, then, their votes — to the success of Hamilton's scheme. So had the real possibility that Hamilton's adherents — the "monarchical" party (Federalists) made up mostly of "merchants" dependent on "British capital," "paper dealers," and the "idle rich of the great commercial towns" — would succeed in their ultimate goal: importing the British system of government complete with a king and house of lords. The one hope for saving the republic lay in the rise of a new party: the Republicans.

Jefferson had tried to make Washington understand. As the notes revealed, the conversations had not gone well. "As to the idea of transforming this government into a monarchy, he [Washington] did not believe there were ten men in the U.S. whose opinions were worth attention who entertained such a thought." For Jefferson, the worst moment came upon discovering that Washington "really" approved "the treasury system." The reforms, Washington insisted, had freed the government from the embarrassing financial crises that had come close to undoing his undersupplied and underpaid army during the Revolution. Much as Jefferson had wanted to put all the blame on Hamilton — to cling to the idea of a president not comprehending his own policies — Washington had rejected it. The very notion struck Washington as an insult, no better than calling him "careless" or "stupid."

What Washington had wanted was for Jefferson and Hamilton to "coalesce in the measures of the government." If the cabinet would come together, so would the country, Washington had said. Even back then,

Jefferson had deemed it delusional. Party differences had begun to mirror geographic differences, with Federalists dominating the North and Republicans the South. Only Washington himself, Jefferson had said, could transcend that divide. Only Washington serving a second term could hold together the country. How much Washington wanted to retire, Jefferson had known. He had seen the "valedictory" or "farewell" address that his closest confidant, then-congressman James Madison of Virginia, had secretly written in 1792 for Washington to publish under his own name in the newspapers. Jefferson and Madison had both begged Washington not to do so. So he had postponed his plan to retire but only after wondering whether he himself had lost the "confidence" of the South. Certainly, his administration had.

Most of Jefferson's notes dated to the second term, not because it had represented most of his time as secretary of state (far from it) but because those final months between the first day of the second term (March 4, 1793) and the last day of his tenure (December 31, 1793) had brought realizations that made him "tremble."

One realization was that Washington had lost trust in the people he led. How else to explain why he had underlined and questioned the word "republic" while editing a letter Jefferson had written? "Ours was a republican government," Washington conceded, "but yet we had not used that style in this way." "Republic" was the word the French had begun using to describe their country in the fall of 1792, just months before guillotining Louis XVI. That the president had begun to identify with the witless king would have stunned Jefferson had he not seen how Washington had looked earlier when told of Louis's capture. "I never saw him [Washington] so much dejected by any event in my life." Federalist friends, Jefferson thought, purposely exaggerated the violence in France so as to scare the president. They showed him newspaper reports that played up the chaos. The strategy succeeded. As for the United States, Jefferson heard Washington once say, "There was more danger of anarchy being introduced [than monarchy]."

The neutrality that Washington had declared after the outbreak of war between Britain and France led Jefferson to another frightening realization: the administration's foreign policy would favor Britain (the country Jefferson had denounced in the Declaration of Independence), even though the heart of the American people beat for France (the country that had given aid during America's Revolution and now desperately needed aid during its own). The instability abroad caused Washington to convene his cabinet more and more. Always hoping for "unanimity," he often settled disputes among his advisers by forcing them to vote. The pro-British position usually started off with two votes because that "plump" "fool" Secretary of War Henry Knox of Massachusetts almost always backed the views that Hamilton presented in the forty-plus-minute speeches he delivered as if addressing a "jury." The swing vote belonged to Attorney General Edmund Randolph, a fellow Virginian who should have been a solid Republican but could change his colors as quickly as a "chameleon." Thus, against overwhelming odds, Jefferson had soldiered on, as if "a gladiator" forced "to descend daily into the arena . . . to suffer martyrdom in every conflict."

Just recalling the memories brought back the misery. Never again, Jefferson swore, would he endure days like August 2, 1793, when the cabinet discussed the so-called Democratic Societies, the local political clubs that had formed in support of the revolution in France and the Republican Party in America. The notes Jefferson had taken told the story:

Met again. Hamilton spoke again 3/4 of an hour [about the danger of the Democratic Societies]. . . .

I answered . . . [by warning that condemning the societies would encroach on] the right of voluntary associations . . . [and would] make the President assume the station of the head of a party instead of the head of the nation. . . .

Knox [at some point] in a foolish incoherent sort of a speech introduced the pasquinade [a satire] lately printed . . . where the President was placed on a guillotine [just as Louis XVI had been]. . . .

The President was much inflamed, got into one of those passions when he cannot command himself. Run on much on the personal abuse which had been bestowed on him. Defied any man on earth to produce one single act of his since he had been in the government which was not done on the purest motives. That he had never repented but once the having slipped the moment of resigning his office, and that was every moment since. That by god he had rather be in his grave than in his present situation. That he had rather be on his farm than to be made emperor of the world and yet that they were charging him with wanting to be a king. . . .

There was a pause. Some difficulty in resuming our question.

To Washington, around this time, Jefferson had confided that he could take no more. For months, he had wished to retire, to return to Monticello, to escape Philadelphia, "where the laws of society oblige me to move always exactly in the circle which I know to bear me peculiar hatred, that is to say, the wealthy aristocrats, the merchants connected closely with England, [and] the new created paper fortunes that thus surrounded." Only Washington's pleading had persuaded Jefferson to stay until the end of 1793. Without "the check of my opinions in the administration," Jefferson remembered, Washington had worried about "things . . . going too far." Indeed, not long after Jefferson's departure, they had.

In the fall of 1794, Washington had led an army west toward Pittsburgh and the Forks of the Ohio, where the "infernal" whiskey excise tax had stirred what authorities denounced as an insurrection but what Jefferson deemed nothing "more than riotous" protest. That Hamilton had stayed with the army even after Washington's return to Philadelphia had not surprised. Jefferson remembered once hearing the treasury secretary call Julius Caesar "the greatest man that ever lived." Meanwhile, in a speech to Congress, Washington had blamed the insurrection on the Democratic Societies, which Federalists, in turn, had blamed on the Republican Party and France. "It is wonderful indeed," Jefferson wrote, "that the President should have permitted himself to be the organ of such an attack on the freedom of discussion, the freedom of writing, printing and publishing." Washington had been warned: there would be no going back if he allowed the Federalists to cast him as their party head. It would not have happened had he not lost "the firm tone of mind, for which he had been remarkable," and had not "a listlessness . . . crept on him, and a willingness to let others act and even think for him."

Soon after had come the day when the cabinet no longer had space for dissenters, not even one as timid as Edmund Randolph. His offense had been to urge a delay before ratifying the Jay Treaty, which amounted to "really nothing more than a treaty of alliance" with Britain. For this heresy, the Federalist successors to Hamilton and Knox (both of whom had resigned after the Whiskey Rebellion) had purged Randolph after accusing him of soliciting bribes from the French. Evidently believing the absurd story, Washington had signed the treaty, despite having previously resolved to postpone ratification, or so went the story Randolph told afterward. Crowds opposing the treaty had taken to the streets up and down the coast, even in New York, where shouting and stone throwing had done what Jefferson never could: cut short one of Hamilton's endless speeches. Only Washington's personal popularity had allowed the Federalists to press on with their unpopular foreign policy. "Nothing can support them but the colossus of the President's merits with the people," Jefferson wrote. "His successor, if a Monocrat [Federalist], will be overborne by the republican sense of his constituents."

It had been in this mind-set that Jefferson had written his old neighbor Mazzei. Had Washington inspired the line about Solomons and Samsons selling out to Britain? No, Jefferson reassured himself, even though, according to his own notes, Washington had undergone exactly such a transformation. The Samson who had won his country's independence had unwittingly signed it away to Britain. The Solomon who had proudly stood above party disputes had finally fallen to the Federalists. According to one rumor, Washington had even said that if "a separation of the Union into Northern and Southern" halves ever happened, "he had made up his mind to remove and be of the Northern." The old man was past saving. "His mind had been so long used to unlimited applause that it could not brook contradiction, or even advice offered unasked."

That included advice from Jefferson. In 1796, he had warned Washington of Federalist "intriguer[s]" trying "to sow tares between you and me." As recently as Adams's inauguration, the intriguers had not completely succeeded, for the two Virginians could still dine and talk, if not about current events, then of days long past and their farms faraway. If publication of the Mazzei letter had not already destroyed that remaining piece of their relationship, publication of the "secret" history needed to clarify the translation errors obviously would. "It would be impossible for me to explain this publicly without bringing on a personal difference between General Washington & myself," Jefferson concluded. "It would embroil me also with all those with whom his character is still popular, that is to say, nine tenths of the people of the U.S. And what good would be obtained . . . ? Very little indeed in my opinion to counterbalance a good deal of harm." The newspapers awaiting a response to the Mazzei letter would receive none. Jefferson would stay silent. The "secret" history would stay secret.

Besides, a sliver of hope had arisen. Adams had ultimately defied his cabinet. Instead of sending two more Federalists to join Pinckney as envoys to France, Adams had sent only one, John Marshall of Virginia. The third appointee would be an independent whom Republicans could cheer: Elbridge Gerry of Massachusetts. Not that Jefferson really wanted the mission to succeed at this point. He had secretly advised the French to "drag out the negotiations at length" with the envoys. In other words, delay until power passed from a Federalist administration to a Republican one.

One day that spring of 1797, the weather turned so hot that Washington "threw off his flannel" only to catch cold by night. For all the years he had recorded the weather in Virginia, the "sudden change" had surprised him. Reacclimating to his old home after so long away would take more time. Having Hercules, the runaway chef, back in the kitchen would have made everyone at Mount Vernon feel more at home, but no reports of his whereabouts had arrived. In his absence, the kitchen fell into chaos. Those trying to fill the void knew "nothing of cooking" or "arranging a table." The "inconvenience" for Martha was especially "great" given that her personal attendant, Oney, "who was brought up and treated more like a child than a servant," had also recently fled.

Perhaps Eliza Willing Powel could suggest a Philadelphia chef willing to relocate to Mount Vernon. Washington drafted a letter for Martha to copy and send under her own signature. She often required a ghostwriter when writing to fashionable friends like Eliza. Washington, on his own, would also ask a few fellow Virginians for their advice on replacing Hercules but did not expect their help to lead anywhere. Most Virginians would simply recommend "another slave." That was not what Washington wanted. He wanted a freeman. He had "resolved never" again to "purchase" a human being.

In the aggregate, Mount Vernon already

contained more slaves than it could profitably hold. Two times too many, Washington
calculated, despite all of his attempts to
diversify the estate's operations and to create new jobs for hands no longer needed in
the fields. "It is demonstratively clear that
on this estate, Mount Vernon, I have more
working Negroes by a full moiety, than can
be employed to any advantage in the farming system." He would have long ago gotten
"quit" of every one of his slaves if not for
being opposed to the usual way of going
about it: "selling negroes, as you would do
cattle in the market."

From time to time came letters from
busybodies suggesting another way he could
"get quit of Negroes": he could emancipate
them. "Shame! Shame!" read a recent one
from an Englishman who had never seen
Mount Vernon. "Ages to come will read
with astonishment that the man who was
foremost to wrench the rights of America
from the tyrannical grasp of Britain was
among the last to relinquish his own op-
pressive hold of poor unoffending negroes.
In the name of justice what can induce you
thus to tarnish your own well-earned celebrity . . . with so foul and indelible a blot." A
letter like that deserved no response. So
Washington had simply returned it, but the

point stayed with him. For the sake of history, he wanted it known that the "unfortunate condition of the persons, whose labor in part I employed, has been the only unavoidable subject of regret."

It was not that he had given no thought to emancipating his slaves. He had. He had even begun to carry out an emancipation plan during his final year in office. In newspapers across the country, he had placed an advertisement offering for rent four of Mount Vernon's farms (all except the one around the mansion house) and offering for sale his prized western lands, the more than thirty thousand acres of "cream of the country" real estate that he had accumulated along the Ohio River and its tributaries. For all the information the advertisement had provided (enough to take up two full newspaper columns), people responding to it fixated on the one detail omitted: What would happen to the slaves? Would they be rented with the land? While he had not wanted to preclude any possibilities (why refuse an offer before hearing the terms?), it was "not . . . [his] intention to let the Negroes." He had "something better in view for them."

So secret was the idea that putting it on paper even for a trusted friend required

95

precautions: an asterisk leading to a separate page labeled "private" and written in euphemisms. "I have another motive which makes me earnestly wish for the accomplishment of these things. It is indeed more powerful than all the rest — namely to liberate a certain species of property which I possess very repugnantly to my own feelings." Renting four of the farms and selling the western lands, it seemed, could break the cycle of economic dependence that bound Washington and his slaves together. By augmenting his income and reducing his responsibilities to just the one farm around the mansion house, he could afford to give up the slaves who accounted for so much of his personal wealth. By hiring themselves out to new tenants needing hands, the slaves could afford to survive without the food, clothing, and shelter he provided. All the pieces of the puzzle would have fit together if not for a pair of protruding problems.

First, months of advertising yielded no tenants capable of meeting the terms he detailed. Only immigrants would do (preferably from Britain) because Americans (especially Virginians) made "slovenly" farmers who thought "of nothing else but to work a field as long as it will bear anything and until it is run into gullies &

ruined." The tired tobacco fields littering Virginia showed the damage. Mount Vernon deserved better. He could not give up all control. It was simply not in his constitution.

Second, most of the Mount Vernon slaves were not his to manumit. They belonged to the estate of Martha's first husband. In a sense, these dower slaves had been what had made the widow such an attractive match for a soldier who had enhanced his reputation during the French and Indian War but still needed to enlarge his fortune. The dower slaves would stay at Mount Vernon as long as she did, and there lay the problem: when Martha passed away, they would pass on to her grandchildren. If marriage to Martha had twisted affairs in ways Washington had not foreseen in 1759, the marriages the slaves had subsequently consummated among themselves completed a Gordian knot. He had known that some of his slaves had married dower slaves. But seeing just how many astonished him. According to a survey he had recently ordered, about two in every three slave marriages at Mount Vernon crossed ownership lists. "When it is considered how much the dower Negroes and my own are intermarried," he wrote, separating them "will be an affecting and trying event." Virginia law might not recognize these unions, but he did. He had pledged to honor them. Any plan that emancipated his slaves while leaving the dower slaves in bondage would break that vow and would leave his estate to the same sad fate befalling his country: a future half-slave and half-free.

There was one way that Mount Vernon and the United States could both avoid that fate, even if, as president, he had feared discussing it: legislative emancipation. Even something so trivial as an "ill-judged" petition advocating the idea had prompted talk of Virginia seceding and forming a southern confederacy. "What would Virginia (and such other States as might be inclined to join her) gain by a separation?" he wondered. "Would they not, most unquestionably, be the weaker party?" Virginia's long-term interest, he believed, aligned with Pennsylvania and the northern states phasing out slavery. No doubt, it was easier for the North. Of the 694,280 slaves counted in the first national census, 645,023 lived in the South. Of those, 292,627 lived in Virginia. Even so, as he saw it, economics dictated Virginia must eventually follow Pennsylvania's course and embrace gradual emancipation. One need only look at land prices in the two states. The numbers were "higher" in the northern one. He wished from his "soul that the legislature of this state [Virginia] could see the policy of a gradual abolition."

No longer, however, did he have faith that he understood the politics of the state where he had won his first elective office (a seat in the House of Burgesses) four decades earlier. Much time had passed since he had "mixed in the politics or much with the people of that state (out of the neighborhood of Alexandria)." At best, the relationship between his administration and Virginia had grown, in a word, "problematical." At worst, the opposition voiced in Virginia had set "the tone" for "all the states south." As Washington's second term had waned, so had any doubt that the two "characters . . . foremost in the opposition to the government and consequently to the person administering of it" were both Virginians: Thomas Jefferson and James Madison.

Friends in Philadelphia had known better than to mention the Mazzei letter when writing to Mount Vernon. They must have known Washington would see it for himself in the newspapers. In truth, the story was not all that new. Rumors of Jefferson making similar comments had begun shortly

99

after he had left Washington's cabinet. "It would not be frank, candid, or friendly to conceal that your conduct has been represented as derogating from that opinion I had conceived you entertained of me," read the letter Washington had written during the final summer of his presidency to Jefferson. "My answer invariably has been that I had never discovered anything in the conduct of Mr. Jefferson to raise suspicions, in my mind, of his insincerity." How Jefferson had interpreted that last line, Washington did not know. Jefferson had never written back.

At the time, Washington had been in the midst of preparing the farewell address he would publish in September 1796. The urge to write something that would "lessen" Jefferson "in the public estimation" had been almost too much to resist. An early draft had included a footnote identifying Madison by name and Jefferson by implication as among the "friends" who had talked Washington out of publishing a similar address four years earlier. Readers, then, would have seen these so-called Republicans as Washington saw them: hypocrites who had opposed his administration while secretly urging its continuation. The justice of revenge had appealed to one part of his personality. But another part wished to rise above petty conflict, to avoid "allusions to particular measures" and "personalities," to write wisdom that would endure.

The task of reconciling these impulses had fallen to Alexander Hamilton. To whom else could Washington have turned for help? Not to a cabinet full of replacements he did not fully trust. Not to Madison again; that would have defeated the point. Only Hamilton possessed the skill and trust. True, he had left the administration at the beginning of 1795, but by that summer, amid the debate over whether to ratify the Jay Treaty, his advice had again become indispensable. No one else had "studied" the nexus between America's commercial and international relations on such a "comprehensive scale." At times, Washington felt almost "ashamed" of the lengths to which Hamilton went to explain these matters, but not so ashamed as to shy away from asking for some writing assistance. Like all good military aides, Hamilton had learned to "possess the soul of the general" he had served during the Revolution. Thus, "from a *single* idea," he could "convey" Washington's "meaning in the clearest & fullest manner."

That was what happened with the farewell address. Hamilton had presented the wisdom Washington wished to share as "the disinterested warnings of a parting friend, who can possibly have no personal motive," and yet this disinterestedness was also what made the address so devastating to the "pretensions" of the Republicans. The address relegated views that sounded suspiciously like theirs to the wrong side not of fleeting factional fights but of "lastingly" important political truths.

Rather than defend the details of the treasury program, the farewell warned of a timeless need to "cherish public credit" and to "bear in mind that towards the payment of debts there must be revenue [and] that to have revenue there must be taxes."

Rather than rebuke Republicans for organizing an opposition party and stirring up the Whiskey Rebellion, the farewell warned how "the spirit of party . . . agitates the community with ill-founded jealousies and false alarms, kindles the animosity of one part against another, [and] foments occasionally riot and insurrection."

Rather than mock the naïve notion that America's foreign policy need always be pro-French and anti-British because of the Revolutionary War, the farewell warned that holding "an habitual hatred or an habitual fondness" for any foreign nation would make the United States "in some degree a slave" or a "satellite," an allusion to the puppet republics that France had begun carving out of conquered lands in Europe.

Rather than accuse French-loving Republicans of betraying the interests of the United States, the farewell warned that "a free people ought to be *constantly*" on guard "against the insidious wiles of foreign influence."

President Adams had echoed that last point in his recent address to Congress. Rightly so, Washington thought. "True Americans," he believed, would rally behind the message. "All will end without shedding of blood . . . if our citizens would advocate their own cause instead of that of any other nation under the sun — that is, instead of being Frenchmen or Englishmen in politics, they would be Americans."

That was how he saw himself. He was neither an Anglophile nor a Francophile. He was "no party man." For the party divide, he blamed only one party: the Republicans, who stood against their own government. He himself stood only for the good of his country, a word that to him did not mean Virginia but the Union. "Think and speak of it as of the palladium of your political safety," his farewell had advised.

"The name of AMERICAN, which belongs to you in your national capacity, must always exalt the just pride of patriotism, more than any appellation derived from local discriminations." Hence why, when printed in the newspapers, the farewell had listed no city, as was customary, in its dateline. The words "United States" stood alone. That was the only location that should matter.

In the real world, of course, where one lived within the United States still mattered a great deal. The cook whose name Eliza passed along from Philadelphia would not do. Among other reasons, the man was "unacquainted with blacks," whom he would need to manage at Mount Vernon, at least for the foreseeable future. "Finding there is no prospect of engaging a suitable character in Philadelphia," Washington instructed Martha to write back to Eliza, "I must take the chance of getting one here."

Suddenly he feared that he might have to "break" the "resolution" he had made against buying more human beings. Renting a slave would technically avoid breaking the pledge. So would apprehending an escaped one. It would not be easy, Washington knew. "If Hercules was to get the least hint of the design, he would elude" it.

■ ■ ■ ■

The many visitors to Mount Vernon that spring included a party of French princes, cousins to the guillotined king. Like young Georges Washington Lafayette, they had fled their homes. For a few days, the general welcomed them to his house and, in a sense, hers, too, for she lived within footsteps, just out of line of sight, of the mansion house. All the mansion house slaves did, many in the large brick wings attached to either side of the greenhouse. As children, when the general was not looking, they had played in his gardens. But she was not a child anymore, even if she looked small for her age. She was over eleven, which usually meant old enough to work and old enough to know to bow to white strangers from afar but not to approach. It was the Frenchmen who engaged her. They had heard about Hercules. Someone attending them said she must be "deeply upset" that she would "never see her father again."*

"Oh," she responded. It was not the first time she had bid her father farewell. That

*Which of Hercules's daughters the princes met cannot be determined with absolute certainty. For competing theories, see the notes.

105

had been in 1790, when he had gone to the president's house in Philadelphia. He had returned a changed man, sporting shiny shoes, a cane, a blue coat with brassy buttons, and a pocket watch that he had purchased from selling kitchen leftovers. He also returned with a realization: the excuses the general gave for sending slaves back to Mount Vernon every so often served as cover to stop them from claiming freedom under Pennsylvania law. The lies had hurt her father's feelings. So perhaps had the mistrust with which the overseers had handled him after his most recent return to Mount Vernon in the fall of 1796. A few months later, amid celebrations of Washington's birthday, her father had fled. This time, she knew, he would not come back.

Everyone seemed to miss him. As to whether she herself resented his escape, however, she could say only this: "I am very glad, because he is free now." Probably he had returned to Philadelphia. Whether she could one day join him remained, at best, uncertain. Talk of the general emancipating his slaves in the future abounded. But, unlike her father, she was not one of the general's slaves. Slaves belonged to their mother's owner, and her late mother had belonged to the Custis estate. Into the servitude of the Custis heirs, she would almost certainly pass, for the ground between Virginia and Pennsylvania — between South and North — had never looked so impassable.

CHAPTER THREE:
SONS OF THE CHILDLESS

Grandpapa liked to say that "honesty is always the best policy." Not so, Wash had discovered near the start of the summer of 1797. "Ashamed" had been the way Grandpapa described his feelings after hearing Wash confess a desire to drop out of the college at Princeton. The guilt had been unbearable. Wash had promised to return and rededicate himself to school. "My very soul, tortured with the sting of conscience, at length called reason to its aid and, happy for me, triumphed," he wrote. "The conflict was long [and] doubtful till at length I obtained the victory over myself and now return like the *prodigal son* a sincere penitent." Nothing did he want so much as Grandpapa's approval.

In search of it, Wash turned his blue eyes to a new piece of paper and wrote home again on July 1. Would Grandpapa be pleased to hear about Wash forgoing a ball on the Fourth of July because he deemed the venue not "consistent with propriety"? He would read in his room instead, even though the mercury rising to ninety-eight degrees had made "study and confinement very disagreeable." Would Grandpapa also be pleased to hear about Wash resuming an edifying correspondence with an old tutor who had attended Yale College?

No and no, came the answers. First, if it was "usual for the students . . . to go to the balls," Wash should have gone, too. Second, corresponding with a Yale man might divert Wash from the course of study advised at Princeton and lead to "evil." Furthermore, Wash had obviously recorded the temperature incorrectly. "At no time this summer has the mercury been above 90, or at most 91, at this place, and . . . Princeton must be as cool *at least* as Mount Vernon, being nearly two degrees North of it." Grandpapa, of course, would know. He had fought a famous battle at Princeton and won.

So it went with letters from Grandpapa. The advice flowed, as if he could not hold back. "Endeavor to conciliate the good will of *all* your fellow students," but "select the most deserving only for your friendship, and before this becomes intimate, weigh their dispositions and character *well*." Join "no society while you are at college that is not sanctioned by the professors." Pursue the "course of reading" the college recommends "whilst your own judgment is locked up in immaturity." That was what most worried Grandpapa: the possibility of Wash following his own judgment. "You are now entering into that stage of life when good or bad habits are formed, when the mind will be turned to things useful & praiseworthy or to dissipation and vice. . . . This, in a strong point of view, shows the propriety of letting your inexperience be directed by maturer advice and in placing guards upon the avenues which lead to idleness and vice. The latter will approach like a thief, working upon your passions." In return for this advice, Grandpapa required "assurances" of it being followed. He "was not to be trifled with."

Grandpapa hoped Wash would one day become "a useful member of society." For now, however, just being part of society — just glimpsing history as a member of the country's first household — pleased Wash. There had been the day in 1793 when he had watched the procession of masons, musicians, and militiamen accompanying a joyful-looking Grandpapa to lay the cornerstone of the Capitol. Most intimate had been the morning that Wash had walked in on Grandpapa dressing and seen the "manly frame" almost completely naked, save for a "miniature portrait" of Grandmama dangling around his neck. Just how "thin he was in person" astonished Wash. So did the abnormality he saw around Grandpapa's chest: where it should have "rounded out" in the center, it instead "indented" as if being sucked into his heart and lungs. Wash had heard that "a pulmonary affection in early life" had "considerably broken" Grandpapa's voice, even though it could still produce words with "distinctness" and "precision."

As for Wash, he liked to puff out his own chest by being the first to inform Grandpapa of political intelligence. Sharing the news, in a sense, made Wash feel part of it. Had Grandpapa heard about the misfortune that had befallen the three largest northern financiers speculating in the federal city real estate market? One had just checked into debtors' prison. The other two, including Robert Morris, who had owned the house Grandpapa had rented in Philadelphia, were "much embarrassed." More uplifting news had arrived from abroad: "It was with heartfelt satisfaction I read that [General] Bonaparte had sued for the liberation of the

Marquis [de Lafayette]." The news, if "authentic," should bring "great relief" to Lafayette's son, Georges, at Mount Vernon.

For one evening in the summer of 1797, Mount Vernon felt at the center of the political universe, thanks to a visit from John Marshall, the dark-eyed forty-one-year-old Virginian en route to Philadelphia and then off to France, where he would be one of three envoys representing the United States. "Worthy of . . . friendship and confidence" was Washington's judgment of Marshall after hearing him talk about the crisis abroad and farming advances at home. Inventions such as the new threshing machine Marshall described were of particular interest to Washington. Mount Vernon needed "one or two" of such machines "with as little delay as possible," he immediately decided.

For days after Marshall's departure, Washington recollected their conversation. Never had he crossed the ocean the younger man soon would. Youthful dreams of seeing Europe had died long ago. The only passage before an aging man was time. The records he kept of it in diaries often showed little more than the clouds passing overhead, the wind blowing, and the mercury rising and falling.

July 12: "Little or no wind. Mercury at 83." The irritation he had felt that day while writing back to Samuel Washington, a nephew begging for a loan, did not deserve entry. Of course, he had given the young man what he could — and interest-free, too — but only after giving a lecture. "I perceive by your letter . . . that you are under the same mistake that many others are, in supposing that I have money always at command. The case is so much the reverse of it." Only with great difficulty had he been able to pull together the money needed to "clear . . . out of Philadelphia."

No longer would he receive the twenty-five thousand dollars that Congress had allotted him annually during his presidency. The sum, delivered in quarterly installments, had not always even sufficed to cover the expenses he encountered in office. In fact, Benjamin Franklin Bache had published a series of articles in the *Aurora* accusing Washington of drawing excess pay from the Treasury when, in reality, he had just taken what his financial friends termed "advances." Either way, nothing of that money remained. Dividends from the thousands of dollars of stocks he owned as well as an annuity from the Custis estate would provide some income flow. So would the rents he charged tenants on lands he owned up the Potomac. As for the farms at Mount Vernon, they made barely enough to "support themselves." The expense of keeping up the mansion house alone would consume any profit they made as well as any deriving from the mill and fishery. The plan to rent the farms had so far come to naught. Ditto for the plan to sell his most prized Ohio Country lands, which he valued at more than three hundred thousand dollars or about ten dollars an acre but for which he found no person yet willing to pay. Although he had not lost faith in the western future he had seen over the mountains, he had lost patience. He needed cash now. He was owed it by various people, whom he would have sued if not so averse to the hassle of litigation. Sometimes these debtors tried to convince him to accept strange and perhaps fraudulent means of payment, when it was, as he found himself repeating, "the money I wanted." Getting it from a bank was out of the question. Just because he had signed a bill creating a national bank did not mean he understood how bank loans worked. He had never taken one. "Debt," he warned his nephew Samuel, builds "like a snow ball in rolling."

One need only look at poor Robert Morris. He was a close friend. In the dark days of the Revolution, he had offered his own credit to the Continental Army because the Congress had possessed so little. Now holed up in a house outside Philadelphia, he could barely fend off his own creditors. It had been with some "repugnance," Washington remembered, that he had allowed Morris and his partners — "men of spirit with large capital" — to buy thousands of lots in the federal city on credit. Washington had hoped to finance the public buildings not by making private deals with "speculators" but by auctioning off lots to settlers. But not enough such bidders had opened their purses, and fear of reopening debate over the site of the federal district had made those involved reluctant to request Congress open its purse. "Something" else had been "necessary to put the wheels in motion," and nothing, Washington believed, moved men faster than "self-interest." Plus, Morris and his partners had promised to build brick houses in a city that had barely a hundred of them in total. But few structures could stand up against the snowball of debt now rolling after Morris and muddying the titles to properties associated with his name.

It was, in sum, "a disagreeable spectacle."

July 17: "Appearances of rain most part of the day but none fell — pleasant. Went up to the Federal City," twelve miles away. That was the entry for the beginning of the first overnight trip away from Mount Vernon since Washington had returned. He had recently heard people express "doubts" about whether the government would move to the new capital. They needed to hear him say that "he did not entertain the least doubt," so he had obliged. What else could he have said? The private investment the city desperately needed would flee even faster without public confidence. Besides, reports of progress since March fueled genuine hope. "One wing of the Capitol (with which Congress might make a very good shift) and the President's house will be covered in this autumn, or to speak more correctly perhaps, the latter is *now* receiving its cover, and the former will be ready for it by that epoch." For the first time, people needing to cross the river running through the federal district could forgo the ferry. "An elegant bridge is thrown over the Potomac at the Little Falls," a few miles above the city.

July 19: "Went by the bridge at the Little Falls to the Great Falls & returned home in the afternoon." He had seen what he wanted to see. The canal bypassing the Little Falls had finally opened. A boat carrying the wealth from the west downriver could proceed to port in the federal district, that is, after being lugged overland around the still-unfinished canal at Great Falls about ten miles farther upriver, where the water dropped more than seventy feet. Part of Washington wanted to preserve the rugged scene; he had just purchased a landscape of it. Another part of him wanted the rocks and rapids obliterated. For too long, they had obstructed passage to the Ohio Country. A dozen years had passed since he had persuaded representatives in Maryland and Virginia to charter a company to improve the river. Until becoming president of the United States, he himself had served as president of the venture. It had given his mind a much-needed mission after the war.

July 31: "Mercury at 76. Wind Easterly — and frequent showers of rain in the afternoon." No mention was needed of how lonely Mount Vernon had felt that day. "I am alone *at present,* and shall be glad to see you this evening," he had written Tobias Lear, the thirty-four-year-old Harvard graduate who had served as Washington's personal secretary until opening a Potomac

Lat Capitol.... 38: 53. N.
Long......... 0. 0.

GEORGE TOWN

PART OF VIRGINIA WITHIN THE TERRITORY OF COLUMBIA.

POTOMAK RIVER

OBSERVATIONS
explanatory of the
Plan.

I. THE positions for the different Edifices, and for the several Squares or Areas of different shapes, as they are laid down, were first determined on the most advantageous ground, commanding the most extensive prospects, and the better susceptible of such improvements, as either use or ornament may hereafter call for.

II. LINES or Avenues of direct communication have been devised, to connect the separate and most distant objects with the principal, and to preserve through the whole a reciprocity of sight at the same time. Attention has been paid to the passing of these leading Avenues over the most favorable ground for prospect and convenience.

III. NORTH and South lines intersected by others running due East and West, make the distribution of the City into Streets, Squares, &c. and these lines have been so combined as to meet at certain given points with those divergent Avenues, so as to form on the Spaces "first determined," the different Squares or Areas.

SCALE OF POLES.

A map showing the 1792 plan for the City of Washington, including the Capitol, the ident's house, and squares out of which lots were to be sold. The diagonal avenues cut across the grid and connecting key points, the caption on the map explains, "have devised . . . to preserve through the whole a reciprocity of sight." At the confluence of Potomac River and its so-called Eastern Branch (the Anacostia), the City of Wash

Within the image:

PLAN

of the CITY of

Washington

(in the Territory of Columbia,)

ceded by the States of

VIRGINIA and MARYLAND

to the

United States of America,

and by them established as the

SEAT of their GOVERNMENT,

after the Year

MDCCC.

BRANCH

OF MARYLAND WITHIN THE TERRITORY OF COLUMBIA.

Breadth of the Streets.

THE grand Avenues, and such Streets as lead immediately to public
places, are from 130 to 160 feet wide, and may be conveniently divided
into feet ways, walks of trees, and a carriage way. The other Streets
are from 90 to 110 feet wide.

IN order to execute this plan, Mr. ELLICOTT drew a true Meridional
line by celestial observation, which passes through the Area intended for the
Capitol; this line he crossed by another due East and West, which passes through
the same Area. These lines were accurately measured, and made the basis on
which the whole plan was executed. He ran all the lines by a Transit Instru-
ment, and determined the Acute Angles by actual measurement, and left
nothing to the uncertainty of the Compass.

originally accounted for only a portion of the larger District of Columbia, which also
...ded Georgetown (shown) to the west and Alexandria (not shown) to the south. "No
...arture from the engraved plan of the City ought to be allowed, unless imperious neces-
...should require it," Washington wrote during the final months of his life. Courtesy of
...Geography and Map Division, Library of Congress.

119

trading company. "Unless someone pops in, unexpectedly, Mrs. Washington and myself will do what I believe has not been done within the last twenty years by us, that is, to set down to dinner by ourselves."

Literary young men like Lear would have once surrounded the table. The aides with whom Washington had often shared his meals during the war constituted what he called "my family." He missed their company. As late as the past spring, he had hoped that forty-five-year-old former aide-de-camp and self-declared poet David Humphreys would join the household. It had been Humphreys whom Washington had authorized to write an official biography in 1785. He had even edited portions of it himself. Unfortunately, portions were all Humphreys had produced. Only a few pages had been published, and those anonymously at the end of a reference book. Word that Humphreys had recently found a wife while overseas in Europe had "annihilated every hope" of his now moving to Mount Vernon and finishing the book. "The desire of a companion in my latter days, in whom I could confide, might have induced me to express myself too strongly," Washington admitted after hearing about the engagement. If Humphreys could not join the house, perhaps Washington's thirty-year-old nephew Lawrence Lewis, son of the late Betty, could. "As both your Aunt and I are in the decline of life," Washington would write Lawrence, "I require some person (fit & proper) to ease me of the trouble of entertaining company," which, the loneliness of this day notwithstanding, the house still usually had.

August 21: "Clear with little or no wind. Mercury at 80." Not since leaving office had Washington heard from the most famous member of his military family: Alexander Hamilton. The name was back in the news. Corruption charges that Hamilton had disproved time and again while treasury secretary had reappeared in the latest Republican smear, a new publication called *The History of the United States for 1796.* Washington did not ask anyone to send a copy. Instead, he decided to send Hamilton a gift. "Not for any intrinsic value the thing possesses, but as a token of my sincere regard and friendship for you, and as a remembrance of me, I pray you to accept a wine cooler." It had been left behind by mistake in Philadelphia. Only recently had Washington remembered it.

September 15: "Great appearances of rain with light drippings in the forenoon —

mercury 78. In the afternoon about 6 o'clock, it began a sober rain & continued till 11 o'clock." He dared not record any reaction to the pamphlet he had just finished. It was Hamilton's response to *The History of the United States for 1796*. "The charge against me is a connection with one James Reynolds for purposes of improper pecuniary speculation," Hamilton had written. "My real crime is an amorous connection with his wife, for a considerable time with his privity and connivance, if not originally brought on by a combination between the husband and wife with the design to extort money from me. . . . I had frequent meetings with her, most of them at my own house; Mrs. Hamilton with her children being absent on a visit to her father." Only by confessing to a personal indiscretion did Hamilton, evidently, believe he could clear his name of official wrongdoing. For being forced to this extreme, Hamilton blamed Francophile "Jacobin[s]" conspiring to destroy faith in the federal government by destroying the reputations "of our most virtuous citizens. . . . Even the great and multiplied services — the tried and rarely equaled virtues — of a WASHINGTON can secure no exemption."

With that, Washington agreed. He tried to

pretend as if he took no notice of the Republican gazettes. Just recently, he had written a letter demanding one such outlet stop sending its paper to Mount Vernon. He did not care to read it, he had said. But, of course, he did. He needed to read it. The compulsion to safeguard his reputation had not receded. He especially longed to know what lies lay on the pages of the *Aurora,* but he dared not give an editor such as Bache the satisfaction of seeing the name George Washington among the subscribers. Instead, he would subscribe under someone else's name. Perhaps Secretary of War James McHenry could send the *Aurora* under cover of the War Department. Someone should also send *The History of the United States for 1796.* Having read Hamilton's response made one want to read the original.

October 3: "Clear & very warm. Wind Southerly — mercury at 68. . . . Washington Custis came home." Nothing else needed to be noted about young Wash returning from Princeton. Despite pledging to submit to the better judgment of elders, Wash had been suspended for "various acts of meanness & irregularity." Worse, professors accused him of undermining their "authority & influence." That Wash would not go back to the college was apparent. The experiment had lasted less than a year. The boy had only himself to "upbraid" for squandering the college education that Washington had once wished for himself but had long ago lost the opportunity to receive. He had been just eleven when his father, Augustine Washington, had died along with all hope of continuing the family tradition of embarking for England for education. A few more years of schooling had been all that Washington could afford. Having never acquired the knowledge of Latin and French a gentleman should possess had implanted an insecurity deep inside him. Even as president, he had felt it: the suspicion that he lacked "many of the essential qualifications" for office.

He had hoped for better for Wash but feared much worse. "From his infancy, I have discovered an almost unconquerable disposition to indolence in everything that did not tend to his amusements, and have exhorted him in the most parental and friendly manner, often, to devote his time to more useful pursuits." That Wash's late father, Martha's son Jacky, had shown the same disposition spoke less to heredity and more to the environment in which Martha raised boys. She coddled them. There was nothing Washington could do. The children had always been more hers than his. The stern discipline Wash required would have caused Martha distress, which Washington dared not inflict. Her happiness, he knew, "is bound up in the boy." Any hope for diverting Wash from the "road to ruin" depended on prying him from her protective embrace.

Where the boy should go next perplexed Washington. He would have already sent Wash to that college in Cambridge, Massachusetts, if not for the knowledge that sending him so far from home would prove "a heart-rending stroke" to Martha. "I believe that the habits of the youths there . . . are less prone to dissipation & debauchery than they are at the colleges [to the] South," for example, Virginia's William & Mary.

What a shame that the national university Washington had proposed for the federal city still existed only in his imagination. Despite the very real pledge he had made in 1795 to endow the institution with the fifty shares of stock that the Virginia legislature had gifted him (unnecessarily and embarrassingly so) in the Potomac Company — despite the pleas he had made to Congress the following year in the conviction that no young man should need to cross an ocean in pursuit of education — the plan had won little support.

October 12: "Cold & frosty morning. . . . Mr. Georges Washington Lafayette & [his tutor] Mr. Frestel left . . . for Georgetown to take the stage for New York to embark for France. I accompanied them to the Federal City." Pleas for Georges to wait for more "authentic accounts" of his father's release were to no avail. Georges had determined to set sail. Even pointing out that his father might be sailing the opposite way — perhaps he would want to live out his days near Mount Vernon — could not dissuade Georges. "It will . . . be a matter of sore disappointment & regret if his parents should have embarked for America before he sees them in Europe & will be a source of much concern to me also, for he is an amiable and sensible youth," Washington wrote. But no argument could overcome the "ardent filial . . . affection" Georges felt.

If the Austrians really had released Lafayette, what would he think when he finally reunited with Georges and heard how the young man had not initially received the reception he had expected? The question troubled Washington. Georges would need to explain the "delicate . . . situation" in which Washington had found himself.

Georges had "leaped for joy" and dashed into a field upon receiving the news: his father was free. For months, Georges had shrouded his sorrows as best he could. He had not wanted to bring them into Mount Vernon. But it had not been easy. Being at the house brought back memories of Father. In the hall hung the key to the Bastille, the infamous Paris prison that Father had ordered torn down during the heady days when he had dared to imagine the French Revolution culminating with a constitution that protected natural rights and contained checks and balances. The key to the Bastille, Father had written then-president Washington, "is a tribute which I owe as a son to my adoptive father, as an aide de camp to my general, as a missionary of liberty to its patriarch." In the parlor off the hall hung another reminder: an old painting showing Father and Mother as well as Georges and his two sisters. The paint around the faces had begun to peel. It was fitting, for no one in the portrait looked now as they had then.

Gone was the handsome military uniform that Father had worn. Instead, "rags" were said to have covered the body that had wasted away until recently in the Austrian prison at Olmütz. Gone was the youth Mother should have still possessed at thirty-seven years old. The radicals forcing Father's flight from France had imprisoned her in his stead and sent her mother, sister, and grandmother to the guillotine along with the thousands of other victims of the Reign of Terror. For a time, Mother had lost faith in all but God. Even Washington had disappointed her. She had implored him to send an envoy demanding Father's release from the Austro-Prussian counter-revolutionary forces who had captured him after his defection. But Washington had sent only money. "I cannot believe it!" she had exclaimed. "I confess to you, Sir, that your silence — and the abandonment of the Marquis Lafayette & his family — is perhaps of all our evils the most inexplicable to me." Nonetheless, after leaving her prison in Paris in early 1795, she had resolved to give Washington another chance before setting off with her two daughters to join Father in his prison in Austria. "Sir," she had written Washington, "I send you my son. Although I have not had the consolation . . . of obtaining from you those good offices which I thought likely to bring about his father's delivery from the hands of our enemies, . . .

I put my dear child under the protection of the United States, which he has ever been accustomed to look upon as his second country."

Thus, Georges had sailed off in search of the namesake whom Father adored but whom Mother struggled to comprehend. Georges had grown up hearing stories about Father's youthful exploits during the Revolutionary War: not only about the glorious part he had played in the critical Yorktown campaign of 1781 but also about the wound he had received at Brandywine in 1777. "Treat him as if he were my son," General Washington had ordered the medic. No words could have pleased Father more. He proudly proclaimed himself Washington's "adoptive son." For Father, the general had once professed "perfect love & gratitude that neither time nor absence can impair." For the general, Father had named his only son. That was Georges. For as long as he could remember, he had heard that he would find a "second father" in the United States.

But it had not turned out that way in August 1795, when Georges had sent a letter announcing his arrival in Boston. President Washington, then in his second term, had sent no invitation to Philadelphia, only an offer to pay for Georges's education at Harvard, and even that had come via a third party. Apparently, Washington had deemed it inappropriate to write directly. Months passed. Not until November 1795 had a personal note from the president arrived. Over and over, "a thousand times repeated," Georges had read that letter. Washington explained that he wanted "to stand in the place of a father" but could not yet offer a place inside his house. Georges had not been able to understand. "The idea of not being permitted" to come to Philadelphia had been "very painful." For a time afterward, he had struggled to eat. Not until early 1796, with talk of a congressional investigation into the whereabouts of Lafayette's son, had the doors of the president's house finally opened to Georges.

Now, all these months later, Georges understood how much the situation had distressed Washington, how much he had wanted to embrace Georges. While an ordinary citizen could simply follow his conscience, a "public character" needed to worry about appearances. A president who had just signed a controversial treaty with Britain could not appear eager to shelter the son of a French defector.

Altogether, while bidding farewell to his

American father, Georges felt grateful. "I have the hope of being after so long and so cruel a separation at last united again to my parents and sisters," he told Washington. "I need not tell you, Sir, that if anything can soften the painful remembrances of all their sufferings, it will be to hear from [me] . . . that the friendship with which you always honored the father has induced you to receive the son under your roof with so much goodness!" Along the way to New York, Georges happily agreed to stop in Princeton as a personal favor to the general. Wash had left unpaid debts at the college. Someone needed to settle them.

By December of 1797, the Potomac had frozen. The ice blanketing the water between Mount Vernon and Maryland made the river appear a barren and hostile wilderness. Washington struggled to remember "an earlier winter . . . for since the beginning of November we have scarcely experienced a moderate day." The fireside warmed the visitors who somehow managed to keep flowing into the house. Among them were the British minister, Robert Liston, and his younger wife, Henrietta, whom Washington had always liked to have seated by his side in Philadelphia. The arrival of nephew

Lawrence Lewis reduced the burden of entertaining guests. So did hiring a housekeeper, whose exorbitant salary Washington countenanced only because efforts to recover Hercules had proved unsuccessful despite a reported sighting of him in Philadelphia. Martha could wait for help no longer. She looked "exceedingly fatigued."

Washington himself felt pent-up energy. Hence, his surprise upon learning that Martha had received a letter from Eliza Willing Powel inquiring about a rumor of his suffering an "apoplectic" fit. Martha, he thought, should send Eliza a witty response. He would draft it. "I am now, by desire of the General, to add a few words on his behalf," Martha should write. "As he has entered into an engagement with . . . several other gentlemen not to quit the theatre of *this* world before the year 1800, it may be *relied upon* that no breach of contract shall be laid to him on that account, unless dire necessity should bring it about. . . . At present there seems to be no danger of his giving them the slip, as neither his health, nor spirits, were ever in greater flow, notwithstanding, he adds, he is descending & has almost reached the bottom of the hill." As to the reports that he had suffered an "apoplectic" fit, Eliza should know that he would much rather suffer some other kind of fit: "a love fit, a fit of laughter, and many other kinds which he could name."

On days when it was too cold to ride around the farms, he would spend an hour pacing from one end of his piazza to the other. He could go miles without going anywhere. An impatience grew inside him. "It is time, now, to hear what the reception of our envoys at Paris has been & what their prospects are." The last letter he had received from Marshall had dimmed hopes. It carried the date of September 15 and came from French-occupied Holland, where the envoys had planned to rendezvous before proceeding to Paris. According to the information then in Marshall's possession, an army-backed coup had resulted in the French Directory's three most radical members ousting the two other members and reversing an election that had brought moderates favoring peace to power in the legislature. "Complete and impartial details concerning it will not easily be obtained as the press is no longer free," Marshall wrote of the coup. "The journalists who had ventured to censure the proceedings . . . are seized." Seeing so-called Republicans in America defend such a tyrannical regime made Washington want to laugh. He had to remind himself that he had "quit politics." His field was the past.

David Humphreys might never produce a definitive Washington biography, but someone else would. The papers Washington had saved needed to be made ready for research. Thus, the resolution he made: "I shall be able to go but little out of the house this winter having appropriated it to the assorting and arranging my voluminous papers — a task of no small magnitude." It would leave little time for looking after his lands. An agreement he had finally reached would put twenty-three thousand acres of his best Ohio Country lands in the hands of a man named James Welch despite there being some "doubt" about his honesty. The fate of the Mount Vernon farms, however, remained as uncertain as ever. An inquiry from an "experienced" English farmer named Richard Parkinson had raised hopes for renting out one of the farms, but no agreement had been reached. In the meantime, Washington would have to rely more on James Anderson, the Scottish immigrant who had recently taken over as Mount Vernon's estate manager.

Many of the ideas the Scotsman brought to Mount Vernon — for example, building a distillery that would make the estate a major whiskey producer — received Washington's approval. The implementation, however, did not. Washington could not ignore the inefficiencies he spotted when inspecting the farms. Why did he see mostly empty carts carrying "trifles" to Alexandria multiple times a day instead of just making one trip with a "full load"? Why did he see slaves sometimes "shifting suddenly from one kind of work to another" and other times "waiting more than half a day before" being put to work? The small problems added up to a systemic one, namely that Anderson followed no system at all. In sum, Mount Vernon's manager needed to manage better. "If a person only sees or directs from day to day what is to be done, business can never go on methodically or well, for in case of sickness or the absence of the director, delays must follow," Washington wrote Anderson. "System in all things is the soul of business." Because man by nature was erratic and frail, systems needed to be strong and lasting.

No one needed "system" more than Martha's grandson. "Now & then," according to the written orders Washington issued at the start of the new year, Wash could "go out with a gun" and hunt "before breakfast" so long as he would promise to "confine" himself to his "studies" afterward until "an hour before dinner." That Wash promised to obey, of course, did not mean he would. He almost always said what elders wanted to hear. Just watching the boy "running up & down the stairs" to no end for "hours" filled the mind with worry as to what other ways he would find to "misspend his time."

Virginia provided endless examples of "opulent" young men disgracing their families. One such story had recently come to Washington's attention courtesy of a man named John Nicholas. Nicholas did not say exactly what he did for a living, only that he monitored the mail in Albemarle County, Virginia, where he lived, as he said, "in cannon shot of the very headquarters of *Jacobinism,*" that is, Monticello.

It had started back in November with an "unclaimed" letter at the post office in Albemarle County. Weeks had passed. The letter would have raised no eyebrows except for the unusual dichotomy between its sender and recipient. The former was George Washington, the most recognized name in America. The latter was John Langhorne, a name the postmaster did not recognize at all. That was why John Nicholas had involved himself. He was the clerk for the county and had made it his business to know every name therein. Plus, he considered General Washington a friend and was confident the general would return the feeling if only they could have cause to meet.

Who was Langhorne? Nicholas knew, as it turned out, "an old gentleman of that name in an adjoining county." Probably the letter had gone to the wrong place. Then, on November 18, a "great surprise" had upended that assumption. A young man definitely not named Langhorne had claimed the mysterious letter after explaining that he had used the pseudonym only to correspond with General Washington. Within hours, Nicholas had rushed off a letter of his own warning the general that Langhorne was not who he claimed and, in fact, was "closely connected with some of your greatest and bitterest enemies." If Nicholas could come to Mount Vernon, he would explain more.

Shortly afterward, Nicholas received his own letter from Mount Vernon. "I know not how to thank you sufficiently," the general wrote. Only politeness, he explained, had induced him to mail a letter to "John Langhorne," who had begun the correspondence by urging Washington to stand tall against Republican attacks on his character. The intent was clear: win the general's confidence and then lure him into divulging some indiscreet thought that could be used against him. Fortunately, the general had responded cautiously. So that Nicholas could see for himself, Washington enclosed copies of the correspondence. "If they should be a mean of detecting any nefarious plan of those who are assailing the government in every shape that can be devised, I shall feel happy in having had it in my power to furnish them."

Indeed, Nicholas did detect a "nefarious plan." Washington surely would, too, once he learned the one critical piece of information Nicholas had withheld: the true identity of John Langhorne. Much as Nicholas had wished to deliver the evidence in person, he could wait no longer. On December 9, he wrote Washington a second letter identifying Langhorne as one Peter Carr, a twenty-seven-year-old "entertaining sentiments, I do assure you of my own personal knowledge, very different indeed towards *you* from those contained in his letter." As to the reason for the ruse, Nicholas had a theory: Carr had sought to obtain information he could use in the service of his loving uncle, the general's "very sincere friend" Thomas Jefferson. Here was a revelation to rouse even the most reticent of retirees.

CHAPTER FOUR:
SECRET LETTERS

The addition of Robert Morris in February 1798 made it a majority. Two of the three most famous financiers speculating in the federal government's future home had now succeeded in procuring a new home for themselves. Anyone needing to do business with them would find them at Philadelphia's Prune Street Debtors' Prison. So that was where Thomas Law had gone shortly after arriving in Philadelphia from the City of Washington, where he had invested the wealth he had earned as a British official in India toward building a home and developing lots around the Capitol. It was not just business that prompted the trip to Philadelphia. There was also pleasure, the joy of showing off the wife he had won in 1796, not long after immigrating to America. She was a "prize" that "delighted all eyes." She was Martha Washington's oldest grandchild, Elizabeth "Betsey" Parke Custis. And at just twenty-one years old, she was about half Law's age. She gave him the connection he desperately sought: a relationship with America's most famous man, her step-grandfather.

That a controversy involving George Washington would dominate the trip never occurred to Law until the morning of February 23, 1798. Just the night before, the Laws had attended a dinner party at President Adams's house, where Betsey had joked about marrying her youngest sister, Nelly, off to one of the Adamses' sons. That the dinner had fallen on George Washington's sixty-sixth birthday had been a co-incidence. The real celebration would happen tonight at the ball that Eliza Willing Powel's brother had helped plan in honor of the old chief. Though Washington no longer lived among them, Philadelphia's Federalists had assumed they would celebrate his birthday, in their usual way, by toasting and dancing, that is, until they opened that day's *Aurora* and found Benjamin Franklin Bache's latest outrage.

On the third page appeared an item leading with this question: "What would be thought of a man high in office refusing to accept a public invitation to a ball given in celebration of the Birth Day of George

Washington and returning a written answer couched in the following impolite & arrogant terms?"

I have received your polite invitation . . . & embrace the earliest opportunity of informing you that I decline accepting it.

The letter was signed by none other than John Adams. Having somehow obtained a copy, Bache gloated over the controversy sure to ensue. "President [Adams] knows too well the respect due to himself. . . . It is to be hoped that the [ball] managers will not again celebrate the birth day of a president politically defunct."

Adams had created a needless controversy. He had acted, Law thought, "ignobly." In "republics," people did not revere "titles." They revered "virtuous actions." To acknowledge that the former president, who had fought for freedom in the field, outstripped his successor in that regard should not have wounded the latter's pride, and yet it manifestly had. Only jealousy, Law wrote in his diary, could have driven Adams to draft such a "petulant & rude" response. "The answer has offended the people, for they all almost adore their old patriot." Most offended was Betsey. Law himself could not soothe the "ardent" and "uncontrollable" temper she claimed to have inherited from her late father. The thought of people following Adams's lead and skipping the ball horrified her. It would insult Washington. In desperation, she pleaded with people — even Republicans — to attend. She told one congressman he could escort her and be her dance partner if only he would go. "It would mortify Mr. Adams and please Mr. Washington," she insisted. Tempted as the congressman must have been, he said no. He would not go.

Others did go, however. Unwilling to appease Adams were the cabinet secretaries he had inherited. Each of them attended the ball in honor of their old chief.

The bones in the family burial ground beside his birthplace downriver: something that February made Washington ponder them. Maybe it was the result of turning another year older. Maybe it was occasionally entertaining the thought of what people would say about him when he died. Maybe it was the realization that more than a year had elapsed without his responding to a genealogist's inquiry into the English origins of his family. He had "paid very little attention," he liked to say, to his genealogy beyond using the family coat of arms and believing that his immigrant forebear, John Washington, had landed in America in "1657 or thereabouts." Having "been so much occupied in the busy and active scenes of life from an early period" had left little time for learning more, that is, until recently. Could a relative living near the cemetery, Washington wrote, send copies of the "inscriptions on the tombs of our ancestors," the dates of birth and death?

In the family Bible, Washington's own birthday had been recorded not as February 22 but as February 11, in accordance with the Old Style calendar used at the time. It was around that date that he celebrated this year by taking Martha and Nelly to Alexandria for a ball. The usual artillery fire welcomed them. Couples filled the dance floor.

Back at Mount Vernon afterward arrived birthday greetings from Virginia's Albemarle County. As promised, John Nicholas had continued to investigate the deceptive letter. Though Nicholas still could not prove it, circumstantial evidence had convinced him that Peter Carr had acted "under the guidance of" Uncle Thomas Jefferson. "Besides the clear proofs of the vile hypocrisy of *that man's* professions of friendship towards you

143

contained in the celebrated letter to Mazzei, he begins now to speak out, in this part of the world, a very different language from what I have formerly heard him express," read Nicholas's letter. Examples followed.

The one that troubled Washington most was the charge that Jefferson had helped draft a disturbing new book by fellow Albemarle County Republican James Monroe. The same Monroe whom Washington had appointed as minister to France in 1794 "after several attempts had failed to obtain a more eligible character." The same Monroe who had convinced the French that the American people were at odds with the very neutrality policy Washington had needed a minister to explain. The same Monroe who, while in Paris, had written dispatches criticizing his own government for Bache to publish in Philadelphia. The same Monroe whom Washington had finally recalled in 1796.

Secretary of State Timothy Pickering had mailed a copy of Monroe's book, *A View of the Conduct of the Executive, in the Foreign Affairs of the United States.* The title itself signaled a personal attack on Washington. How could he read it otherwise? The "executive" referenced was Washington himself, and the "view" was a malicious lie. Ratifying the Jay Treaty with Britain, went the book's argument, had betrayed America's true ally, France, as well as Monroe himself, who had suffered the "embarrassment" of promising to let the French review the terms beforehand only to discover that he himself could not obtain a copy of them. "None but a party man, lost to all sense of propriety, . . . would have brought himself into such a predicament," Washington wrote in the margin.

The urge to write a response built inside him. Never had he done anything like this before. But the more he read of Monroe's book, the more the pages filled with angry annotations. Not only did the book disclose confidential communications, but also it revealed the pretentious "self-importance" of its author. What gave Monroe the right to criticize, for example, the exclusion of the word "France" from the 1795 annual message to Congress? It had been Washington's speech. "If Mr. Monroe should ever fill the chair of government," Washington scribbled, "he may (and it is presumed he would be well enough disposed) let the French Minister frame his speeches." President Monroe! The words sounded absurd. Monroe, it was said, had written his own political "death warrant." In no way, however, did that mean Jefferson deserved pardon for the part he had played in the literary production. If Nicholas was to be believed, Jefferson had said he hoped Monroe's book would help "overturn the government of the United States."

That did it. No longer would Washington evade responding, as he had done to this point, to Nicholas's insinuations of Jefferson's involvement in Peter Carr's plot. A response was required. "Nothing short of the evidence you have adduced — corroborative of intimations which I had received long before, through another channel — could have shaken my belief in the sincerity of a friendship, which I had *conceived* was possessed for me *by the person* to whom you allude," Washington wrote Nicholas on March 8. "But attempts to injure those who are supposed to stand well in the estimation of the people . . . is one of the means by which the Government is to be assailed and the Constitution destroyed." The air in the house suddenly felt warm. The snow outside had melted. For the first time in months, the mercury in Mount Vernon's thermometer struck sixty degrees. The long winter had ended. Emotions flowed.

Still, something held them back: the fear

of producing one's own Mazzei letter. Prudence dictated Washington first send what he had written to his nephew Bushrod Washington, a respected thirty-five-year-old lawyer. "[Nicholas] seems very desirous of drawing me into a correspondence on party subjects, which — of all others — is not the most pleasant. And even civil answers upon this topic to one of whose character I know nothing might be imprudent." If Bushrod thought the response unwise, he should destroy it. Otherwise, he should send it on to Nicholas. "Misrepresentation & party feuds have arisen to such a height, as to distort truth" and to make it impossible for a man to know whom he could trust. So often people deceived and disappointed.

Even President Adams had recently delivered a "surprise" and "not of the pleasing sort." Word of the fuss that he had created over the birthday celebration in Philadelphia had spread. That sad story by itself would not have surprised; Adams's "high-toned" attitude toward protocol had embarrassed Washington before. But the controversy cast a darker shadow in light of a series of unsettling letters that Washington received and that provided him with a window into the inner workings of Adams's presidency.

The reports came from Alexander White,

one of the three presidentially appointed commissioners (holdovers all from Washington's administration) overseeing the new federal city. With no hope of receiving payment from the speculators, White had gone to Philadelphia in search of congressional financial support. Washington himself now accepted its necessity. President Adams did, too. But when White had met with Adams and pushed him to express that view publicly, he had shown "an uncommon degree of warmth." He had exclaimed that "he should not make himself a slave to the Federal City." The city was Washington's. Adams would do "no more" for it than "official duty required." The words "astonished" White. Adams must have thought better of them, too, because not long after he recanted. White reported returning for another meeting and hearing the president say that "he had a great regard for the opinion of his predecessor and would not reverse any of his orders without weighty reasons."

At present, White added, Adams supported just one change to the city: building the offices for the cabinet secretaries not in the neighborhood around the president's house, as proposed by Washington, but in the neighborhood around the Capitol, as favored by Thomas Law, whose lots in the latter area would surely rise in value as a result. Adams liked the idea because it would encourage cooperation between cabinet members and members of Congress. Washington's own thinking had been the "reverse"; that is, placing the cabinet members near the Capitol would not only make them inaccessible to the president with whom they should have "daily intercourse" but also expose them to congressmen eager to meddle in executive matters. Did Adams not understand that a president needed to keep the keys to his own cabinet? Or was he just "ignorant," Washington wondered, of the careful planning that had gone into selecting the sites for the federal city's buildings? Either way, the situation required monitoring. White should keep sending updates to Mount Vernon on the fate of the federal city. And if so inclined, he could include reports on other subjects he heard discussed, too.

The reports that Washington had requested the cabinet secretaries send from time to time had not satisfied his need to know. Too often their letters began with apologies for not responding to his sooner, and always did they insist they had no answer to the one question he most wished to know: What of the envoys? Since their arrival in Paris in September, no one had heard from them. Lots else had been heard from France and her most feared general, Bonaparte. The treaty that he had imposed on the Austrians had taken them out of the war. Rumor said that he would cross the English Channel next. Little could be known for sure. Much depended on the envoys. Benign explanations for the silence dwindled with the days. "Are our Commissioners guillotined?" Washington wrote Secretary of War James McHenry on March 4.

Then, at last, news came. Dispatches from the envoys had reached Philadelphia. On March 5, Adams forwarded one of them to Congress. "We can only repeat that there exists no hope of our being officially received . . . or that the objects of our mission will be in any way accomplished," the envoys wrote from Paris. The other dispatches were said to require deciphering. Adams, however, already seemed to have "some knowledge of their contents," or so read the letter that Alexander White sent to Mount Vernon after dining with Adams in mid-March. "[Adams] said the letters might contain facts which would implicate individuals on either side of the water, or even endanger the personal safety of our ministers," White wrote. "I would not have communicated these sentiments expressed in the private manner which I have related [to you] to any other person."

Too bad the American people could not see the rest of the dispatches. Abigail Adams knew how much her "dearest friend" and husband, the president, wished he could share them. "It is a very painful thing to him that he cannot communicate to the public dispatches in which they are so much interested," she wrote. "But we have not any assurance that the Envoys have left Paris and who can say that in this critical state of things their dispatches ought to be public." The envoys could face retribution while still in a country whose revolution and resulting wars had killed, according to a report currently circulating, more than a million of its own men, to say nothing of women and children. At sea, the French had given their "piratical . . . robbers" newly widened latitude to terrorize American ships. And yet despite all the evidence, Republicans loyal to Vice President Jefferson continued to accuse her husband of being the one seeking war, of covering up dispatches proving France favored peace.

If George Washington had still been president, the people would not have needed to see the rest of the dispatches. They would have seen enough already. "How different is the situation of the President from that of Washington?" Abigail wrote. Where Washington had possessed the loyalty of his vice president, Abigail's husband had a vice president leading the opposition. Where Philadelphians had celebrated Washington, they insulted her husband over and over again. Of course, he had refused to attend the ball for Washington's birthday. She herself had happily celebrated the occasion the previous year. But that had been before her husband had accepted the country's first office. "Placing himself in a secondary character" to anyone would degrade that office. What would foreign ministers think? "The President of the United States [in his public character] to attend the celebration of the birth day . . . of a private citizen!" A private citizen — that was all Washington was now.

Abigail envied him. "The task of the President is very arduous, very perplexing, and very hazardous. I do not wonder Washington wished to retire from it." Her husband had begged her to join him in Philadelphia after taking office the previous year, so she had set off from their farm in Quincy, Massachusetts. She resented some of the precedents greeting her in Philadelphia: for example, the five hundred dollars' worth of "cake, punch, and wine" that the Washingtons had provided for "all the gentlemen of the city" every Fourth of July. "You will not wonder that I dread it or think President Washington to blame for introducing the custom, if he could have avoided it."

The one notable precedent her husband broke caused an uproar. He had appointed a relative — their oldest son, John Quincy Adams — as minister to Prussia. "Mr. Washington made it a rule not to appoint his relations. But if Washington had been blessed with sons — and those sons had been qualified — I presume to say he never would have observed the rule," her husband had said. Indeed, Washington himself had encouraged the appointment. It had been the one piece of parting advice he had given. "If my wishes would be of any avail, they should go to you with a *strong hope* that you will not withhold merited promotion from Mr. John Quincy Adams because he is your son, for without intending to compliment the father or the mother, or to censure any others, I give it as my *decided opinion* that Mr. [John Quincy] Adams is the most valuable public character we have abroad, and there remains no doubt in my mind that he will prove himself to be the ablest of all our diplomatic corps." Abigail had saved the letter. Her oldest son had just married. One day his children would cherish those words. If Washington had served a third term, he probably would have tapped John Quincy for the country's most sensitive diplomatic assignment: the mission to France. Then it would have been her son's life that releasing the rest of the dispatches would have risked.

Nevertheless, the Republicans continued demanding disclosure. Her husband would resist no more. His enemies would get what they wanted. They would then repent. In the first days of April 1798, Congress learned the full story of what had happened to the envoys in Paris. After arriving, they had met with the French foreign minister, Charles Maurice de Talleyrand-Périgord, who declared his government not ready to receive them. Then, three mysterious men — referred to as X, Y, and Z in dispatches scrubbed of their names — had informed the envoys that negotiations could not commence until the American government met certain demands: apologize for the most bellicose lines in the speech Abigail's husband had delivered to the special session of Congress the previous year; extend a loan to France, which desperately needed money for its wars; and deliver a bribe to Talleyrand and the Directory. The bribe was what mattered most to X, Y, and Z. Would the United States pay? "No, not a sixpence," one of the envoys answered.

Republicans reading the dispatches, Abigail exclaimed, "were struck dumb." What could they say? The fallen few who dared defend France now — who dared don the French tricolor cockade once so widely worn in Philadelphia — were not "real Americans," she thought. For the first time, the people rallied to her husband as they had rallied to Washington. From across the country, they sent addresses supporting the stand her husband had taken. In Congress, their representatives began enacting the defensive measures he had proposed "with a degree of spirit which has not before appeared." At the theater, where "it has been customary to play and sing French songs and airs," crowds demanded American ones like the "President's March" in honor of her husband. Abigail herself went to hear it played. Benjamin Franklin Bache published an article accusing her of crying during the performance. "That was a lie," she wrote.

"However, I should not have been ashamed if it had been so."

There was solace in knowing that Bache had treated Washington little better. Nothing would stop the attacks on Abigail and her husband save for a "sedition bill." She hoped one would pass soon. Someone who admired France as much as Bache "richly deserve[d] that *French freedom* and *liberty* which has been exercised against . . . printers in France." In the meantime, Bache would go on mocking her husband as "old, querulous, bald, blind, crippled, [and] toothless." In truth, her husband's appearance troubled her, too. Proud as she felt to see him don a military uniform while urging crowds of young men to do the same and go "to arms," he did not look quite right. Something was off. "I never saw Mr. Adams look so pale, and he falls away," she wrote. "But I dare not tell him so."

Between seeing clients in his New York law office, Alexander Hamilton pondered the possibility of himself wearing a new military uniform: a buff and blue coat with golden epaulettes covering his trim shoulders, a plumed hat shielding his light skin and brilliant blue eyes. The governor of New York had almost appointed Hamilton to a vacant

Senate seat without asking his permission. It was fortunate the governor had thought better of it, because Hamilton did not want the office. Unlike corrupt French ministers, Hamilton had never sought personal profit from public office, never cashed in on the inside financial information he had possessed. Only out of office could he adequately provide for his family. "There may arrive a crisis when I may conceive myself bound once more to sacrifice the interest of my family to public call. But I must defer the change as long as possible." He would accept office only if "invited to *a station in which the service I may render may be proportioned to the sacrifice.*" A Senate seat could not meet that test. A commission as a line officer in the army might.

To be a line officer — to command in the field — was what he had wanted all those years during the Revolutionary War while drafting letters for Washington and sharing his living quarters as one of his staff officers. "I always disliked the office of an aide de camp as having in it a kind of personal dependence," Hamilton had confided. It had seemed as if the general had expected Hamilton to accept a role he had not wanted: that of surrogate son. Quite simply, he "felt no friendship" for the general. "The

truth is our own dispositions are the op-
posites of each other & the pride of my
temper would not suffer me to profess what
I did not feel. Indeed, when advances of
this kind have been made to me on his part,
they were received in a manner that showed
at least I had no inclination to court them,
and that I wished to stand rather upon a
footing of military confidence than of
private attachment." Thankfully, a tiff in
1781 over keeping Washington waiting "two
minutes" — "ten minutes," he had claimed
in his usual "ill humor" — had given Hamilton the excuse he needed to "part" from
the general's staff, take to the field, and lead
a last glorious assault on the British defenses
at Yorktown.

Even as Hamilton had gone off to make
his own name in battle, however, he had
not forgotten that one could achieve more
under the guise of Washington's name. "The
General is a very honest man. . . . His
popularity has often been essential to the
safety of America and is still of great importance to it," Hamilton had written. "These
considerations have influenced my past
conduct respecting him and will influence
my future." It had been why during the final
months of the war, after Hamilton had left
the army and taken a seat in the Continental

Congress, he had urged Washington to take advantage of the unrest spreading among the officers at Newburgh: harness it to force the Continental Congress into enacting much-needed financial reforms. It had been why Hamilton had urged Washington to accept the presidency and had ridden beside him to put down the Whiskey Rebellion ("the crisis was arrived when it must be determined whether the Government can maintain itself"). It had been why the prospect of an Adams presidency had so worried Hamilton.

Even after many other Federalists had reconciled themselves to Adams's candidacy in 1796, Hamilton had clung to hope that the emerging crisis with France would force Washington to serve a third term and that, if not, then gaming the electoral system would elevate some other Federalist, someone whose "habitual discretion" and "self-command," at least, resembled Washington's. That was not Adams. "Egotism" and "jealousy" — those were the qualities that defined Adams. Hamilton could not forget how the "journal" Adams had sent home from his assignment in Europe during the closing days of the Revolutionary War had "extremely embarrassed his friends." One entry proudly noted how a French minister's wife had dubbed Adams "the Washington of Negotiation," as if a man so unacquainted with "sarcasm" could hold such a title. Nor did Hamilton forget having heard Adams more than once ponder "theories at variance with" the Federalist financial program, that is, Hamilton's financial program. To be fair, Washington had never accepted all of Hamilton's views. But to the credit of the old man, he had always "consulted much, pondered much, resolved slowly, resolved surely." If Adams would do the same, all might be well. He just needed the right advice.

Hamilton could not give it directly, for he knew that "Mr. Adams never could forgive" the Federalists who he believed had conspired against his election. But just because the president held a grudge did not mean his cabinet secretaries did. Through them, Hamilton found a secret "channel" for influencing Adams. The advice they sent to the president's desk often originated on Hamilton's. "I am sure I cannot do such justice to the subject as you can," wrote James McHenry. It was true. Mac, as Hamilton called the Irish-born secretary of war who had also served in Washington's military family, could not do justice to a subject as sensitive as the French crisis.

There was no need to declare war, Hamilton advised McHenry to advise the president. "A mitigated hostility," or quasi war, would leave "a door open to negotiation" while giving the country time to take measures such as these: allow merchant vessels "to arm for defense"; endow the essentially nonexistent embryonic navy with new ships ("tis not impossible these may be procured from Great Britain") and authorize them to go after French privateers; "fortify" key ports; expand the United States army to twenty thousand men; create a thirty-thousand-man provisional force that the president could mobilize if needed; and raise new revenue, which should not be difficult in a country where "many of the principal sources of taxation [remain] yet untouched."

Adams, Hamilton recommended, should also declare a day of prayer and fasting. "On religious ground, this is very proper. On political, it is very expedient. The Government will be very unwise, if it does not make the most of the religious prepossessions of our people," in contrast not only to the atheism of the French regime but also to Thomas Jefferson's well-known indifference to whether his fellow citizens worshipped "twenty gods, or no god." Adams should borrow a line from Washington's farewell address: "Of all the dispositions and habits which lead to political prosperity, religion and morality are indispensable supports. In vain would *that man* claim the tribute of patriotism, who should labor to subvert these great pillars of human happiness." Saying *"that"* man instead of *"a"* man had raised the question of whom Washington had in mind or, rather, whom Hamilton had in mind, for it was he who had written the line. In an anonymous article published afterward, Hamilton had explained the intent. "[The address] seems to point at Jefferson!" Even now, after the XYZ revelations, according to reports from Philadelphia, the Republican "high priest" continued to preach the French cause. Fortunately, Jefferson's flock had begun to thin.

The course Hamilton urged to the cabinet secretaries rolled over the opposition in Congress. Legislation increasing the number of American war vessels and founding the Department of the Navy sailed through both chambers and onto the president's desk. The recommendations that Hamilton feared would meet the most resistance, however, regarded the institution that most concerned his own future: the army. If the

French could land an army across the English Channel, as he thought possible, what would stop them from later landing an army across the Atlantic Ocean? The United States needed to prepare. Unreliable state militias made up of seldom drilled citizen soldiers would not do. They had almost lost the Revolution. The fear many Americans held of standing armies must not stand in the way. A new professional federal army would command the people's support if their old beloved general would agree to command it. Washington had emerged from retirement before. He would again if told that no one else would do. To the news-papers, Hamilton took his case. "Experienced officers," he wrote under the name Titus Manlius, "[are] ready to form an army under the command of the same illustrious chief who before led them to victory and glory, and who, if the occasion should require it, could not hesitate again to obey the summons of his country."

Left unsaid was that Washington was not the same man he had been during the Revolution. A man past his sixty-sixth birthday would need to delegate. He would need a deputy he could trust. If offered the job, Alexander Hamilton would accept.

■ ■ ■ ■

By the spring of 1798, Wash had started at yet another college, St. John's in Annapolis. Suspicions that he "misspent [his] time" at taverns in the town soon arose. Why else, Washington wondered, did the young man need to ask where to "apply for money in case of want"? For some reason, he had also begun expressing opinions on whom Nelly should marry, as if his views mattered. So far as Washington could see, she had shown no interest in any man. For now, politics engaged her. She described her own as "perfectly federal" and denounced the French rulers as "democratic murderers" or "demons." If they invaded, she joked of painting "whiskers" on her face and raising a "corps of independent volunteers," of which she would naturally serve as "commander in chief."

All would be well, Washington thought, if all Americans showed the same spirit. But even after the XYZ dispatches had exposed the "corruption and profligacy" of the French Directory for all to see, he doubted that the "leaders of the opposition" would open their eyes. Rumors spread up the Potomac that "some" Republicans had written "treasonable" letters urging the French Directory to embarrass the envoys.

On May 9, Washington attended a sermon in Alexandria. Adams had asked his countrymen to dedicate the day to "humiliation, fasting and prayer." It seemed as if the new president basked in receiving the laudatory addresses Washington had once received. Adams deserved them, and Washington wanted the world to know he thought so. "No one has read the various approbatory addresses . . . with more heartfelt satisfaction than I have done." All in all, the measures the government had begun taking to prepare for armed conflict as a last resort pleased him. He himself had just one recommendation: build the arsenal he had long hoped to see at a strategic point called Harpers Ferry, sixty miles up the Potomac from the City of Washington.

Thankfully, Congress had finally approved new financial support for the federal city. Visiting Mount Vernon after returning from Philadelphia with Betsey, Thomas Law radiated optimism. "The late progress of the public buildings in the City give the greatest hopes," he said. "An example alone is wanting to encourage private buildings." If Washington would agree to build a house near the Capitol, Law would supply the lot and even lend money for construction. "Your name would effect much."

No doubt that it would, Washington thought. Everyone wanted the name. That was why he had made a point of purchasing the same number of lots around the Capitol as he had around the president's house. Landowners around both those places had formed factions at odds with each other. A former president building a house in one of the neighborhoods would increase real estate prices there while increasing "jealousy" in the other. Besides, even with a loan, he did not think he could afford to build at present. "It has been a maxim with me from early life, never to undertake anything without perceiving a door to the accomplishment, in a reasonable time & with my own resources." If he gave the name Washington to yet another project, he would need to give all of himself, whatever there was left.

CHAPTER FIVE:
THE ONCE AND FUTURE
COMMANDER IN CHIEF

"Five and twenty years, nearly, have passed away since I . . . have been in a situation to indulge myself in familiar intercourse with my friends, by letter or otherwise." With those words on May 16, 1798, Washington began the letter he had long waited to write Sally Cary Fairfax. A quarter century had passed since he had last seen the married woman whom he had called "the object of my love" in 1758, since she and her husband had left Belvoir, the estate they owned just downriver from Mount Vernon, for Britain on the eve of a revolution they would not join. At the war's end, Washington had written Sally's husband letters encouraging him and her to return home. They had not. In 1787, her husband had died across the ocean. Sally's marriage, like Washington's, had yielded no children. Washington "wondered often" what kept her in a "foreign country" when she still had relations in her native one.

The Potomac had changed so much since she had seen it. "During this period," he wrote, "so many important events have occurred, and such changes in men and things have taken place, as the compass of a letter would give you but an inadequate idea of." Still, he would try. He wanted Sally to see what he saw upriver. Alexandria, the town whose first lots Sally could remember Washington surveying as a young man, "has increased in buildings, in population, in the improvement of its streets by well executed pavements, and in the extension of its wharves, in a manner of which you can have very little idea." Just up the river, on the other side, rose the City of Washington, which "a century hence" would be "of a magnitude inferior to few . . . in Europe." That he had never crossed the ocean — never seen cities larger than New York and Philadelphia — mattered not. He had seen all he needed upriver. The District of Columbia would be the gateway to a western empire. Navigation of the Potomac, he told Sally, already extended "upwards of 200 miles," which was true as long as one looked past the still-untamed Great Falls. Rocks and rapids would not stand in the way. Upriver lay the future.

His own future, he told Sally, lay at Mount Vernon. But for reasons he could not explain, the sentence stating his wish to "spend the remainder of my days (which cannot be many) in rural amusements" fit best in a paragraph focused largely on the new crisis with France. "Those whom we have been accustomed to call our good friends and allies are . . . provoking us to acts of self-defense, which may lead to war. What will be the result of such measures, time, that faithful expositor of all things, must disclose."

As he wrote, the wind, as if whisked along with the water, blew downriver. More and more "often," he admitted to Sally, "I cast my eyes" in that direction, "towards Belvoir." The house had burned during the Revolution. For a time afterward, looking at the "ruins" had saddened him. Memory was a muscle that defied control. Even in a fading mind like his own, old flames better extinguished burned on. Long ago, he had predicted that Sally would haunt him. "I feel the force of her amiable beauties in the recollection of a thousand tender passages that I could wish to obliterate, till I am bid to revive them," as he did now. History would remember him for the life he had lived after Sally's departure: the eight years of his generalship, the eight years of his presidency. "None of which events, however, nor all of them together," he wished Sally to know, "have been able to eradicate from my mind, the recollection of those happy moments — the happiest of my life — which I have enjoyed in your company."

Why write Sally this now? There was the practical: her brother-in-law living near Mount Vernon had planned a voyage to England and could deliver the letter. There was also the wistful: having finally found time to sort through his "voluminous" old papers had conjured old memories. Letters written during the French and Indian War required special attention. The way he had written back then embarrassed him. No one need know if he made revisions. He had actually already made some in the years after the Revolutionary War. Now he would make more. When done, he would order a clerk to incorporate both sets of edits into clean copies, which, if all went according to plan, would be the only ones passed to posterity. Revising the letters required reentering the mind-set of a younger self: the twenty-three-year-old audacious enough to commence a letter-writing campaign to his neighbor's wife; courageous enough to cross the mountains walling off the civilized world from the uncharted territory beyond; ambitious enough to dictate the terms by which he would emerge from the first of several self-imposed retirements and accept the title he would hear many times again: commander in chief.

"In order to engage your correspondence, I think it is incumbent on me to deserve it, which I shall endeavor to do, by embracing the earliest, and every opportunity, of writing to you," he wrote Sally. It was the last day of April 1755 and the start of a new military campaign up the Potomac River and into the Ohio Country. "It will be needless to dwell on the pleasures that a correspondence of this kind would afford me, let it suffice to say [that] a correspondence with my friends is the greatest satisfaction I expect to enjoy in the course of the campaign and that from none shall I derive such satisfaction as from yours — for to you I stand indebted for many obligations."

He had almost sat out the campaign. His mother had not wanted him to go. Who would tend to her needs was her usual complaint. She had made him miss a meeting in Alexandria with Edward Braddock, the general whom the king had sent to lead British regular soldiers against the French and Indian forces fortifying the Forks of the Ohio. Twice already, Washington had tried to expel the French from over the mountains: first, in 1753, as a messenger delivering an ultimatum; then, in 1754, as a colonial Virginia officer leading an attack party against a smaller French force before being forced to surrender to a larger French one. He had resigned his commission afterward not because he had tired of the fight — "my inclinations are strongly bent to arms," he had admitted — but because he felt unappreciated. He had learned that the lowliest officer in the British regular army could claim to command the highest-ranked colonial officer. Worse, a reorganization of Virginia's forces would have reduced his own rank from colonel to captain. Not even from Braddock, who carried the power to award brevet rank in the regular British army, would Washington accept a captaincy.

That said, opportunities for colonials to forge connections with British generals as well regarded as Braddock did not often arise. Invited to accompany the general on his mission, Washington needed to say yes. So up the Potomac he went as a "volunteer" member of Braddock's military family. "I am not a little biased by selfish considerations," Washington admitted. "To explain,

Sir, I wish earnestly to attain some knowledge on the military profession, and . . . a more favorable opportunity cannot offer than to serve under a gentleman of General Braddock's abilities and experience."

No experience, however, had prepared Braddock for moving an army over the mountains and into a wilderness confounding white men unschooled in the ways of the Indians threading the trees. The march of the British regulars up the Potomac slowed after reaching Fort Cumberland, where the river arches north toward Pennsylvania. Rather than stand around with the army, Washington wondered if he should stand for a seat in the Virginia colonial legislature. Only with his younger brother John Augustine could Washington discuss that particular ambition, for fear of being seen as too ambitious. Could John Augustine measure the people's interest in the idea without letting on to Washington's own interest? "I hope & think you may do without disclosing much of mine," Washington wrote, "as I know your own good sense can furnish you with contrivances." It was impossible for Washington himself to test the waters because the mountains he had crossed cut him off from the colony's coastal elite.

During an express mission back east, he stopped to see Sally, who hinted that he should send future messages via a third party. "Am I to consider the proposed mode of communication as a polite intimation of your wishes to withdraw your correspondence?" Once back with the army, he received few letters at all. The ones he did brought little pleasure. His mother wrote asking for butter. "Honored Madam," he responded, "butter cannot be had here to supply the wants of the camp army."

In mid-June, Braddock finally heeded Washington's advice to leave the baggage trains bogging down the march behind and send the best troops ahead. Washington would have been among them had he not fallen "excessively ill." Only by riding in rickety wagons could he catch up to Braddock just miles from the Forks of the Ohio.

A gap in the correspondence followed. The letter book Washington kept for the campaign contained no correspondence for a week on either side of July 9. To an official back east, he later reported what had happened on that day. "We were attacked (very unexpectedly) by about 300 French and Indians. Our numbers consisted of about 1,300 well-armed men, chiefly regulars, who were immediately struck with such an inconceivable panic that nothing but confusion and disobedience of orders prevailed amongst them. . . . In short the dastardly behavior of the regular troops exposed all those who were inclined to do their duty to almost certain death." Among the mortally wounded lay Braddock. A report circulated that Washington himself had died. To John Augustine, Washington wrote, "As I have heard . . . a circumstantial account of my death and dying speech, I take this early opportunity of contradicting the first, and of assuring you that I have not, as yet, composed the latter. But by the all-powerful dispensations of Providence, I have been protected beyond all human probability & expectation, for I had four bullets through my coat and two horses shot under me yet, although death was levelling my companions on every side of me, escaped unhurt." Responsibility for coordinating the army's retreat had fallen to him.

Only those who had looked into the "impervious darkness" of the night that followed — only those who had felt their way through the forest by "groping on the ground with their hands" — would understand "the gloom & horror" he had encountered. "The shocking scenes which presented themselves in this night's march are not to be described: the dead — the dying — the groans, lamentations and cries along the road of the wounded for help — . . . were enough to pierce a heart of adamant."

Back east, for the second straight summer, he returned defeated. Braddock bore most of the blame, and somewhat unfairly so, Washington thought. As for himself, "I have been upon the losing order ever since I entered the service." But for all that he had lost — time, horses, and a connection to a British general who could have granted a career in the British army — Washington had won something greater: "the esteem and notice the Country has been pleased to honor me with." He was a hero. "At present, [that] constitutes the chief part of my happiness." Sally castigated him for not having rushed to Belvoir upon his return. She would have to come see him at Mount Vernon.

Almost immediately began talk of putting Washington in charge of a new Virginia force that would go back over the mountains. Whether to accept, as he saw it, depended on how best to protect — or, better yet, augment — the "reputation" he had earned. If the terms accompanying the offer presented little hope of success, accepting command would set him up for humiliation and rid him of the respect of his country-men. If, however, the terms accompanying the offer proved more favorable, refusing command at a moment when Virginia's frontiers lay exposed to Indian war parties would bring, as he tried explaining to his mother, "dishonor."

In such a situation, neither an unqualified acceptance nor an outright refusal would do. A negotiation needed to occur. If the colony's leaders expected him to risk what he coveted most, they must give what he needed most: power to select his own subordinates. The glory he had gained over the mountains meant he had more to lose. He would not wager the name of Washington on the whims of men not of his own choosing:

I think a commanding officer not having this liberty appears to me to be a strange thing, when it is considered how much the conduct and bravery of an officer influences the men; how much a commanding officer is answerable for the behavior of the inferior officers; and how much his good or ill success in time of action depends upon the conduct of each particular one. . . . [Consider] how little credit is given to a commander who after a defeat, in relating the cause of it justly lays the blame on some individual whose cowardly behavior betrayed the whole to ruin; how little does the world consider the circumstances; and how apt are mankind to level their vindictive censures against the unfortunate chief, who perhaps merited least of the blame. Does it not appear then that the appointing of officers is a thing of the utmost consequence — a thing that should require the greatest circumspection? Ought it to be left to blind chance?

The demand had surprised some. But ultimately the crown's representative in the colony had largely acceded. The colony needed Washington. No one else's name would do.

In August 1755, Washington received a commission appointing him "Colonel of the Virginia Regiment & Commander in Chief of all the forces now raised & to be raised for the defense of this His Majesty's colony & for repelling the unjust & hostile invasions of the French & their Indian allies." He was, in short, commander in chief, a title that he would hold through the year 1758, when he would see the French fort at the Forks of the Ohio finally fall, win a seat in the colonial legislature, write Sally a cryptic letter of which he kept no copy, and then pledge to "say no more."

There was more to tell Sally now. The letter Washington finished on May 16, 1798, gave no update on his family. Those details he delegated to a different letter, one that Martha would send. He prepared a draft for her the next day. "With respect to my own family," she should tell Sally, "it will not, I presume, be new to you to hear that my son died in the fall of 1781. He left four fine children — three daughters & a son, the two oldest of the former are married and have three children. . . . The youngest daughter, Eleanor [Nelly], is yet single & lives with me, having done so from an infant; as has my grandson George Washington [Wash], now turned of seventeen, except when at college, to three of which he has been." To this, Martha added little more than a few words calling Wash "a fine promising youth." That was her opinion.

More important than what Martha wrote was that she write something. Her letter would conceal Washington's own. "Mrs. Washington begs the favor of you to put her letter to her old neighbor and friend Mrs. Fairfax into a channel for safe delivery, if you should not see her yourself," Washington told Sally's brother-in-law as he left for England. Only upon breaking the seal would Sally learn that Martha's letter had not traveled alone.

In the meantime, Washington and his wife would set off for the federal city so she could see the great-grandchildren she had mentioned in her letter and he could see the progress of the buildings he had mentioned in his. The greatest activity surrounded the scaffolding on the Capitol, where hundreds of laborers — some freemen, some hired slaves — worked on the roof that they should have already finished. The children had grown more to schedule. Betsey Law's daughter had just learned to walk. Carefully did an imposing six-foot man need to plan his approach to a toddler. "Here is something for you," he said, dangling a piece of cheese before the girl. In return, she gave a hug.

He tried to relax. He reacquainted himself with billiards, a game he had often played for money before the Revolution; introduced himself to Julian Ursyn Niemcewicz, a prominent Polish exile staying with the Laws while touring the federal city; and steered conversation away from unpleasant subjects. Asked how the city could possibly welcome members of the House, Senate, and executive departments in just two years' time given the shortage of housing, Washington deflected with humor. "Oh well, they can camp out," he joked. "The Representatives in the first line, the Senate in the second, the President with all his suite in the middle."

Mostly he talked about farming. Not enough rain had fallen that spring, and the fields had suffered. The unexpected arrival of a letter from James Anderson, the estate manager back at Mount Vernon, stating his "intention to withdraw from . . . employment, at the end of the year" added to the worries. The length to which Anderson had gone to avoid giving the news in person was evident by the date on the letter. He had written it on May 19, the very day Washington had left for the city. The reasons Anderson gave for resigning sounded comical given how often he had heard his "strict integrity," "industry," and "zeal" praised. Nonetheless, he claimed his feelings hurt. He accused Washington of being an overbearing boss who meddled too much, as if one could meddle in one's own affairs.

Finding fault from time to time with subordinates did not make a manager overbearing. Anderson had simply proved himself oversensitive. "Strange & singular indeed would it be if the proprietor of an estate . . . should have nothing to say in, or control over, his own expenditures," responded Washington from the federal city on May 22. "If I cannot remark upon my own business — passing every day under my eyes — without hurting your feelings, I must discontinue my rides or become a cypher on my own estate." That he could not do, especially not when he saw so many of his plans for the estate thwarted: fields planted with disregard for crop rotation schedules; carpentry projects commenced but never completed; carts and plows broken down in record numbers; hedges weeded only after being "suffocated," which "is like applying to the doctor [only] when the paroxysm of death has fast hold of the patient."

In spite of these problems, losing Anderson would present a larger problem. The Scotsman would quickly find a new job at another estate if he had not already secured one. How would Washington find someone new to run the distillery? He would never have built it if not for Anderson's expertise in the whiskey business. Perhaps Anderson would continue managing the distillery and mill as well as perhaps the fishery if, without reducing his pay, Washington "relieved

[him] from the responsibility of other matters," including the farms. If necessary, for the time being, Washington could manage those himself. There was room for negotiation on the specifics so long as Anderson understood the one principle upon which there could be no negotiation: "I have no hesitation in declaring that I shall never relinquish the right of judging in my own concerns . . . to any man living while I have health & strength to look into my own business."

It looked as if rain might finally fall. "Clouds gathering from all quarters," Washington noted the next morning, and, as forecast, the afternoon brought "a very fine rain." The downpour continued the day after and the day after that, at which point he set off for home. He wanted to see the puddles forming in the fields for himself.

In the pile of mail welcoming him home lay a letter proposing he prepare to leave his fields again. It was from Alexander Hamilton. "At the present dangerous crisis of public affairs, I make no apology for troubling you with a political letter." What followed amounted to an argument for returning to public life. Washington, Hamilton argued, need not issue any formal announcement. It would be better to begin subtly by scheduling a tour of the states south of the Potomac, where Hamilton sensed that sympathy for France still outweighed support for the American military buildup. Southerners needed to hear from Washington. The dinners and dances thrown in his honor during the tour would present an opportunity, Hamilton explained, "[to] throw the weight of your character into the scale of the Government and revive an enthusiasm for your person that may be turned into the right channel." Having promised to live out his days around Mount Vernon, Washington, of course, would need an excuse for heading south. Hamilton suggested claiming a health problem necessitating warmer air.

That excuse would not do. No one would believe it. "The state of my health . . . never was better," Washington responded. Besides, the revelations contained in the XYZ dispatches had accomplished more than he ever could. Even in the South, he sensed the current of public opinion shifting against the Republican collaborators who had deluded the French into believing they could raid American ships without repercussions. Learning otherwise had given the French a much-needed warning. "Although I think them capable of *anything bad,*" he wrote, "I cannot believe . . . they will attempt to do more than they have done . . . when they perceive the spirit & policy of this country rising into resistance and that they have falsely calculated upon support from *a large* part of the *people* thereof." The odds of a French invasion, as he saw it, had fallen.

The logic soothed. "If I did not view things in this light, my mind would be infinitely more disquieted than it is," more disquieted by what Hamilton had written in closing. "You ought also to be aware, my dear Sir, that in the event of an open rupture with France, the public voice will again call you to command the armies of your Country. . . . All who are attached to you will . . . deplore an occasion which should once more tear you from that repose to which you have so good a right, yet it is the opinion of all those with whom I converse that you will be compelled to make the sacrifice."

What, the letter tacitly asked, would Washington do? He did not want to say. The question seemed premature. "There is no conviction in my breast that I could serve my country with more efficiency in the command of the armies . . . than many others," he responded. Elevating "generals of juvenile years" had produced "astonishing success" for the French. The now famous General Bonaparte had not even turned thirty. President Adams might prefer to appoint someone else, "a man more in his prime." All other options deserved first consideration if for no other reason than so Washington could know that his name had surfaced as a last resort, that there had been no other option.

In that case, he already knew the answer he would give because he had "once before departed from a similar resolution" to spend his days at Mount Vernon. He had worried that attending the Constitutional Convention and accepting the presidency would open him to charges of "inconsistency" and "ambition" — and risk his legacy as the American Cincinnatus — given he had pledged never again to "intermeddle in public matters" after the Revolutionary War. "A citizen of so much consequence as yourself . . . has no option but to lend his services if called for," Hamilton had written at that time. "Permit me to say [that] it would be inglorious in such a situation not to hazard the glory, however great, which . . . [you] might have previously acquired."

That was no less true now for Washington. He would leave his "present peaceful abode," he wrote, with "as much reluctance" as if summoned downriver to the "tombs of my ancestors." That the "recollection of . . . happy moments" had already turned his eyes downriver — toward the place where Sally dwelt in his mind — the world had "no business to know." In the direction of duty, there had always been hidden desire. Now they flowed together as if carrying his past and future to the same end. If the "crisis" should "leave . . . no choice," he would return to public life. But before he again risked "the esteem and notice the Country has been pleased to honor me with" — before he again exposed "what at present constitutes the chief part of my happiness" to the fields of fire and to the pens of posterity — there was one more question he must ask. "It may well be supposed," he wrote Hamilton, "that I should like, previously, to know who would be my coadjutors, and whether you would be disposed to take an active part."

The haste with which Hamilton responded suggested he had already considered the question. "If you command," he wrote less than a week later, "the place in which I should hope to be most useful is that of Inspector General with a command in the line. This I would accept." As to what arrangement President Adams would accept, Hamilton took it "for granted" that the "executive" would defer to whatever choice of subordinate officers Washington wished.

General Washington's recent visit to the federal city had given Julian Ursyn Niemcewicz his first glimpse of the great man. Just laying eyes on him was sufficient to accelerate the heartbeat. Washington little resembled the portraits that Niemcewicz had seen on the other side of the Atlantic, the ocean he had crossed after a failed revolution in his native Poland. "[The general] is a majestic figure in which dignity and gentleness are united . . . He is nearly six feet tall, square set, and very strongly built; aquiline nose, blue eyes, the mouth and especially the lower jaw sunken, a good head of hair." The way he had behaved had stood out at a time when many Americans extended their anger at the French to anyone speaking with a continental European accent. For his part, the general had extended hospitality: an invitation to Mount Vernon.

For twelve nights in June, Niemcewicz stayed at the house. He felt as if "a member of the family." When alone, he wandered the rooms. In the parlor off the hall running between the front door and the piazza facing the Potomac, he gazed at the portrait of a young Washington wearing "a blue uniform, red vest and breeches, the whole trimmed with narrow silver braid." Here stood the Virginian who had gone off to fight against the French and Indians in the forests. "He is represented in the attitude of an officer on the march; lest there should be any doubt, he takes out of the pocket of his vest a paper on which is written *march order.* He has a gun slung across his back and a violet sash over his shoulders." Beside this portrait was another one of the young woman who became his wife, in a "blue gown," with "her hair dressed" and "her ears uncovered. In her right hand she carries a flower." The painting of Mrs. Washington had been "badly damaged." Niemcewicz suspected it "was never good." Looking now at Mrs. Washington, all these years later, with her "lively eyes" staring out beneath the "bonnet of white gauze . . . [hiding] half of her white hair" made Niemcewicz suppose she had been "at one time one of the most beautiful women in America." She "loves to talk and talks very well about times past," he noted. She seemed proud of her husband and "showed [off] . . . a small collection of medals struck during the Revolution."

The general himself was more eager to show off a plow he had invented. From the plow, it was said, Cincinnatus had raced to the rescue of Rome, and to the plow he had rushed back afterward. He had made the plow his symbol. Now Washington had made that symbol his own. "[The general] has shown that he was not eager for glory," Niemcewicz found himself thinking. "For being able to remain all his life at the head of the government, he resigned voluntarily from the office of President."

Only once did Niemcewicz hear Washington ponder what might have been had he stayed in power. On the last night of the visit, after dinner, the general sat out on the piazza, where the grass sloped toward the river. "It is from there," Niemcewicz noted, "that one looks on perhaps the most beautiful view in the world. One sees there the waters of the Potomac rolling majestically over a distance of four to five miles. Boats which go to and from make a picture of unceasing motion." To Niemcewicz, Washington began reading aloud a letter from a correspondent in France. The letter described the "formidable military preparations" the French had undertaken for an invasion of England and the insults the French had imposed on the puppet republics now littering the map of Europe. Never had Niemcewicz heard Washington "speak with so much candor . . . with such heat."

Such degradation must not be America's fate, Washington said. "Continued patience and submission will not deliver us any more than submission delivered . . . others. Submission is vile. Yea, rather than allowing herself to be insulted to this degree, rather than having her freedom and independence trodden under foot, America [will] . . ." He stopped, then began again, as if correcting himself. "Every American [will] . . ." Another pause followed. Suddenly he found it, the true subject of the sentence. "I, though old, will pour out the last drop of blood which is yet in my veins."

Then it happened: Washington imagining himself back inside the president's house. "They censure Mr. Adams for haste in deeds and excessive boldness in words. From the moment that I left the administration, I have not written a word to Mr. Adams, nor yet received a word from him except the dispatches which we have seen in the papers. I do not know what are those other sources of information on which he acts. With all this, I am certain . . . that he cannot do other than he does. I, in his place, perhaps would be less vehement in expression but I would prepare myself stealthily and boldly in the same fashion."

The next morning, "for the last time," Niemcewicz gazed across the grass tumbling away toward the Potomac. "I looked out on the open view, on the clear and beautiful stream." As he rode back up the Potomac toward the District of Columbia, he bade farewell to Mount Vernon and the American Cincinnatus.

Partway down King Street was where the troops would find Washington waiting to review their ranks. Toward him marched the men in their uniforms. He had put on his own earlier that morning before departing Mount Vernon, where his manager had opted to continue supervision of most of the farms, and heading to Alexandria's July 4 celebration. Smoke clouded the clear sky as cannons fired sixteen times, one for every state in the country that had stretched over the mountains to the west in the twenty-two years since severing its connections to the king across the ocean to the east.

That a European power would threaten America's freedom again at this moment in history — that a crisis would "turn . . . [his] eyes from the shades of Mount Vernon" so soon after his return — Washington could not have "contemplated" when he had left Philadelphia the previous year. He thought back to his last days there, the moment he had parted with his successor. The silence between them could last no longer, not with so much talk of forming a new army. So Washington had finally written a letter: an invitation to Mount Vernon if Adams needed a place to stay while touring the federal city, which he should have visited long ago. That subtle message was lost on Adams, who declined the invitation. If one of them were to pay the other a visit, the letter that Adams had sent back on June 22 suggested, it would be Washington making the trek to Philadelphia. "I must tap you sometimes for advice," Adams wrote. "We must have your name, if you, in any case, will permit us to use it. There will be more efficacy in it than in many an army." Adams admitted that he himself was in over his head as commander in chief. "I have no qualifications for the martial part of it," he wrote. "If the Constitution and your convenience would admit of my changing places with you or of my taking my old station as your lieutenant civil [vice president], I should have no doubts of the ultimate prosperity and glory of the country."

The words were "delicate," but their

meaning was "not to be misunderstood." A letter a few days later from Secretary of War James McHenry made it explicit. Here was an offer to command the armies of the United States. What would people say? Would they view Washington accepting as a "restless act" by a man "discontent in retirement"? Would they declare the farewell address a "sham"? Would they pass him off as past his prime? He did not know. Worried as he was for his reputation, however, he knew it rode with the fortunes of the country he had forged. Today, on the anniversary of its independence, he would provide his conditional answer in a letter to McHenry.

Yes, Washington would write, "provided my declining years is not considered as an objection to the trust" and "provided also that I can have such characters associated with me as will render the turmoils of war and the burthen of the command as light as the nature of it will admit, for it is well known that the vicissitudes of war are not within the reach of human control and that the chances of adding to are not greater than the hazard of taking from that reputation [that] the partiality of the world has been pleased to confer for past services." Regard for that reputation ruled out accepting responsibility for men who did not enjoy his "entire confidence." The selection of general officers, like inspector general, especially concerned him. These officers, President Adams must be made to understand, needed to operate as if "limbs" of the commanding general. "Viewing them then in this light, it will readily be seen how essential it is that they should be agreeable to him. Such characters are within my view if they would accept." Washington already knew one.

As the procession continued through King Street, Washington could not hide his pleasure. The pageantry of soldiers marching to the beat pleased him. It was the life he had envisioned for himself as a young man still learning to control his emotions. "Many considerations besides the mere gratification of the passions . . . are essential to happiness," he had recently written after hearing rumors of Wash "devoting much time to paying particular attentions to a certain young lady" in Annapolis. The "boy" needed to remember a favorite saying: "There is a time for all things."

Now Sally knew. The letter she received that summer confirmed it. All these years later, the general still cast his eyes downriver. She could remember her late husband reading aloud the "description" that Washington had sent after the Revolutionary War of himself wandering among the ruins of Belvoir, where, he said, "the happiest moments of my life had been spent . . . [where] I could not trace a room in the house (now all rubbish) that did not bring to my mind the recollection of pleasing scenes." The "contrast" between past and present had eventually overcome him. "I was obliged to fly from . . . painful sensations," he had written. She had felt the sensations, too. She had restrained them in the presence of her husband at first but could not do so for long. Hearing what Washington had written back then had "produced many tears & sighs."

At least now, Washington wrote, he could see the ruins for what they were: "memento of former pleasures." She, too, had mementos: old letters that had come to her from a young man crossing into the wilderness beyond the constraints of civilization. Inside the place where she preserved the papers — if not still inside their author, where his chest caved so distinctly and unexpectedly into the center of his being — beat the passions of the soldier she had known, passions he had said "the world has no business to know."

■ ■ ■ ■

PART II
COMMANDER

■ ■ ■ ■

CHAPTER SIX:
SEDITION ACT

Not since the Revolution had Independence Day served as such a call to arms. In Philadelphia, the soldiers and militiamen parading down Market Street stopped before the president's house for a review. Benjamin Franklin Bache could only hope that the "young men" would not proceed to his house next, as they had several weeks earlier when they had "battered" its outside and terrified his family inside. He had recently heard himself called a "prostitute" lying at the pleasure of the French and a disgrace to the late legendary grandfather from whom he had inherited not only his printing press but also his first two names, Benjamin Franklin. For the sake of "his country" and "mankind," Bache would not let his enemies "awe him into a base dereliction of his duty." The sun on the masthead of his newspaper would rise again the next day. During these dark times, the American people needed the *Aurora* for light.

The July 4, 1798, paper featured the most jarring of juxtapositions. In the third column of page 3 appeared this item: "GEORGE WASHINGTON, of Virginia, [appointed] Lieutenant General and Commander in Chief of the Armies of the United States of America." In the columns beside it ran the Declaration of Independence in case Americans had forgotten the reasons they had "dissolved" their connection to another power-hungry George, the British king. Reprinting the Declaration of Independence also served as an implicit rebuke to the senators preparing for a vote that very day on a sedition bill imposing jail time — some had favored the death penalty — for printers, like Bache, daring to wield their pens and presses against the government. "Anything in the shape of persecution against the cause which I have espoused," Bache wrote, "will meet with the countenance from our Federal Executive."

Already the government had begun proceedings against Bache under common law. He had gotten out on bail. But the "prosecution" — rather, "persecution" — would continue because he had dared to print the truth: the French wanted peace. Talleyrand, the French foreign minister, had asked Elbridge Gerry, the one independent-minded American envoy, to stay behind in Paris after his two Federalist colleagues, John Marshall and Charles Cotesworth Pinckney, had departed. Gerry had agreed in the hopes of preventing a formal war, which, of course, was what the hard-liners in the American government really wanted. Just a few days after the Fourth of July came news of hostilities off the New Jersey coast: an American vessel chasing down a French privateer and giving John Adams's new navy its first capture. Bells rang in Philadelphia as the Federalists and their "mercantile" friends celebrated the small engagement as a stupendous "victory."

It was not supposed to be this way when Adams assumed the presidency. The clothes he had worn to his inauguration — the number of horses that had pulled his carriage to Congress Hall — had heralded the beginning of a more republican era. Promising-sounding predictions had filled the pages of the *Aurora*. Adams, their authors wrote, would not place "himself at the head of a party as his predecessor has done." In "striking contrast," Adams would welcome Republicans into his administration. Most important, unlike Washington, Adams would "not be the tool of any man," especially not of someone who had intrigued against his election, as everyone knew Alexander Hamilton had. As Washington had departed Philadelphia, the *Aurora* had celebrated. "If ever there was a period for rejoicing, this is the moment. Every heart, in unison with the freedom and happiness of the people, ought to beat high with exaltation that the name of WASHINGTON from this day ceases to give currency to political iniquity."

Yet less than a year and a half later, Adams had brought the name back into the news by nominating Washington for commander in chief of the army. Some senators whispered that commander in chief, a title given to the president by the Constitution, could not be given away by the president. But ultimately they had approved the appointment unanimously. Whether the general himself would approve, Bache could only speculate. The nomination had proceeded before anyone in Philadelphia had heard from the general. "He retired from *civil* life on account of his years and to seek the repose which age requires," Bache wrote. "If this was a good reason a year ago, is it not now better, when called to a *military* employment?" Even in his prime, Washington had hardly possessed a great military mind. The shortcomings he had shown as a strategist during the Revolution had resulted in a string of catastrophic defeats for his army. Credit for Yorktown belonged more to the French. Victory would have come sooner had the United States found a general as brilliant as Bonaparte had proved himself for the French. In a fight against Bonaparte, Bache believed, Washington would be no match. "He would be like a puny shrub in the midst of a stupendous forest."

Bache would have let this history lie had not Federalists used Washington's name as the aegis behind which they advanced their aims. They needed Washington's name again now to provide legitimacy to the military establishment they had begun to erect: a new army, which added twelve regiments totaling twelve thousand soldiers to the four frontier regiments currently in existence, as well as a provisional army, which offered the president ten thousand more soldiers he could call up in the event of war.

Readers of the *Aurora* already knew the real reason for the military buildup. The Federalists wanted a "standing army" for the same reason they wanted a sedition law: so they would have the force needed "to suppress opinions," specifically, those of the opposition. They would not silence Bache's. "The cloud with which the *George* of America has covered himself has been large enough to hide his own want of merit and that of others whom he has placed in office. But when it drops, all will be exposed together," Bache believed. As the saying went, "Truth will out!"

As far as one could see from Mount Vernon in the wake of the Fourth of July, nothing had changed. Washington remained a retiree. As long as that remained so, he would resist the urge to retrieve his mail daily from the post office in Alexandria. Whatever letters awaited him there could wait a few more days. He needed to stay focused on his fields and his finances, as best he could. The pleas to return to public life had already diverted his eyes too much. "I have been so much engaged for the few days past that I have been unable to look into any accounts." As a result, they had turned into a "jumble." Only by good fortune had he noticed that rent payments collected on his behalf by his old secretary Tobias Lear had gone elsewhere. For some reason, without asking, Lear had decided to treat the money as a personal loan. "I never had the most distant suspicion," Washington wrote. "It would be uncandid and inconsistent with the frankness of friendship not to declare that I have not approved . . . of having my money received and applied to uses not my own." In sum, his personal affairs presented enough problems. The world's must wait.

But the world would not wait any longer. That was the message that the Independence Day editions of the Philadelphia newspapers delivered when they finally reached Mount Vernon several days after their publication. All the hours that Washington had devoted to deciding whether to accept the command had been for nothing. If his appointment as commander in chief could appear in July 4 papers, then there could be no doubt that President Adams had made the appointment without knowing the terms Washington had mailed to Secretary of War James McHenry in a letter of that same date.

The note McHenry attached to one of the newspapers offered a lame explanation. "The crisis — and almost universal wish of the people to see you at the head of the armies of the United States — has been too strong to be resisted: the President has yielded to causes so powerful and nominated you accordingly." In the letter's most ironic passage, McHenry claimed to "know what must be your feelings" upon reading the news. How could anyone in Philadelphia know? The president had proceeded "without any previous consultation" as to those feelings.

Under any circumstance, there would have been "sorrow," Washington would have explained if given the opportunity, "at being drawn from my retirement, where I had fondly hoped to have spent the few remaining years which might be dispensed to me, if not in profound tranquility, at least without public responsibility." But under these circumstances, there was also shock, embarrassment, and "regret": shock because he had not "the most distant suspicion" that the president would act so presumptuously; embarrassment because the command could not be accepted without knowing whether Adams would accept conditions he had not yet seen; "regret" because McHenry himself had already set off to deliver the commission to Mount Vernon.

On the evening of July 11, with "sensations . . . easier to conceive than describe," Washington watched as the carriage carrying the secretary of war snaked its way up the drive to the house. At once, McHenry presented a letter from the president. "To you, Sir, I owe all the apologies I can make.

The urgent necessity I am in of your advice and assistance, indeed of your conduct and direction of the war, is all I can urge, and that is a sufficient justification to myself and the world," Adams wrote. "If it had been in my power to nominate you to be President of the United States, I should have done it with less hesitation and more pleasure." Had the cares of office not detained him in Philadelphia, Adams himself would have made the trip to Mount Vernon. Instead, he explained, he had sent McHenry "to wait on you, in my behalf."

It was probably for the best that the errand had fallen to McHenry, even if the office of secretary of war had fallen to him only because everyone else imaginable for the job had said no. That McHenry's "talents were unequal to great exertions" and unfit for the war office did not mean he was unfit for this particular mission: having served as a personal secretary to Washington for a time during the Revolution had qualified McHenry to carry the sensitive message Washington needed to send back to the president.

"Take the commission back [to Philadelphia]," Washington instructed McHenry, so "that it might be restored or annulled, according to the President's determination to accept or reject the terms on which I . . . offered to serve."

Returning the commission, McHenry countered, "[would] be considered as an evidence of distrust." Once the president heard the conditions, he would surely consent. Returning the commission would turn a personal miscommunication between Washington and Adams into a public controversy that would divide the government's friends at a time when they needed to stand united.

On into the next morning stretched the conversation. Eventually Washington relented. He would accept the commission, he said, on a "conditional" basis.

Talk then turned to who else should receive commissions as general officers. McHenry shared a list of candidates the president had begun to consider. Looking at the list confirmed an observation that Alexander Hamilton had recently sent to Mount Vernon: "It may be well, however, to apprise you that the arrangement of the army may demand your particular attention. The President has no *relative* ideas & his prepossessions on military subjects in reference to such a point are of the wrong sort."

Wrong, indeed! A number of the men on

Adams's list did not deserve discussion for any position, let alone that of general. Some had disgraced themselves during the Revolution or had grown too old in the years since. Some, like that master of "intrigue" Aaron Burr, Washington knew to be Republicans! They could have no place in an army formed to repel the very foreign invasion their perfidy and propaganda had invited. "All violent opposers of the Government and French partisans should be avoided," Washington believed, "or they will disseminate the poison of their principles in the Army and split what ought to be a band of brothers into parties," just as they had done to his first cabinet, the Congress, and the country itself. "What pity it is," he thought, "this expense [of raising an army] could not be taxed upon" the Republicans necessitating it. Federalists, of course, would ultimately share the financial burden, but they would not share the command. It would be theirs alone.

Unable to use Adams's list of names, McHenry and Washington began assembling their own. Only one choice had already solidified in Washington's mind: the physician general must be his own personal physician, James Craik. As younger men, they had traveled together over the mountains to the Forks of the Ohio and seen General Braddock defeated by surprise. Energetic as Washington had felt in recent months, he would not let his own health take him by surprise. Already he contemplated an "occasion" when he would need a "physician or surgeon."

Facing that possibility raised the most important question: Who would serve as Washington's second-in-command, the "chief" in his "absence"? Such an absence was all but assured given one of the other conditions Washington had put on his service: that he be allowed to stay at Mount Vernon unless absolute necessity demanded he take the field. Below the rank of lieutenant general, which Washington alone would possess, stood openings for three major generals, one of whom would also be inspector general. That Henry Knox, Charles Cotesworth Pinckney, and Alexander Hamilton would fill these three openings required almost no deliberation. Which of them would be Washington's overall second-in-command required much.

If rank during the Revolution decided the question, the honor would go to former secretary of war Knox. Of the three, only Knox had reached the rank of major general during the previous war. Hamilton had not risen above a colonelcy, Pinckney a brigadier generalship. But as to why rank in an old army that had "disbanded" a decade and a half earlier should dictate rank in a new army, Washington could not see. "If we entered into a serious contest with France," he reasoned, "the character of the war would differ materially from the last we were engaged in. In the latter, time, caution, and worrying the enemy until we could be better provided with arms & other means . . . was the plan for us. But if we should be engaged with . . . [the French], they ought to be attacked at every step, and, if possible, not suffered to make an establishment in the Country."

Besides, just because Knox had outranked the other two in the last war did not mean he still outranked them in the "public estimation." Manifestly, he did not. During the Whiskey Rebellion, Knox had not shown the dispatch duty demanded. He had temporarily abdicated control of his department to Hamilton, who had gladly added the responsibilities of the War Department to his own at the Treasury and had ridden west by Washington's side. The "abilities and integrity" that Hamilton had displayed had "made him a conspicuous character in the United States and even in Europe." Likewise, Pinckney being twice refused by the French — first as the American minister, then as one of the three envoys — had "much advanced [him] in the estimation of the public."

Only in personal friendship to Washington did Knox still stand above the others. The nearly three-hundred-pound Knox had always brought welcome levity to camp and cabinet meetings. "With respect to General Knox," Washington said, "there is no man in the United States with whom I have been in habits of greater intimacy; no one whom I have loved more sincerely; nor any for whom I have had a greater friendship. But esteem, love & friendship can have no influence on my mind when I conceive that the subjugation of our Government and independence are the objects aimed at by the enemies of our peace." The choice for second-in-command would come down to Pinckney versus Hamilton. Knox, Washington assured himself, would understand.

At first, Pinckney seemed the strategic pick. Esteemed as Hamilton had become, he "did not possess the confidence of the country," not the complete country, anyway. Washington could not forget Thomas Jefferson warning that Hamilton's financial system would tear the country in two. By contrast, choosing Pinckney (a member of a prominent South Carolina clan) would shore up support in the region where the government most needed it: the South, the underdefended underbelly of the Union. Washington still struggled to believe that the French — deluded as they were — would "be so *mad* as openly and formidably to invade these United States in expectation of subjugating the Government." But if they did, he reasoned "their operations will commence in the Southern quarter: first, because it is the weakest; second, because they will expect, from the tenor of the debates in Congress, to find more friends there; third, because there can be no doubt of their arming our own Negroes against us." There was a fourth reason, too: having subdued Spain in Europe, the French could use the Spanish colonies of Florida and Louisiana as a convenient base of operations against the South. In that event, the army would benefit from having a true southerner as its second-in-command.

That consideration would have carried the question for Pinckney if not for a "confidential" letter that had come from Secretary of State Timothy Pickering. "The enemy whom we are now preparing to encounter — veterans in arms led by able and active officers and accustomed to victory — must be met by the best blood, talents, energy and experience that our country can produce," Pickering wrote. "You too well know Colonel Hamilton's distinguished ability, energy and fidelity to apply my remark to any other man. But to ensure his appointment, I apprehend the weight of your opinion may be necessary. From the conversation that I and others have had with the President, there appears to us to be a disinclination to place Colonel Hamilton in what we think is his proper station and that alone in which we suppose he will serve — the *second* to you — and the *chief in your absence.*" The most surprising revelation followed. "Even Colonel Hamilton's political enemies [aside from Adams], I believe, would repose more confidence in him than in any military character that can be placed in competition with him," Pickering wrote. When asked to confirm this, McHenry did not go so far but did assure that the Federalists in Congress, "whence alone anything like a public sentiment relative thereto could be deduced," certainly favored Hamilton for second-in-command. In other words, putting Hamilton in any other place would disappoint the people providing the army with its base of support.

If what Pickering said was true, putting Hamilton in any other place would also disappoint Hamilton himself. Hamilton had previously specified only his wish to be "Inspector General with a command in the line." That he would serve beneath no one but Washington was new. Of course, for all Washington knew, Pinckney would not serve under anyone else either. Whichever way the names ranked risked rankling someone. For a moment, Washington almost regretted inserting himself into the controversy certain to follow. "[It] is not a little embarrassing." He wished he could consult more before deciding. But that would take time, and there was no more time. McHenry had already stretched his stay to three nights. He needed to get back. A decision could not wait.

So Washington decided to defer to public sentiment not as he had previously understood it but as the cabinet secretaries now presented it. The chain of command would follow this order: Hamilton, Pinckney, Knox. Hamilton would be, all at once, inspector general, the first major general, and second-in-command overall. That this outcome accorded with Washington's own personal "wish" made it all the much easier to accept. Having served during the Revolu-

A version of a map George Washington requested the War Department send him m
after his appointment as commander in chief in July 1798. Made in London, the
sprawls across four sheets, measuring about four feet by four and a half feet when
pieced together. "I have seen a map of the United States on a large scale," Washir
wrote. "It is very necessary the Commander in Chief should be possessed of such a

own, the United States had not yet acquired the Spanish colonies of Louisiana Florida, both of which Washington worried the French would use as a base of tions against the southern United States. Courtesy of the Geography and Map ion, Library of Congress.

tion as the "most confidential aide of the commander in chief" — having read his correspondence and learned to anticipate his answers — had given Hamilton "the means of viewing everything on a larger scale than those whose attentions were confined to divisions or brigades." Though he had "never acted in the character of a general officer," he had studied the part of commander in chief more closely than any of the other men mentioned for major general. To no one else could Washington so comfortably and completely, if necessary, delegate.

Who would deliver the decision to the president? That he was said to be "in opposition" to Hamilton — and did not yet know the full conditions of Washington's acceptance — complicated the question. "Encumber[ing]" the acceptance letter Washington himself would write Adams with too many "stipulations . . . would be improper" given the president would surely want to publish it. McHenry would have to explain the conditions privately upon presenting the list of "suggested" officers to the president. These were the men, McHenry should say, whom Washington considered "best qualified" and "without whom I think he would not serve."

■ ■ ■ ■

The breakfast dishes still sat on the table of their house in Philadelphia when John Adams and his wife welcomed the day's first caller between seven and eight on July 18, 1798. It was McHenry, just off the carriage from Mount Vernon, which he had left four days earlier with the answer to the question Adams waited to hear: Would Washington accept command? The sooner the answer arrived, the sooner Adams could depart the sweltering city soon to be beset by yellow fever. Adams needed a break. Being at his desk every day for nine hours, including three devoted to discovering different ways of wording his appreciation for the addresses praising his policies, had taken a toll on his body. He pined for the "purer air" and "tranquil shades" of his Massachusetts home.

The House of Representatives had already adjourned. The Senate would, too, as soon as it received more nominations for command of an army that now included more regiments than Adams himself thought the threat demanded. Any escalation in the fighting against France would take place at sea, he thought. On the growing navy rode his hopes for protecting the country. By contrast, the army introduced its own risks. History had shown how quickly a standing army could turn into a "many bellied monster" that would "tyrannize" over the people who had created it.

As of yet, Adams had nominated only the one man whom Americans could trust to wield such power. Until knowing whether Washington would accept, Adams would appoint no one else. In truth, he would not have even submitted Washington's name yet had not circumstances necessitated the move. Nominating Washington had been the only way to hold off the advisers pushing for Hamilton to hold the top spot. "Whom shall we appoint commander in chief?" Adams had asked Secretary of State Timothy Pickering three times. Three times, Pickering had given the same answer, Hamilton. Finally, Adams had snapped and stopped seeking advice.

No wonder Hamilton had become so "conceited." That he had some real "talents," Adams did not deny. That Hamilton had "debauched morals," all Americans now knew. Adams had long known it. He had heard Abigail speak of seeing "the very devil" in Hamilton's "wicked eyes." Hamilton's admission to adultery only proved the point: a man who could not be trusted to control his sexual appetite could not be trusted with control of an army. To see the danger, one needed to look only to Europe, where General Bonaparte increasingly dictated terms not only to foreign governments but also to his own. His ambitions grew with his every triumph. Hamilton, Abigail predicted, "[would] become a second Bonaparte if he was possessed of equal power." Hence, why she had taken to repeating what Adams had said in his inaugural about Washington. "The knowledge that he lives [is] a bulwark." Washington could not say no. He must say yes.

And he did say yes, according to the letter McHenry delivered. "Feeling how incumbent it is upon every person, of every description, to contribute at all times to his country's welfare, and especially in a moment like the present, when everything we hold dear & sacred is so seriously threatened, I have finally determined to accept the commission of Commander in Chief of the Armies of the United States, with the reserve only that I shall not be called into the field until the Army is in a situation to require my presence, or it becomes indispensable by the urgency of circumstances," Washington had written. The letter mentioned no other condition. The words "pleased" Adams. He would publish them.

Only later in the day did McHenry mention a second condition. "General Washington made the right to name the general officers and general staff a condition of his acceptance," McHenry explained. The presumptuousness of it would have offended Adams had not McHenry added that Washington understood, of course, that all final decisions must "rest with the President." So said the Constitution. The only consent required was the Senate's. Even during the most desperate days of the Revolution, when some in the Continental Congress had considered letting Washington appoint his own officers, Adams had resisted. "In this house," Adams had said, "I feel myself his [Washington's] superior." That did not make Washington's "opinion" unwelcome. In truth, Adams very much wanted it. Where possible, he would heed it.

Only a few of the suggestions McHenry presented really bothered Adams. They happened to be the first few. "Colonel Hamilton, former rank considered, was not entitled to stand so high," Adams told McHenry. "Knox for various reasons (among others his former rank in the army) was clearly entitled to rank next to General

Washington."

McHenry tried to explain Washington's reasoning for the rankings. It was then that Adams realized "extraordinary pains" had been taken to persuade Washington that "the unanimous wish of the Federalists was that General Hamilton might be first." Part of Adams blamed McHenry. Another part suspected that McHenry, being his usual good-natured but simpleminded self, had performed a part in a plan beyond his own understanding. Whatever had convinced Washington that Hamilton had "popular" support would not convince Adams. Nothing would. Hamilton did not even "rank . . . among the [great] Revolutionary characters." Few would have even recognized the name back then. Even now, Hamilton seemed as if in perpetual "puppyhood." Besides, Hamilton was "not a native of the United States but a foreigner." The idea that the people would support a foreigner for high command at a time when their representatives in Congress had just passed multiple laws restricting aliens in the country defied common sense. Only one arrangement made any sense: reversing the three major generals so they would rank as they had during the Revolution: Knox, Pinckney, Hamilton.

Back and forth the discussion went. Eventually, a compromise emerged. The names would go to the Senate in the order Washington wished but with the understanding that the three men themselves must reach agreement as to their own relative rank. What would happen if they could not agree went almost undiscussed, because the Constitution left no room for debate: the president himself would decide.

No matter the final order, Adams would keep a close watch over the commander in chief's orders. According to custom, every one of those orders would pass across the desk belonging to the powerful administrative officer known as the adjutant general. That position would go to William S. Smith, Adams's son-in-law, or so Adams had thought until people began questioning Smith's fitness for the job. First Pickering, then three other Federalists accused Smith of being "a bankrupt" and even a Republican sympathizer and demanded Adams withdraw the nomination. He refused. Washington himself had suggested Smith for the job. And had there been any "solid foundation" as "to the charge of his [Smith's] being antifederal," Washington would have never done so. The arguing did no good. The Senate rejected the nomination.

All the other nominations received confirmation in the order Washington wished. On July 25, without saying farewell to his cabinet secretaries, Adams and his wife set off for Quincy, Massachusetts, over recently rained-upon roads. The clouds followed their carriage northward. It felt as if there was a conspiracy. Maybe there was. To what purpose, he did not know. Probably Washington himself did not know. Hamilton's friends could have played the former president for a "dupe." They would not play the current president for one. Hamilton had catapulted his name to the top of the list, but he would not connive his way to the top of the army. That, Adams swore. "If I should consent to the appointment of Hamilton as second in rank, I should consider it as the most [irresponsible] action of my whole life and the most difficult to justify."

A letter from George Washington! Not since Washington's retirement had Henry Knox received one. Now here before him in Boston on July 28 lay an envelope from Mount Vernon. "I opened [it] with all the delightful sensations of affection which I always before experienced upon the receipt

225

of . . . [such] letters." Since the early days of the Revolution, Washington's words had been the ramparts upon which Knox guarded his own self-worth against those doubting whether an overweight former bookseller who had once shot off a few of his own fingers in a recreational accident could serve as the artillery chief for the Continental Army and later as the country's first secretary of war. With Washington's "esteem and respect," Knox had always "flattered" himself. Even after receiving Washington's reprimand for leaving the War Department unmanned during the Whiskey Rebellion — Hamilton had happily taken charge — Knox told himself that "a sincere, active, and invariable friendship" had endured.

Evidently it had not. That was as clear as the position that Washington explained he had ranked Knox among the major generals: third. In that position Knox would not serve. "I find that others greatly my juniors in rank have been, upon a scale of comparison, preferred before me. Of this, perhaps the world may also concur . . . that I have no just reason to complain. But every intelligent and just principle of society required either that I should have been previously consulted on an arrangement in which my feelings and happiness have been so much wounded or that I should not have been dragged forth to public view at all to make the comparison so conspicuously odious." How someone so sensitive as Washington to rank could be so insensitive, Knox could only wonder. "I read it with astonishment," he wrote Washington the next day. "For more than twenty years, I must have been acting under a perfect delusion."

There was one other possibility: that Washington himself had been deluded. "There has been," Knox found the courage to tell Washington, "a species of management in the affair of which you are not apprised." The public had accepted Hamilton's nomination only because it had come from Washington. But Washington had made the recommendation, he himself admitted, only because it complied with the "public estimation as declared to me." Declared by whom? Not by Washington's fellow Virginians or southerners. Most of them hated Hamilton. Not by New Englanders. Knox's having such a lowly place in the high command would insult them. Not by the Senate. Some of the senators, Knox imagined, had "silenced" their objections to the arrangement for fear of offending Washington. Upon the force of circular logic, Hamilton had begun to spin his way to command. Soon the situation might spin out of control.

CHAPTER SEVEN: SECOND-IN-COMMAND

Having one commander in chief to the north in Quincy and another to the south at Mount Vernon made Secretary of War James McHenry the mailman in the middle. Distance delayed every decision, especially given the reluctance of the commanders in chief to write each other directly. If General Washington had a question for President Adams, for example, providing an answer required several days just for McHenry to receive the question in Philadelphia, a day to compose a letter relaying it to Adams, another ten days for the letter to reach Quincy, a week more for the president's response to arrive in Philadelphia, and a few more days for McHenry to send it to Mount Vernon, where the general, by that time, had lost what little patience nature had given him.

McHenry had first felt the impatience during the Revolution. "When I joined his

Excellency's suite," he remembered, "I gave up soft beds, undisturbed repose, and the habits of ease and indulgence which reign in some departments for a single blanket, the hard floor or the softer sod of the fields, early rising, and almost perpetual duty." Twenty years' time had not made General Washington any less demanding.

Why, he now complained, had McHenry not immediately replied to a letter requesting an update on plans for building the arsenal at Harpers Ferry? "I expected no more than . . . you would have said it *had,* or had *not,* been forgotten."

Why, the general asked, did McHenry provide no information on the controversy over who would serve as adjutant general? "I am thrown entirely into the field of conjecture to account for the cause of your silence on these interesting points."

Why, the general wrote, was he kept "ignorant of every step that has been taken in the appointment of the battalion officers [and] for recruiting" soldiers? "Having staked my life — my reputation — my fortune — my ease, tranquility & happiness — in support of the government & independence of our Country, it is not a little interesting & important for me to be advised of the measures which you are pursuing to organize & provide for the augmented force," Washington wrote.

As if the general himself did not make enough demands, the ladies of his house added their own. Mrs. Washington (the general wrote on her behalf) asked McHenry to design and deliver a flag that she could present to a group of old men in Alexandria who had formed their own infantry company called the Silver Grays. Young Nelly Custis sent a separate letter asking for help adorning a flag for some volunteer dragoons whom she had taken to calling *"my"* company. "You will perhaps be a little surprised when you see from whom this letter comes, as it is not *very common* for ladies to begin a correspondence," she wrote McHenry. "I hope you will excuse me for adding to your weight of business, which must already be almost too much to bear."

Nelly had no idea. Nor did her grandpapa. "If you could know how much I have had to do and how much I have been compelled to neglect to do," McHenry wrote the general, "you would most heartily and readily pity and forgive me had I utterly overlooked [your concerns]." Congress had charged McHenry with forming a new army but had given the War Department only a few clerks, all of whom now faced the specter of yellow fever in Philadelphia. Having long ago trained as a doctor, McHenry recognized the beginnings of yet another epidemic: the blackish vomit, the yellowish skin, the reddish eyes, the corpses filling the cemeteries, the living fleeing the city. The executive departments would soon have no choice but to evacuate to Trenton. McHenry himself would have already gone if not suffering from an "old bilious complaint." So, in sickness and increasing solitude, he labored. Often he had time only to recopy — not to reword — the recommendations he received from his old friend Hamilton before sending them on to the president.

Such was the case with the advice "Ham" gave McHenry on July 30, 1798, during a visit to Philadelphia. "I observe you plunged in a vast mass of details. I know from experience that it is impossible for any man whatever be his talents or diligence to wade through such a mass without neglecting the most material things and attaching to his operations a feebleness and sloth of execution. It is essential to the success of the minister of a great department that he subdivide the objects of his care, distribute them among competent assistants and content himself with a general but vigilant superintendence."

Insulting as Hamilton's imperiousness was, McHenry dutifully wrote the president on August 4. "I find myself plunged in a vast mass of details and know from experience that it is impossible for any man, whatever be his talents, to wade through it without neglecting perhaps the most material objects or attaching to his operations . . . feebleness and sloth of execution. It is essential to the success of the minister of a great department that he be enabled to subdivide the objects of his care, distribute them among competent assistants, and content himself with a general but vigilant superintendence."

Hamilton had offered a solution, which McHenry passed off as his own to the president. That solution was Hamilton himself. The government had not yet called him into active service. It should at once. It should also commence paying his salary. McHenry needed to delegate authority. "If these suggestions meet with your approbation," McHenry wrote Adams, "it will make me extremely happy."

One week passed without hearing back from President Adams, then another. Finally arrived a response: Hamilton could not enter active service until all parties agreed to their rank. "If it shall be consented that the rank shall be Knox, Pinckney, and Hamilton, you may call the latter, too, into immediate service," the president wrote. "Any other plan will occasion long delay and much confusion." McHenry had recognized that Adams had gone away from Philadelphia angry over the arrangements for the army, but had not realized until this moment that the president had gone totally mad. General Washington would never agree to having his rankings reversed. An army barely in existence faced its first fight: a battle between two commanders in chief.

Thunder sounded in the distance on the morning of August 20. A fever that had stirred Washington from his sleep a few nights earlier lingered. Nonetheless, he said, "I endeavored to shake [it] off by pursuing my usual rides." The fields needed his attention, and he desperately needed the distraction from the indolence, insecurity, infidelity, and incompetence threatening his reputation.

The indolence was Wash on break from St. John's College. He would return to Annapolis soon, or so Washington had assumed, until hearing the boy ask if he could stay at Mount Vernon permanently. "The question . . . really astonishes me!" Washington said. "It would seem as if *nothing* I could say to you made more than a *momentary* impression. Did I not, before you went to that seminary, and since by letter, endeavor to fix indelibly on your mind, that the object for which you were sent there was to finish a course of education?" The boy offered no answer, only a "moped and stupid" expression. "[He] says nothing and is always in some hole or corner excluded from company," Washington noted. Such behavior, he worried, reflected poorly on the master of the house.

The insecurity was Henry Knox letting "little jealousies" keep him from duty, letting down an old friend counting on help from "coadjutors" on whom he "could place entire confidence." Knox had no right to complain about his "feelings" not being consulted, Washington responded. No one had inquired as to Washington's own feelings before drawing him out of retirement. "If giving in your name . . . is considered as a wound to your feelings, might I not complain upon ground equally strong & hurtful to mine, brought, as I was, without the least intimation before the public?" If Knox made a "stand upon punctilios" at this moment, he would sit out whatever fighting ensued.

The infidelity was Thomas Jefferson. While traveling back to Monticello from Philadelphia earlier in the summer — passing but once again not stopping at Mount Vernon — he was said to have "used every indirect means of damping the patriotic spirit of the people." Too bad that the people still did not know the true story of the counterfeit letter his nephew had sent Washington. The "informer" John Nicholas wished to publish the "history of the whole affair." He just needed more evidence. "If he could prove indubitably" that Jefferson had sanctioned the scheme, "it would be a pity not to expose him to public execration," Washington agreed.

The incompetence was James McHenry. A letter Alexander Hamilton had recently sent to Mount Vernon summed up the situation this way: "McHenry is wholly insufficient for his place, with the additional misfortune of not having himself the least suspicion of the fact!" Unfair as it was, blame for the "ill success of the operations of the war department" would ultimately fall on Washington himself as commander in chief. Such was the way of war. The worst part was how ungrateful McHenry seemed for the lengthy letters Washington took the time to write. McHenry's responses looked so "short" by comparison. In light of the "sacrifices" Washington had made — in light of how he had tied his fate to the army's — he deserved timelier information about its formation. As it stood now, if war commenced, "I would be called to the Army in the moment of danger as ignorant of its formation . . . as if I had just dropped from the clouds."

So, through a "heavy fog," Washington rode. He sensed "rain around" him but felt none. He struggled to clear his mind. Even the horse he rode fed the fear of looking foolish. "My *present* want of a riding horse is great, but if I should be called to the field, it will be much greater." He needed a younger horse, one possessing an attractive symmetry. If it were too "long-legged," he would struggle to get his own long legs over it. "For color, I will not contend, but would prefer a *perfect* white, a dapple grey, a deep bay, a chestnut, [or] a black, in the order they are mentioned. The size & strength must be equal to my weight, which without the saddle may be estimated at 210 lbs.," just a pound more than he had weighed at the end of the Revolutionary War. People back then had admired his appearance on horseback. They must be able to do so again.

Often, as he made his way back to the mansion house from his rides, someone would rush out to put letters in his hand as he dismounted. Inevitably they would be from, or on behalf of, young men hoping to advance in the army on the "mistaken idea" that such decisions rested with the new commander in chief. Little did they know that he had requested the right to choose only the general officers and staff. More junior-level applicants should have written to the War Department. Nonetheless, letters on their behalf flowed into Mount Vernon.

From an ambitious mother came a complaint about her son's rank. "Should you, Sir, be induced once more to head our armies, will you forgive the solicitations of maternal tenderness in favor of a worthy object & place my son in such a point of view as will prevent his abilities being obscured by ignorance?"

From powerful men came requests for preferential treatment for protégés seeking army posts. Nothing about the practice troubled Washington. It was the way of the world, the reason he had long ago accompanied General Braddock to the Forks of the Ohio. In fact, said Washington, "nothing can be more grateful to my sensibility than the numberless offers of a similar kind from gentlemen of the first families [and] fortunes." Reading these letters gave him an idea. He dared not mention it for fear of upsetting Martha. But if war came, he would request a commission for Wash. "If real danger threatened the country," went the thinking, "no young man ought to be an idle spectator of its defense."

From people Washington barely knew came applications for a place in his military family. Alexander Hamilton forwarded one such request from a European. "No foreigner will be admitted as a member of my family, while I retain my present ideas. Nor do I think they ought to be in any situation where they can come at secrets & betray a trust," Washington responded, never mind Hamilton himself not being native born.

In truth, choosing the members of the military family could wait. The need for a secretary — someone who could beat back the letters flooding the mansion — stood as the exception. "I am assailed from all quarters, and by all descriptions of people, for commissions, introductions, recommendations, etc., to *all* of which common civility makes some sort of reply necessary," Washington wrote. No longer could he go more than a day without sending the mailbag to Alexandria. No longer did he have "leisure hours" to look over his old letters. When the mailbag returned, it contained too many new ones. Even the post office could not keep track of them all. Letters he had mailed out sometimes ended up in his incoming mail. So he, who already had too many letters to write, had to send one more rebuking Alexandria's postmaster for his "inattention."

It was all too much. The frustrations added to the fever that had beset his body. He had felt fever like this a few times before, the first time being as a young man exploring the forests over the mountains. The chills shook his body. His energy and appetite fell as his temperature rose. By August 21, he could not write a letter, let alone ride a horse. To Mount Vernon that evening reported Washington's old doctor, James Craik, now the army's new physician general, along with other doctors he wished to consult. By this time, Washington could barely take notice of them or anything else.

Lying there with his body at the mercy of doctors left his mind to search for its own comfort. "A thousand other matters" would "fall in" place, he told himself, as soon as McHenry brought Hamilton into active service and accepted his "assistance." Because being an aide long ago had taught

Hamilton to "possess the soul" of the commander in chief, having Hamilton in the service again now would allow Washington to dispossess himself of some of his concerns.

But then came a new concern: disturbing reports that the president had decided to rank Hamilton third among the major generals. There was nothing Washington could do. He lacked the strength to write. For now, others would have to write on his behalf. To their good judgment, he entrusted his reputation.

Trenton, August 22, 1798

To John Adams, President of the United States

. . . After what has passed with and [given] the conceptions of General Washington respecting the relative grades of Generals Hamilton, Pinckney & Knox . . . , I cannot help apprehending some disagreeable consequences to the public service should a different relative grade be now known to be decisively contemplated. . . .

Your faithful & humble servant,
James McHenry,
Secretary of War

Quincy, August 29, 1798

To James McHenry, Secretary of War
. . . You speak to me of the expediency of attempting an alteration in the rank of the gentlemen in question. You know, Sir, that no rank has ever been settled by me. . . .

The power and authority are in the President. I am willing to exert this authority at this moment, and to be responsible for the exercise of it. All difficulties will in this way be avoided. . . . I foresee it will come to me at last after much altercation and exasperation of passions, and I shall then determine it exactly as I should now — Knox, Pinckney & Hamilton.

There has been too much intrigue in this business with General Washington and me. . . .

Your most obedient & humble servant,
John Adams,
President of the United States

New York, September 8, 1798

To James McHenry, Secretary of War
 . . . My mind is unalterably made up. I shall certainly not hold the commission on the plan proposed [by President Adams], and only wait an official communication to say so. . . .

Adieu,
A[lexander] Hamilton,
Major General

Trenton, September 10, 1798

To Alexander Hamilton, Major General
 . . . I cannot blame you for your determination. . . . [The cabinet secretaries] have agreed to make a respectful representation on the subject to the President. You will not, of course, hear from me, relative to the commands of the President, 'till the result is known to me.

Yours affectionately,
James McHenry,
Secretary of War

Trenton, September 17, 1798

To John Adams, President of the United States

. . . Considering all the circumstances of General Washington's services and retirement, it was certainly a serious question for him to determine whether he should again encounter the perils of public life. Having consented, it will be expected by all dispassionate men that his reasonable wishes should be consulted. . . .

. . . If he [General Knox] is allowed the rank he claims — and [if] General Hamilton declines, contrary to what, in my opinion, is his duty — the evil will not end with the wound to General Washington's feelings nor with the public disappointment. There will be, really, no character high in rank . . . possessed of that various information of the resources of the country and skilled in the formation of those systematical arrangements which the state of our country indispensably requires. . . .

Your most obedient servant,
Oliver Wolcott,
Secretary of the Treasury

Mount Vernon, September 25, 1798

To John Adams, President of the United States
... The subject, on which I am about to address you, is not less delicate in its nature than it is interesting to my feelings. It is the change which you have directed to be made in the relative rank of the Major Generals, which I had the honor of presenting to you, by the Secretary of War. . . .
... To increase the powers of the Commander in Chief — or to lessen those of the President of the United States — I pray you to be persuaded, was most foreign from my heart. To secure able coadjutors in the arduous task I was about to enter upon was my sole aim. . . .
... By some, he [Hamilton] is considered as an ambitious man and, therefore, a dangerous one. That he is ambitious, I shall readily grant, but it is of that laudable kind which prompts a man to excel in whatever he takes in hand. He is enterprising, quick in his perceptions, and his judgment intuitively great — qualities essential to a great military character, and therefore I repeat that his loss will be irreparable. . . .

I have addressed you, Sir, with openness and candor, and I hope with respect, requesting to be informed whether your determination to reverse the order of the three major generals is final. . . .
Your most obedient and
most humble servant,
Go: Washington,
Lieutenant General

As Washington looked over what he had written, he deemed it a "rough draft," one still missing something. Only after signing it did he realize what. On a new page, he wrote: "Lengthy as this letter is, there is another subject not less interesting to the commander in chief of the armies (be him whom he may). . . ." In truth, the "subject" that followed was far less important than the threat implied within the parentheses. If the president reversed the rankings, he would need to find a new commander in chief. Washington would resign. How, he thought, could "[I] retain the commission under such violation of the terms on which I accepted it"? He did not see how he could "with propriety" and with "due respect" for his "character." The controversy could not continue. The letter went in the mail. Too much time already had been lost.

Not until days after falling ill at the end of August had he been well enough to take "the bark" prescribed.* Suspicious of medicine, he avoided it when he could. But even he conceded the bark's effectiveness, and Doctor Craik had a pleading expression to which even the most stubborn patient had to submit. By mid-September, the twenty pounds Washington had lost had begun to return at "nearly a pound and a half a day," a pace, he joked, that would soon bring his weight to four or five hundred pounds.

By September 20, sufficient strength had mustered inside him to allow for a journey to the City of Washington. The next day had gone toward inspecting land around the Capitol. By comparison to Philadelphia's low-lying streets, which the newspapers said the yellow fever had emptied of people, the land around the Capitol looked "as high" and "as healthy as any in the United States." A balustrade had begun to crown the roof covering the north wing. The rooms inside where Congress would carry out its business required little more than plaster and woodwork. Where the members would live, however, remained unknown. Jokes aside,

*The quinine in the bark made it a treatment for malaria.

they could not "camp out."

Hence, the decision he now made to put aside concerns regarding neighborhood jealousies and construction costs and to purchase a lot to his liking just above the Capitol for the purpose of building a pair of three-story town houses that could serve boarders. He had already begun sketching designs. The "earlier" digging began for the cellar, the "better," he said. "I never require much time to execute any measure after I have resolved upon it."

That others did not execute the same way was the root of the frustration he felt at Mount Vernon. "[The] negroes," he observed, "are growing more & more insolent & difficult to govern." Estate manager James Anderson had once again begun sending "long letters of complaint" as if afraid to meet face-to-face for a conversation that could have resolved his "remonstrances" in "five" minutes. Wash had delayed going back to college for so long that hope he ever would had disappeared.

Away from Mount Vernon, business followed a similar pattern. That recruiting for the new army had not yet begun defied comprehension. "It is for the Executive to account for this delay," Washington said. "Sufficient it is for me to regret, and I do regret it sorely, because that spirit & enthusiasm, which was inspired by the dispatches from our Envoys, . . . is evaporating fast, and the recruiting service, which might have been successful (of the best men) a month ago, may be found very difficult a month hence (of the worst kind)." Republicans, he worried, would use the delay to infiltrate the ranks. So might the "Illuminati," that "nefarious" society about which he now "heard much." Such types, he thought, "will leave nothing unattempted to overturn the Government."

The fate of the government could turn on the outcome of the midterm elections. The country needed good Federalists — especially Virginians like John Marshall, who had returned from France a hero — to stand against the Republicans by standing for seats in Congress. Never had Washington so involved himself in congressional electioneering. "The temper of the people of this State in many (at least in some) places are so violent and outrageous that I wish to converse with General Marshall . . . on the elections which must soon come on." Marshall had resisted the call of office until visiting Mount Vernon and joining Washington on the piazza overlooking the river. "Every man who could contribute to the success of sound opinions was required by the most sacred duty to offer his service to the public," Washington explained. If he himself could "surrender the sweets of retirement" after having vowed "never again, under any circumstances, to enter public life," what excuse did Marshall have? "No man could make a stronger sacrifice than" Washington himself had by "breaking a resolution thus publicly made."

That sacrifice would be in vain if the president did not honor the conditions Washington had set for his service. He would have risked his reputation for no end. Some damage had already resulted. What would people say if they saw the letters passing back and forth between him and the cabinet secretaries at present? Washington had begun labeling his own not just "private" or "confidential" but *private and quite confidential*" and including instructions to "burn" once read. Evidently, the president had not done the same, for McHenry forwarded the private letters he received from Quincy.

Not until mid-October did Washington finally receive a letter directly from Quincy. "There is no doubt to be made that, by the present Constitution of the United States, the President has authority to determine the rank of officers," President Adams wrote. "But," he added, "they will of course be submitted to you as Commander in Chief, and if after all, anyone should be so obstinate as to appeal to me from the judgment of the Commander in Chief, I was determined to confirm that judgment." The names would rank as Washington wished. Hamilton would be second-in-command. The crisis had ended. The president had yielded. Washington felt almost grateful.

Perhaps Adams would feel grateful, too, when he heard that his image would appear on the flag Martha had requested for the Silver Grays of Alexandria. Washington himself had approved the design. Given how jealous Adams had been when the people of Philadelphia had celebrated Washington's birthday earlier that year, a decision had been made: Martha would present the flag at a parade in Alexandria on October 30, the sixty-third birthday of John Adams.

The "most gloomy summer" had ended. The winter might be "more dismal still," Adams thought. His wife had fallen sick. She was "confined to the bed," he to a trap of his own cabinet's making. He was, he thought, "no more at liberty than a man in a prison, chained to the floor and bound hand and foot." To decide the relative rank of the major generals, the cabinet secretaries had appealed to the one man outranking the president. If George Washington walked away from the army, as he had threatened to do, he would probably run for president in 1800. And once he was back in office, which he would surely win, Hamilton would receive the command he wished, anyway. Despite swearing never to "consent to the appointment of Hamilton as second in rank," Adams had no choice but to consent.

It was the same story when a seat on the Supreme Court opened. The cabinet secretaries suggested George Washington's nephew Bushrod. Adams liked Bushrod but worried about his relative youth. "I know by experience that seniority at the bar is nearly as much regarded, as it is in the army," Adams said, before catching himself and consenting.

Thankfully, the secretaries had not gotten their way on another appointment: the decision to include Elbridge Gerry on the mission to France. Gerry would embarrass the country, Adams remembered the secretaries saying. For a time, even he had feared their predictions had come true. Gerry's decision to stay behind in France and continue unofficial talks with Minister Talleyrand had mystified everyone. Only after meeting with Gerry in October, just days after his return to the United States, did Adams finally understand. Badly as the French had behaved, peace was possible, Gerry said. Letters from other sources in Europe confirmed the message. "At present," Adams concluded, "there is no more prospect of seeing a French army here than there is in Heaven."

At some point, the American people would tire of financing an army for a war that would never happen. The new army had necessitated new taxes. "One thing I know [is] that regiments are costly articles," Adams wrote. "If this nation sees a great army to maintain without an enemy to fight, there may arise an enthusiasm that seems to be little foreseen." The army's backers, then, would have to find some other purpose for it.

A series of letters that Rufus King, the American minister to Britain, had forwarded to Adams suggested one possibility: Britain and the United States joining forces for an offensive against the New World colonial empire of Spain, so her ally France could not use these possessions as a base of operations. The "plan," according to the documents, would culminate with the "complete independence of South America." It was Francisco de Miranda, a Venezuelan-born soldier, who had dreamed up the scheme while in exile in England. Having visited the United States during the Revolution, Miranda had ingratiated himself to Continental Army officers and was said now to be in communication regarding his plan with one of his "most intimate" American friends: Major General Alexander Hamilton, now second-in-command of the new army.

Adams "knew not whether . . . to laugh or to weep." The details of the plan read as if Miranda had stolen them from the "Hero of La Mancha" out of the pages of *Don Quixote.* Did Miranda's friends sincerely "believe the South Americans capable of a free government?" Adams did not. "It appeared . . . as absurd as . . . [plans to] establish democracies among the birds, beasts, and fishes." Moreover, just because France and Spain had entered an alliance did not mean the United States had the sudden right to invade Spanish territories. And even if such a right did exist, where would the United States get the several thousand troops Miranda requested? At the moment, the new army had basically none.

No doubt that was why the secretary of

war had suddenly called a meeting on the subject of recruiting. To Philadelphia in November, when the risk of yellow fever would fall with the temperatures, McHenry would summon Generals Washington and Hamilton. Adams was in no rush to join them. He had lost the battle over relative rank. But he could still win the war by preventing one. His thoughts had turned to peace.

CHAPTER EIGHT:
BEWITCHED

Up the Potomac to Alexandria, across the river to Georgetown, through the broad avenues slicing through the City of Washington, and into the woods beyond rolled the carriage, crossing the twenty-mile radius beyond which Washington remembered having vowed never again to stray from Mount Vernon. His traveling party included a half-dozen horses, four "servants," and Tobias Lear, whom Washington had hired as his personal secretary as soon as President Adams had granted permission to employ one. Ahead lay Philadelphia and days of secretive meetings with the secretary of war and Major Generals Alexander Hamilton and Charles Cotesworth Pinckney. Henry Knox had officially refused to serve. Too much time had already gone toward trying to change his mind. Never again would he receive another letter from Washington.

There were other concerns for Washington

to contemplate. An awkward question that had loomed over his departure from Mount Vernon on the morning of November 5, 1798, still nagged at him. Why had his nephew Lawrence Lewis not joined the others in seeing off the carriage? Surely Lawrence had not intended "disrespect." Perhaps he was sick. Had he even come downstairs for breakfast? Washington tried to "recollect." As usual, when under "the pressure of many things," his memory failed.

Such had been the distraction created by the letter he had received shortly before leaving from Richard Parkinson, the "experienced" English farmer whom Washington had corresponded with in 1797 about renting one of Mount Vernon's farms but had not heard back from until now. Parkinson had apparently liked the idea, because he had decided to set off for America. In fact, he had done so weeks earlier. Soon his ship would sail up the Potomac, land in Alexandria (if not at Mount Vernon itself), and unload what he described as the finest animals one could find in England: "five stallions of the first blood," "eight full blood mares of good extraction," "one hunting mare," "four different sorts of bulls & cows of the best this island produces," "some sheep (rams & ewes)," and "a number of boars & sows of the best kind." Noah and his ark docking at Mount Vernon would hardly have "surprised" Washington more. No "arrangements" had been made, no official "terms" struck.

It was not just the prospect of Parkinson's arrival that worried Washington. There was word of another transatlantic traveler en route. According to a letter Lafayette had sent in May but that had arrived only recently, he and his son had reunited near Hamburg and planned to return to America. Unless their schedule had subsequently changed, they, too, could show up at Mount Vernon any day. To have embraced Lafayette would have pleased Washington at almost any other moment save this one. How would it look for the commander in chief of the armies of the United States to embrace a Frenchman at a time when Congress had authorized the president to remove meddling aliens? Meddling was exactly what, it seemed, Lafayette had in mind to do. Already he wrote of the ways he could help negotiate peace between his native country and his adopted one. In trying, he would humiliate himself. Probably he would humiliate Washington, too.

As if Washington needed another reason to feel self-conscious en route back to the "public theatre," the new riding horse he had recently bought had unusually large teeth that would surely attract notice. He feared his own teeth would also. By this time, his dentures had pushed his upper lip out so far that it rested "just under the nose." The lower lip, meanwhile, had curled into a state of permanent "pouting." A dentist Washington liked in New York had promised to send a better-fitting apparatus to the War Department in Philadelphia, where it would await Washington's arrival.

The last time Washington had driven these roads — the opposite way — he had tried to avoid military processions. Now he made no effort. On November 10, horsemen escorted him the rest of the way up the Delaware River. Advised to ride in such a way as to avoid the yellow fever refugee camps that the poor with nowhere else to go had formed on the outskirts of Philadelphia, even though he himself had no "apprehension of the desolating fever," he entered the city and found some of the troops there assembled in the hopes of receiving his approval. They had it. On he then rode to the quarters reserved for him at a boardinghouse on Eighth Street, just a few blocks away from the vacant president's house from which he had ridden away the previous year and to which his successor had not yet returned from Quincy, Massachusetts.

Not until President Adams returned to Philadelphia would Thomas Jefferson even contemplate leaving Monticello. If he could, he would delay his departure long enough so as to miss having to sit through the spectacle surrounding the president's annual message to Congress and so as to have the opportunity to complete some more renovations at his home. Many of the rooms still lacked floors. Others lay exposed to the elements. Before the winter, Monticello desperately needed cover. So did Jefferson himself.

"Spies," he believed, monitored his every move. He feared they even opened his letters. How else to explain why letters that had formerly taken eight days to reach Monticello from Philadelphia suddenly took a minimum of sixteen? No doubt, his letters attracted scrutiny from the post office. He warned his correspondents to check the seals. Such was life under the Sedition Act. The printer who had forced Hamilton into divulging his affair had fled Philadelphia. The brave Benjamin Franklin Bache had stayed and published on only to perish in the yellow fever epidemic. Even elected officials had not escaped prosecution. A congressman had gone to jail for "words" no more "seditious" than "general censures of the proceedings of Congress & of the President."

To conceive the government trumping up a similar case against a vice president no longer classified as paranoia. "I know not which mortifies me most: that I should fear to write what I think, or [that] my country [should] bear such a state of things," Jefferson wrote. Already he heard himself accused of having conspired with the late Bache. For having met with Bache, Jefferson would not apologize; Bache had been the grandson of Benjamin Franklin, "the greatest man & ornament of the age and country in which he lived." And for calling Franklin so, Jefferson would not apologize to George Washington. "It was the irresistible influence & popularity of General Washington, played off by the cunning of Hamilton, which turned the government over to antirepublican hands" and ushered in what Jefferson deemed the "reign of witches" — a massive conspiracy to commence war with France, conquer Spanish colonies, concoct laws allowing the president and senators to serve for life, and cheat the people out of natural rights over which the federal government should have possessed no power.

Should states such as Virginia secede rather than submit? Some Virginians thought so. Jefferson himself thought not. If given time, the rest of the country would turn against the Federalists, who would not always have a Washington to hide behind. In the meantime, a way to protect the "friendless alien" subjected to the Alien Act — and the poor printer prosecuted under the Sedition Act — had occurred to Jefferson. If these laws violated the Constitution — if they violated the "compact" into which the states had entered — "a nullification of the act is the rightful remedy." Each state could "judge for itself." A resolution he had written declaring the Alien and Sedition Acts "void and of no force" would go before the legislature of Kentucky. That he had written the resolution needed to remain a secret from most everyone except his fellow Virginian James Madison.

With Madison, Jefferson had "no secrets." To Madison, Jefferson would entrust the task of drafting a similar resolution for Virginia, Washington's native state. Madison had recently assured Jefferson that the most "hotheaded" of the federal government's measures would not find receptive soil "in the cool climate of Mount Vernon." Jefferson was not so sure. He remembered something else Madison had observed about Washington after his return to private life in the wake of the Revolutionary War. "A mind like his," Madison had written, "cannot bear a vacancy."

Washington's first few days back in Philadelphia conjured memories of the days after he had taken the presidential oath for the first time in 1789. "No business could be done [then]," he remembered, "for by the time I had done breakfast, thence 'till dinner & afterwards 'till bed time, I could not dispatch one (ceremonious) visit before I was called to another." So it was again now, as he settled into the house on Eighth Street. With no designated visiting hour like the one he had eventually set for levees during his presidency, the "many" visitors paying their respects came whenever they wished.

On November 13, Washington had just sat at his desk when he heard one of his "servants" announce yet another visitor, a Doctor Blackwell, waiting in the parlor. Only upon entering the room and extending his hand did Washington notice that the doctor had not called alone. There was another man waiting to grasp Washington's hand.

Reflexively, Washington withdrew it. The man looked surprised and said his name as if thinking his face had gone unrecognized when just the opposite had happened. Washington recognized the face all too well.

It belonged to a man whose name Washington shuddered to say: George Logan, a Pennsylvania farmer and Republican who had recently returned from an expedition to France taken on the notion that he could succeed where the envoys had failed, never mind that he lacked any right to represent his own government and gave every reason for his fellow citizens to suspect him of sedition. If the servant announcing Doctor Blackwell had provided any warning as to Logan's presence, Washington would have thought better of rising from his desk in the first place. Saying anything that the self-appointed "Envoy Logan" could deem supportive of his freelancing diplomacy could undermine America's elected government, to say nothing of Washington's own reputation.

Thus, the need immediately after the meeting to document the hesitancy, nay, the hatred, with which Washington "finally" offered his hand.

With an air of much indifference, I gave

264

him [Logan] my hand and asked Doctor Blackwell to be seated. The other [Logan] took a seat at the same time. I addressed all my conversation to Doctor Blackwell; the other all his to me, to which I only gave negative or affirmative answers, as laconically as I could, except asking how Mrs. Logan did. . . .

About this time, Doctor Blackwell took his leave. We all rose from our seats, and I moved a few paces towards the door of the room, expecting the other [Logan] would follow and take his leave also — instead of which, he kept his ground & proceeded to inform me . . . that he had seen General Lafayette at Hamburg. . . . But as I wished to get quit of him [Logan], [I] remained standing and showed the utmost inattention to what he was saying. . . .

He observed that the situation of our affairs in this Country — and the train they were in, with respect to France — had induced him to make the voyage in hope . . . to their amelioration. This drew my attention more pointedly to what he was saying and induced me to remark that there was something very singular in this. That he who could only be viewed as a private character . . . should suppose he could effect what these gentlemen of the first respectability in our Country specially charged under the authority of the Government were unable to do.

With this observation, he seemed a little confounded but, recovering, said that not more than five persons had any knowledge of his going; that he was furnished by Mr. Jefferson [the vice president] . . . with certificates of his citizenship; that . . . [the] President of the Directory of France had discovered the greatest desire that France & America should be on the best terms. I answered that he was more fortunate than our Envoys, for they could neither be received nor heard by . . . the Directory. . . .

He said that the Directory was apprehensive that [America's government] . . . was not well disposed towards France. . . . I conceived his object . . . to be, that we should be involved in a dangerous situation if we persisted in our hostile appearances. To this I finally replied that we were driven to those measures in self-defense, and I hoped the spirit of this Country would never suffer itself to be injured with impunity by any nation under the sun.

Logan had eventually gone away. But the

repercussions of his peace mission would not go away, Washington knew. The foreign propaganda that Logan had brought back would spread "by means of the presses which are at the command of that party." It was as if the Republicans complaining most about the "unconstitutionality" of the Alien and Sedition Acts simultaneously sought to prove the necessity of these laws.

Washington himself "scarcely" had time to read any newspapers. The strict schedule imposed after the encounter with Logan rarely varied. Every morning at ten, Hamilton and Pinckney reported to the house for discussion of the questions upon which Secretary of War McHenry had asked advice. For example, how many commissions for regimental officers should each state receive? To whom should the appointments go? And once raised, where should the soldiers assemble? That last question required less thought, for Washington had already decided on one place: Harpers Ferry on the Potomac.

To McHenry's questions, Washington added some of his own, a plurality of which involved uniforms. "Smaller matters," he called them, "which may give a tone to measures which may prevail hereafter." For starters, "would not cotton or (still more so) flannel be advisable for shirting and linings for the soldiery?" And that decided, "what had best be the distinctions in dress, in the badges and other peculiarities, between the commander in chief and his suite, and the major generals & their aides?" All the uniforms, he thought, ought to make use of a "small eagle" that could be made of "pewter," "tin," or even "silver" and be "fixed by way of button in the center of a rose cockade, which was not only very distinguishable but somewhat characteristic."

With so many important issues to discuss, the daily morning meeting would continue until three in the afternoon, when the generals would break for dinner. By seven in the evening, however, they had returned to the house, and work resumed. Never before nine at night and sometimes not before ten did the sessions end.

This is not to say the schedule precluded pleasure. There was time for long walks during which Washington looked at the city's buildings with his mind focused on the ones he himself would soon build in the federal city. "If . . . not incongruous with rules of architecture," he wished to have his buildings "executed in . . . [the] style" of a pair of town houses he observed with "doors in the center," "a pediment in the roof," "dormer windows on each side of it in front," and "skylights in the rear."

There was also time for a bittersweet meal with his old friend Robert Morris inside the debtors' prison that had become his lot after he had lost all the ones he had purchased in the federal city. There was time, too, for meals in more elegant settings: at the houses of cabinet secretaries eager to share the state of their departments; at the governor's house, where a large party heard Hamilton rage about the ways "Virginia was threatening" the Union; and at the president's house at which John Adams, who had finally returned to Philadelphia in late November, asked whether Aaron Burr deserved reconsideration for a generalship in the army (he did not).

Each of these dinners merited entry in the diary Washington kept. The meals he shared with Eliza Willing Powel did not. "Did the love of variety so preponderate that because you had never blundered as President . . . , you [were] determined to try its delights as a private gentleman?" she had teased after he had left Philadelphia the previous year. Now back, he asked if he could have "the honor of drinking tea" at her house one evening and the "pleasure of breakfasting with her" one Sunday "at her usual hour," after which he had stepped out and walked through the rain.

The next day, she sent a "book of prints" to his lodgings. She had "also taken the liberty to add" a few prints of her own choosing, "on a presumption" that he would "admire fine representations of the work of God in the human form."

Eliza's "heart" felt "so sincerely afflicted," her "ideas so confused," as she searched for the words to send the general as his days in the city dwindled. "I can only express my predominant wish," she wrote him on December 7. "That God may take you into his holy keeping and preserve you safe both in traveling and under all circumstances — and that you may be happy here and hereafter — is the ardent prayer of your affectionate afflicted friend."

She saw little of him afterward. He attended the president's annual message to Congress the next day and turned down an invitation to eat with her the day after that. He needed to bring his work in the city "to a close," he wrote, and no longer had time to dine out, not even on the Sabbath, the observance of which he had secretly "dispensed with."

His thoughts were already back home. He asked her help picking out presents for the women awaiting his return. For Nelly, he wanted "handsome muslin" for a dress. Eliza worried it would cost more than he wished to pay. "The difference between thirty & sixty (or more) dollars is not so much a matter of consideration as the appropriate thing," he answered. So Eliza had spent sixty-five of his dollars on the fabric. For his wife, he wished to spend less. "Is there anything — not of much cost — I could carry Mrs. Washington as a memento that she has not been forgotten in this city?" She always seemed to like thread cases. A seven-dollar one, Eliza thought, should do.

On December 19, 1798, Mount Vernon appeared between the trees as it always did when Washington approached. He had returned just in time. By the next morning, three inches of snow covered the ground. So "extreme" had been his "impatience" to leave Philadelphia "on account of the season & weather" that "erasures" had marred the reports that represented the result of his many meetings with his major generals. "In contemplating the possibility of our being driven to unqualified war, it will be wise to anticipate that frequently the most effectual

271

way to defend is to attack. There may be imagined enterprises of very great moment to the permanent interests of this Country," read one of the reports that Hamilton had drafted and that Washington had not had time to render a fair copy of. "I am really ashamed," he admitted.

There had not even been time to properly calculate how much money the government owed for the travel expenses he had incurred. In truth, he desperately needed the money refunded. The estimate he had received for building the two houses in the federal city "far" exceeded the "sum" he had settled upon in his own mind and far exceeded the cash he either had on hand or had any hope of soon having. The way Richard Parkinson had begun his trip to the United States left little hope it would end with a deal to rent one of Mount Vernon's farms. Meanwhile, the tenants leasing Washington's properties up the Potomac blamed a bout of bad weather and pests for destroying their harvests and rendering them unable to make rent payments. None of the money James Welch had promised for the rich western lands he wished to purchase had materialized so far, and probably none of it ever would. Unless cash came from some unexpected source, a lack of liquidity would leave Washington no "recourse" but to apply for the first time for a bank loan at what he presumed would be a "ruinous" rate.

Had he been the man the Republicans caricatured him as — he had not forgotten how their newspapers had accused him of overdrawing his pay from the Treasury as president — he would have simply requested the full compensation to which his command now entitled him: more than five hundred dollars a month dating back to July 4, the day given on his commission. But he had never served the public for private gain. He wished only for what he had asked at the start of both the Revolutionary War and his presidency: his expenses paid. So, at the end of the trip to Philadelphia, even though McHenry had urged drawing three months' pay, Washington had requested only two, which left him seventy-six dollars and five cents poorer for his travels. "I had rather sustain the loss and the fatigues of the journey than it should be thought I was aiming to draw an iota more from the public," he wrote.

The experience reinforced his resolve to remove himself from the army's day-to-day chain of command. "You know the ground," he wrote McHenry, "on which I accepted the command of the Army, and that it is a part of my plan to decline the occupations of the office unless and until my presence in the field should be required for actual operations or other imperious circumstances might require my assistance. Persevering in this plan, I cannot undertake to assume a direct agency incompatible therewith, and a halfway acting might be more inconvenient than totally declining it. The other general officers will, I am persuaded, execute with alacrity any service to which they may be destined." Pinckney could oversee the southern states. Hamilton could oversee the middle and northern ones as well as the West. He could also take charge of "the whole of the recruiting service, [which] should be under one direction, and this properly appertains to the Office of Inspector General."

Only too late had Washington remembered his delinquency in discharging one last army-related duty: obtaining Martha's permission for the appointment he had recommended for Wash in the cavalry as a cornet. If she would not give her "consent" for fear of losing her only surviving male descendant — the last hope for carrying his family name into a new century — "it would be better" that Wash not suffer the "disappointment" of knowing the opportunity had existed. But it was too late. Wash had caught word. Thankfully — surprisingly — his grandmama did "not seem to have the least objection."

Assuming President Adams also had no objection (how could he?), Wash would ride in a troop under the command of his house-mate, soon-to-be-captain Lawrence Lewis. Washington had been sure Lawrence would be "glad of some appointment," especially given he had expressed "regret" for not hav-ing joined the rest of the family in seeing Washington off to Philadelphia. The young man apologized for being so "awkward." As it turned out, he had the best reason for it.

After Washington had left for Philadelphia, Lawrence had asked Nelly to marry him. Yes, she had said. The news stunned Wash-ington. He had not seen it coming. In fact, he had not possessed the "smallest suspicion that such an affair was in agitation." Mar-tha had reservations about the match. Lawrence showed an inclination for "idle-ness," though thankfully "unaccompanied by vicious habits." Not that it would have made a difference, anyway. Long ago, Wash-ington had learned not to "intermeddle" when members of the opposite sex had set their minds on matrimony. "I am too well

275

acquainted with women to give advice to any of them when they are bound for the Port of Matrimony, because I never shall advise *any one* to marry the man she does not like and because I know it is to no purpose to advise them to refrain from the man they do."

The soon-to-be spouses went their separate ways for Christmas. Nelly celebrated with her birth mother, Lawrence with Wash on a trip across the mountains.

Washington himself cast his thoughts across the ocean he would never cross. More than a year had passed since he had written Lafayette despite receiving from him six letters, including two in recent weeks. The futility of sending a letter to Europe to a man on the eve of embarking for the United States had previously provided the excuse Washington needed for postponing unpleasantness. No longer could he, however, given that Lafayette had reported temporarily postponing his trip to America.

So on a "perfectly clear" Christmas Day, Washington began writing. "No one in the United States would receive you with opener arms or with more ardent affection than I should after the differences between this Country & France are adjusted and harmony between the nations is again restored. But it would be uncandid, and incompatible with that friendship I have always professed for you, to say . . . that I wish it before." If Lafayette came now, he would have to choose sides not only between his native land and his adopted one but also between Federalists and Republicans. He could not stay neutral. Not even Washington could, not so long as those who went by Republican "oppose[d] the government in all its measures and are determined . . . by clogging its wheels, *indirectly* to change the nature of it and to subvert the Constitution," not so long as the Republicans accused anyone defending their own government of being "monarchists" and "aristocrats." He had not intended to say more than "a few words" about politics in his letter, but those few soon became a few hundred and then a thousand.

Thousands of more words about politics poured out with the wine at Christmas dinner. He found himself wanting to pass around a new pamphlet he had read in defense of the sedition law. The pamphlet would not persuade "the leaders of [the] opposition," he knew. Not even an argument with "conviction as clear as the sun in its meridian brightness" would convince them. But the argument did convince him. A constitution empowering Congress "to make all laws which shall be necessary and proper for carrying" out powers granted to the government surely allowed Congress to pass laws prescribing punishment for publications that threatened the very existence of the government.

The compulsion to turn the talk at the table to farming had faded. A year that had brought dramatic revelations from abroad ended with a realization at home. "When I offered my valedictory address to the people of the United States," Washington noted, "I little thought that any event would arise in my day that could withdraw me from the retreat in which I expected to pass the remnant of a life worn down with cares. . . . But we know little of ourselves & much less the designs of Providence."

A true farmer could never settle at Mount Vernon. "The whole of the different fields were covered with either stalks of weeds, cornstalks, or what is called sedge — something like spear-grass [that no animal] . . . would eat." There was "no green grass there, except in the garden," "very little" clover, and "no grass hay of any kind." All this was hard to see beneath the blanket of snow around Christmas. But Richard Parkinson had seen the "barrenness" during a visit on a "hot and dry" day earlier in the month.

The only reason for his return now was that General Washington had been in Philadelphia then and deserved a face-to-face explanation for why Parkinson had decided against accepting the farm he had sailed from Liverpool to rent. In fact, he would not even let his animals lodge for a time on it for fear that they would leave looking as "poor" as Washington's. "The General . . . seemed at first to be not well pleased with my conversation," Parkinson noted. "To convince the General of the cause of my determination, I was compelled to treat him with a great deal of frankness." What passed for a poor estate in England, Parkinson said, would produce ten times more wheat per acre than Mount Vernon, not to mention sheep with about three times as much wool.

The general looked "surprised." Nonetheless, he remained "friendly," Parkinson thought, at least in the "mild" sense of the word. Only when slaves appeared did Washington show a different side. "When he spoke to them, he amazed me by the utterance of his words. He spoke as differently as if he had been quite another man, or had been in anger." It was as if the general were once again disciplining raw soldiers, willing a ragtag army onward. The general could call himself a farmer all he wished. At heart, however, he would never be one at Mount Vernon.

Hell Broke Loose, or, the Murder of Louis, by William Dent, 1793. Just four years after the shocking news that Louis XVI of France had gone to the guillotine, as depicted here by a British artist, power passed peacefully in America from one head of state, George Washington, to another, John Adams, on March 4, 1797.

George Washington, by Joseph Wright, circa 1784. This portrait, showing Washington as he looked at the end of the Revolutionary War, hung in the house of Eliza Willing Powel, who said that Washington's "countrymen gaze[d] on him like a God." Washington himself was said to have called the portrait a "good likeness but not flattering."

Residence of Washington in High Street, Philadelphia, by William L. Breton, 1830. To this house, Washington bade farewell at the end of his presidency in 1797. He said that he "counted" the days until he could ride away from its walls.

An early painting of Mount Vernon, by Edward Savage, circa 1787–1792. The house as it appeared from the direction George Washington would have approached on March 15, 1797, the final day of his journey home from the presidency. "I am once more seated under my own vine and fig tree," he wrote.

4

5

Life of George Washington: The Farmer, by Junius Brutus Stearns, circa 1853. After returning to Mount Vernon, Washington devoted his time between breakfast and dinner to inspecting his farms. He expected the slaves depicted here to labor from dawn to dusk.

6

View of Mount Vernon with the Washington Family on the Piazza, by Benjamin Henry Latrobe, 1796. George and Martha Washington, pictured here sitting at a table, would often lead their guests out to the piazza overlooking the river. "It is from there," one guest wrote, "that one looks out on perhaps the most beautiful view in the world. One sees there the waters of the Potomac rolling majestically over a distance of four to five miles."

A close-up of the Athenaeum portrait of Martha Washington, by Gilbert Stuart, 1796. Martha Washington as she looked while awaiting the end of her husband's presidency and the fulfillment of her long-deferred wish of living out their days in "the still enjoyments of the fireside at Mount Vernon."

7

A portrait of Eleanor "Nelly" Parke Custis Lewis, by Gilbert Stuart, 1804. A granddaughter of Martha Washington by her first marriage to Daniel Parke Custis, Nelly grew up with her younger brother, Wash, under the same roof as George Washington and looked upon him as "the most affectionate of fathers." She married Washington's nephew Lawrence Lewis.

8

A portrait of George Washington "Wash" Parke Custis, by Charles Balthazar Julien Févret de Saint-Mémin, 1808. Martha Washington's grandson, Wash, as he appeared early in adulthood, the stage of life for which he had seemed so unprepared in the eyes of George Washington. "It would seem," Washington wrote Wash, "as if *nothing* I could say to you made more than a *momentary* impression."

9

John Adams, by Gilbert Stuart, circa 1800–1815. In 1797, Adams succeeded George Washington in office. One of the opposition newspapers described the second president as "old, querulous, bald, blind, crippled, [and] toothless."

10

Abigail Smith Adams (Mrs. John Adams), by Gilbert Stuart, circa 1800–1815. Abigail resented the way people treated her husband as president. "How different," she complained, "is the situation of the President from that of Washington?"

11

Thomas Jefferson, by Rembrandt Peale, 1805. Jefferson believed that only the "popularity" of George Washington sustained the Federalists. Their reign, he predicted, would come to an end when Washington came to his.

12

Alexander Hamilton, by John Trumbull, circa 1792. Hamilton, pictured here as treasury secretary, later said he would return to public service only if "invited to *a station in which the service I may render may be proportioned to the sacrifice.*" The position he had in mind was inspector general of the new army.

13

A portrait of Timothy Pickering, based on a painting by Gilbert Stuart. John Adams retained Secretary of State Pickering along with the other men George Washington had appointed to his final cabinet. "Washington saddled me with . . . secretaries who would control me," Adams later said.

14

James McHenry, by Charles Balthazar Julien Févret de Saint-Mémin, 1803. McHenry, as he looked a few years after resigning from the War Department, succeeded in pleasing no one while in office. To George Washington, Alexander Hamilton wrote that McHenry was "wholly insufficient for his place, with the additional misfortune of not having himself the least suspicion of the fact!"

15

Mrs. Samuel Powel, a painting of Eliza Willing Powel, by Matthew Pratt, circa 1793. A prominent Philadelphia widow, Eliza had once warned George Washington that retirement might not suit him. "Have you not," she asked, "on some occasions, found the consummation of your wishes the source of the keenest of your sufferings?"

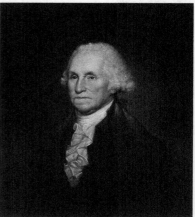

George Washington, by Rembrandt Peale, 1795. A copy of one of the last portraits for which Washington sat. "He really felt himself growing old, his bodily health less firm," Thomas Jefferson recorded Washington saying.

16

17

18

"Washington's Last Birthday, February 22, 1799, from the Painting by H. A. Ogden," as published in *Harper's Weekly*, February 19, 1898. George Washington agreed to serve as guardian to Nelly Custis so she could marry on his sixty-seventh birthday. The new army uniform she wanted him to wear did not arrive in time for the celebration.

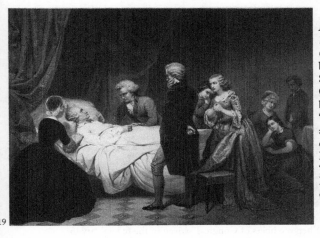

Life of George Washington: The Christian Death, by Junius Brutus Stearns, circa 1853. George Washington believed that the "disorder" that awoke him in the early hours of December 14, 1799, "would prove fatal." It did. "Let me go off quietly," he said.

19

20

High Street, from the Country Market-place Philadelphia: With the Procession in Commemoration of the Death of General George Washington, December 26, 1799, by William Birch, 1800. An illustration of the mock funeral staged in Philadelphia for George Washington. The procession led to the German Lutheran Church, where Congressman Harry Lee of Virginia eulogized Washington as "first in war, first in peace, and first in the hearts of his countrymen."

21

A View of the Capitol of Washington, by William Birch, circa 1800. When members of Congress arrived in the federal city in 1800, they found just one wing of the Capitol ready to receive them. Architect William Thornton hoped that dedicating the space below the unbuilt dome as a final resting place for George Washington's body would give "inducement to the completion of the whole building."

22

A drawing of Mount Vernon, by Theodore R. Davis, as published in *Harper's Weekly*, February 28, 1874. The illustration shows the usually eastbound Potomac traveling south for a stretch from the City of Washington (in the background) to Alexandria before turning unexpectedly to the west just before Mount Vernon. The new tomb, which Washington ordered his executors to construct in his will, is shown on the far left of the picture, just downriver from the mansion house.

CHAPTER NINE:
GUARDIANSHIP

Just when Nelly had begun to doubt what Grandpapa had said about love ("that the passions of your sex are easier roused than allayed") — just when she had discarded his warning ("do not therefore boast too soon, nor too strongly, of your insensibility to or resistance of its powers") — it happened exactly as he warned it would. "Cupid, a small mischievous urchin, who has been trying sometime to humble my pride, took me by surprise. . . . When I had abused & defied him & thought my heart impenetrable, he slyly called in Lawrence Lewis to his aid & transfixed me with a dart." Upon returning from Philadelphia, Grandpapa asked for all the details. He "was very curious about all my love letters." So she "showed him" the ones she had "received."

Lawrence had wooed her for months. Only after she had learned of his appointment to the army did his tactics triumph.

She would marry him, she had said, but only under the condition that he agree to decline the commission. Grandpapa would have to wait to hear that particular detail until closer to the wedding.

It was impossible not to see a certain family "resemblance" between Grandpapa and the groom-to-be. According to family lore, Lawrence's recently deceased mother had appeared "so strikingly like her brother [Grandpapa]" that soldiers would have obeyed her orders had she donned "a military hat on her head." Lawrence himself had Grandpapa's enormous eye sockets and conspicuous nose, albeit on a thinner face.

What Lawrence did not have was Grandpapa's vigor. The younger man preferred to recede into himself. He did not seem cut out for a career in the army. He spoke of making a home over the mountains. Nelly dreaded leaving Mount Vernon. "My prospects of happiness, although very great, are yet clouded when I think of leaving my beloved grandparents who have been everything to me hitherto and this dear spot, which has been my constant *home* since my first remembrance, to which I must ever feel the strongest attachment." Knowing, however, that Lawrence as "Grandpapa's nephew" would have "the same inducement" to visit Mount Vernon assuaged the fear. "I am perfectly reconciled & neither think 'the day evil or the hour unlucky' that witnessed my solemn promise to become Mrs. Lewis & take said Lawrence for better or worse," Nelly wrote.

According to custom in Virginia, she would need a guardian to give her away. Though Grandpapa had refused the role many years ago, she hoped he would accept it now. And he did. On January 21, 1799, he rode to Alexandria and returned later that day as her guardian. "There will be no impediment to your union," he said.

She knew what she wanted Grandpapa to wear to the wedding: that "splendidly embroidered uniform" being prepared for the commander in chief of the army. The uniform should look exactly how Grand-papa described it. The "silver stars" on either shoulder would number three. They would lie on "gold epaulettes" topping a blue coat cut from the "best & softest French or Spanish" cloth. The buttons would be "plain, flat, and of the best double gilt." The cuffs would be "neither large nor tight." The linings would look, he hoped, "buff," not "yellow or orange." He had asked the secretary of war to consult sartorial "connoisseurs" as to the specifics. None of them mattered so much as the delivery date. All of the parts needed to arrive in time for the ceremony, which would take place on Grandpapa's sixty-seventh birthday, February 22, 1799.

There were no uniforms to wear. That was the reason the War Department gave for delaying recruiting. If mustered, the soldiers would shiver in the cold, as they had during the Revolutionary War. The embarrassments needed to end. The letters that Alexander Hamilton received from fellow Federalists begged him to assume control of operations. Now that the War Department had agreed to provide his full pay, he would. Only the "rich," like General Washington, could afford to spurn a salary. Hamilton needed to provide for his family. The hours he had spent, especially in Philadelphia, had already cost him half of his law practice. The meetings with Washington and Charles Cotesworth Pinckney had taken too much time and accomplished too little. "But that is not my fault," Hamilton explained. "I cannot make everybody else as rapid as myself." The real work of forging an army would happen in New York, to which he had returned for the winter.

Then and there arrived a letter dated

February 7 from Theodore Sedgwick, a Massachusetts senator fresh from presenting Hamilton's proposals for reorganizing the military (for example, tripling the size of the provisional force) to President Adams. Adams had asked but one question: "What additional authority it was proposed to give the commander in chief?" And by commander in chief, of course, Adams meant Washington.

"None," Sedgwick had answered. "All that was proposed was giving him a new title, that of [full] general," a symbolic promotion from his current rank of lieutenant general.

"What?" Adams had said as if stunned. Then his voice, reportedly, had grown louder. "Are you going to appoint him general over the President? I have not been so blind but I have seen a combined effort, among those who call themselves the friends of government, to annihilate the essential powers given by the president."

The conversation had turned to the "delays in the military department." As Sedgwick told the story, Adams had finally said, "If you must have an army, I will give it to you, but remember it will make the government more unpopular than all their other acts. They [Americans] have submitted with

285

more patience than any people ever did to the burden of taxes which has been *liberally laid on,* but their patience will not last always." Among those out of patience, evidently, was the president himself.

Strange as it seemed to say given the primitive state of preparations, the military program was a victim of its own success, thought Hamilton. America's increasingly formidable navy had chased French privateers off the United States coast and turned the tide against them in the Caribbean. A dramatic reduction in attacks on American merchant vessels and insurance rates for shipping had followed. Meanwhile, just hearing the call to arms in the United States in the wake of the XYZ revelations had forced the French to reconsider their belief that Americans would flock to the French flag in the event of invasion. "Some late occurrences," Hamilton wrote, "have rendered the prospect of invasion by France less probable or more remote." The most important of these "occurrences" had happened on the other side of the world. General Bonaparte had landed his troops not in England, as expected, but in Egypt, where they were now said to be stranded. A British admiral named Horatio Nelson had wrecked Bonaparte's fleet and, with it, fears of French troops landing in America. In no way, however, did these developments diminish the need for an army. Protection against "internal disorders alone," Hamilton wrote, required as many troops as Congress had authorized. Whatever anyone thought about the Alien and Sedition Acts — he himself thought the former could benefit from "revision," even if the "mass [of the aliens] ought to be obliged to leave the Country" — the resolutions that the Virginia and Kentucky legislatures had passed against these laws would render the Constitution null and void and "destroy" the Union. "In times like the present," Hamilton wrote, "not a moment ought to have been lost to secure the Government so powerful an auxiliary" as an army. "When a clever force has been collected, let them be drawn towards Virginia for which there is an obvious pretext, and then let measures be taken to act upon the laws & put Virginia to the test of resistance." The test might come soon. Republicans in the state legislature were said to be moving to "purchase . . . arms" and awaiting an opportunity to "throw themselves in the way" of a federal marshal enforcing the laws. "Thus," read a letter to Hamilton, "the signal of Civil War will be given." If faced with such rebels, the federal government could not afford to rely on state militias of questionable loyalty, as it had in 1794 against the whiskey rebels. Preserving the Union would require deploying a professional federal force, that is, the new army.

Preserving the Union might also justify another use Hamilton had in mind for the new army: preemptive "offensive operations." If negotiations with the French did not resume by the summer, the United States should consider escalating hostilities on its own terms by seizing and annexing the Spanish colonies of Louisiana and Florida, "tempting objects," which he had "long" considered "essential to the permanency of the Union" and which would give southerners and westerners a stake in the war and thereby turn regions that had been Republican strongholds into fertile ground for Federalism.

Once begun, offensive operations against the Spanish could end only after the liberation of their empire in South America. The secret plan that the "adventurer" Francisco de Miranda had sent was hardly new to Hamilton. The logic for it had come to him on his own. "If universal empire is still to be the pursuit of France, what can tend to defeat the purpose better than to detach

South America from Spain, which is only the channel through which the riches of *Mexico* and *Peru* are conveyed to France?" The British would supply the ships needed. The United States should "furnish the whole land force necessary." Who would command the expedition? Not General Washington. His age, Hamilton reasoned, would preclude his participation. "The command in this case would very naturally fall upon me." The bureaucratic battle over relative rank had assured it. A soldier on the threshold of such glory could be forgiven for telling one of his children that his name might "descend to a grateful posterity as the Liberator of Southern America." Indeed, to few others did Hamilton dare disclose his full thinking.

Not since leaving Philadelphia had he communicated with General Washington. There had been no need. Washington had entrusted his powers and, thus far, requested no updates (even said they might be "inconvenient"). Besides, Hamilton had not previously seen much worth communicating. That changed only upon learning what President Adams had told Senator Sedgwick. "It may be useful," Hamilton began to think, to arrange a system for communicating with General Washington about "confidential matters relating to our administration without the mention of names." The letter *X*, for example, could stand in for President Adams.

The day he dreaded neared. There was no avoiding it this year. John Adams would have to attend the ball, the one the Philadelphians had planned in honor of yet another of George Washington's birthdays. The amphitheater where the guests would gather would be so frigid, Adams predicted, that staying warm would require one to be willing to dance, which he was unwilling to do. "I shall get a cold and have to eat gruel for breakfast for a week afterwards." In fairness, the Philadelphians had tried to placate his feelings by holding a ball a few weeks earlier in his honor. The ladies had worn their finest dresses. Washington, everyone remembered, had always known just what to say to them. Adams struggled to say a word. He blamed it on his teeth hurting. In truth, there was just one woman he wished to see: the "talkative wife" he had once again left in Quincy. He worried about her poor health, even if it did bring her one benefit: the excuse she needed to decline attending the Washington birthday celebration in Boston.

As if Adams and his wife needed another reason to resent Washington's birthday this year, they had it. The wedding planned at Mount Vernon — Custis weddings always caused chatter — would kill the joke the Adamses loved about arranging a marriage between Nelly and their youngest and last remaining unmarried son, twenty-six-year-old Thomas Boylston Adams. The "poor boy" had just returned from Europe, where he had served as a secretary to his oldest brother, John Quincy Adams. Sometimes, as when thinking about his disgraced son-in-law, William S. Smith, Adams envied Washington for having no children. "I do not consider George Washington at all a happier man because he has not children," Abigail had responded. "If he has none to give him pain, he has none to give him pleasure." She was right, of course. Adams felt the "pleasure" as soon as Thomas appeared in Philadelphia and delivered the best of presents: more evidence of the French change of heart.

By now, enough evidence had accumulated to convince a fair mind — one free of party prejudice — that the greatest threat to the United States came not from Bonaparte's army but from Hamilton's. Receiving secret reports of what Hamilton hoped to achieve with the army while remembering what he had already done to achieve his rank in it revealed two truths to Adams: first, Hamilton was "stark mad"; second, the true purpose for the army was to give him "the command of it & then to proclaim a regal government [and] place Hamilton at the head of it." Time and time again, Hamilton had invoked Washington's name for purposes and plans beyond Washington's understanding.

Little did Hamilton know, however, that Washington had given Adams an opportunity to do the same. It had begun with an unexpected letter from Washington, who reported receiving a letter from one Joel Barlow, an American poet and duplicitous "wretch" who had moved to Paris. Barlow had written to assure Washington that the French government would accept a new American envoy without preconditions. If Adams agreed that the Directory might be using Barlow as a backdoor channel for communicating, Washington offered to respond. It was as if the general wished to serve his country in a new capacity, as an unofficial diplomat. The offer did not interest Adams. What did interest him was what Washington wrote in closing. "Restoring peace and tranquility to the United States upon just, honorable and dignified terms . . . is the ardent desire of all the friends" of the country. "What," Adams wondered upon reading the sentence, "could I understand by this hint but an expression of his opinion that I ought to endeavor to make peace if I could?"

Here was the cover Adams needed. Here were words that he could quote if the Federalists protested, as they surely would, the decision he had just made. He would keep it secret even from his cabinet secretaries. He would surprise them all. On February 18, 1799, just four days before Washington's sixty-seventh birthday, Adams sent a message to the Senate, where Thomas Jefferson, who had finally returned to Philadelphia, presided in his capacity as vice president. "Always disposed and ready to embrace every plausible appearance of probability of preserving or restoring tranquility," read the message, which Jefferson recited, "I [John Adams] nominate William Vans Murray, our minister resident at The Hague, to be minister plenipotentiary of the United States to the French Republic." Perhaps Washington would recognize a few of the words as his own. It was he, after all, who had recommended "restoring . . . tranquility."

Shortly afterward, Adams sent a letter explaining the decision to Mount Vernon. Without apology, the letter dismissed Washington's offer to render diplomatic service. Adams had no need for it. With a little luck, the message would arrive at the general's house just in time for his birthday celebration.

The woman whom Washington would give away wore white. The woman with whom he had marked his fortieth wedding anniversary the previous month (without note in his diary) wore a satin dress with flowers. He wore a blue and buff uniform but not the new one he had requested only, he insisted, for Nelly's sake.

He had done everything in his power to procure the new uniform: sent multiple reminders to the secretary of war, who might otherwise have deemed the business "trifling"; provided precise dimensions for a custom portmanteau in which the tailor making the uniform in Philadelphia could pack it for the journey to Mount Vernon; and volunteered the newest member of the Supreme Court (nephew Bushrod) for the job of courier. In the end, none of the arrangements mattered. The French cloth that the tailor had cut never left the shop. No store in America, the tailor discovered after searching ones in Philadelphia, New York, and Baltimore, possessed gold thread in the quantities required for the embroidery. The coat would need to wait for a shipment from across the Atlantic.

As the hour of the nuptials neared, the sky turned clear. Martha invited some of the mansion house slaves inside for the ceremony. "Miss Custis was married about candlelight to Mr. Lawrence Lewis," Washington noted in his diary for February 22.

He had celebrated his birthday eleven days earlier by riding into Alexandria, which observed the occasion, once again, according to the Old Style calendar. The troops welcoming him into town had promptly split into opposing forces. One group boarded ships so as to play, as the newspapers explained afterward, the part of an "invading enemy" staging a "landing," which the other group opposed block by block until finally triumphing at the corner of Fairfax and King Streets. It was, Washington now knew, the only fighting he would see for the foreseeable future.

He had never believed an invasion imminent. The chances of the French undertaking one — even with the encouragement that the opposition party had shamefully given — had always seemed small. But the chances looked essentially nonexistent after opening the letter President Adams had sent explaining his latest decision.

It came as a "surprise" and "not a little" one. Why had the president taken the "formal" step of announcing a new diplomatic mission before receiving "formal" assurances that the French would receive it? A sitting president should not have responded to an unofficial communication from a foreign government. A former president, however, could have. Thus, the real question: Why had President Adams not accepted Washington's offer? True, there were reasons to suspect the poet Joel Barlow, but none of those reasons precluded the government from pursuing another means of backdoor communication with Talleyrand, the French foreign minister. "Had we approached the antechamber of this gentleman when he opened the door to us and *there* waited for a formal invitation into the interior, the governments would have met upon equal ground, and we might have advanced, or receded, according to circumstances, without commitment," Washington thought. Now, instead, Adams had set the United States up for another round of Talleyrand's "roundabout game."

Adams's own cabinet secretaries could not hide their contempt for his decision. "We were all thunderstruck when we heard of it," Secretary of State Timothy Pickering wrote Washington. "Confidence in the President is lost. . . . The *honor* of the country is prostrated in the dust. God grant that its *safety* may not be in jeopardy."

For a moment, in the midst of drafting a response to Pickering, Washington imagined himself as president again. He began to lay out "the course I should have pursued." Then, just as suddenly, he stopped. "But, not being acquainted with all the information & the motives which induced the measure, I may have taken a wrong impression & therefore shall say nothing further on the subject at this time."

Besides, what could he do from Mount Vernon? Responding to an update from Hamilton — the first one to arrive in months — filled the mind with fatalism. There had been a moment in 1798, Washington thought, when the country could have raised such an army as "the world had never seen, but the golden opportunity is passed & probably will never occur again." Public opinion had shifted. Hamilton needed to understand that "the zeal and enthusiasm which were excited by the publication of the dispatches from our commissioners at Paris . . . are evaporated." The army "is not only viewed with indifference but deemed unnecessary by that class of people whose attentions . . . [are] turned to other matters." With spring approaching, the "reputable yeomanry" from which the new army should have drawn its ranks would increasingly turn away from potential fields of battle to the fields of their family farms. Only the "riff-raff of the country & the scape-gallowses of the large cities" would respond to the recruiting calls. "Unless a material change takes place," Washington wrote, "our military theatre affords but a gloomy prospect to those who are to perform the principal parts in the drama."

Young men looking to make a name should look elsewhere. One wrote to ask whether to accept a commission as a major in the army if it meant surrendering a seat he had won in the Virginia state senate. He should keep the senate seat, Washington responded. More lay at stake in the fights on the floor of the commonwealth's capitol. If the "friends of order & good government" did not stand up against measures like the Virginia and Kentucky Resolutions, the Union would "dissolve."

Other young men submitted less noble

reasons for rejecting their commissions. Only a few days before Nelly's wedding had Washington learned of her insistence that Lawrence Lewis not join the army. Making matters more awkward was that Washington had just written a letter quibbling over his nephew's relative rank among the captains in the cavalry. Regardless, there was no choice but to inform the War Department of Lawrence's determination. "The condition of the marriage is that he is to relinquish the field of Mars for the sports of Venus," Washington wrote.

For Grandpapa, the quip never got old. Over and over again, he joked of men laying down the arms of Mars and leaping into the arms of Venus. It was, however, the reverse of what he wanted for Wash, and Wash knew it. A commission should "divert his attention from a matrimonial pursuit," Grandpapa said. So when other young men spurning the cavalry service created an opening for a lieutenant, Grandpapa asked about getting Wash's rank raised. "If I mistake not," Grandpapa wrote Secretary of War McHenry, Wash "stands the first for promotion, that is, he was made the senior cornet." Would there "be any impropriety" in promoting him to lieutenant? McHenry would know not to regard the inquiry as a request for a "favor," for everyone knew that Grandpapa would "never," as he put it, "solicit anything for myself or connections."

Grandpapa need not have worried so much about Wash. The woman with whom he had formed an attachment before quitting college had rejected his advances. The women he saw the most now lived in the quarters near the greenhouse: for example, the "housemaid" Caroline. Someday, depending on how he and his sisters divided the lot, Caroline and many other prominent mansion house slaves might belong to him.

That was the future. The past was what interested Wash, the stories he could hear about the "cold" the soldiers had endured at Valley Forge from Billy Lee, the "body servant" whom Grandpapa had purchased before the Revolutionary War and who had ridden beside him during it. Billy's days on horseback had ended because of "an accident" that had wrecked his "stout athletic form." The job of "body servant" now belonged to a younger slave named Christopher. Though Billy had found a new job as a shoemaker, he had not given up all his old duties. Just as he had during the war, he "carefully reconnoitered" the visitors waiting to see Grandpapa. The ones who had

300

served in the Continental Army knew to report to Billy first.

"Ah," Wash heard Billy say to the veterans, "glad to see you. We of the army don't see one another often in these peaceful times. . . . I am a poor cripple [and] can't ride now, so I make shoes and think of the old times." The old times — that was where the glory lay, where it would always lie.

CHAPTER TEN:
TESTAMENT

"Here, in the language of geographers, is a fine champaign country, well stored with woods, abounding in various sorts of game; a majestic river, navigable, full of fish & wild fowl, and other natural advantages too numerous to be enumerated." Here was "a city growing in the midst of wood," buildings rising so far apart as to be "scarcely visible" from one to the next. There on the east end of Pennsylvania Avenue was the nearly completed north wing of the Capitol. There on the west end stood the president's house, that "fine spacious & magnificent pile" whose polished stone exterior concealed a cavernous void that Father moving into could not possibly fill.

Some member of the family had needed to see the city before the move the next year. So in the spring of 1799, Thomas Boylston Adams had set off from Philadelphia for a tour of his parents' future home. More money would solve every problem, the people welcoming Thomas to Washington said. What happened to the sums already spent — what happened to the money that supposedly would fall from the tree-covered lots sold to the speculators — no one would say with the same surety. "Affairs," Thomas concluded, "have been unfortunately managed. The title to a considerable portion of the soil is liable to dispute. Private speculation has so interwoven itself with everything relating to the concerns of the City that no one who does not court difficulty & embarrassment will venture to purchase there." What about, the people countered, General Washington himself? Only by a few weeks had Thomas missed seeing the cornerstone laid for the town houses the general had begun to build.

No failure, Thomas learned, could fall so flat as to deter the people of Washington from raising it into a reason for hope. The lack of buildings? Rural grandeur, they said. The roads to nowhere cutting through the trees? A healthful contrast with crowded cities teeming with yellow fever. A shortage of supplies? Wait till the canal circumventing Great Falls opens and the wealth of the West rides down the Potomac. When arguments failed, Thomas found other means of persuasion employed. "I was . . . feasted & flattered in that quarter more than elsewhere in order . . . that I might make *a good report.*" It was Father the people wished to impress. They had hoped he would come in person.

Instead, he had elected to join Mother in Quincy for the summer. He did not expect to occupy the new president's house for long, anyway, he said. The Federalists, whose support he most needed for reelection, were the ones who most opposed his decision to send a new mission to France. Agreeing to their demands to increase the number of envoys to three did little to decrease the anger. He would not have undertaken such "an ill-timed & *unadvised* measure," his former friends said, had "the old woman," by which they meant Mother, been with him in Philadelphia. Cabinet secretaries let it be known that the president had not consulted them. General Washington, they said, would never have made such a decision in seclusion. He would have known to ask for advice.

To see the general, Thomas headed downriver to Mount Vernon, where he received a "flattering" welcome. The weather provided the one disappointment. "Excessive heat" prevented the general from leading one of his "eight to ten mile walking [tours] about his grounds." Nonetheless, Thomas complimented them. "I told the General that if the President were to see Mount Vernon, he would be quite ashamed of his own place. . . . [The general] smiled at the remark as if to say, I like the compliment, though I am not sure of your sincerity." Thomas was not sure either. It was for every man to estimate the value of his own estate.

The mailbag still went to Alexandria at least every other day and "frequently" every day. But the urge to put off responding to letters from the War Department grew until the realization that a pair of possibly important letters from Secretary of War McHenry (saying, among other things, something about deploying soldiers to parts of Pennsylvania said to be revolting against the new taxes) had gone a few weeks without a full response.

An explanation was owed. So Washington wrote one on April 23, 1799. "Six days do I labor, or, in other words, take exercise and devote my time to various occupations in husbandry and about my mansion. On the seventh . . . day, for want of a place of worship (within less than nine miles), such letters as do not require immediate acknowledgment, I give answers to." That answered why months had passed without Washington attending church but still left unanswered why two Sabbaths had passed without him responding to McHenry. In truth, Washington had already answered that question. He had warned that interest in the army would wither with the warmer weather. Everyone's attention would turn elsewhere. Certainly, his had. In the diary he kept, the days marched on.

April 24: "Mercury at 52. Morning clear, no wind — afterwards at northwest & high. . . . I went up to Alexandria to an election of a representative from the district to Congress." A piece of unpleasantness greeted Washington in one of the town papers. Words he had written "in much haste" the previous day were quoted in support of a congressional candidate he most definitely did not support. Federalists had accused Republican Roger West of opposing the new army — or "standing" army, as he called it — only because he had been refused a commission in it. West had appealed to Washington's memory. Had West asked for a commission in the new army or just the provisional one, which would be raised only in the event of an invasion? The latter, Washington had conceded in the let-

306

ter West had published. In spite of it, West's opponent (a Federalist) prevailed.

So did the Federalist candidates in the two congressional elections that most interested Washington. By little more than a hundred votes, John Marshall won the seat representing Richmond. Had the election turned out otherwise, Washington could not have "easily forgive[n]" himself for having pushed Marshall into the contest.

By an even closer vote, the right to represent the area around Washington's birthplace down the Potomac went to Harry Lee, the forty-three-year-old former Virginia governor who had lost the good name he had earned as a light-horse commander during the Revolutionary War by afterward making bad land deals, the worst of which involved the land around the canal at Great Falls. Of all of the debtors with whom Washington dealt, no one surpassed Lee in terms of dishonesty and double-dealing. Not even selling one property to two different buyers was beyond him. Yet the public good required looking past private shortcomings. Although Lee had once flirted with the opposition, he had ridden against the whiskey rebels and spoken against the dangerous Virginia and Kentucky Resolutions. A victory for Lee was a victory for the Union.

Overall, Federalists won eight of the nineteen congressional seats belonging to Virginia and would have won a majority but for what Washington deemed "some egregious mismanagement" of the election. Nonetheless, he saw it as a step toward reclaiming Virginia from the Republicans. "That we are gaining strength must console us for the present and stimulate Federal men to greater exertions in [the] future," he said.

May 6: "Morning clear, wind brisk from the southward. . . . Mr. & Mrs. Lewis set out on their journey." Mrs. Lewis, of course, was Nelly, and the journey would eventually take them over the mountains to where Lawrence Lewis wished to live. Nelly looked sad. She "dropped" hints that she wished she could stay. Perhaps she could. She and Lawrence could rent the farm on Mount Vernon's northwest corner. They could even build a house there, for that part of the estate would one day be theirs, according to the new plan Washington had conceived. To make it so, he would revise his will.

The task would demand all the "leisure hours" he could muster. The motivation, however, was easy to find. It came not from glimpsing an imminent end but from seeing the opportunity for a new beginning: for Nelly as she commenced married life; for Martha as she awaited the great-grandchildren she hoped would follow; for himself as he freed his thoughts from an army that would never take the field and returned to the retirement he sought among his own fields. With the newlyweds taking one farm — and the distillery, mill, and fishery also being put up for rent — he would finally relieve his manager of responsibility for the other farms in the belief that they "would be no more than amusement *for me* to superintend, if I should not be drawn again into public life."

May 15: "Clear & warm. Mercury at 60, and wind brisk from the southward especially towards night when it lowered. . . . [Neighbors] dined here, as did a Mr. Searson." The pursuit of poetry brought John Searson. He wished "to obtain an adequate idea of Mount Vernon," so he could immortalize the house in verse. He climbed to the cupola, looked in every direction, and pronounced the spot "beauteous." Most of the land one could see from up there — about half the total estate, including the mansion house and outbuildings — would belong, Washington had decided, after his

309

death to his most distinguished nephew, Justice Bushrod Washington, but only after Martha died, too. For as long as she lived, she would have "use, profit, and benefit" of the "whole estate."

May 31: "More rain last night. Morning clear, wind at northwest & mercury at 60 — blowing hard all day. Went up to the Federal City." There Washington could see his new houses rising and, with them, his finances sinking. A few weeks' time would force him into a "new scene" where people spoke in strange terms he struggled to comprehend. "This business of borrowing & discount," he admitted, "I am quite a novice in." Nevertheless, he would accept the terms a bank in Alexandria would set for a loan of fifteen hundred dollars.

Venturing into the City of Washington meant venturing into the latest dispute dividing its people. This one involved whether private owners had the right to build on the "small" and "irregular" slices of land formed by the diagonal avenues cutting across the grid. Two of the three commissioners said yes. One had objected and appealed to Washington on the grounds that the original plan that he had approved for the city called for preserving these spaces for "fountains, statues, obelisks," and other public purposes. "No departure from the *engraved* plan of the City ought to be allowed, unless *imperious* necessity should require it," Washington responded after first saying, "I must beg leave to premise that, when I left the Chair of Government, it was with a determination not to intermeddle in any public matter which did not immediately concern me."

No one could think the creation of a national university in the federal city did not concern him given the promise he had made to endow it. The four years since that pledge had further shown the need for an institution that would unite young men from "all parts of this rising empire" so as to encourage them to form "friendships in [their] juvenile years" and "thereby to do away local attachments and state prejudices." Faced with resistance in Congress, he had awaited "a moment" when he "could devise some plan by which . . . [his] wishes could be carried into effect." Such a moment, he now knew, would come only in death. A provision for the university had appeared in an earlier version of his will, but the new one would make an additional point: lest anyone accuse him of meddling from beyond the grave, everyone should know that much as the university would appreciate congressional appropriations, it did not need them.

Dividends from the fifty shares of Potomac Company stock that the Virginia legislature had awarded him after the Revolution and that he had set aside for education would flow to the university as surely as the riches would roll down the river, across the mountains, and over the falls. Yes, the Great Falls remained impassable years after a canal should have opened. No, he could not explain why the work had proceeded, in a word, "limpingly." Nonetheless, the construction would conclude soon enough if the company could just raise more capital from its investors. He would have given the full sum himself had he possessed it. "I would predict, without fear of having my judgment arraigned by the result, that it would be found one of (if not) the most productive funds (with the least risk to the stockholders) . . . in the United States."

The national university would have received a second stream of revenue from stock the Virginia legislature had awarded him at the same time in a company carrying out improvements on the James River to the south. But unlike the Potomac, which ran between states, the James never left the borders of the Old Dominion. Thus, the very "state prejudices" that he prayed the national university would eventually wash away forced him to leave the James stock to an in-state seminary. Modesty required that his will refer to the college he had selected in the Shenandoah Valley by its old name, Liberty Hall, rather than the new name its trustees had chosen: Washington Academy.*

July 4: "Morning heavy. Mercury at 74 and wind southeast. Clouds in every quarter & sprinklings of rain. Mercury 80 at night. Went up to Alexandria and dined with a number of the citizens there in celebration of the anniversary of the Declaration of American Independence." The newspapers noted afterward that he had looked in "excellent health" while inspecting the troops. He would have unveiled his new uniform at long last but for another "disappointment": no craftsman in the country had the skill needed to embroider the gold thread, which had arrived from Europe. Twenty-three years after the Declaration of Independence, the United States Department of War could not do its own needlework. The coat would need to go to London

---

*The academy would soon become Washington College and eventually Washington and Lee University.

for finishing.

Here was the truth laid bare about the country's preparedness for war. There was no dressing up the disarray. The letters he received from the new army's most ardent backers read as if increasingly detached from reality.

Liberate Spain's colonies and go into history "not merely as the Father of the United States but of the United Empires of America," read a suggestion from one Federalist, who imagined Washington could move soldiers across continents as easily as he could slide figurines (the War Department had recently sent a set for the "practice of tactics") across a game board. A country with an opposition party protesting even basic "defensive measures" could not summon the unity needed for "offensive operations."

Recruit more officers from Virginia, read a request from Secretary of War McHenry, who said he needed them for a revamped provisional force, which he called the "eventual army," never mind that there was nothing "eventual" about this "army" given the government could only mobilize it in the event of a war that the new peace initiative had rendered extremely unlikely. Never mind also that Washington had already exhausted every eligible name he knew in the state. Besides, the War Department could not even properly equip the officers whom he had already recruited.

When would the sword Washington had ordered for Wash arrive? Not a day went without Wash asking. Washington would present the sword, when ready, with the same injunction he had decided to place on the swords he would leave in his will to his nephews: "Not to unsheathe them for the purpose of shedding blood, except it be for self-defense, or in defense of their Country and its rights; and in the latter case, to keep them unsheathed, and prefer falling with them in their hands, to the relinquishment thereof."

July 9: "Clear with a very light air from the northwest. Mercury at 70 in the evening & morning both. Much appearances of rain, but a sprinkling only fell." The hours hunched over the desk had led to this day: the one when he would set his "hand and seal" to the twenty-nine pages constituting his last will and testament. "It will readily be perceived that no professional character has been consulted or has had any agency in the draft," he wrote. "It may, notwithstanding [the days devoted to the document], appear crude and incorrect. But having endeavored to be plain and explicit in all devises, . . . I hope, and trust, that no disputes will arise concerning them."

If disputes did arise, they would probably involve the 317 men, women, and children he had counted in recent weeks while conducting a survey of Mount Vernon's slaves. As he had written the clause regarding their fate, he had struggled to even settle the disputes he felt within himself: the dread of discussing slavery with the duty to do so in detail near the beginning of a document destined for public disclosure; the embarrassment of holding human beings in such an "unfortunate condition" with the entitlement he felt to profit from the bodies his farms fed; the desire to "get quit" of slavery with the disappointment of knowing that emancipating the Custis dower slaves would never be in his "power" (even now, his wife urged him to arrange another attempt to apprehend her runaway "body servant," Oney Judge); the conviction that slaves deserved "a destiny different from that in which they were born" with the concern that the seven executors appointed in his will (five of his nephews as well as Martha and Wash) would conspire to thwart a decision upon which he knew his own legacy depended: the decision to emancipate his slaves.

Future generations might ask why he had waited, especially when he claimed to own twice as many slaves as he could profitably employ. Future generations might ask why even now, instead of freeing the surplus slaves, he had begun to consider a plan for employing them on new plantations he would form on lands he had previously rented out upriver. The will would explain. Of the 124 slaves he owned outright, 123 would receive freedom only after both he and Martha died so as to delay as long as possible "the most painful sensations" of what he could not avoid: splitting up the marriages his slaves had formed with the dower slaves destined to be split up among Martha's grandchildren. Only one slave, Washington wrote in the will, "my mulatto" Billy Lee, "as a testimony of my sense of his attachment to me and for his faithful services during the Revolutionary War," would receive, if he chose it, "immediate freedom" and, "in either case," thirty dollars a year for life on account of "accidents which have befallen him and which have rendered him incapable of walking."

Other slaves once freed would also need support. The emancipation clause would do no credit to its author if it left those too old to find new employment to shiver and starve and those too young to labor without the education needed for "useful occupation." Providing for them would require not a onetime payment but "a regular and permanent fund." And here was where the will needed to "most solemnly enjoin [the executors] . . . to see that *this* clause respecting slaves and every part thereof be religiously fulfilled."

July 20, 1799: "Morning a little cloudy. Wind at northeast & mercury at 66. . . . Appearances of rain." One of the letters carried back from the post office that day looked suspicious not because of who had written it (Governor Jonathan Trumbull of Connecticut had served as a military aide during the Revolution) but because of how long it had taken to arrive (nearly a month). There appeared no "marks of violence" that would indicate tampering. The only clue lay in the contents: Trumbull claimed to write not for himself alone but for many fellow Federalists. President Adams had lost the support of the party. If the Federalists did not unite around "some [other] eminently prominent character" before the election of 1800, they would lose control of the government. Surely, Trumbull wrote, "you will not disappoint the hopes & desires of the wise & good in every state by refusing to come forward once more to the relief & support of your injured Country."

Similar letters had come to Mount Vernon many times in the past. Always they claimed that only he, George Washington, could save his country. Never had the words sounded this deluded. They were based on the premise that he remained a singular force in American politics when there was no longer anything singular about him. "The line between parties" had become "so clearly drawn" as to reduce everyone into one of two things: Federalist or Republican. "Any other respectable Federal character would receive the same suffrages that I should," he reasoned, because no Federalist (himself included) could "obtain a *solitary* vote from" the Republicans. "Let that party [the Republicans] set up a broomstick — and call it a true Son of Liberty, a Democrat, or give it any other epithet that will suit their purpose — and it will command their votes in toto!" And since the name Washington could no longer give Federalists any advantage, they should give their suffrage to someone else. Besides, "thankful" as he was for his "good health," he was not "insensible" to his decline "in other respects," which would make it "criminal . . . to accept an office . . . which another would discharge with more ability."

Dare he say who among his countrymen was most deserving of the office? The question had arisen while drafting his will because of the need to make a provision for an oak box said to be cut from a tree under which William Wallace, the medieval Scottish patriot, had sought shade after battling the English. A Scottish lord had sent the relic in 1791, Washington recalled, "in terms too flattering for me to repeat, with a request to pass it, on the event of my decease, to the man in my country, who should appear to merit it best." Who that was, Washington decided, was "not for me to say." Upon his death, the box would return to Scotland.

As for the current president, he should return to "the seat of government" at once. His months-long stay in Quincy, Washington wrote, "in the present critical conjuncture affords matter for severe animadversion by the friends of government." Adams had lost control of the government. Soon, if predictions held, he would lose his place in it.

The letter from Jonathan Trumbull had not gone directly to General Washington. For weeks that summer, while President Adams had stayed in Quincy, the Trumbull letter had secretly circulated in Philadelphia among a few cabinet secretaries, including Secretary of State Timothy Pickering, involved in deliberations over whether to forward it, as they finally did, to Mount Vernon. Whether President Adams could win reelection if the new mission to France proceeded did not require any deliberations. Simply put, he would stand no chance. That was clear to Pickering. Speaking, as he had no trouble doing, for "all the ablest and best supporters of the government," he declared the mission "the most unfortunate and the most humiliating event to the United States which has happened since the commencement of the French Revolution."

Fortunately, for a variety of reasons, the envoys had not yet sailed. The hope lay in further delaying their departure by delaying completion of their instructions. The few days that Pickering promised the president it would take to prepare a draft for his review in August had stretched into weeks thanks, in part, to a timely yellow fever outbreak forcing the government once again to flee to Trenton. By mid-September, when the instructions finally went in the mail to Quincy, so did news that Pickering hoped would postpone the mission permanently: "what the newspapers . . . called 'another explosion,' " rumblings of a revolution against the Directory in France. There were rumors that a relative of the late Louis XVI would seize power. If the president agreed that these "new facts" merited indefinite "suspension" of the mission, he could save himself the "trouble" of traveling to join his cabinet in Trenton.

But the president did come to Trenton. And once there, he astonished everyone by announcing the envoys would depart at once. No one — not even Alexander Hamilton, who happened to be in town — could change Adams's mind. "This great question I supposed (& my colleagues had formed the same expectation) would be a subject of *consultation,* but we have been disappointed," Pickering wrote Washington. "The *President alone* considered and decided. . . . He did not consult us, [he said], *because he had long deliberated on the subject [and] had made up his mind, and this was unchangeable.*" No one could have imagined the "modest" Washington speaking such words. It was as if Adams wished to illuminate the "splendor" of his predecessor.

Adams's "vanity" would ruin his country internationally and domestically. Internationally, it would align the United States against the royalist forces in Europe just when they looked likeliest to triumph. Domestically, it would "change the whole administration." With the Federalists divided, their administration would fall. A Republican reign would commence. The highest office would go to Thomas Jefferson, Pickering's own office at the State Department to James Madison. "There is but one way in which these evils can be prevented," Pickering predicted. "It is the only way in which the mischiefs of this French mission can be repaired [and] the only atonement which the President can make to his country for this fatal error: his announcing publicly, at the close of the next session of Congress, *that he will retire.* Then the Federalists, uniting in one man for his successor, might yet save the country from ruin."

All this Pickering freely told Federalist friends, including one who immediately responded this way: "I have flattered myself that the great Washington would again come upon the stage, if the occasion should be made to appear worthy of his reappearance."

His "dear Patcy" had been ill most of September. Multiple times to her bedside, Washington had summoned Doctor Craik. Every time Martha had shown signs of improving, the fever had returned. Not until October when Nelly and her husband returned to the house did Martha fully recover. Suddenly she found new reason to rise. The house needed to be made ready for the baby Nelly wished to deliver there.

Amid the anticipation of new life was mourning. Washington's only surviving sibling, baby brother Charles, had passed. "The death of near relations always produce awful and affecting emotions," Washington wrote. "I was the *first,* and am now the *last,* of my father's children by the second marriage who remain. When I shall be called upon to follow them is known only to the giver of life. When the summons comes, I shall endeavor to obey it with a good grace." The black seal he affixed to his letters after learning about the loss signified his grieving.

More and more, he resisted the urge to call for the mail daily, even though he had "departed" from another "resolution": the one "not to take charge of any military operations, unless the army should be called into the field." Orders to the soldiers building a winter encampment up the Potomac, near the proposed arsenal at Harpers Ferry, would flow from Mount Vernon. The exceptional strategic value he attached to the arsenal there merited the exception. He had "no doubt of this arsenal being their principal place of arms," if the states were "wise enough to keep united."

How the future would unfold, he did not pretend to know. Over and over again, the news "surprised" him. Word of the mission departing for France came from cabinet secretaries seemingly afraid to ask but desperate to discover if he would somehow intervene. He would not, he responded. "I have, for some time past, viewed the political concerns of the United States with an anxious and painful eye. They appear to me to be moving by hasty strides to some awful crisis. But in what they will result, that Being, who sees, foresees, and directs all things, alone can tell. The vessel is afloat, or very nearly so, and considering myself as a passenger only, I shall trust to the mariners whose duty it is to watch to steer it into a safe port." Occasionally, his mind strayed and wandered back to what Jonathan Trumbull had written. "No tongue" must mention it.

On Sunday, November 17, Washington did what he had not done in months. Through a "very heavy & thick fog," he rode to the Episcopal church in Alexandria. He would not take communion, but he would occupy the pew he owned. Across the universe reigned a divine force he called Providence, whose ways defied man's comprehension but whose designs no man should doubt. Surely not by chance had he stood tall when others around him had fallen in the forests and fields in which he had fought. Surely not by chance had a member of a "short-lived family" not yet finished his journey downriver.

That evening, with Wash and Lawrence as companions on the ride home, Washington stopped for a respite. Just as he began to remount his horse, embers from an old campfire along the road spooked the steed. Away it sprinted. Down he tumbled. Off from their own horses, which disappeared into the darkness after his, the younger men sprang. They asked if he was injured. Not physically. The fall, he answered, "was owing to a cause that no horseman could well avoid or control." He had lost his horse but not that "most precious gift of Heaven," health.

There was much he wished to see in the year ahead: the government relocated to the federal city; his town houses there finished with a faux stone look matching Mount Vernon's; a surveying expedition undertaken in the spring with members of the Fairfax family to lots he and they owned near the Great Falls; boats lifted and lowered on the locks of the canal there; Harpers Ferry made into the central arsenal of the Union; the surplus Mount Vernon slaves resettled up the waters beyond. All these aspirations lay upriver. It had grown late. He needed to get home. Knowing his fellow travelers would follow, he rose, wiped his clothes, and stepped into the darkness. Somewhere downriver, the banks of Mount Vernon beckoned.

CHAPTER ELEVEN:
WASHINGTON SINKS

The pleas to return to public life never ceased. Friends dangled every conceivable office. Finally, in 1799, they offered a post from which they said he could "correct" the "abuses" associated with "executive powers," a post for which he must surrender the "enviable . . . domestic life" he had found in the Virginia countryside. If elected, he could not refuse. To the governorship of Virginia, James Monroe would say yes.

Federalists, of course, would oppose the nomination. They wished "to exclude from offices" any man willing to stand against their corruption, any man who proved "honest and inflexible," the very words Monroe used to describe himself. Already Federalists acting through their patron George Washington had excluded Monroe once before by recalling him in 1796 from his post as a minister to France (a country whose culture he loved almost as much as his own) all because he had cherished the relationship with America's fellow republic. For this crime, the Federalists fabricated sensational stories about Monroe's misdeeds abroad. They said he had shown disrespect during an obligatory toast to George Washington at a Fourth of July celebration in Paris.

It was James Madison who would defend Monroe against these charges in the Virginia assembly, which would choose the next governor. In early December, Madison asked Monroe for evidence that he had intended no insult to Washington at the celebration. Monroe had not; in fact, he had drunk to Washington's name, even as less polite lips had hissed. Not that Monroe had blamed them. Only for so long would people continue to "dance" on Washington's "birth night" and call him and his friends "great & good men" without noticing what they truly were: "little people."

Surely, Washington would not wish to insert himself into the gubernatorial election. If for some reason he did, however, Monroe would meet the challenge. He had once scripted out what he would say to the old man if given the chance. "Your military career gained you the unreserved confidence of your countrymen, and your political career availed itself of that confidence for the purpose of oppressing them. It was the unceasing effort of your administration to wrest the government from the people and place it in the hands of an oligarchic faction. . . . If I were to select out from the general & comprehensive roll of your fellow citizens the person who had done most harm to his country for eight or ten years past, it would be yourself. Others had the will and did all the harm they could, but unaided by you, their efforts had been impotent and vain."

Not even Washington, however, could save the Federalists from their greatest foe: themselves. "The more . . . that party is left to itself, the sooner will its ruin follow," Monroe had told his mentor, Thomas Jefferson, the year before during the height of the war hysteria. "The administration will overwhelm itself by its folly & madness." The currents that had carried the Federalists to power would soon sweep them from it. If Washington could not free his legacy from the Federalists, it would "sink to nothing."

The wind rushing downriver was no reason not to ride. The "large circle" Washington had observed around the moon the previous night augured "falling weather." The mercury in the thermometer he had checked that morning stood just one degree above freezing. He needed to see his fields while he could. By ten in the morning on December 12, he had mounted his horse. Off he went on the circuit of his farms.

Snowflakes began to fall. The cattle would need to move to their winter quarters. He stopped to inspect one of the pens. The conditions disappointed. "Such a pen as I saw . . . would, if the cattle were kept in it one week, destroy the whole of them." If he could not provide them suitable shelter, he would have no choice but to leave them to the "open fields" and a winter of wandering that would give him no "ease."

There was so much he could not control: the feuding "interests" and "jealousies" forcing the federal city "to pass through a fiery trial"; the hundreds of newspapers, including those belonging to "infamous scribblers" smearing pages with libels and lies intended to "destroy all confidence" in the government; the political parties fueling "ill-founded jealousies and false alarms" pitting "one part" of the people "against another"; the countries of Europe unleashing upon the world "a more destructive sword" than ever recorded in "modern times." In all this, a man could see but "mere chaos." Only Providence could see the script to which the confusion conformed.

It should be otherwise at Mount Vernon. He regretted leaving back at the mansion the long letter he had written for his underlings. In it lay the directions for what he called an "entire new scene," one that would commence in the year 1800. He had scripted every role in detail, so he could have what he had always wanted: the "ease" of knowing that "all who are actors . . . [are] enabled to play their parts to advantage."

The stage was nearly set. Nelly had given birth to a daughter in late November. Her husband had agreed to rent one of the farms as well as the mill and the increasingly profitable distillery. The process of identifying lands over the mountains for relocating surplus slaves had begun. Estate manager James Anderson would embark on a scouting expedition farther west to Washington's holdings in the Ohio Country "so soon as the weather becomes temperate and settled in the spring." Washington himself would assume management of Mount Vernon. The nineteen-page plan he had prepared for how the "exhausted . . . fields in some measure [might be] restored by a rotation of crops" would bring the estate to the threshold of a new century. Not long ago he had joked about a contract he had made "not to quit the theatre of *this* world before" 1800. Only weeks remained until the new year. It had come quickly, just as he had warned it would to the men making ready the city bearing his name.

The snow turned to sleet, then to a "cold rain." A little past three o'clock — later than he liked — he returned to the mansion, where his secretary, Tobias Lear, waited with letters he had prepared for Washington's signature. One was a response to a detailed proposal Alexander Hamilton had sent for a military academy. "The establishment of an institution of this kind . . . has ever been considered by me as an object of primary importance to this Country, and while I was in the chair of government, I omitted no proper opportunity of recommending it in my public speeches and other ways to the attention of the Legislature. But I never undertook to go into a *detail* of the organization of such an Academy, leaving this task to others . . . better qualified. . . . For the same reason, I must now decline making any observations on the details of your plan," read the response Lear recommended. Washington signed on the spot but told Lear to wait a day to mail it. "The weather was too bad to send a servant up to the [post] office."

Gesturing toward the water dripping from Washington's neck and the snow "hanging upon his hair," Lear said that he was "afraid" that Washington had allowed himself to get so "wet," and worried he would "take cold."

"There was no danger," Washington assured. The "great coat" he had worn outside "had kept him dry." There was no time to change clothes, as he usually did, before dinner. The meal was already on the table, and he hated to keep people waiting.

The rain reverted to snow as the mercury fell to twenty-eight degrees. In the morning, three inches covered the ground. He would not repeat yesterday's ride. His throat hurt. Not until the afternoon, when the snow had stopped, did he venture outside, behind the piazza. The sky, he noted while looking beyond the bluff, "became perfectly clear." There was nothing before him but the cloudless blue above and the untrodden snow sloping to the river below. A mind like his needed something else — those trees over there! They obstructed the view. He would have them chopped down later.

A rider had made it to the post office and returned with the newspapers. Washington

would read them in the parlor with Martha
and Lear. It would be just the three of them
that evening. Lawrence Lewis and Wash
were traveling together. Nelly was confined
upstairs with her baby. Discussion of the
news downstairs would proceed in hushed
voices, which was as well, for Washington
could muster no more. His voice was always
weak. Now it was hoarse, too. Nevertheless,
he could not resist reading certain articles
aloud as he pored over the papers. The
anxiety of needing to know had eased but
not ceased. A vestige would always linger.
There would always be unanswered questions.

What facts would surface from the sedition prosecution the government had commenced against William Duane, the successor to the late Benjamin Franklin Bache at
the *Aurora*? Duane had alleged that hundreds of thousands of dollars of British
bribes had worked their way into the hands
of "high" officers of the United States.
"Pray, my good Sir, what part of the
$800,000 have come to your share?" Wash-
ington had written in jest to Secretary of
War McHenry, before being informed about
the shocking evidence that Duane planned
to submit in his defense: an old letter by
John Adams insinuating that the British had

influenced an appointment Washington himself had made as president. If the letter proved authentic, Adams owed an "explanation."

What explanation except for a willful "blind side" would do for reports of Lafayette still contemplating a voyage to the United States? Maybe he had already sailed. The last accounts, which were months old, had Lafayette musing of "buy[ing] a farm near Mount Vernon" and making himself "useful in uniting [America's] parties," that is, Federalists and Republicans. What he would be, of course, was "embarrassing to himself, embarrassing to his friends, and possibly embarrassing to the Government." If Washington's Christmas letter had not freed Lafayette of his fantasies, nothing would. Any day could bring word of his ship steering its way up the Potomac.

And what of the world Lafayette would leave behind? Just as some had begun to predict the fall of the French, the newspapers brought reports of the British and their Russian allies suffering a major defeat in Holland. "What will be the final result . . . is not for a man at the distance of 3000 miles from the great theatre of action to predict," Washington said, even as he began to wonder if a man three thousand miles away might be the only hope for peace. "A bystander sees more of the game, generally, than those who are playing it, so neutral nations may be better enabled to draw a line between the contending parties than those who are actors in the war." Who among the American people could possess the prestige needed to bring the Europeans to the negotiating table was not for someone who had never crossed the ocean to say. He would say only this: "My own wish is to see everything settled upon the best and surest foundation for the peace & happiness of mankind, without regard to this, that, or the other nation."

At some point, Martha excused herself and went upstairs. He would join her but only after seeking an answer to a final question: Who had won the governorship of Virginia? The answer lay at the end of the long account that a Richmond paper had produced of the debate preceding the December 6 vote in the Virginia House of Delegates. No longer, however, could Washington himself read the story aloud. He had already strained his voice too much. Soon he might lose it altogether. Someone else would need to take over. Would Tobias Lear read these lines?

■ ■ ■

"The house were then proceeding to the choice of a Governor," began the article Tobias Lear had agreed to read, "when a motion was made to postpone the order of the day." Not having sufficient votes to prevent James Monroe's election, Federalists tried to delay a vote altogether. "To choose the gentleman to so high and important an office as that of governor of this commonwealth was a step deserving the most serious deliberation," one Federalist argued. "The election would amount to saying that the executive had been wrong in recalling" Monroe from France. And because everyone recognized that the word "executive" here stood in for George Washington, no one could feign ignorance of what the vote would mean for Virginia: a rebuke of its most famous resident.

As the newspaper correspondent reported, "Mr. [James] Madison rose next, and his appearance produced such a general rustling in the house that, for several minutes, we could not hear one word which he said." As the room quieted, people heard Madison question why Monroe's election should constitute a "condemnation" of George

Washington. Monroe had already explained his actions in France. "Was he to be debarred from serving his country upon vague suspicions?" No, the delegates answered. By a large margin, they elected Monroe governor of Virginia.

Lear stopped reading there and looked up at the face of the man he had served for the better part of the thirteen years since first stepping foot in Mount Vernon as a twenty-three-year-old Harvard graduate. Lear had once dreamed of making it on his own, but the business venture he had launched on the Potomac had sunk and left him suicidal and so short of cash that he had embezzled funds. Yes, from the general, too. A man could not labor as long as Lear had for Washington and not have seen his wrath: how it "broke out suddenly," how "his very frame shook," and how "he threw his hands up" repeatedly. "Awful" was the word for this anger, and here it was upon hearing what the Virginia assembly had done. "He appeared much affected and spoke with some degree of asperity on the subject." Being more sympathetic to the Republicans — sometimes even commiserating with Thomas Jefferson during his final months as secretary of state — Lear "endeavored to moderate," as he "always did," when the general fell too far under the influence of the Federalists. If nothing else, the general could not afford to tax his voice. The "hoarseness" had "increased" as the evening approached its end. "He had better take something to remove his cold," Lear suggested before the general went upstairs for bed.

"No," Washington responded. "You know I never take anything for a cold. Let it go as it came."

At first light on Saturday, December 14, 1799, Lear received a summons to the bedroom the Washingtons shared. "I found the General breathing with difficulty, and hardly able to utter a word intelligibly." What had happened? Mrs. Washington explained. The general had woken her at two or three o'clock in the morning. He felt as if he had "an ague," he had told her. "She observed that he could scarcely speak and breathed with difficulty, and [she] would have got up to call a servant, but he would not permit her lest she should take cold." Only after the housemaid Caroline had lit a fire had he allowed Mrs. Washington to call for help. He needed to be bled, he said. George Rawlins, an overseer at one of the farms, was said to be skilled in the science. Fetch him, the general ordered.

In the meantime, perhaps swallowing a "mixture of molasses, vinegar, and butter" would relieve the throat pain. "But he [the general] could not swallow a drop. Whenever he attempted it, he appeared to be distressed, convulsed, and almost suffocated."

Into the bedroom stepped George Rawlins. He looked nervous as he prepared the arm for the incision. "Don't be afraid," said the general. The blood began to flow "freely" but not fast enough to satisfy the patient. "The orifice is not large enough," he said in a voice that sounded "low & broken."

Mrs. Washington had an uneasy look as if unsure "whether bleeding was proper or not in the General's situation." She "begged that much might not be taken from him, lest it should be injurious." At some point, she could bear no more. "Stop it," she said.

"More," the general said. Only after losing "half a pint" did he surrender to his wife's pleas. Christopher, the slave attending to the general, dressed him and moved him to a chair, where he could soak his feet in warm water. Being upright, however, brought "no relief," so he returned to bed, where he would wait for the doctors en route.

The first to arrive was the general's old

friend James Craik, who immediately ordered a second bleeding and, seeing no improvement, a third. He applied a blistering agent to the throat and gave the general a solution of "sage tea and vinegar" for gargling. "But when he held back his head to let it run down, it put him into great distress and almost produced suffocation." Lear feared the general would drown in tea. "When the mixture came out of his mouth, some phlegm followed it." Craik urged the general to cough, but he could not. At noon, the general submitted to an enema, "which produced an evacuation but caused no alteration in his complaint." He could not swallow.

By this time, Mrs. Washington and Craik had requested reinforcement. It arrived in the afternoon in the form, first, of Doctor Elisha Cullen Dick from Alexandria and, then, of Doctor Gustavus Richard Brown from just across the river in Maryland. The doctors bled Washington a fourth time. No longer did the blood rush out. It "ran slowly [and] appeared very thick." By this time, the general gave a look of "resignation." Nevertheless, he did what the doctors asked as if to respect the part they must play in the drama. He had a part, too. "He uttered," Lear noted, "not a sigh nor a complaint."

Maybe it was because the other two doctors were older men and Elisha Cullen Dick was only in his thirties. Maybe it was because the other two had known the patient longer. Whatever the reason, they would not listen. Dick had warned against bleeding the general a fourth time. "He needs all his strength," Dick had said. "Bleeding will diminish it." Only after Doctor Craik and Doctor Brown had proceeded to take another thirty-two ounces had they finally conceded the futility of further bleeding.

Outside the bedroom, the doctors tried to agree on a new course of action but could not even agree on the name of the disease. "Inflammatory quinsy," Craik insisted on calling the illness as if not wanting to use the name he had given to a condition he had recently diagnosed among some children in Alexandria: "sore throat." He had been as wrong then as he was now. The children and the general, Dick explained, suffered from the same disease: "croup." The name did not matter at the moment so much. There would be time enough to concoct a technical name (maybe "cyn-

343

anche tracheitis") and debate it later.* Craik and Brown now accepted Dick's basic diagnosis: "a violent inflammation of the membranes of the throat, which . . . had almost closed."

The time for bleedings, which even Dick himself believed the best cure for the croup if caught early enough, had passed. The one chance for saving "a man whose loss every virtuous man in the community would deplore" lay in a more radical procedure known as a tracheotomy, by which the doctors would cut a hole in the windpipe so as to bypass whatever obstructed the airflow. "At first," Dick thought, "I had reason to flatter myself that I had obtained the concurrence of the other physicians, and was about to make preparation for carrying the measure into immediate execution when I was rendered unhappy." The two older doctors vetoed the idea. Having achieved more renown in the profession than Dick had, they had more to risk. "Increased timidity, which is, perhaps, a common attendant on old age, seemed not only to have extinguished all ardor in the pursuit of additional celebrity but also to have created a steady

* Modern medical opinion has largely settled on acute epiglottitis.

determination to hazard no part of that stock which had been already acquired."

Whether a tracheotomy would have saved General Washington, Dick did not know. But he did know that it had offered hope. That was more than the doctors had now. They would try more purgatives and blisters even as they could see "the disease was manifestly hastening to a fatal termination." The general could not breathe.

The realization had struck Washington as soon as he had woken in the wee hours of the morning. "The disorder would prove fatal." He would die in the large bed his wife had custom ordered for them to share. The pictures hanging on the walls of her progeny reminded that he would leave none of his own. A clock made in the Louis XVI style crowned the mantel over the fireplace. Nearby was a chest Sally Fairfax had kept in her bedroom at Belvoir. He had purchased the piece and brought it to Mount Vernon after bidding her farewell on the eve of the Revolution. That had been a long time ago.

In the desk in the office downstairs now, Martha would find two wills. Would she bring both to the bedside where he could see them? This one she should "burn" in the fireplace, for it had been "superseded." The other she should "put . . . away" somewhere secure. She and the other executors would need it soon. "I find I am going."

The grave had never really been that far downriver from the mansion, just footsteps really, in the "old vault" burrowed into the bluff overlooking the Potomac. Talk of drifting "down the stream of life" as far as the ancestral burial ground near the river's mouth — "the dreary mansions of my fathers" — had always been metaphor. None of them had lived this long, a few months shy of sixty-eight years.

The time had come for a "change" of "scene," maybe to a "happier place" but most surely to one "from whence no traveler is permitted to return." Any fear of what waited in "the world" beyond had faded long ago. Neither prayers nor conversations with clergy would consume the little breath left. "The keys," after all, to "the gate by which patriots, sages, and heroes are admitted to immortality" belonged not to ministers but to "bards," the poets who wrote history. Would Tobias Lear continue to "arrange and record all my late military letters and papers," and would he ensure that George Rawlins's brother, Albin, who had started as a clerk at the house, "finish[ed] recording my other letters?" It would "be done," Lear promised.

Was there "anything" else "essential . . . to do?" Little could be done for Christopher, Caroline, Molly, and Charlotte, the slaves standing around and shuffling in and out of the room. All four belonged to the Custis estate. A letter "found in . . . [the] yard" by chance a few months earlier had revealed that a person or people living outside Mount Vernon had concocted a plan to entice Christopher to run away. The plot had failed. Christopher had been on his feet since first light. Have him sit there by the bed.

What about farewells? Nelly could not leave her room. When would Wash return? Not in time. What about Martha's two other grandchildren? Lear would need to send letters to their husbands. The doctors reentered. Speaking to them required being propped up. "I feel myself going. I thank you for your attentions, but I pray you to take no more trouble about me. Let me go off quietly." Doctors Brown and Dick left the room. Craik stayed to sulk in front of the fireplace. "Doctor, I die hard, but I am not afraid to go."

The light faded. "What hour . . . was [it]?"

Around eight in the evening, when the last application of blisters occurred. The faces around the bed looked bleak. Only the body itself refused to submit as it wrenched and rolled in search of air.

"What hour . . . was [it]?" When asked the last time, about nine. By now, probably ten. The struggle could not last much longer. But what if it looked over before it was? What if, while in the vault burrowed into the bluff, the eyes shot open to the sound of the river rushing by but saw only darkness? Just imagining the feeling of paralysis could fill the mind with terror. The first few attempts to give Lear a final order failed. Finally, out came the words. "Do not let my body be put into the vault in less than two days after I am dead." Lear nodded. Did he understand? He promised he did. "Tis well." Nothing more needed to be said. Nothing more could be. The throat had all but closed.

Martha sat by the bottom of the bed. Lear lay in it so he could assist with position changes from time to time. Doctor Craik maintained his post near the fire. Caroline, Charlotte, and Molly blocked the door. Christopher lengthened his shadow by returning to his feet. For the first time since waking in the dark, the struggle eased. The muscles relaxed. So this was what it meant to "glide gently down the stream of life." The arms could still move but barely. With the little strength left, one hand grasped the wrist above the other in search of the pulse, the beat of the blood flowing through the body. Did the current carry on?

■ ■ ■ ■

PART III
CITY

■ ■ ■ ■

Part III
City

Chapter Twelve: Washington Rises

The body had gone down the stairs into the large room around midnight. Somehow lying there the next afternoon, it looked larger than it had in life. Stretching its limbs and straightening its spine yielded a final measurement of six feet, three and a half inches. The flesh felt "frozen," Doctor William Thornton thought as he hovered over the body, as if death had cast it into the same stone being laid across the river in the City of Washington. Thornton had come as soon as he could. He owed his career to George Washington. "No sorrow for his loss is more real than my own," Thornton thought, "for I have lost one of the best friends I ever had."

It was then-president Washington who had made Thornton the winner of the design contest for the United States Capitol. Thornton had submitted a late entry in 1793, "presumptuous" as it was given he had received his formal training not as an architect but as a doctor at the University of Edinburgh. He had only recently begun "to study architecture." The inspiration for his "extensive" plan with its Corinthian columns had arisen from contemplating "the amazing extent of our country and . . . the apartments that the representatives of a very numerous people would one day require." Washington had appreciated how the design balanced "grandeur" and "simplicity." He had then gone on to appoint Thornton one of the three commissioners for the federal city.

Messengers carrying word that General Washington did not have long to live had reached the federal city late on Saturday, December 14. With Mrs. Washington's grandson-in-law Thomas Law, Thornton had set off for Mount Vernon the next day in the hopes of saving the general only to find him "a stiffened corpse." He had died, Thornton reasoned, from "want of air" and "loss of blood." Neither seemed irreversible to a scientific mind such as Thornton's. If allowed to "thaw" in a bath and rubbed under "blankets," the body could spring back to life once given a tracheotomy and a transfusion of lamb's blood. "There was no doubt . . . restoration was possible," Thornton argued. Washington's family quickly rejected the idea of a resurrection. "It was doubted by some whether, if it were possible, it would be right to attempt to recall to life one who had departed full of honor and renown, free from the frailties of age, in the full enjoyment of every faculty, and prepared for eternity."

In that case, the funeral could not wait for Wash and Lawrence Lewis to return to Mount Vernon from their travels. "Considering the disorder of which the General died," Thornton argued, "it would not be proper, nor perhaps safe to keep the body so long."

So at eleven in the morning on Wednesday, December 18, 1799, a crowd formed around the piazza. The funeral would have begun at noon had the soldiers from Alexandria not insisted on participating. "It is my express desire that my corpse may be interred in a private manner, without parade or funeral oration," the general had written in his will. But that was an order the troops would not obey. Not until after three o'clock when they had fully assembled did the procession begin winding its way toward the vault to the sound of a band performing a dirge and guns firing from a ship in the river below. The pallbearers carried the general in a coffin made of mahogany and draped with black, behind a pair of slaves guiding the horse he would have ridden. Then followed the few family members and friends able to attend. Evidently, Mrs. Washington did not wish to join them, for she did not appear outside. At the vault, the reverend performed the service and the Masons their rites for one who had called himself their brother.

As the sun set, the body receded into the chamber through the opening the slaves had cleared in the brick wall. Rather than re-lay the brick afterward, Mrs. Washington had asked them to construct a door. The vault would need to "open . . . again," she said, for her body. Plus, her husband had left instructions in his will for his executors to move all the bodies in the vault, which looked old and rickety, to a new one he wished to have constructed "upon a larger scale" elsewhere on the property.

A larger scale was exactly what Thornton had in mind, just not at Mount Vernon. He imagined a different resting place for the general, one upriver. "At the time of his death, I doubted not [that] the nation . . . would consider his remains as appertaining too much to our country to permit them to be deposited without the most public mark of their admiration and affection . . . [and]

that the Congress would place him in the center of that national temple which he approved of for a Capitol," Thornton wrote. That was the point from which future generations of Americans would "calculate" their "longitudes," and it was Washington more than anyone who had made it so. It was he who had drawn the ten-mile-square federal district straddling the Potomac. It was he who had conceived a new capital city growing out of the trees along the banks and uniting a people destined to disperse across a vast continent long after he departed the earth. It was he who belonged beneath the Capitol dome.

Only two obstacles stood in the way. First, the widow: the prospect of the country once again summoning her husband from his home would deprive her of what she called her "last temporal consolation." Congress could "restore to her mind a calm and repose," Thornton believed, "merely" by leaving space for her body beside his in the Capitol. The second obstacle to laying the general under the Capitol dome was, well, the Capitol had no such dome, not even the beginnings of the center rotunda over which it would go. But this was less of an obstacle than an opportunity. What could provide a better "inducement to the completion of the whole building," Thornton thought, than promising to deposit "the remains of the virtuous Washington" in the center? If the great man could not rise from his grave, the Capitol of a great country could rise over his grave.

By the spring of 1800, John Adams had read enough eulogies. "An eminent character and example of public virtue has now been sufficiently celebrated," he said. "I hope we shall now let him enjoy his heaven in tranquility and no longer disturb his ghost with fulsome adulation." Europeans, Adams's wife noted, did not mourn their princes for as long as the citizens of America had mourned their first president. They had worn black, rung bells, shuttered stores and theaters, and arranged elaborate tributes.

News of Washington's death had not reached Philadelphia until December 18, the day of the funeral. At the urging of Congress, Adams had sent his personal secretary to Mount Vernon with the request that Mrs. Washington allow the people whom her husband had served to eventually reinter his remains in the City of Washington. That the people had not yet taken possession of the body had not stopped them from staging "mock funerals" the likes of which America had never seen. In Philadelphia on December 26, troops stepping to a "muffled" beat had paraded through the streets at the command of Alexander Hamilton, who had ridden close to a bodiless coffin and riderless horse as if to suggest himself as the man best suited to fill the now vacant post of commander in chief of the army. Two of Adams's department heads had served as honorary pallbearers while the other cabinet members had marched behind the senators and representatives. They had filed in to the German Lutheran Church, where Adams and his wife had joined to hear that newly elected Virginia congressman Harry Lee, a debtor to put Adams's embarrassing son-in-law to shame, eulogize Washington as "first in war, first in peace, and first in the hearts of his countrymen."

Adams's wife took to the "expression" and began repeating it. The more Adams himself heard it, the more it bothered him. Had there been a moment in the wake of the publication of the XYZ dispatches when he himself could have supplanted Washington as "first in the hearts of his countrymen"? To judge by the "millions" of approving addresses Adams had received "from all quarters" of the country, yes, he thought. Perhaps those addresses had "piqued" Washington's "jealousy." Perhaps they explained why the general had accepted the offer "to return to public bustle again" despite all of his talk about "his aversion to public life and his attachment to retirement." It was not, Adams thought, that Washington had lied. It was that he "did not know his own heart. . . . He knew not himself." He did not know that "he could not be easy in retirement."

Eulogists across the country insisted otherwise. They said Washington had returned to the public theater time and time again not because he longed for the stage but because no one else could play his part. They called him the "savior of his country," as if he was something more than "a man," as if he had performed miracles, as if he had died like Moses "a few steps" short of leading his people into a new capital.

To say any one man had saved America, of course, did "injustice" to countless other men, most significantly Adams himself. Could he not have achieved military glory had he followed a different course earlier in life? Of course, he could have, he reminded people. Had he not saved America from a catastrophic and costly war with France? Probably he had. The French had promised to welcome the envoys he had sent.

As Adams had expected, the stories his cabinet members had so easily swallowed about the restoration of the French royal family had proved fanciful. Instead, that "Corsican ruffian," as Adams's oldest son called General Bonaparte, had made himself dictator. The shocking news reached America just weeks after General Washington's death and gave people yet another reason to exalt his character. Washington had always respected civilian rule, proclaimed the eulogists recounting his life in speeches that would inevitably live on in pamphlet form. Unmentioned in these productions was how Washington had turned into a pawn for one who did possess the "pretension" of a "perpetual dictator": Hamilton.

Adams's irritation over the inaccuracies had swelled until finally exploding during a private meeting on May 5, 1800, with Secretary of War James McHenry, who had somehow managed to turn a report recommending the creation of a military academy into a eulogy for Washington. "General Washington's death and the eulogiums upon him have been made use of as engines to injure and lower me in the eyes of the public, and you know it," Adams told McHenry. "It was you who biased General

Washington's mind (who hesitated) and induced him to place Hamilton on the list of Major Generals, before Generals Knox and Pinckney. . . . You are subservient to Hamilton, who ruled Washington and would still rule if he could."

McHenry denied it. He also denied rumors that Hamilton had used his influence over the army to work against Adams's reelection. But reviewing the recent election results from New York (the state that "bastard . . . foreigner" Hamilton called home) left little doubt. The legislative body that would select the state's all-important presidential electors had fallen into the hands of Adams's enemies. Ironically, Hamilton's machinations benefited not his preferred candidate, Major General Charles Cotesworth Pinckney, but Vice President Thomas Jefferson. In the resulting desperation, Hamilton would probably have persuaded Washington to stand for a third term had he still stood among the living. But having lost Washington, Hamilton would lose the command he so coveted. Adams would sign legislation disbanding the new army.

That would leave Hamilton with one other major source of power: his influence over the cabinet. But Adams would "take care of that," too. "Washington saddled me with . . .

secretaries who would control me," Adams told McHenry. "You cannot, Sir, remain longer in office." McHenry agreed to resign. When asked to do the same afterward, Secretary of State Timothy Pickering declined. So exercising a power Washington never had, Adams dismissed a member of his cabinet. Some would see political calculations in the timing, as if he wished to run away from the military buildup that his advisers had urged and that he had warned would grow, as it had, "unpopular."

In truth, it would have been far more convenient to retain McHenry and Pickering past June 15, the day by which Adams had requested the cabinet secretaries finish relocating their departments from Philadelphia to the Potomac, even though the new federal city at this stage offered only one of the departments (the Treasury, which happened to be the biggest) a permanent headquarters ready to accept its staff of sixty-nine. Given the turnover, Adams would need to oversee part of the move. The summer respite he had planned in Quincy with Abigail, who had already gone north, would have to wait. There were papers to pack and ships to load. The City of Washington awaited.

Adams had not personally favored the

Potomac site. If Congress had heeded his advice at the time of the selection, the capital would have permanently rotated every four years between New York and Philadelphia. He had, of course, heard his predecessor go on about the possibilities the Potomac presented, how it would make the federal city a "nexus." Everyone who had spent time with Washington had heard the claims. "The federal city would . . . bind together not only the northern and southern states but the trans-Alleghenies with the Atlantic states." What Adams never heard was Washington confess how much he personally would benefit from placing the capital so close to Mount Vernon. "How far his interest and the consideration of the rise in the value of his lands . . . [influenced] him," Adams would "leave to the searcher of all hearts." According to his own rough estimate, the move had probably "raised" the worth of Washington family lands "a thousand percent." Adams had no such stake in the success of the city. Who could blame him, then, for having declined to take as active a role in its affairs? He had still never seen the place despite the plea for a visit from Washington himself.

Thus, upon crossing into the District of Columbia for the first time on June 3, 1800,

Adams had not known what to expect. He had known only that he would stay in a hotel. The president's house could not accommodate him yet. He would find the house, people said, "uncomfortably cold, situated [apart] from all society, [and] without furniture." They advised he look for housing elsewhere for when he returned in the fall for the first session of Congress in the city. The heirs to General Washington had not yet found buyers for the two town houses he had built in the city. Perhaps Adams could rent one. But one of Washington's houses was not what Adams wanted. For however much longer he occupied the office, he wanted the president's house. It looked close enough to completion. On the whole, he liked what he saw during his brief visit. Come the fall he and Abigail would "sleep or lie awake" inside the whitish-looking walls.

What was it like inside the president's house? The answer depended on who asked. Members of the public needed to hear how pleased Abigail had felt upon first reaching the city on November 16, 1800. "The president's house is in a beautiful situation in front of which is the Potomac with a view of Alexandria," she wrote. Out the windows, she could see the ships heading up and down the river. The house itself stood on such a "grand and superb scale" as to surpass any other in the United States.

With friends and family, Abigail could be more honest. The property did not have a garden or a yard or even a fence. Slaves shoveled dirt right outside the front. Inside, laundry hung in the large room designed for public receptions on the east side of the house. The oval room upstairs would one day make a "beautiful" drawing room but only after the installation of the house's "principal stairs." From the otherwise bare walls stared out George Washington, a portrait of the general with his hand extended and his lips pursed. Walking the great hall — peering into the unfinished and underfurnished rooms — fixed the mind on the future. The house had not been built for Abigail and her husband. It had been built, as he reminded her, for "all that shall hereafter inhabit it." In "ages to come," its size would serve it well. For now, it seemed a curse whose upkeep required more servants than she could afford and whose fireplaces consumed more wood than she could find for sale in the city.

Only the indolence and incompetence of a people dependent on slave labor — the sight of which disgusted Abigail — could explain the shortage of wood given that the federal city stood in the middle of what amounted to a vast wood. En route, Abigail had seen almost nothing but trees. Washington itself, she concluded, was "a city in name" alone. It would have better resembled one had the buildings risen closer together instead of "scattered" on opposite ends of muddy avenues.

The process of paving the main artery, Pennsylvania Avenue, had only begun. Down it a carriage had ceremoniously carried her husband on November 22 for his annual message to Congress. The officials escorting him past the pools of stagnant water and construction debris surrounding the one-winged Capitol wanted the speech to serve as the city's formal opening. A painting of Louis XVI, the king who had lost his head, greeted Abigail's husband as he entered the columned Senate chamber, where members of both houses had assembled. "In this city," he began, "may that piety and virtue, that wisdom and magnanimity, that constancy and self-government, which adorned the great character whose name it bears, be forever held in veneration!"

The wisdom of convening in a city so

short of housing eluded many of the senators and representatives listening while stewing over the size of the sleeping quarters they shared. To them, Abigail's husband conceded, "There is cause to apprehend that accommodations are not now so complete as might be wished, yet there is great reason to believe that this inconvenience will cease with the present session." At least, one could imagine a respectable community forming out of the boardinghouses clustered around the Capitol and the printer, cobbler, grocer, tailor, and launderer doing business nearby.

It was a different story by the president's house. For the foreseeable future, living there would mean living as if a settler in a "new part of the world," Abigail wrote. The Treasury Department stood next door on one side, an unfinished building that would house other departments next door on the other. But there were no residences in sight. "My nearest neighbor is at lodgings almost half a mile from me," Abigail wrote. "I feel as though I was much further removed from all my friends and connections."

Her isolation would not last much longer, she knew. The election had shaped up as expected, with Republicans united around Thomas Jefferson for president and Aaron

Burr of New York for vice president and with the Federalists "split to pieces." Old friends who had "been firm supporters of the administration of Washington," she noted, had "become the most inveterate opposers" of her husband. The "Little General," as she called Alexander Hamilton, had published a book of "gross lies" accusing her husband of envying Washington and of being unworthy of a second term like the one he had received. By this time, she did not know who to fear more: the Republicans riding the mob to victory or the Federalists bowing before a "second Bonaparte" like Hamilton. Either extreme would lead the United States to a similar end. If anyone besides her husband won the election, it would be the country's last election, she said.

Hope, however small, held out until December 12, when word reached the capital that South Carolina had given its electoral votes to Jefferson and Burr, which meant that both of them had beaten her husband overall. Around the same day arrived the treaty resulting from the mission for which the Federalists could not forgive her husband. Pursuing peace had cost him the presidency. She would leave Washington early in the new year, never to return. He would follow on March 4, the day his successor would take office. As if she and her husband needed more to mourn, they received word that one of their sons had drunk himself to death. Amid the sorrow over their "private troubles" and bitterness at the "public ingratitude," there was a strange relief. They would have the rest of their days in Quincy. If her husband could muster the money, he would follow another of his predecessor's precedents and become a farmer.

Just days after learning her husband's fate, Abigail accepted a "pressing invitation" from Mrs. Washington, her granddaughter Nelly, and her grandson, "Major Custis," as he now styled himself, and set off for the famous estate to which General Washington had retired. Abigail had never before seen Mount Vernon. What she saw now did not impress her. Her own house in Quincy looked "handsomer." If the president's house in the federal city upriver gestured toward the future, the former president's house looked as if already part of history. "The house has an ancient appearance and is really so," she wrote. "It required the ready money of large funds to beautify and cultivate the grounds so as to make them highly ornamental. It is now going to decay."

Even with "all her fortune," Mrs. Washington could not maintain the estate as the general would have. In truth, the will he had left — newspapers across the country had published it in full — had left her in a perilous position. In postponing the "painful sensations" of separating slaves from their spouses, he had subjected his own spouse to a life among people who would receive their freedom only upon her death. "She did not feel as though her life was safe in their hands, many of whom would be told that it was their interest to get rid of her," Abigail learned. Friends "advised" Mrs. Washington to free her husband's slaves "at the close of the year" not for their good but for her own.

Mrs. Washington's health had visibly deteriorated. She no longer displayed the "beautiful" teeth Abigail had admired when they had first met a decade earlier. But the widow still showed what had most impressed then: "manners" best described as "modest and unassuming, dignified and feminine." She was said not to have "shed a tear" after the general's death until reading the letter from Abigail's husband requesting the body. "Taught by the great example which I have so long had before me never to oppose my private wishes to the public will, I must consent to the request made by Congress," Mrs. Washington had responded. "In doing this, I need not — I cannot — say what a sacrifice of individual feeling I make to a sense of public duty." Some doubted whether the widow could have "penned" such a poignant letter herself. She had, Abigail believed. "It bears the strong marks of a heart deeply wounded."

In the months since, the plans for what to do with the body had grown unseemly. A resting place under the Capitol dome would not suffice, some said. The great man deserved a stand-alone pyramid in the city. The irony irritated Abigail. "At the very period when they are voting to raise trophies to his memory, they are placing those very men in the seat, which he occupied with so much dignity to himself and benefit to his country, who they know will pull down the edifice which he and his successor have labored to preserve, beautify, strengthen, and adorn." Towering monuments to Washington, Abigail feared, would "cast into a shade" the true legacy for which he had labored and conceal the contrasts that set his views apart from those of his opponents. They would capitalize on the confusion by claiming his name for their own purposes.

No one needed the name Washington

more than Jefferson. He had defeated Abigail's husband but had not yet won the presidency as a result of a quirk in the Constitution, which gave every elector two votes but no way to specify which one was for president and which one was for vice president.* Jefferson had needed at least one elector voting for him to stray from the party ticket and cast a second vote for someone other than Burr so as to avoid a tie. But no Republican elector had shown the slightest independence. As a result, Jefferson and Burr had tied, and the choice between them would pass from the Electoral College to the House of Representatives, where Republicans controlled a plurality of the state delegations by which members would vote but not the majority the Constitution required to elect a president. Federalists controlled just enough for their members to play kingmaker. So at the mercy of the self-appointed guardians of Washington's legacy, Jefferson would stand with memories still fresh of his Mazzei letter mocking Washington's legacy.

The balloting for president in the House of

*Ratification of the Twelfth Amendment in 1804 corrected this quirk.

Representatives would commence on February 11, 1801, which would have marked General Washington's sixty-ninth birthday on the Old Style calendar. The day was barely a month away. Not much time remained, Thomas Jefferson knew, to find the few Federalist votes he needed in the House. To suggest, as some Federalists had, that he had purposely avoided all tributes to their hero Washington after his death was not fair. Yes, Jefferson had missed the mock funeral in Philadelphia, but he had appeared at a memorial event in the city just weeks later and had acknowledged letters from people enclosing their own eulogies, which he said he enjoyed when they steered clear of "impiety" and "extravagance," which they rarely did. The purpose of the odes immortalizing Washington as a "firm believer" in Christ could have eluded no one reading the Federalist newspapers deriding Jefferson day after day as an "unbeliever," never mind that it was Washington who had seemingly gone out of his way to avoid the mere mention of the name Jesus.

Had the people wished for a more honest eulogy of their general, years of "intimately" and "thoroughly" observing "the great man" would have allowed Jefferson to oblige. Of course, Jefferson issuing any official statement during the mourning period would have raised howls of hypocrisy. So he had not. But had he done so, there was much he could have said. He could have described Washington's mind ("slow in operation, being little aided by invention or imagination, but sure in conclusion"), his circumspection ("never acting until every circumstance, every consideration was maturely weighed"), his resolution ("once decided, going through with his purpose whatever obstacles opposed"), his courage ("incapable of fear, meeting personal dangers with the calmest unconcern"), his morality ("most pure" and "inflexible"), his finances ("honorable but exact"), his charity ("liberal in contributions to whatever promised utility, but frowning and unyielding on all visionary projects and all unworthy calls"), his speech ("possessing neither copiousness of ideas nor fluency of words"), his temperament ("naturally irritable and high toned"), his self-control ("firm and habitual"), his letters (written "in an easy & correct style . . . acquired by conversation"), his heart ("not warm in its affections but . . . [calculating] every man's value and . . . [giving] solid esteem proportioned to it"), his athleticism ("the best horseman of his age"), and his appearance ("easy, erect, and noble").

Jefferson would have told the people that they had lost the "greatest man that ever lived" had not Washington shown a more "despotic" side during his last years. Probably it had been there from the beginning, the inheritance of a child "brought up to govern slaves," the nature of a man so "naturally distrustful" as to have "no idea of people being left to themselves to act" and to be incapable of ever fully ceding control. It was why Republicans, Jefferson had predicted, would need to "lie" on their "oars" as long as the general lived. Only after he lay buried in the banks of the Potomac would the "vessel" of state return to its rightful "republican tack."

Yet more than a year after his death, the prediction had not yet fully come to pass. The name Washington had not lost all control of the currents carrying the ship of state. Because the Federalists miring the House in debate over "a mausoleum" for Washington retained some say over who would serve as his second successor — because having seen how little they trusted public opinion left Jefferson uncertain as to whether they would "yield to the known will of the people" and approve his election — he had no choice but to do what he had avoided for months. On January 2, 1801, the second day of a new century, Jefferson rented a horse and prepared to ride back into the past. The journey would take him out of the City of Washington, across the Potomac, and down its banks. Mount Vernon lay ahead. And so did a long-overdue reckoning with the widow Washington.

The condolence letters she received could not address her as "dear Patcy," as her husband's letters had. Martha would burn the correspondence he and she had shared rather than share that part of her marriage with random writers. So the letters they sent instead came addressed to Mrs. Washington and usually began with some version of "Dear Madam." The condolences came in such quantities and from such faraway places that Congress voted to exempt her from paying postage for the rest of her life.

From across the Atlantic came a letter from Lafayette regretting that, contrary to the rumors, he had not set sail for America and now would never again see his American father. "Nor could I forgive myself . . . had I not the remembrance of the advice by which you know he has repeatedly deferred my departure for America. . . . Alas, in this world, we can no more meet!"

From New York came a letter from Alexander Hamilton assuming Martha would remember "the numerous and distinguished marks of confidence" he had received from her husband. "I cannot say in how many ways the continuance of that confidence and friendship was necessary to me in future relations."

From Philadelphia came a letter from Eliza Willing Powel saying she, too, had "lost a much-valued friend" but assuring that "he is removed to regions of bliss."

From a town called Dumfries, down the Potomac, came a letter from a parson named Weems enclosing a "little book" that he would dedicate to Martha under the title *A History of the Life and Death, Virtues and Exploits, of General George Washington.* "Should it contribute in any wise to diffuse the spirits of WASHINGTON [and] in any degree to promote those *virtues,* which rendered him the *greatest,* because the most serviceable of mankind," Weems wrote, "it will be a matter of great joy."

"Grateful" as Martha was for the tributes to her husband, she found "comfort" only in God for what she had lost. She had not wanted her "old man," as she had playfully dubbed her slightly younger husband, to accept the presidency in 1789. She had weathered the worst winters of the Revolution by his side on the assumption that they would live thereafter in "the still enjoyments of the fireside at Mount Vernon." It had seemed, even then, a decade before his death, "much too late for him to go in to public life again," but he had submitted to the people and gone north, and she had followed.

Now she would "never" venture beyond the bounds of Mount Vernon again. Nor would she return to the bedroom where she had watched her husband die. Afterward, she had moved upstairs to the garret, where she squeezed a bed, a mirror, a table, and a few chairs beneath a sloping ceiling. Friends urged her to return to a healthier part of the house. But she did not "expect to be well as long" as she lived. "There was now nothing to attach her to the earth," she said, even though there were still some things: Wash and the worries he always gave her, a parrot she loved to pet, and the one-year-old great-grandchild she could spoil courtesy of Nelly and Lawrence Lewis.

There were also still visitors eager to hear about her husband and to see his tomb. All received the hospitality her husband would have shown. None upset her more than the man who arrived on January 3, 1801. Not since her husband's death had any "occurrence" at Mount Vernon proved so "painful" as welcoming Thomas Jefferson.

In the more than a year since her husband had died, the vice president had sent not a word of condolence. He had waited until now, when the election results had rid the members of her household of all their hopes not that John Adams would win the presidency but that Hamilton's candidate, Charles Cotesworth Pinckney, would. Jefferson had waited until now, when he needed the Washington name. His timing could not have been worse.

Just two days earlier, she had emancipated her husband's slaves in the knowledge that the unions they had formed with the dower slaves would dissolve as a result. "What [else] could she do?" she asked. The dower slaves belonged to her first husband's estate. Freeing them was no more in her "power" than it had been in her second husband's. And even if she could have emancipated them, she probably would not have. "The blacks are so bad in their nature that they have not the least gratitude for the kindness that may be showed to them," she thought, while doubting if freeing them even classified as kindness. She worried for them, she said, "as a parent." They would go "adrift

380

into the world without house, home, or friend."

Jefferson could not have known how slavery had divided the house in two. But what "he must have known" was that she, its mistress, possessed "evidence of his perfidy." His tears over the tomb would not fool her. She had no choice but to sit with him and feign acceptance of his condolences, but he would not spend the night. He was "one of the most detestable of mankind," she would be sure to tell her Federalist friends afterward. Her husband during his final months had begun deriding Republicans as "Democrats," a word synonymous, in his definition, with the disorder that had so disgusted him about the French Revolution. No member of the Mount Vernon family would cheer the "triumph of democracy" in America. But there was no stopping it. Jefferson would go back upriver and claim the new capital city in the name of the people. What they would do with Washington then would be for them to choose.

EPILOGUE:
WE ARE ALL

So Thomas Jefferson will go back upriver to Washington. And on March 4, 1801, shunning the sword his predecessors strapped to their sides, he will set off on foot for the Capitol. Four years after John Adams gazed into the eyes of George Washington and wondered whether the incoming or outgoing president would be happier, Jefferson will not face the same question, for Adams, having departed for Quincy before dawn, will not be among the people packing the Senate chamber. So tightly will the bodies crowd together that they will obstruct the doors. There will be no exit till the end.

Jefferson will struggle to project his voice across the chamber. But the more important audience, the one below and beyond Capitol Hill, will see the words clearly in the newspapers. "I have learnt to expect that it will rarely fall to the lot of imperfect man to retire from this station with the reputation, and the favor, which bring him into it," Jefferson will say before immediately disclaiming any "pretensions to that high confidence you reposed in our first and greatest revolutionary character." To no one will the identity of this character be a mystery. "[Washington's] pre-eminent services had entitled him to the first place in his country's love, and destined for him the fairest page in the volume of faithful history."

The inaugural address will go into the pages of history for these lines: "We have called by different names brethren of the same principle. We are all republicans: we are all federalists," never mind that Jefferson will have won the election not because any of the House Federalists agreed to vote for him but because just enough of them agreed not to vote at all. In no sense, except the most literal lowercase one in which Jefferson will write the words, will the people he addresses be all Republicans and all Federalists. They will be, as quoted in the preceding pages of this book, "speculators" and "farmers," "paper dealers" and "bankrupts," "reputable yeomanry" and "riffraff," "bastards" and "wealthy aristocrats," "aliens" and heirs "of the first families," "scribblers" and "spies," "monarchists" and "Jacobins," "chameleons" and "party men," "intriguers" and "tools," "geniuses" and "fools," "believers" and "unbelievers," "prostitutes" and "ladies," "great men" and "second-rate" ones, and many "ambitious" and "jealous" others. They will switch names and roles, but they will never be all the same. What they will be is all together in Washington, part of the city. They will write its future just as they told the story of its namesake's end.

Martha Washington will go to the grave barely a year after Jefferson's inauguration without knowing whether her body and her husband's would ever go upriver to the federal city. "Remember," she will say in her final hours, "to have my remains placed in a leaden coffin, that they may be removed with those of the general at the command of the government." The decision that Tobias Lear will make before her death to leave the service of the Washington family for service in the Jefferson administration will subject him to endless speculation of having expunged the harshest words about his new boss from his old boss's papers. Lear will commit suicide many years later by means of a pistol shot to the head. John Nicholas, the clerk of Albemarle County, will take it upon himself in 1803 to "fully" inform the world of his role in the fallout between the first and third presidents: that it was he who discovered that Jefferson's nephew had written to Washington under a false name. The story will barely suffice for scandal among the people of Washington. No one will ever prove that Jefferson himself had any knowledge of the plan. At the end of Jefferson's presidency in 1809, the federal city will number only about eight thousand people and more resemble the kind of rural community that he so romanticized than the vast metropolis that Washington envisioned.

Among the people of the federal district at one time or another will be many of the slaves George Washington could not free. Of Martha's four grandchildren, only Nelly will not have a house inside the four ten-mile boundary lines. Some share of the slaves she will inherit (Hercules's daughters among them) will go to the house that she and her husband will build on Mount Vernon's northwest corner. From there, she will gaze out upon the old mansion house and long for the life she once had. Wash will attempt to purchase the old place but, failing, will succeed in carting upriver its finest portraits and most intimate relics, including the bed on which Washington died and the four dower slaves who tended to him on his last day. They will all go to Arlington, the columned house Wash will build on the Virginia side of the federal district, directly across the Potomac from the City of Washington.

In 1814, Wash, still going by "Major Custis," will retreat with the ranks in the face of a foreign army (a British one, not a French one) marching on the city. The town houses Washington built during his last days will burn along with all the public buildings save for the few Doctor William Thornton will persuade the British to spare. The task of seeking terms for Alexandria's surrender downriver will fall to a committee, which will include Doctor Elisha Cullen Dick. Only the defiance of Baltimore's Fort McHenry, named for the compliant former secretary of war, will turn the tide against the British in the Chesapeake Bay.

Former secretary of state Timothy Pickering, now an antiwar congressman and an apostle for the necessity of the North seceding from the South, will oppose rebuilding Washington, whose construction he will call a "capital error" conceived at an arbitrary point that only a cryptic compromise in Congress and the whims of one man could explain and encompassing a vast space and wide avenues that people would never fill. Underlying these criticisms will be Pickering's unwavering belief that Washington himself was a middling man undeserving of a monument striving for such majesty. Hamilton accomplished more and sacrificed more (his life itself in a duel with Aaron Burr in 1804), Pickering will claim. He will vote to move the federal government back to its old home in Philadelphia. But he will not carry the majority. Thomas Law, whose tumultuous union with Martha Washington's oldest granddaughter will end in divorce, will join others in preparing accommodations for the government for however long it takes for the Capitol and president's house to rise out of the ruins where George Washington willed them to go. The first man to reoccupy the building to be known as the White House will be James Monroe.

In 1824, after receiving a letter from Monroe, Lafayette and his son finally will embark for the United States and then on a grand tour of a country clinging together only because of congressional compromises over slavery. They will be in the City of Washington when, for the second time in history, a presidential election will head to the House of Representatives. This time, an Adams will prevail. Abigail will not live to hear the news. But her husband will. Just as his critics predicted, his oldest son will succeed to the presidency. On July 4, 1828, President John Quincy Adams will shovel the first dirt for a new canal along the river whose waters George Washington predicted would bind the nation and whose profits would finance a national university. The new company, like the original one, will struggle to stay above water. The Potomac will never be the economic engine Washington envisioned. Speculators such as Washington's most quoted eulogist, Harry Lee, will never recover. His youngest son, Robert, will marry Wash's only daughter at the columned house across the Potomac from the City of Washington in 1831, inherit the sword Wash received from his "grandpapa," and eventually lead a rebel army fighting for slavery and a Southern confederacy over the river.

Around the time of the Custis-Lee wedding, the bodies in the old vault at Mount Vernon will be moved to a new one on the property. They will never go upriver to the city. Instead, in 1848, shortly after the retrocession of Alexandria to Virginia will fracture the perfect ten-mile-square diamond that George Washington plotted for the federal district, Wash will help position the cornerstone for the Washington Monument, the towering obelisk that will not reach its full height of 555 feet until after the Civil War, when the city will finally grow into a place of more than one hundred thousand people.

In time, as Abigail Adams feared and biographers will bemoan, the monument will "cast into a shade" the actual human being. People will hear the word "Washington" and think only of the city, even though they will speak of it in the same polarizing ways their forebears whispered about its aging namesake. They will marvel at its influence and decry the influences under which it has fallen; complain that it moves too slowly and shudder at the speed of its wrath; plead for it to do more and wish it would go away; view it as worthy of its memorials and see it as a betrayal of a revolutionary past. They will look to it to contain the feuding and factions tearing them apart and wonder how much longer it itself can hold together. In every succeeding generation, they will talk as if they are living in the last days of Washington. It shall be as if they never ended.

ACKNOWLEDGMENTS

"Arrange & record all my late military letters & papers." In a life full of giving orders, those words were among the last orders George Washington gave. Responsibility for carrying out the charge has passed to the men and women who edit *The Papers of George Washington,* and thank goodness. Their meticulous and methodical work serves as the starting point for any writer seeking the American Cincinnatus. Early on in this project, however, I discovered that following Washington's paper trail alone, critical as it was, would not produce a full portrait of an aging patriarch ceding control of his name and his legacy and that I would also need to follow the trails editors have cut through the papers of other prominent personalities of the era. Many of these volumes are now available not only in print but also digitally, in some cases at Founders Online, a National Archives website through which all Americans can meet their country's fathers.

Other primary sources upon which this book relies remain unpublished in archives like the one that George Washington hoped to build at Mount Vernon upon returning home but never did. Two centuries later, Mount Vernon finally has the repository it deserves thanks to the completion of the Fred W. Smith National Library for the Study of George Washington. My visit there was a success thanks to Mark Santangelo, Samantha Snyder, Dawn Bonner, and Katherine Hoarn, who directed me to papers that would otherwise have eluded me. The archivists at the Library of Congress's Manuscript Reading Room, the Historical Society of Pennsylvania, the American Philosophical Society, and the Maryland Historical Society made me feel at home among their treasures. Frances Pollard, John McClure, and Matthew E. Guillen kindly assisted me at the Virginia Historical Society, as did Stacey Swigart at the Philadelphia History Museum and Jobi O. Zink at the Rosenbach in Philadelphia. The Massachusetts Historical Society allowed me to make use of its rich collections.

When not hunched over old letters, biographers must walk the ground where history actually happened. My research for this book as well as my previous one has taken me up and down the river Washington called home. I have met many wonderful guides along the way, and I am especially grateful to those at Mount Vernon, which continues to set the standard for historic sites under the leadership of Douglas Bradburn. Special thanks to Meagan Regina and Matt Iannone for being so generous as to give me a memorable personal tour of the Powel House in Philadelphia.

Many great writers have set off in search of the Father of Their Country. I have benefited tremendously from what they found. Robert L. O'Connell published the brilliant book *Revolutionary: George Washington at War* too late for my research but kindly agreed to give my manuscript an early read nonetheless. Given that I have gone from writing about Robert E. Lee to George Washington, I owe one more mention of Douglas Southall Freeman, who traveled the path long before me. Reading Freeman's inimitable biography of Lee and books about his lieutenants introduced me to the "fog-of-war" style. Whatever fault the reader finds in my telling of this story reflects not on Freeman, who interestingly did not strictly follow his own once-famous rules when writing about Washington, but on the decision I made to adapt the style to my own end.

It was my editor, Colin Harrison, who encouraged me to look for a different way to tell this story. At the time, I could not have imagined where the search would lead, how long it would take, and what extraordinary patience Colin would show. At every stage, this book has benefited from his wisdom as well as from the support of his talented colleagues at Scribner, including Mia O'Neill, Jason Chappell, and the incredible Sarah Goldberg, who sent a thoughtful response to every question I asked (even the irritating ones). The pages of this book received a thorough copyediting from Barbara Wild and a stirring cover courtesy of the outstanding Scribner art department. From the beginning, my wonderful agent, Glen Hartley, stood behind this project and provided the judicious and reassuring counsel an author needs.

I owe the greatest debt to my family, which includes Horns, Luses, and Shaskans, as well as the Nathans into whose family I was so lucky to marry. In helping care for my family, Macarena Reardon became a part of it. My sister-in-law Marjorie Galler, a doctor possessing a rare mix of genius and compassion, demonstrated both qualities in addressing the questions I encountered while writing about Washington's death. Any errors I have made are a result of me straying from the course she prescribed. Though no ancestor of mine came to this country until decades after the events described in this book, Myra and George Shaskan, my much-missed grandparents, wove early American history into our family history by surrounding us with the styles and stories of the era. The dedication to this book credits my parents, Carol and Lawrence Horn, for the best of beginnings, which is both inadequate and misleading because the love they show never ends. Credit for this book reaching its actual end belongs to my wife, Caroline. She is my compass, and her conviction and commitment pointed the way when I could not find it.

Our daughter, Laura, grew as I wrote and astonished me with her awareness of the world. "Are you done with your book?" she asked daily. "Yes," I tell her now, as I write the last sentence with Berkeley, a special dog named for an enchanting place Washington knew well, waiting at my feet, just where she was when I began.

NOTES

Abbreviations

APAFC *The Adams Papers: Adams Family Correspondence*

APS American Philosophical Society

DGW *The Diaries of George Washington*

HSP Historical Society of Pennsylvania

LOC Library of Congress

MHS Massachusetts Historical Society

MV The Fred W. Smith National Library for the Study of George Washington at Mount Vernon

PAH *The Papers of Alexander Hamilton*

PGWCF *The Papers of George Washington: Confederation Series*

PGWCL *The Papers of George Washington: Colonial Series*

PGWP *The Papers of George Washington: Presidential Series*

PGWR *The Papers of George Washington: Retirement Series*

PGWRW *The Papers of George Washington:*

Revolutionary War Series
PTJ *The Papers of Thomas Jefferson*
VHS *Virginia Historical Society*
WGW *The Writings of George Washington from the Original Manuscript Sources, 1749–1799*

The words quoted in this book belong to an earlier time. In places, the author has updated capitalization, punctuation, and spelling. When citing from the published collections listed above, the author has generally omitted page numbers because the National Archives has made digital versions of most of these volumes available through the website Founders Online and because letters cited in volumes not available digitally can be located according to their dates in the print versions. Citations containing incomplete dateline information reflect omissions in the originals.

Prologue: History's Current
noon: *Philadelphia Gazette,* March 6, 1797; *Claypoole's American Daily Advertiser,* March 6, 1797; J. Thomas Scharf and Thompson Westcott, *History of Philadelphia, 1609–1884* (Philadelphia: L. H. Everts, 1884), 1:488; Constance M. Greiff, *Independence: The Creation of a National Park* (Philadelphia: University of Pennsylvania Press, 1987), 173; Ron Chernow, *Washing-*

ton: A Life (New York: Penguin Books, 2010), 29–30; John Ferling, John Adams: A Life (New York: Oxford University Press, 1992), 169. • "Washington!": Scharf and Westcott, History of Philadelphia, 1:488. • gallery: Edward M. Riley, "Philadelphia, the Nation's Capital, 1790–1800," Pennsylvania History 20, no. 4 (October 1953): 367 and 370–73; Henry Wansey, An Excursion to the United States of North America, in the Summer of 1794, 2nd ed. (Salisbury, England: J. Easton, 1798), 98. • light-headed: John Adams to Abigail Adams, Philadelphia, March 5, 1797, in APAFC, vol. 12; John Adams to Abigail Adams, Philadelphia, March 17, 1797, in APAFC, vol. 12. • wind: George Washington, March 1797, in DGW, vol. 6; Edward M. Riley, "The Independence Hall Group," Transactions of the American Philosophical Society 43, no. 1 (1953): 17–18 and 24. • "handsome": John Adams to Benjamin Rush, Quincy, November 11, 1807, in Alexander Biddle, ed., Old Family Letters: Copied from the Originals for Alexander Biddle (Philadelphia: J. B. Lippincott, 1892), 168–70. • envied: John Adams to Abigail Adams, Philadelphia, May 29, 1775, in APAFC, vol. 1. • "[His] excellent": John Adams, The Adams Papers: Diary and Autobiography of John

Adams, vol. 3, ed. L. H. Butterfield (Cambridge: Harvard University Press, 1961), 322–23. • idol: Douglas Southall Freeman, *George Washington: A Biography* (New York: Charles Scribner's Sons, 1948–1954), 4:395 and 545. • "splendid": John Adams to Abigail Adams, Philadelphia, February 24, 1797, in *APAFC,* vol. 11. For adulation of Washington, see Barry Schwartz, *George Washington: The Making of an American Symbol* (New York: Free Press, 1987), 33–38 and 77–80. • socialites: Elizabeth Willing Powel to George Washington, February 8, 1797, George Washington Papers, LOC; John Adams to Abigail Adams, Philadelphia, February 2, 1797, in *APAFC,* vol. 11. • "a few": John Adams to Abigail Adams, Philadelphia, January 31, 1797, in *APAFC,* vol. 11. • the calendar: John Adams to Abigail Adams, Philadelphia, February 24, 1797, in *APAFC,* vol. 11; George Washington Parke Custis, *Recollections and Private Memoirs of Washington* (New York: Derby & Jackson, 1860; Bridgewater, VA: American Foundation Publications, 1999), 397n–98n; John Adams to Abigail Adams, Philadelphia, March 11, 1797, in *APAFC,* vol. 12; Ferling, *John Adams,* 11. • slept: John Adams to Abigail Adams, Philadelphia, March 3, 1797, in *APAFC,* vol. 12; John Adams to

Abigail Adams, Philadelphia, March 5, 1797, in *APAFC,* vol. 12; John Adams to Abigail Adams, Philadelphia, March 17, 1797, in *APAFC,* vol. 12. • "fill": Abigail Adams to Ruth Hooper Dalton, September 24, 1796, in *APAFC,* vol. 11. • education: John Adams to Benjamin Rush, Quincy, April 22, 1812, in Biddle, ed., *Old Family Letters,* 377; James Thomas Flexner, *George Washington: The Forge of Experience, 1732–1775* (Boston: Little, Brown, 1965), 24; Chernow, *Washington,* 12 and 18. • "there are thousands": John Adams to John Jebb, Grosvenor Square, September 10, 1785, in *The Adams Papers: Papers of John Adams,* vol. 17, ed. Gregg L. Lint et al. (Cambridge: Belknap, 2014), 422–27. • fame: Ferling, *John Adams,* 19; Joseph J. Ellis, *Passionate Sage: The Character and Legacy of John Adams* (New York: Norton, 2001), 67. • "immense elevation": John Adams to Benjamin Rush, Quincy, November 11, 1807, in Biddle, ed., *Old Family Letters,* 168–70. For Washington's height, see Chernow, *Washington,* 29–30; Custis, *Recollections and Private Memoirs of Washington,* 481–84 and 527. • no biological: John Adams to Benjamin Rush, Quincy, September 1807, in Biddle, ed., *Old Family Letters,* 162; Dumas Malone,

Jefferson and the Ordeal of Liberty (Boston: Little, Brown, 1962), 283; John Adams to Benjamin Rush, Quincy, August 28, 1811, in Biddle, ed., *Old Family Letters,* 353. • "self-command": John Adams to Benjamin Rush, Quincy, November 11, 1807, in Biddle, ed., *Old Family Letters,* 170. • "rivers": John Adams to Benjamin Rush, Quincy, January 25, 1806, in Biddle, ed., *Old Family Letters,* 90–91. For Washington keeping his mouth closed, see Freeman, *George Washington,* 3:6. For Adams on Washington's teeth, see Adams, *The Adams Papers: Diary and Autobiography of John Adams,* 3:280. • "a strain": John Adams to Benjamin Rush, Quincy, June 21, 1811, in Biddle, ed., *Old Family Letters,* 287. • "darted": Adams, *The Adams Papers: Diary and Autobiography of John Adams,* 3:323. • "solemn": John Adams to Benjamin Rush, Quincy, June 21, 1811, in Biddle, ed., *Old Family Letters,* 287. • faster: Scharf and Westcott, *History of Philadelphia,* 1:488. • "He must": John Adams to Abigail Adams, Philadelphia, December 20, 1796, in *APAFC,* vol. 11. • "His skin": John Adams to Abigail Adams, Philadelphia, January 31, 1793, in *APAFC,* vol. 9. • every electoral: George Washington to Alexander Hamilton, Philadelphia, June 26, 1796, in *PAH,* vol.

20. • three votes: John Adams to Abigail Adams, Philadelphia, January 18, 1797, in *APAFC,* vol. 11. • "the most insignificant": David McCullough, *John Adams* (New York: Simon & Schuster, 2001), 447. • powdering: Scharf and Westcott, *History of Philadelphia,* 1:488; Dumas Malone, *Jefferson the Virginian* (Boston: Little, Brown, 1948), 3 and 48; *Philadelphia Gazette,* March 6, 1797; *Claypoole's American Daily Advertiser,* March 6, 1797; John Adams to Charles Adams, Philadelphia, January 2, 1794, in *APAFC,* vol. 10. • "is as": John Adams to Abigail Adams, Philadelphia, March 13, 1797, in *APAFC,* vol. 12. For the quotation's context, see Abigail Adams to John Adams, Quincy, March 25, 1797, in *APAFC,* vol. 12. • "awake": John Adams to Abigail Adams, Philadelphia, January 18, 1797, in *APAFC,* vol. 11. For Adams's predictions, see Ellis, *Passionate Sage,* 92–98. • Franco-American: Christopher Hibbert, *The Days of the French Revolution* (New York: Harper Perennial, 2002), 185–89 and 193; William Doyle, *The Oxford History of the French Revolution* (New York: Oxford University Press, 1989), 210–14; John Adams to Abigail Adams, Philadelphia, December 16, 1796, in *APAFC,* vol. 11; Gordon S. Wood, *Empire of*

Liberty: A History of the Early Republic, 1789–1815 (New York: Oxford University Press, 2009), 177 and 181–82; Alexander DeConde, *The Quasi-War: The Politics and Diplomacy of the Undeclared War with France, 1797–1801* (New York: Charles Scribner's Sons, 1966), 3–12; Alexander DeConde, *Entangling Alliance: Politics and Diplomacy Under George Washington* (Durham: Duke University Press, 1958), 472–76; Ferling, *John Adams,* 339; Stanley Elkins and Eric McKitrick, *The Age of Federalism* (New York: Oxford University Press, 1993), 520–21 and 537–39. • "short": Ferling, *John Adams,* 53, 129, 133, 159, and 176. • "Adams!": Scharf and Westcott, *History of Philadelphia,* 1:488. For more details of the inauguration, see John Alexander Carroll and Mary Wells Ashworth, *George Washington* (New York: Charles Scribner's Sons, 1957), 7:436–37; *Claypoole's American Daily Advertiser,* March 6, 1797. • "I have been": John Adams to Abigail Adams, Philadelphia, March 9, 1797, in *APAFC,* vol. 12. • "seem to be": John Adams to Abigail Adams, Philadelphia, March 17, 1797, in *APAFC,* vol. 12. For Federalist concerns about Adams, see Elkins and McKitrick, *The Age of Federalism,* 515 and 524. • support of her:

John Adams to Abigail Adams, Philadelphia, January 11, 1797, in *APAFC,* vol. 11. • oath required: John Adams to Abigail Adams, Philadelphia, March 17, 1797, in *APAFC,* vol. 12; Chernow, *Washington,* 687; John Adams to Benjamin Rush, Quincy, January 25, 1806, in Biddle, ed., *Old Family Letters,* 90. • "open to": John Adams to Abigail Adams, Philadelphia, March 9, 1797, in *APAFC,* vol. 12. • "get through": John Adams to Abigail Adams, Philadelphia, March 5, 1797, in *APAFC,* vol. 12. • "In that retirement": *Claypoole's American Daily Advertiser,* March 6, 1797. • "as serene": John Adams to Abigail Adams, Philadelphia, March 5, 1797, in *APAFC,* vol. 12. • bows: *Claypoole's American Daily Advertiser,* March 6, 1797. • "more weeping": John Adams to Abigail Adams, Philadelphia, March 9, 1797, in *APAFC,* vol. 12. • "dry eye": John Adams to Abigail Adams, Philadelphia, March 5, 1797, in *APAFC,* vol. 12. • freezing air: George Washington, March 1797, in *DGW,* vol. 6; Carroll and Ashworth, *George Washington,* 7:445; Riley, "Philadelphia, the Nation's Capital," 363, 363n, and 376–77; United States Bureau of the Census, *Population of the 33 Urban Places: 1800* (1998). • "a child": James C. Nicholls, "Lady Henrietta Liston's Journal of Washington's

'Resignation,' Retirement, and Death,"
Pennsylvania Magazine of History and Biography 95, no. 4 (October 1971): 516. • slow:
George Washington to Matthias Slough,
Philadelphia, February 6, 1796, in *WGW,*
35:385–86; George Washington to Tobias
Lear, Chester, March 9, 1797, in *PGWR,*
vol. 1; Patricia Brady, *Martha Washington:
An American Life* (New York: Viking, 2005),
186. • "dear Patcy": George Washington to
Martha Washington, Philadelphia, June 18,
1775, in Joseph E. Fields, ed., *"Worthy
Partner": The Papers of Martha Washington*
(Westport, CT: Greenwood, 1994), 159–
60. • white hair: Brady, *Martha Washington,*
27 and 204; Martha Washington to Mr.
Whitelock, April 14, 1794, in Fields, ed.,
"Worthy Partner," 265; Abigail Adams to
Mary Smith Cranch, Richmond Hill, June
28, 1789, in *APAFC,* vol. 8; Martha Washington to Fanny Bassett Washington, New
York, June 8, 1789, in Fields, ed., *"Worthy
Partner,"* 215. • "the first": Martha Washington to Mercy Otis Warren, New York, December 26, 1789, in Fields, ed., *"Worthy
Partner,"* 223. For why Washington would
have known the contents of this letter, see
Chernow, *Washington,* 219. • "the faculty":
George Washington to George Augustine

Washington, Mount Vernon, October 25, 1786, in *PGWCF,* vol. 4. • "violent": George Washington to James McHenry, Mount Vernon, April 3, 1797, in *PGWR,* vol. 1. • "remember": George Washington to Tobias Lear, Chester, March 9, 1797, in *PGWR,* vol. 1. • "poor little": Eleanor Parke Custis to Elizabeth Bordley, Hope Park, October 19, 1795, in Patricia Brady, ed., *George Washington's Beautiful Nelly: The Letters of Eleanor Parke Custis Lewis to Elizabeth Bordley Gibson, 1794–1851* (Columbia: University of South Carolina Press, 2006), 22–23. For background on Nelly and Frisk, see Brady, ed., *George Washington's Beautiful Nelly,* 6; Eleanor Parke Custis to Elizabeth Bordley, Hope Park, March 30, 1796, in Brady, ed., *George Washington's Beautiful Nelly,* 26; Mary Custis Lee, "Memoir of George Washington Parke Custis," in Custis, *Recollections and Private Memoirs of Washington,* 37; Editorial Note, George Washington to Tobias Lear, Chester, March 9, 1797, in *PGWR,* vol. 1. • "should not": George Washington to Tobias Lear, Chester, March 9, 1797, in *PGWR,* vol. 1. • carriage sick: George Washington to William Pearce, Head of Elk, October 19, 1795, in *PGWP,* vol. 19; George Washington to Tobias Lear,

Philadelphia, November 16, 1796, in *WGW,* 35:284–85; Lee, "Memoir of George Washington Parke Custis," 37. • another namesake: William Spohn Baker, *Washington After the Revolution, 1784–1799* (Philadelphia, 1897), 319–20; Mme de Lasteyrie, *Life of Madame de Lafayette,* trans. Louis de Lasteyrie (London: Barthes and Lowell, 1872), 173. • "reconcile": George Washington to Alexander Hamilton, Philadelphia, November 28, 1795, in *PGWP,* vol. 19. For background on Georges Washington Lafayette's arrival and appearance, see George Washington Motier Lafayette to George Washington, Boston, August 31, 1795, in *PGWP,* vol. 18; Harlow Giles Unger, *Lafayette* (New York: John Wiley & Sons, 2002), 320; Alexander Hamilton to George Washington, New York, December 24, 1795, in *PGWP,* vol. 19. • "the man I": George Washington to Lafayette, Philadelphia, January 4–5, 1782, in *WGW,* 23:431. For background on Lafayette, see Unger, *Lafayette.* For background on Washington's political concerns and Georges Washington Lafayette's gloom, see George Washington to Alexander Hamilton, Philadelphia, November 23, 1795, in *PGWP,* vol. 19; Henrietta Liston to James Jackson, Germantown, September 6, 1796, in Bradford Perkins, "A Diplomat's Wife in

Philadelphia: Letters of Henrietta Liston, 1796–1800," *William and Mary Quarterly* 11, no. 4 (October 1954): 603. • attacks so: George Washington to Thomas Jefferson, Mount Vernon, July 6, 1796, in *PTJ,* vol. 29. • "Every act": George Washington to Alexander Hamilton, Mount Vernon, June 26, 1796, in *PAH,* vol. 20. • "pains": George Washington to Jeremiah Wadsworth, Philadelphia, March 6, 1797, in *PGWR,* vol. 1. • "posterity": George Washington to Timothy Pickering, Philadelphia, March 3, 1797, in *WGW,* 35:414–16. For the history of the letters, also see James Tagg, "Benjamin Franklin Bache's Attack on George Washington," *Pennsylvania Magazine of History and Biography* 100, no. 2 (April 1976): 221–22; Freeman, *George Washington,* 4:582. • "To the wearied": George Washington to Henry Knox, Philadelphia, March 2, 1797, in *WGW,* 35:409. • "cankered": Malone, *Jefferson and the Ordeal of Liberty,* 307. • "just": George Washington to John Armstrong, Philadelphia, February 23, 1797, in *WGW,* 35:397. For background on Newburgh, see John Ferling, *The Ascent of George Washington: The Hidden Political Genius of an American Icon* (New York: Bloomsbury, 2009), 223–35; Richard H. Kohn, "The Inside History of the

Newburgh Conspiracy: America and the Coup d'Etat," *William and Mary Quarterly* 27, no. 2 (April 1970): 187–220; William M. Fowler Jr., *American Crisis: George Washington and the Dangerous Two Years After Yorktown, 1781–1783* (New York: Walker, 2011), 174–88. • "To some": George Washington to James McHenry, Mount Vernon, April 3, 1797, in *PGWR,* vol. 1. • horseback: Eleanor Parke Custis to Elizabeth Bordley, Mount Vernon, March 18, 1797, in Brady, ed., *George Washington's Beautiful Nelly,* 30–31. • "buildings": George Washington to John Sinclair, Philadelphia, December 11, 1796, in *WGW,* 35:324–29. For a description of the roads, see Isaac Weld Jr., *Travels Through the States of North America and the Provinces of Lower Canada, During the Years 1795, 1796, and 1797,* 4th ed. (London: John Stockdale, 1800), 37–43. • disappeared: George Washington to William Pearce, Philadelphia, November 14, 1796, in *WGW,* 35:279; Editorial Note, George Washington to Tobias Lear, Head of Elk, March 10, 1797, in *PGWR,* vol. 1; George Washington to Frederick Kitt, Mount Vernon, January 10, 1798, in *PGWR,* vol. 2; Custis, *Recollections and Private Memoirs of Washington,* 422–24; Mount Vernon Farm Accounts, February 25, 1797, in Mount

410

Vernon Farm Accounts, January 7, 1797–September 10, 1797, MV; Tobias Lear to George Washington, Philadelphia, June 5, 1791, in *PGWP,* vol. 8. For the Pennsylvania law, see George Washington to Tobias Lear, Richmond, April 12, 1791, in *PGWP,* vol. 8; Tobias Lear to George Washington, Philadelphia, April 24, 1791, in *PGWP,* vol. 8. • "If he can": George Washington to Tobias Lear, Head of Elk, March 10, 1797, in *PGWR,* vol. 1. • "Met": George Washington, March 1797, in *DGW,* vol. 6. • trees have stood: Thomas Twining, *Travels in America 100 Years Ago: Being Notes and Reminiscences* (New York: Harper and Brothers, 1893), 95–98; Weld, *Travels Through the States of North America and the Provinces of Lower Canada,* 47–48. For Washington's conception of his own ancestry, see George Washington to William Augustine Washington, Mount Vernon, February 27, 1798, in *PGWR,* vol. 2. • "experience": George Washington to the People of the United States, United States, September 17, 1796, in *Claypoole's American Daily Advertiser,* September 19, 1796. • permanent seat: Bob Arnebeck, *Through a Fiery Trial: Building Washington, 1790–1800* (Lanham, MD: Madison, 1991), 24–36; George Washington, Proclamation, January 24, 1791, in

PGWP, vol. 7; Joel Achenbach, *The Grand Idea: George Washington's Potomac and the Race to the West* (New York: Simon & Schuster, 2004), 170–83; George Washington to John Sinclair, Philadelphia, December 11, 1796, in *WGW,* 35:328–29; George Washington to Arthur Young, Philadelphia, December 5, 1791, in *PGWP,* vol. 9; George Washington to Alexander Hamilton, Philadelphia, September 1, 1796, in *PAH,* vol. 20; Jeffrey L. Pasley, *The First Presidential Contest: 1796 and the Founding of American Democracy* (Lawrence: University Press of Kansas, 2013), 406. • artillery echoes: Editorial Note, George Washington, March 1797, in *DGW,* vol. 6; Twining, *Travels in America 100 Years Ago,* 100–2; William C. Allen, *History of the United States Capitol: A Chronicle of Design, Construction, and Politics* (Washington, DC: Government Printing Office, 2001), 19–20, 26, and 33–34; George Washington to David Stuart, Philadelphia, March 8, 1792, in *PGWP,* vol. 10. • "doubt": George Washington to the Commissioners of the District of Columbia, Philadelphia, February 15, 1797, in *WGW,* 35:389. • "The year 1800": George Washington to Thomas Sim Lee, Philadelphia, July 25, 1794, in *PGWP,* vol. 16; George

Washington to the Commissioners of the District of Columbia, Philadelphia, May 22, 1796, in *WGW,* 35:64. • avenues radiating: Twining, *Travels in America 100 Years Ago,* 100–2. • "genius": George Washington to David Stuart, Philadelphia, November 30, 1792, in *PGWP,* vol. 11. • "every person": George Washington to Pierre L'Enfant, Philadelphia, December 2, 1791, in *PGWP,* vol. 9. For tearing down the house, see Fergus M. Bordewich, *Washington: The Making of the American Capital* (New York: Amistad, 2008), 82–89. • "It is much": George Washington to David Stuart, Philadelphia, November 20, 1791, in *PGWP,* vol. 9. • "huzzas": Editorial Note, George Washington, March 1797, in *DGW,* vol. 6. For the description of Pennsylvania Avenue and the president's house, see Arnebeck, *Through a Fiery Trial,* 192, 342, 386, and 572–74; Weld, *Travels Through the States of North America and the Provinces of Lower Canada,* 72. • amount of land: David Stuart to George Washington, Hope Park, February 26, 1792, in *PGWP,* vol. 9. • "A house": George Washington to the Commissioners for the District of Columbia, Philadelphia, March 3, 1793, in *PGWP,* vol. 12. • grown comfortable: James Thomas Flexner, *George Washington: Anguish and Farewell, 1793–*

1799 (Boston: Little, Brown, 1972), 330. • "whistle": George Washington to John Augustine Washington, Camp in the Great Meadows, Pennsylvania, May 31, 1754, in *PGWCL,* vol. 1. • screams: Rosemarie Zagarri, ed., *David Humphreys' "Life of General Washington" with George Washington's "Remarks"* (Athens: University of Georgia Press, 1991), 14–18; Joseph J. Ellis, *His Excellency: George Washington* (New York: Vintage Books, 2005), 53–58. • "I will": George Washington to Lafayette, Mount Vernon, February 1, 1784, in *PGWCF,* vol. 1. • bodies: John W. Wayland, *The Washingtons and Their Homes* (Baltimore: Clearfield, 1944; Baltimore: Genealogical Publishing, 1998), 10–14. • lips: George Washington to John Greenwood, Philadelphia, January 20, 1797, in *WGW,* 35:370–71; George Washington to John Greenwood, Philadelphia, January 25, 1797, in *WGW,* 35:374–75; Bernhard Wolf Weinberger, *An Introduction to the History of Dentistry in America: Washington's Need for Medical and Dental Care; Houdon's Life Mask Versus His Portraitures* (St. Louis: C. V. Mosby, 1948), 2:296–334; Chernow, *Washington,* 437–39, 568, 642–44, and 821; Custis, *Recollections and Private Memoirs of Washington,* 482 and 520; Thomas Jefferson, Conversation with Washington, July 10, 1792, in *PGWP,* vol. 10; Edmund Randolph, *A Vindication of Edmund Randolph* (Philadelphia, 1795; Richmond: Charles H. Wynne, 1855), 75; Nicholls, "Lady Henrietta Liston's Journal of Washington's 'Resignation,' Retirement, and Death," 515–16; J. H. Mason Knox Jr., "The Medical History of George Washington, His Physicians, Friends and Advisers," *Bulletin of the Institute of the History of Medicine* 1, no. 5 (June 1933): 179. • "His memory": Thomas Jefferson, Memorandum of Conversations with Washington, March 1, 1792, in *PGWP,* vol. 10. • blur: George Washington to David Rittenhouse, Newburgh, February 16, 1783, in *WGW,* 26:136–37; Arnebeck, *Through a Fiery Trial,* 192 and 594–96. • "The remainder": George Washington to Henry Knox, Philadelphia, March 2, 1797, in *WGW,* 35:409–10. • "public theatre": George Washington to James Anderson, Mount Vernon, July 25, 1798, in *PGWR,* vol. 2. • final sentence: Freeman, *George Washington,* 6:xxxv and xlii–xliii. • "no information": Douglas Southall Freeman, *R. E. Lee* (New York: Charles Scribner's Sons, 1934; Safety Harbor, FL: Simon Publications, 2001), 1:ix and xiv. Freeman often strayed from the rule that had guided his earlier work while writing about Washington.

Chapter One: Private Life

"a large": Elizabeth Willing Powel to George Washington, Philadelphia, March 11, 1797, in *PGWR*, vol. 1. For background on the Powels, see David W. Maxey, *A Portrait of Elizabeth Willing Powel, 1743–1830* (Philadelphia: American Philosophical Society, 2006). • "Suppose": Elizabeth Willing Powel to George Washington, Philadelphia, March 11, 1797, in *PGWR*, vol. 1. • "radiant": Maxey, *A Portrait of Elizabeth Willing Powel*, 17–19, 27, 29–30, 35–36, and 38–39. For the yellow fever, see J. H. Powell, *Bring Out Your Dead: The Great Plague of Yellow Fever in Philadelphia in 1793* (Philadelphia: University of Pennsylvania Press, 1993). • "no propriety": Elizabeth Willing Powel to George Washington, September 9, 1793, in *PGWP*, vol. 14. • mourned: Flexner, *George Washington: Anguish and Farewell*, 100; Maxey, *A Portrait of Elizabeth Willing Powel*, 38. • "good likeness": Nicholas B. Wainwright, "The Powel Portrait of Washington by Joseph Wright," *Pennsylvania Magazine of History and Biography* 96, no. 4 (October 1972): 419–23. For details of

Washington's appearance, see Custis, *Recollections and Private Memoirs of Washington*, 484 and 527; Weld, *Travels Through the States of North America and the Provinces of Lower Canada*, 86n. • "flattery": Elizabeth Willing Powel, "Sketch of a Panegyric of General Washington," Powel Family Papers, HSP. • "abilities": Elizabeth Willing Powel to George Washington, Philadelphia, November 17, 1792, in *PGWP*, vol. 11. • fleeting glimpse: Robert F. Dalzell Jr. and Lee Baldwin Dalzell, *George Washington's Mount Vernon: At Home in Revolutionary America* (New York: Oxford University Press, 1998), 6–11; George Washington to William Pearce, Philadelphia, November 14, 1796, in *WGW*, 35:279–80; Joseph Manca, *George Washington's Eye: Landscape, Architecture, and Design at Mount Vernon* (Baltimore: Johns Hopkins University Press, 2012), 52. • "I am once": George Washington to James Anderson, Mount Vernon, April 7, 1797, in *PGWR*, vol. 1. • "No estate": George Washington to Arthur Young, Philadelphia, December 12, 1793, in *PGWP*, vol. 14. • "woodland": George Washington, Advertisement, Philadelphia, February 1, 1796, in *PGWP*, vol. 19. • "going fast": George Washington to Oliver Wolcott Jr., Mount

Vernon, May 15, 1797, in *PGWR,* vol. 1. For details of the disrepair, see George Washington to Tobias Lear, Mount Vernon, March 25, 1797, in *PGWR,* vol. 1; George Washington to Elizabeth Willing Powel, Mount Vernon, March 26, 1797, in *PGWR,* vol. 1. • "I am already": George Washington to James McHenry, Mount Vernon, April 3, 1797, in *PGWR,* vol. 1. • memory back: George Washington to George Lewis, Mount Vernon, April 9, 1797, in *PGWR,* vol. 1; Chernow, *Washington,* 7; Dalzell and Dalzell, *George Washington's Mount Vernon,* 30–31, 43, 47–53, and 104–11. • "At no": George Washington to Thomas Pinckney, Mount Vernon, May 28, 1797, in *PGWR,* vol. 1. • "Mrs. Washington's": George Washington to William Pearce, Philadelphia, November 20, 1796, in *WGW,* 35:286. For the private staircase and sunrise, see Dalzell and Dalzell, *George Washington's Mount Vernon,* 16 and 201; Custis, *Recollections and Private Memoirs of Washington,* 162–63 and 527–28. • "If my": George Washington to James McHenry, Mount Vernon, May 29, 1797, in *PGWR,* vol. 1. • hoecakes: Eleanor Parke Custis Lewis to Elizabeth Bordley Gibson, February 23, 1823, MV; Julian Ursyn Niemcewicz, "Acute Observations: From Domestic Pursuits to Concern for the

Nation," in Jean B. Lee, ed., *Experiencing Mount Vernon: Eyewitness Accounts, 1784–1865* (Charlottesville: University of Virginia Press, 2006), 82. • "This over": George Washington to James McHenry, Mount Vernon, May 29, 1797, in *PGWR,* vol. 1. • twenty miles: James Thomas Flexner, *George Washington and the New Nation, 1783–1793* (Boston: Little, Brown, 1970), 42. • "broad-brimmed": Custis, *Recollections and Private Memoirs of Washington,* 168–69. For the cancer, see George Washington to Thomas Pinckney, Philadelphia, February 25, 1795, in *PGWP,* vol. 17. • "No pursuit": George Washington to James Anderson, Philadelphia, December 24, 1795, in *PGWP,* vol. 19. • "eye-sore": George Washington to William Augustine Washington, Mount Vernon, April 5, 1798, in *PGWR,* vol. 2. • diversifying: Freeman, *George Washington,* 3:117, 152, 195–96, and 242; Edward G. Lengel, *First Entrepreneur: How George Washington Built His — and the Nation's — Prosperity* (Boston: Da Capo, 2016), 154–55. • "It is more": George Washington to Anthony Whitting, Philadelphia, December 2, 1792, in *PGWP,* vol. 11. • "I am really": George Washington to William Pearce, Philadelphia, December 21, 1794, in *PGWP,* vol. 17. • "In nothing":

George Washington to William Pearce, Philadelphia, January 18, 1795, in *PGWP,* vol. 17. • "What kind": George Washington to William Pearce, Philadelphia, March 8, 1795, in *PGWP,* vol. 17. • "in scarcely": George Washington to Anthony Whitting, Philadelphia, October 14, 1792, in *PGWP,* vol. 11. • "Lost labor": Henry Wiencek, *An Imperfect God: George Washington, His Slaves, and the Creation of America* (New York: Farrar, Straus and Giroux, 2003), 95–96 and 123–24. • "to the grown": George Washington to William Pearce, Philadelphia, November 29, 1795, in *PGWP,* vol. 19. • "[not] an ounce": George Washington to Anthony Whitting, Philadelphia, May 26, 1793, in *PGWP,* vol. 12. • "no ambition": George Washington to Arthur Young, June 18, 1792, in *PGWP,* vol. 10. • surname: Philip D. Morgan, " 'To Get Quit of Negroes': George Washington and Slavery," *Journal of American Studies* 39, no. 3 (December 2005): 409. • "my people": George Washington to William Pearce, Philadelphia, November 29, 1795, in *PGWP,* vol. 19. • "master's eye": George Washington to Arthur Young, June 18, 1792, in *PGWP,* vol. 10. For the whip, see George Washington to Anthony Whitting, Philadelphia, January 20, 1793, in *PGWP,* vol. 12. • decreased the demand: Ellis, *His Excellency,* 165 and 258. • "hauling": James Anderson, Farm Reports, April 2–8, 1797, *PGWR,* vol. 1; James Anderson, Farm Reports, April 9–15, 1797, *PGWR,* vol. 1; James Anderson, Farm Reports, April 16–22, 1797, *PGWR,* vol. 1; James Anderson, Farm Reports, April 23–29, 1797, *PGWR,* vol. 1. For other details, see Lengel, *First Entrepreneur,* 65–66; Dennis J. Pogue, *Founding Spirits: George Washington and the Beginnings of the American Whiskey Industry* (Buena Vista, VA: Harbour Books, 2011), 80–89; George Washington to John Sinclair, Mount Vernon, July 15, 1797, in *PGWR,* vol. 1. • chain of command: Mary V. Thompson, " 'I Never See That Man Laugh to Show His Teeth': Relationships Between Whites and Blacks at George Washington's Mount Vernon," Mount Vernon Ladies' Association, 1995, online, 2–3; Wiencek, *An Imperfect God,* 98–99. • "plebeian": Flexner, *George Washington and the New Nation,* 47–49. • sheep: George Washington to William Pearce, Philadelphia, May 25, 1794, in *PGWP,* vol. 16; George Washington to Harry Dorsey Gough, Mount Vernon, August 23, 1797, in *PGWR,* vol. 1. • hurry his horse: Custis, *Recollections and Private Memoirs of Washington,* 169 and 446. • "servants": George Washington to

George Washington Parke Custis, Mount Vernon, January 7, 1798, in *PGWR,* vol. 2. • "I rarely": George Washington to James McHenry, Mount Vernon, May 29, 1797, in *PGWR,* vol. 1. • "may be compared": George Washington to Mary Ball Washington, Mount Vernon, February 15, 1787, *PGWCF,* vol. 5. • table stocked: Dalzell and Dalzell, *George Washington's Mount Vernon,* 191–98; Custis, *Recollections and Private Memoirs of Washington,* 169; John Greenwood to George Washington, New York, December 28, 1798, in *PGWR,* vol. 3. • mouth shut: Thompson, " 'I Never See That Man Laugh to Show His Teeth,' " 17; Freeman, *George Washington,* 3:6; Benjamin Henry Latrobe, "Washington Has Something Uncommonly Majestic and Commanding in His Walk, His Address, His Figure and His Countenance," in Lee, ed., *Experiencing Mount Vernon,* 60–66; Eleanor Parke Custis Lewis to Jared Sparks, Woodlawn, February 26, 1833, in Jared Sparks, *The Life of George Washington* (Boston: Ferdinand Andrews, 1839), 2:522; Chernow, *Washington,* 482 and 580–81; George Washington to George Washington Parke Custis, Philadelphia, November 28, 1796, Custis Family Papers, VHS; Hamilton B. Staples, "A Day at Mount Vernon, in 1797," in *Proceedings of the American Antiquarian Society* (Worcester: Charles Hamilton, 1879), 74–77; Elkanah Watson, "Two of the Richest Days of My Life," in Lee, ed., *Experiencing Mount Vernon,* 23; Niemcewicz, "Acute Observations: From Domestic Pursuits to Concern for the Nation," 74 and 80–82. • "All our friends!": Custis, *Recollections and Private Memoirs of Washington,* 169. • to the study: George Washington to James McHenry, Mount Vernon, May 29, 1797, in *PGWR,* vol. 1; George Washington to Timothy Pickering, Mount Vernon, April 28, 1797, in *PGWR,* vol. 1; Flexner, *George Washington: Anguish and Farewell,* 379. • "a piece": George Washington to Howell Lewis, Philadelphia, August 11, 1793, in *PGWP,* vol. 13. • "Having gone": George Washington to William Pearce, Germantown, August 31, 1794, in *PGWP,* vol. 16. • "where and how": George Washington, February 1768, in *DGW,* vol. 2. For Washington's obsession with preserving paper, see W. W. Abbot, "An Uncommon Awareness of Self: The Papers of George Washington," in Don Higginbotham, ed., *George Washington Reconsidered* (Charlottesville: University Press of Virginia, 2001), 278–82; Flexner, *George Washington: The Forge of Experience,* 20–

23; George Washington to William Charles Cole Claiborne, Mount Vernon, May 30, 1797, in *PGWR,* vol. 1. • "voluminous": George Washington to James McHenry, Mount Vernon, April 3, 1797, in *PGWR,* vol. 1. • Drooping: George Washington to James McHenry, Mount Vernon, May 29, 1797, in *PGWR,* vol. 1. • "serious alarm": George Washington to Elizabeth Willing Powel, Mount Vernon, March 26, 1797, in *PGWR,* vol. 1. • "one thing": George Washington to Sarah Cary Fairfax, Camp at Fort Cumberland, September 12, 1758, in *PGWCL,* vol. 6. For background on Sally, see Peter R. Henriques, *Realistic Visionary: A Portrait of George Washington* (Charlottesville: University of Virginia Press, 2006), 72–73. • "misunderstand": George Washington to Sarah Cary Fairfax, Camp at Rays Town, September 25, 1758, in *PGWCL,* vol. 6. • "the fine tales": George Washington to Elizabeth Parke Custis, Germantown, September 14, 1794, in *PGWP,* vol. 16. • found "friendship": George Washington to Elizabeth Willing Powel, Mount Vernon, March 26, 1797, in *PGWR,* vol. 1. • dined alone: George Washington to Tobias Lear, Mount Vernon, July 31, 1797, in *PGWR,* vol. 1. • "More permanent": George Washington to Armand, Mount Vernon, August 10, 1786, in *PGWCF,* vol. 4. • "unless prevented": George Washington to Lawrence Lewis, Mount Vernon, August 4, 1797, in *PGWR,* vol. 1. For the suppertime routine, see Custis, *Recollections and Private Memoirs of Washington,* 171 and 453; Eleanor Parke Custis Lewis to Elizabeth Bordley Gibson, February 23, 1823, MV. • "The history": George Washington to James McHenry, Mount Vernon, May 29, 1797, in *PGWR,* vol. 1. For the number of books, see Paul K. Longmore, *The Invention of George Washington* (Charlottesville: University of Virginia Press, 1999), 217. • "The melancholy": George Washington to George Lewis, Mount Vernon, April 9, 1797, in *PGWR,* vol. 1. • "Since I left": Eleanor Parke Custis to Elizabeth Bordley, Mount Vernon, March 18, 1797, in Brady, ed., *George Washington's Beautiful Nelly,* 31–32. • harpsichord: David L. Ribblett, *Nelly Custis: Child of Mount Vernon* (Mount Vernon: Mount Vernon Ladies' Association, 1993), 26 and 37–38. • "his lips": Eleanor Parke Custis Lewis to Jared Sparks, Woodlawn, February 26, 1833, in Sparks, *The Life of George Washington,* 2:522. For how the Custis children interpreted this gesture, see Custis, *Recollections and Private Memoirs of Washington,*

171. • flashbacks: George Washington to Henry Knox, Mount Vernon, February 20, 1784, in *PGWCF,* vol. 1. • first recollection: Ribblett, *Nelly Custis,* 2–4. • "the most affectionate": Eleanor Parke Custis to Elizabeth Bordley, Hope Park, October 19, 1795, in Brady, ed., *George Washington's Beautiful Nelly,* 21. For Washington's refusal to accept legal guardianship, see Freeman, *George Washington,* 5:401n–2n; George Washington to Bartholomew Dandridge, Newburgh, April 20, 1782, in *WGW,* 24:139–41. • envy: Eliza Parke Custis to David Bailie Warden, April 20, 1808, in William D. Hoyt Jr., "Self-Portrait: Eliza Custis, 1808," *Virginia Magazine of History and Biography* 53, no. 2 (April 1945): 96–97; Eleanor Calvert Custis Stuart to Tobias Lear, Abingdon, July 8, 1789, MV; Eleanor Calvert Custis Stuart to Tobias Lear, Abingdon, October 8, 1789, MV. • "Everything appears": Eleanor Parke Custis to Elizabeth Bordley, Mount Vernon, March 18, 1797, in Brady, ed., *George Washington's Beautiful Nelly,* 31. • "Grandmama [had]": Lee, "Memoir of George Washington Parke Custis," 38. • a rigorous: Martha Washington to Fanny Bassett Washington, Philadelphia, November 22, 1794, in Fields, ed., *"Worthy*

Partner," 281; George Washington to Tobias Lear, Philadelphia, November 16, 1796, in *WGW,* 35:284–85; George Washington Parke Custis to George Washington, Nassau Hall, March 25, 1797, in *PGWR,* vol. 1; George Washington to George Washington Parke Custis, Mount Vernon, April 3, 1797, in *PGWR,* vol. 1. • Tub: Murray H. Nelligan, *Old Arlington: The Story of the Lee Mansion National Memorial* (Columbia University Dissertation, 1953), 32. For Wash's physical description, see Lee, "Memoir of George Washington Parke Custis," 72; Martha Washington to Fanny Bassett Washington, Philadelphia, December 15, 1794, in Fields, ed., *"Worthy Partner,"* 282; Chernow, *Washington,* 421. • "My dearest": Eleanor Parke Custis to Elizabeth Bordley, Washington, April 24, 1797, in Brady, ed., *George Washington's Beautiful Nelly,* 33. • "Eleanor": Eleanor Parke Custis to Elizabeth Bordley, Hope Park, March 30, 1796, in Brady, ed., *George Washington's Beautiful Nelly,* 26. • raising children: Eleanor Parke Custis to Elizabeth Bordley, Mount Vernon, March 18, 1797, in Brady, ed., *George Washington's Beautiful Nelly,* 31. • "adopted brother": Ribblett, *Nelly Custis,* 40–41. • "danger": Eleanor Parke Custis to Elizabeth

Bordley, Hope Park, October 19, 1795, in Brady, ed., *George Washington's Beautiful Nelly,* 23. • loved dancing: Eleanor Parke Custis to Elizabeth Bordley, Hope Park, March 30, 1796, in Brady, ed., *George Washington's Beautiful Nelly,* 26; Custis, *Recollections and Private Memoirs of Washington,* 143–44. 32• "ladies": George Washington to Eleanor Parke Custis, Philadelphia, March 21, 1796, in *PGWP,* vol. 19. For Washington's interest in counting "ladies," see Chernow, *Washington,* 612–13 and 653. • eligible men: George Washington to Elizabeth Washington Lewis, Philadelphia, April 7, 1796, in *WGW,* 35:15. • "Men and women": George Washington to Eleanor Parke Custis, Philadelphia, March 21, 1796, in *PGWP,* vol. 19. • subscriptions: Ellis, *His Excellency,* 243; George Washington to Tobias Lear, Chester, March 9, 1797, in *PGWR,* vol. 1. • "strong and coarse": George Washington to David Stuart, Philadelphia, January 8, 1797, in *WGW,* 35:360. • "a rallying": Eric Burns, *Infamous Scribblers: The Founding Fathers and the Rowdy Beginnings of American Journalism* (New York: Public Affairs, 2006), 340 and 434. • "refused": James McHenry to George Washington, Philadelphia, March 24, 1797, in *PGWR,* vol. 1; Timothy Pickering to George Washington, Philadelphia,

April 5, 1797, in *PGWR,* vol. 1. For the Directory, see Hibbert, *The Days of the French Revolution,* 282; Jay Winik, *The Great Upheaval: America and the Birth of the Modern World, 1788–1800* (New York: Harper, 2007), 410. • "The conduct": George Washington to James McHenry, Mount Vernon, April 3, 1797, in *PGWR,* vol. 1. • "It was": George Washington to Mary White Morris, Mount Vernon, May 1, 1797, in *PGWR,* vol. 1. For the lost opportunity, see Tobias Lear to George Washington, Philadelphia, March 15, 1797, in *PGWR,* vol. 1; George Washington to Bartholomew Dandridge, Mount Vernon, April 3, 1797, in *PGWR,* vol. 1. • "second-rate": Alexander Hamilton to George Washington, New York, November 5, 1795, in *PGWP,* vol. 19. For Washington's approval of Adams keeping the cabinet, see Ferling, *John Adams,* 333; Carroll and Ashworth, *George Washington,* 7:443. • "friends": George Washington to Charles Cotesworth Pinckney, Philadelphia, August 24, 1795, in *PGWP,* vol. 18. For excluding Republicans and for the many refusals, see George Washington to Timothy Pickering, Mount Vernon, September 27, 1795, in *PGWP,* vol. 18; George Washington to Alexander Hamilton, Philadelphia, October 29, 1795, in *PGWP,* vol. 19; Elkins and Mc-

Kitrick, *The Age of Federalism,* 625–30. •
"No apology": George Washington to James
McHenry, Mount Vernon, April 3, 1797, in
PGWR, vol. 1. • "in the course": George
Washington to Oliver Wolcott Jr., Mount
Vernon, May 29, 1797, in *PGWR,* vol. 1. •
"Let me pray": George Washington to James
McHenry, Mount Vernon, April 3, 1797, in
PGWR, vol. 1. • "Every good": George
Washington to Oliver Wolcott Jr., Mount
Vernon, May 15, 1797, in *PGWR,* vol. 1.

Chapter Two: Place in History
"detained": Timothy Pickering, "Report of
the Secretary of State Respecting the Depredations on the Commerce of the United
States, Since the First of October, 1796," in
American State Papers: Foreign Relations
(Washington, DC: Gales and Seaton, 1832),
2:28–29 and 57–62. For background on
Pickering, see Gerard H. Clarfield, *Timothy
Pickering and the American Republic* (Pittsburgh: University of Pittsburgh Press,
1980). • "scene": Timothy Pickering to John
Adams, Department of State, May 1, 1797,
in Adams Family Papers, reel 384, MHS. •
one remedy: Gerard H. Clarfield, *Timothy
Pickering and American Diplomacy, 1795–
1800* (Columbia: University of Missouri
Press, 1969), 96–101; Timothy Pickering to

Alexander Hamilton, Philadelphia, March 26, 1797, in *PAH,* vol. 20. • would return: Clarfield, *Timothy Pickering and the American Republic,* 183–84; Octavius Pickering and Charles W. Upham, *The Life of Timothy Pickering* (Boston: Little, Brown, 1873), 3:367. • Republican leanings: Clarfield, *Timothy Pickering and American Diplomacy,* 52–57, 109–10; DeConde, *Entangling Alliance,* 342–44, 371–87, and 438–44; DeConde, *The Quasi-War,* 17 and 23. • "extremely slow": Timothy Pickering, "Washington," August 19, 1818, in Timothy Pickering Papers, reel 46, MHS. • conspired: Timothy Pickering, "Franklin," May 8, 1827, in Timothy Pickering Papers, reel 46, MHS. • glasses: Clarfield, *Timothy Pickering and the American Republic,* 6–7 and 35. • "So extremely": John Adams to Benjamin Rush, Quincy, April 22, 1812, in Biddle, ed., *Old Family Letters,* 380. • improved: Timothy Pickering to Richard Peters, City of Washington, January 5, 1811, in Timothy Pickering Papers, reel 14, MHS. • "saw that": Timothy Pickering, "Washington," September 21, 1825, in Timothy Pickering Papers, reel 46, MHS. • what Adams needed: Clarfield, *Timothy Pickering and American Diplomacy,* 109–11; Elkins and McKitrick, *The Age of*

Federalism, 555–56. • "An Anglo": *New York Minerva,* May 2, 1797, in *PTJ,* vol. 29. For background on the letter, see Editorial Note: Jefferson's Letter to Philip Mazzei, in *PTJ,* vol. 29. • "There is no": Timothy Pickering, *Letters Addressed to the People of the United States of America, on the Conduct of the Past and Present Administrations of the American Government, Towards Great Britain and France* (London, 1811), 68. • "patriotism": Timothy Pickering, "Washington," August 19, 1818, in Timothy Pickering Papers, reel 46, MHS. • "I am told": Timothy Pickering to Noah Webster, Philadelphia, May 19, 1797, Noah Webster Papers, New York Public Library, online. For more about what Pickering did with the original, see Editorial Note: Jefferson's Letter to Philip Mazzei, in *PTJ,* vol. 29; *Gazette of the United States,* May 31, 1797. • "It is not": Thomas Jefferson to Edward Rutledge, Philadelphia, June 24, 1797, in *PTJ,* vol. 29. • had suffered: Joseph J. Ellis, *American Sphinx: The Character of Thomas Jefferson* (New York: Vintage Books, 1996), 57–58; Malone, *Jefferson and the Ordeal of Liberty,* 299. • "military preparations": Thomas Jefferson to James Madison, Philadelphia, May 18, 1797, in *PTJ,* vol. 20. For Bonaparte's victories, see James Madison to Thomas Jefferson, Philadelphia, February 11, 1797, in *PTJ,* vol. 29; Thomas Jefferson to James Madison, Philadelphia, June 8, 1797, in *PTJ,* vol. 29; Doyle, *The Oxford History of the French Revolution,* 211–16. • cabinet deliberations: Thomas Jefferson to James Madison, Monticello, January 22, 1797, in *PTJ,* vol. 29; Thomas Jefferson to Thomas Mann Randolph, Monticello, March 23, 1797, in *PTJ,* vol. 29; Thomas Jefferson to Volney, Monticello, April 9, 1797, in *PTJ,* vol. 29; Ellis, *American Sphinx,* 161–62; Malone, *Jefferson and the Ordeal of Liberty,* 221–38. • "disavow": Thomas Jefferson to James Madison, Monticello, August 3, 1797, in *PTJ,* vol. 29. For passing Mount Vernon, see Thomas Jefferson, 1797, in *Jefferson's Memorandum Books,* vol. 2., ed. James A. Bear Jr. and Lucia C. Stanton (Princeton: Princeton University Press, 1997), 960. • "harlot": Thomas Jefferson to Philip Mazzei, Monticello, April 24, 1796, in *PTJ,* vol. 29. For Jefferson's objections, see Thomas Jefferson to James Madison, Monticello, August 3, 1797, in *PTJ,* vol. 29. • "I must": Thomas Jefferson to James Madison, Monticello, August 3, 1797, in *PTJ,* vol. 29. • contemporaneously: Editorial Note: The "Anas," in *PTJ,* vol. 22;

Thomas Jefferson, Explanations of the Three Volumes Bound in Marbled Paper, February 4, 1818, in *The Papers of Thomas Jefferson: Retirement Series,* vol. 12, ed. J. Jefferson Looney (Princeton: Princeton University Press, 2015), 416–29. • "fervor": Thomas Jefferson, Explanations of the Three Volumes Bound in Marbled Paper, February 4, 1818, in *The Papers of Thomas Jefferson: Retirement Series,* 12:416–29. • "gentlemen": Thomas Jefferson, Notes on Ceremonial at New York, June 10, 1793, in *PTJ,* vol. 26. • visiting hour: Chernow, *Washington,* 576–78. • "The President of": Thomas Jefferson, Notes on Levees and Assumption, February 16, 1793, in *PTJ,* vol. 25. • "He had been": Thomas Jefferson, Notes of a Conversation with George Washington, February 7, 1793, in *PTJ,* vol. 25. • Constitutional Convention: Thomas Jefferson to George Washington, Philadelphia, May 23, 1792, in *PGWP,* vol. 10; Thomas Jefferson to George Washington, Monticello, September 9, 1792, in *PGWP,* vol. 11; Thomas Jefferson, Explanations of the Three Volumes Bound in Marbled Paper, February 4, 1818, in *The Papers of Thomas Jefferson: Retirement Series,* 12:416–29; Thomas Jefferson, Notes of a Conversation with Alexander Hamilton, August 13, 1791, in *PTJ,* vol. 22. • "assumption": Thomas Jefferson, Account of the Bargain on the Assumption and Residence Bills, [1792], in *PTJ,* vol. 17. For northern speculation in state debt, see Elkins and McKitrick, *The Age of Federalism,* 138. • "I was duped": Thomas Jefferson to George Washington, Monticello, September 9, 1792, in *PGWP,* vol. 11. • "commerce": Thomas Jefferson to George Washington, Philadelphia, May 23, 1792, in *PGWP,* vol. 10. • "corruption": Thomas Jefferson, Notes of a Conversation with George Washington, July 10, 1792, in *PTJ,* vol. 24. • "monarchical": Thomas Jefferson to George Washington, Philadelphia, May 23, 1792, in *PGWP,* vol. 10. • "merchants": Thomas Jefferson to James Monroe, Philadelphia, June 4, 1793, in *PTJ,* vol. 26. • new party: Thomas Jefferson to George Washington, Philadelphia, May 23, 1792, in *PGWP,* vol. 10. • "As to": Thomas Jefferson, Notes of a Conversation with George Washington, Bladensburg, October 1, 1792, in *PTJ,* vol. 24. • "really": Thomas Jefferson, Notes of a Conversation with George Washington, July 10, 1792, in *PTJ,* vol. 24. • embarrassing: Thomas Jefferson, Notes of a Conversation with George Washington, Bladensburg, October 1, 1792, in *PTJ,* vol. 24. • "careless": Thomas Jefferson,

Notes of a Conversation with George Washington, July 10, 1792, in *PTJ,* vol. 24. For another example of Jefferson doubting Washington's comprehension, see Thomas Jefferson, Notes on a Conversation with Tobias Lear and John Beckley, in *PTJ,* vol. 25. • "coalesce": Thomas Jefferson, Notes of a Conversation with George Washington, February 7, 1793, in *PTJ,* vol. 25. • geographic: Thomas Jefferson to George Washington, Philadelphia, May 23, 1792, in *PGWP,* vol. 10. • "valedictory": Thomas Jefferson to William Johnson, Monticello, June 12, 1823, in Thomas Jefferson, "Letters from Thomas Jefferson to Judge William Johnson," *South Carolina Historical and Genealogical Magazine* 1, no. 1 (January 1900): 6. • "confidence": Thomas Jefferson, Notes of a Conversation with George Washington, Bladensburg, October 1, 1792, in *PTJ,* vol. 24; Thomas Jefferson, Notes of a Conversation with George Washington, February 7, 1793, in *PTJ,* vol. 25. • "tremble": Thomas Jefferson, Notes of Cabinet Meeting on the President's Address and Messages to Congress, November 28, 1793, in *PTJ,* vol. 27. • "republic": Thomas Jefferson, Notes of a Conversation with George Washington, May 23, 1793, in *PTJ,* vol. 26. For France as a republic, see Hibbert, *The*

Days of the French Revolution, 180–81. • "I never": Thomas Jefferson, Memoranda of Consultations with the President, March 11, 1792–April 9, 1792, in *PTJ,* vol. 23. For the newspaper bias, see Thomas Jefferson to George Washington, Monticello, September 9, 1792, in *PGWP,* vol. 11. • "There was more": Thomas Jefferson, Notes of a Conversation with George Washington, May 23, 1793, in *PTJ,* vol. 26. • heart of the American: Thomas Jefferson to James Monroe, Philadelphia, May 5, 1793, in *PTJ,* vol. 25. • "unanimity": Thomas Jefferson, Notes of Cabinet Meetings on Edmond Charles Genet and the President's Address to Congress, November 18, 1793, in *PTJ,* vol. 27. For Jefferson's views on how decisions emerged from Washington's cabinet meetings, see Malone, *Jefferson and the Ordeal of Liberty,* 85–86; Thomas Jefferson, Notes on the Sinking Fund and the Proclamation of Neutrality, May 7, 1793, in *PTJ,* vol. 25; Thomas Jefferson to James Madison, May 27, 1793, in *PTJ,* vol. 26; Thomas Jefferson to James Madison, Philadelphia, August 11, 1793, in *PTJ,* vol. 26. • "plump": Thomas Jefferson, Notes of Cabinet Meeting on Edmond Charles Genet, August 20, 1793, in *PTJ,* vol. 26. • "fool": Thomas Jefferson, Notes on Washington's Questions on Neutrality and the Alliance with France, May 6, 1793, in *PTJ,* vol. 25. • "jury": Thomas Jefferson, Notes of Cabinet Meeting on Edmond Charles Genet, August 1, 1793, in *PTJ,* vol. 26. • "chameleon": Thomas Jefferson to James Madison, Philadelphia, August 11, 1793, in *PTJ,* vol. 26. • "a gladiator": Thomas Jefferson to James Madison, January 22, 1797, in *PTJ,* vol. 29. • "Met again": Thomas Jefferson, Notes of Cabinet Meeting on Edmond Charles Genet, August 2, 1793, in *PTJ,* vol. 26. For the original, see Thomas Jefferson Papers, LOC. For background on Democratic Societies, see Wood, *Empire of Liberty,* 162–64. • "where the laws": Thomas Jefferson, Notes of a Conversation with George Washington, August 6, 1793, in *PTJ,* vol. 26. • "the check": Thomas Jefferson, Notes of a Conversation with George Washington, Bladensburg, October 1, 1792, in *PTJ,* vol. 24. • "infernal": Malone, *Thomas Jefferson and the Ordeal of Liberty,* 189; Thomas Jefferson to James Madison, Monticello, December 28, 1794, in *PTJ,* vol. 28. For background on the Whiskey Rebellion, see William Hogeland, *The Whiskey Rebellion: George Washington, Alexander Hamilton, and the Frontier Rebels Who Challenged America's Newfound Sovereignty* (New York: Simon & Schuster, 2006).

• "the greatest man": Jon Meacham, *Thomas Jefferson: The Art of Power* (New York: Random House, 2013), 260. For Hamilton staying with the army, see James Madison to Thomas Jefferson, Philadelphia, November 16, 1794, in *PTJ,* vol. 28. • blamed: James Madison to Thomas Jefferson, Philadelphia, November 30, 1794, in *PTJ,* vol. 28. • "It is wonderful": Thomas Jefferson to James Madison, Monticello, December 28, 1794, in *PTJ,* vol. 28. • "the firm": Thomas Jefferson, Explanations of the Three Volumes Bound in Marbled Paper, February 4, 1818, in *The Papers of Thomas Jefferson: Retirement Series,* 12:416–29. • "really nothing": Wood, *Empire of Liberty,* 198–99. • Randolph told: Randolph, *A Vindication of Edmund Randolph,* 19–29 and 37–41; Thomas Jefferson to James Monroe, Monticello, March 2, 1796, in *PTJ,* vol. 29; Malone, *Jefferson and the Ordeal of Liberty,* 248; Ron Chernow, *Alexander Hamilton* (New York: Penguin Books, 2004), 489–90. • "Nothing can": Thomas Jefferson to James Monroe, July 10, 1796, in *PTJ,* vol. 29. • reassured himself: Malone, *Jefferson and the Ordeal of Liberty,* 306–7; Editorial Note: Jefferson's Letter to Philip Mazzei, in *PTJ,* vol. 29. • "a separation": Thomas Jefferson,

Notes of a Conversation with Edmund Randolph, in *PTJ,* vol. 28. • "His mind": Thomas Jefferson to Archibald Stuart, Monticello, January 4, 1797, in *PTJ,* vol. 29. • "intriguer[s]": Thomas Jefferson to George Washington, Monticello, June 19, 1796, in *PTJ,* vol. 29. • dine: Thomas Jefferson, Notes on Conversations with John Adams and George Washington, *PTJ,* vol. 29; George Washington to Thomas Jefferson, Mount Vernon, July 6, 1796, in *PTJ,* vol. 29. • "It would be": Thomas Jefferson to James Madison, Monticello, August 3, 1797, in *PTJ,* vol. 29. • Gerry: Thomas Jefferson to Elbridge Gerry, Philadelphia, June 21, 1797, in *PTJ,* vol. 29; Thomas Jefferson, Notes on Conversations with John Adams and George Washington, *PTJ,* vol. 29; Malone, *Jefferson and the Ordeal of Liberty,* 316. • "drag out": Elkins and McKitrick, *The Age of Federalism,* 555–56 and 566–67. • "threw off": Martha Washington to Elizabeth Willing Powel, Mount Vernon, July 14, 1797, in Fields, ed., *"Worthy Partner,"* 306. • whereabouts: George Washington to Frederick Kitt, Mount Vernon, January 10, 1798, in *PGWR,* vol. 2. • "nothing of cooking": Martha Washington to Elizabeth Willing Powel, Mount Vernon, May 1, 1797, in Fields, ed., *"Worthy Partner,"* 301–2.

• "who was brought": George Washington to Oliver Wolcott Jr., September 1, 1796, in *WGW,* 35:201–2. • ghostwriter: Editorial Note, Martha Washington to Elizabeth Willing Powel, Mount Vernon, May 1, 1797, in Fields, ed., *"Worthy Partner,"* 302; Fields, ed., *"Worthy Partner,"* xxxi. • "another slave": George Washington to George Lewis, Mount Vernon, November 13, 1797, in *PGWR,* vol. 1. • "It is": George Washington to Robert Lewis, Mount Vernon, August 17, 1799, in *PGWR,* vol. 4. • "quit": Morgan, " 'To Get Quit of Negroes,' " 416. • "selling negroes": George Washington to Alexander Spotswood, Philadelphia, November 23, 1794, in *PGWP,* vol. 17. • "get quit": Morgan, " 'To Get Quit of Negroes,' " 416. • "Shame!": Dorothy Twohig, " 'That Species of Property': Washington's Role in the Controversy over Slavery," in Higginbotham, ed., *George Washington Reconsidered,* 115 and 129. • "unfortunate": Morgan, " 'To Get Quit of Negroes,' " 422. • "cream": *Claypoole's American Daily Advertiser,* February 10, 1796. For the questions that arose, see Tobias Lear to George Washington, Washington, March 2, 1796, in *PGWP,* vol. 19. • "not . . . [his]": George Washington to William Pearce, Philadelphia, March 13, 1796, in *PGWP,* vol. 19. • "something better": George Washington to Arthur Young, Philadelphia, November 9, 1794, in *PGWP,* vol. 17. • "private": Editorial Note, George Washington to Tobias Lear, Philadelphia, May 6, 1794, in *PGWP,* vol. 16. • hiring themselves: George Washington to Arthur Young, December 12, 1793, in *PGWP,* vol. 14; George Washington to Arthur Young, Philadelphia, November 9, 1794, in *PGWP,* vol. 17. • no tenants: George Washington to Stephen Milburn, Mount Vernon, May 15, 1797, in *PGWR,* vol. 1. • "slovenly": George Washington to William Pearce, Philadelphia, February 7, 1796, in *PGWP,* vol. 19. • all control: George Washington, Lease Terms, February 1, 1796, in *PGWP,* vol. 19; George Washington to James Anderson, Federal City, May 22, 1798, in *PGWR,* vol. 2. • slave marriages: Morgan, " 'To Get Quit of Negroes,' " 407 and 421; Jonathan Horn, *The Man Who Would Not Be Washington: Robert E. Lee's Civil War and His Decision That Changed American History* (New York: Scribner, 2015), 71–72; Chernow, *Washington,* 79–80; Brady, *Martha Washington,* 52–54; George Washington to William Pearce, Philadelphia, January 27, 1796, in *PGWP,* vol. 19. For the survey results, the author has relied on Morgan's numbers, which presumably are similar to

Washington's. • "When it is": George Washington to David Stuart, Philadelphia, February 7, 1796, in *PGWP,* vol. 19. • Virginia law: Mary V. Thompson, " 'They Appear to Live Comfortable Together': Private Life of the Mount Vernon Slaves" (Lecture, Mount Vernon, November 3, 1994), 2–3. • feared discussing: George Washington, March 1790, in *DGW,* vol. 6. • "ill-judged": George Washington to David Stuart, New York, June 15, 1790, in *PGWP,* vol. 5. For the Union breaking up, see David Stuart to George Washington, Abingdon, March 15, 1790, in *PGWP,* vol. 5. • "What would": George Washington to David Stuart, New York, March 28, 1790, in *PGWP,* vol. 5. • national census: Joseph J. Ellis, *Founding Brothers: The Revolutionary Generation* (New York: Vintage Books, 2000), 89–90 and 102; Robert Middlekauff, *The Glorious Cause: The American Revolution, 1763–1789* (New York: Oxford University Press, 2005), 571–72. • "higher": George Washington to John Sinclair, Philadelphia, December 11, 1796, in *WGW,* 35:328. • "soul that": George Washington to Lawrence Lewis, Mount Vernon, August 4, 1797, in *PGWR,* vol. 1. • first elective: Chernow, *Washington,* 88–89. • "mixed": George Washington to Tobias Lear, Philadelphia, December 14,

1794, in *PGWP,* vol. 17. • "problematical": George Washington to Charles Lee, December 27, 1796, in *WGW,* 35:349. • "the tone": George Washington to Edward Carrington, Philadelphia, May 1, 1796, in *WGW,* 35:31. • "characters": George Washington to Alexander Hamilton, Philadelphia, May 15, 1796, in *PAH,* vol. 20. • "It would not be": George Washington to Thomas Jefferson, Mount Vernon, July 6, 1796, in *PTJ,* vol. 29. • "lessen": George Washington to Alexander Hamilton, Philadelphia, May 15, 1796, in *PAH,* vol. 20. • "friends": George Washington, First Draft for an Address, in Victor Hugo Paltsits, ed., *Washington's Farewell Address* (New York: New York Public Library, 1935), 164. • "allusions": George Washington to Alexander Hamilton, Philadelphia, May 15, 1796, in *PAH,* vol. 20. • "studied": George Washington to Alexander Hamilton, Philadelphia, July 3, 1795, in *PGWP,* vol. 18. For Washington's difficulty finding information, see George Washington to Edmund Randolph, Philadelphia, October 21, 1795, in *PGWP,* vol. 19. • "ashamed": George Washington to Alexander Hamilton, Philadelphia, July 13, 1795, in *PGWP,* vol. 18. • "possess": George Washington to James McHenry, Mount Vernon, July 29, 1798, in *PGWR,* vol. 2. •

"the disinterested": *Claypoole's American Daily Advertiser,* September 19, 1796. • "pretensions": George Washington to Alexander Hamilton, Philadelphia, May 15, 1796, in *PAH,* vol. 20. • "lastingly": Alexander Hamilton to George Washington, New York, July 30, 1796, in *PAH,* vol. 20. • "cherish": *Claypoole's American Daily Advertiser,* September 19, 1796. • "True Americans": George Washington to Thomas Pinckney, Mount Vernon, May 28, 1797, in *PGWR,* vol. 1. • "All will": George Washington to William Heath, Mount Vernon, May 20, 1797, in *PGWR,* vol. 1. • "no party man": George Washington to Thomas Jefferson, Mount Vernon, July 6, 1796, in *PTJ,* vol. 29. • "Think": *Claypoole's American Daily Advertiser,* September 19, 1796. • "United States": George Washington, Facsimile of the Final Manuscript, in Paltsits, ed., *Washington's Farewell Address,* 136. • "unacquainted": Martha Washington to Elizabeth Willing Powel, Mount Vernon, July 14, 1797, in Fields, ed., *"Worthy Partner,"* 305–6. • "break": George Washington to George Lewis, Mount Vernon, November 13, 1797, in *PGWR,* vol. 1. • "If Hercules": George Washington to Frederick Kitt, Mount Vernon, January 10, 1798, in *PGWR,* vol. 2. • French princes: Louis-Philippe, *Di-*

ary of My Travels in America, trans. Stephen Becker (New York: Delacorte, 1977), 2–4 and 31–33. • small for: Dalzell and Dalzell, *George Washington's Mount Vernon,* 136, 138, and 267n; George Washington to William Pearce, Mount Vernon, October 27, 1793, in *PGWP,* vol. 14; George Washington, Slave List, June 1799, in *PGWR,* vol. 4; George Washington, February 1786, in *DGW,* vol. 4; Louis-Philippe, *Diary of My Travels in America,* 32. Louis-Philippe describing the young woman as a six-year-old has led many to assume that she was eleven-year-old Delia, the youngest child of Hercules and Lame Alice. The author believes it is far more likely that the prince mistook Delia's slightly older sister Eve or Evey for a six-year-old given that she was said by Washington to be "a dwarf" on the 1799 slave list. • "deeply upset": Louis-Philippe, *Diary of My Travels in America,* 32. • shiny shoes: Editorial Note, George Washington to Tobias Lear, Mount Vernon, September 17, 1790, in *PGWP,* vol. 6; Custis, *Recollections and Private Memoirs of Washington,* 422–24; Tobias Lear to George Washington, Philadelphia, June 5, 1791, in *PGWP,* vol. 8; George Washington, Memorandum, Philadelphia, November 5, 1796, in *WGW,* 35:265; George Washington to

William Pearce, Philadelphia, November 14, 1796, in *WGW,* 35:279; Erica Armstrong Dunbar, *Never Caught: The Washingtons' Relentless Pursuit of Their Runaway Slave, Ona Judge* (New York: Atria, 2017), 73. • "I am very": Louis-Philippe, *Diary of My Travels in America,* 32. • her late mother: George Washington, February 1786, in *DGW,* vol. 4; Dunbar, *Never Caught,* 72.

Chapter Three: Sons of the Childless

"honesty": *Claypoole's American Daily Advertiser,* September 19, 1796. For other examples, see George Washington to Edward Newenham, Mount Vernon, August 6, 1797, in *PGWR,* vol. 1. • "Ashamed": George Washington to George Washington Parke Custis, Mount Vernon, June 4, 1797, in *PGWR,* vol. 1. • "My very": George Washington Parke Custis to George Washington, Nassau Hall, May 29, 1797, in *PGWR,* vol. 1. • "consistent": George Washington Parke Custis to George Washington, Nassau Hall, July 1, 1797, in *PGWR,* vol. 1. • "usual": George Washington to George Washington Parke Custis, Mount Vernon, July 10, 1797, in *PGWR,* vol. 1. • "At no": George Washington to George Washington Parke Custis, Mount Vernon, July 23, 1797, in *PGWR,* vol. 1. • "Endeavor": George

Washington to George Washington Parke Custis, Philadelphia, November 15, 1796, in Custis, *Recollections and Private Memoirs of Washington,* 74. • "select": George Washington to George Washington Parke Custis, Philadelphia, November 28, 1796, Custis Family Papers, VHS. • "no society": George Washington to George Washington Parke Custis, Philadelphia, February 27, 1797, in *WGW,* 35:403. • "course of reading": George Washington to George Washington Parke Custis, Philadelphia, December 19, 1796, Custis Family Papers, VHS. • most worried: Nelligan, *Old Arlington,* 40–41. • "You are now": George Washington to George Washington Parke Custis, Philadelphia, November 28, 1796, Custis Family Papers, VHS. • "assurances": George Washington to George Washington Parke Custis, Philadelphia, January 11, 1797, in Custis, *Recollections and Private Memoirs of Washington,* 79–80. • "was not": Augusta Blanche Berard to Mother and Sisters, Pelham Priory, April 18, 1856, in Clayton Torrence, "Arlington and Mount Vernon, 1856," *Virginia Magazine of History and Biography* 57, no. 2 (April 1949): 162. • "a useful": George Washington to George Washington Parke Custis, Philadelphia, November 28, 1796, Custis Family Papers, VHS. • Capitol: Nelligan, *Old Arlington,* 39; *Philadelphia Federal Gazette,* September 27, 1793; Eliza Parke Custis to David Bailie Warden, Philadelphia, September 8, 1814, Custis-Lee Family Papers, LOC. • "manly frame": Custis, *Recollections and Private Memoirs of Washington,* 171 and 527–28. • "much embarrassed": George Washington Parke Custis to George Washington, Nassau Hall, July 30, 1797, in *PGWR,* vol. 1. For renting the house, see Edward Lawler Jr., "The President's House in Philadelphia: The Rediscovery of a Lost Landmark," *Pennsylvania Magazine of History and Biography* 126, no. 1 (January 2002): 24n. • dark-eyed: Jean Edward Smith, *John Marshall: Definer of a Nation* (New York: Henry Holt, 1996), 4, 21, and 187–89; John Marshall to Mary W. Marshall, Alexandria, June 24, 1797, in *The Papers of John Marshall,* vol. 3, ed. William C. Stinchcombe and Charles T. Cullen (Chapel Hill: University of North Carolina Press, 1979), 92. • "Worthy": George Washington to Charles Cotesworth Pinckney, Mount Vernon, June 24, 1797, in *PGWR,* vol. 1. • "one or two": George Washington to Edward Carrington, Mount Vernon, June 26, 1797, in *PGWR,* vol. 1. • seeing Europe: Flexner, *George Washington: The Forge of*

Experience, 18. • "Little or no": George Washington, July 1797, in *DGW,* vol. 6. • "I perceive": George Washington to Samuel Washington, Mount Vernon, July 12, 1797, in *PGWR,* vol. 1. • "clear": George Washington to Henry Lee, Mount Vernon, September 8, 1797, in *PGWR,* vol. 1. • quarterly: Chernow, *Washington,* 552; Carroll and Ashworth, *George Washington,* 7:320–22; Tagg, "Benjamin Franklin Bache's Attack on George Washington," 212–15; Freeman, *George Washington,* 6:194–95 and 225; Flexner, *George Washington: Anguish and Farewell,* 371. For "advances," see Editorial Note, Alexander Hamilton to George Washington, New York, October 26, 1795, in *PAH,* vol. 19. • Dividends: George Washington, Ledger C, *The George Washington Financial Papers Project,* ed. Jennifer E. Stertzer et al. (Charlottesville: Washington Papers, 2017), online; George Washington, Schedule of Property, Mount Vernon, July 9, 1799, in *PGWR,* vol. 4; Freeman, *George Washington,* 6:59. • "support themselves": George Washington to James Anderson, Mount Vernon, September 16, 1798, in *PGWR,* vol. 3. For the balance sheet that Washington would later receive for 1797, see Pogue, *Founding Spirits,* 109. • patience: George Washington to Presley Nevill, Philadelphia, June 16, 1794, in *PGWP*, vol. 16; George Washington, Schedule of Property, Mount Vernon, July 9, 1799, in *PGWR*, vol. 4. • "the money": George Washington to Henry Lee, Mount Vernon, April 2, 1797, in *PGWR*, vol. 1. For being averse to litigation, see George Washington to Israel Shreve, Mount Vernon, September 1, 1797, in *PGWR*, vol. 1. • bank loans: George Washington to William Herbert, Mount Vernon, September 1, 1799, in *PGWR*, vol. 4; George Washington to Alexander Addison, Mount Vernon, November 24, 1799, in *PGWR*, vol. 4; Flexner, *George Washington: Anguish and Farewell,* 118. • "Debt": George Washington to Samuel Washington, Mount Vernon, July 12, 1797, in *PGWR*, vol. 1. • close friend: Martha Washington to Elizabeth Willing Powel, Mount Vernon, July 14, 1797, in Fields, ed., *"Worthy Partner,"* 306; Bordewich, *Washington,* 24–25 and 220–21; Custis, *Recollections and Private Memoirs of Washington,* 325. • "repugnance": Arnebeck, *Through a Fiery Trial,* 172–78 and 261–62. For how Washington remembered this, see George Washington to Daniel Carroll, Philadelphia, January 7, 1795, in *PGWP*, vol. 17. • "self-interest": Edward J. Larson, *The Return of George Washington: Uniting the States, 1783–1789* (New York:

William Morrow, 2014), 58. • brick houses: Arnebeck, *Through a Fiery Trial,* 193, 447, and 452. • "a disagreeable": Charles Rappleye, *Robert Morris: Financier of the American Revolution* (New York: Simon & Schuster, 2010), 504. • "Appearances": George Washington, July 1797, in *DGW,* vol. 6. For twelve miles, see George Washington, Advertisement, Philadelphia, February 1, 1796, in *PGWP,* vol. 19. • "doubts": Staples, "A Day at Mount Vernon, in 1797," 76. • "One wing": George Washington to David Humphreys, Mount Vernon, June 26, 1797, in *PGWR,* vol. 1. For the first bridge and the position of Little Falls, see Donald Beekman Myer, *Bridges and the City of Washington* (Washington, DC: United States Commission of Fine Arts, 1974), 3; Tobias Lear, Observations on the Potomac River, November 3, 1793, in *PGWP,* vol. 14. • "Went by": George Washington, July 1797, in *DGW,* vol. 6. • still-unfinished: Corra Bacon-Foster, "Early Chapters in the Development of the Potomac Route to the West," *Records of the Columbia Historical Society* 15 (1912): 181–86; Tobias Lear, Observations on the Potomac River, November 3, 1793, in *PGWP,* vol. 14; Flexner, *George Washington: Anguish and Farewell,* 368–69; Achenbach,

The Grand Idea, 121–37; Larson, *The Return of George Washington,* 55–61 and 279; Louis-Philippe, *Diary of My Travels in America,* 29–30. • "Mercury at 76": George Washington, July 1797, in *DGW,* vol. 6. • "I am alone": George Washington to Tobias Lear, Mount Vernon, July 31, 1797, in *PGWR,* vol. 1. For background on Lear, see Ray Brighton, *The Checkered Career of Tobias Lear* (Portsmouth, NH: Portsmouth Marine Society, 1985), 16, 24, and 112–13. • "my family": George Washington to John Laurens, City Tavern, August 5, 1777, in *PGWRW,* vol. 10. • Humphreys would join: George Washington to David Humphreys, Philadelphia, June 12, 1796, in *WGW,* 35:92; Zagarri, ed., *David Humphreys' "Life of General Washington" with George Washington's "Remarks,"* xiv–xxii and xxvii–xxxi; Jedidiah Morse, *The American Geography, or A View of the Present Situation of the United States* (Elizabethtown, NJ, 1789), 127–32. For evidence that Washington was aware that Humphreys had anonymously published portions of the book in Morse's *The American Geography,* see George Washington to Richard Henderson, Mount Vernon, June 19, 1788, in *PGWCF,* vol. 6; Jedidiah Morse to George Washington, Charlestown,

June 25, 1793, in *PGWP,* vol. 13. • "annihilated": George Washington to David Humphreys, Mount Vernon, June 26, 1797, in *PGWR,* vol. 1. • "As both": George Washington to Lawrence Lewis, Mount Vernon, August 4, 1797, in *PGWR,* vol. 1. For Lawrence Lewis's date of birth, see Wayland, *The Washingtons and Their Homes,* 55. • "Clear with": George Washington, August 1797, in *DGW,* vol. 6. • Corruption charges: Editorial Note, Oliver Wolcott Jr. to Alexander Hamilton, July 3, 1797, in *PAH,* vol. 21; Chernow, *Alexander Hamilton,* 528–32. • "Not for any": George Washington to Alexander Hamilton, Mount Vernon, August 21, 1797, in *PGWR,* vol. 1. • Only recently: George Washington to James McHenry, Mount Vernon, August 14, 1797, in *PGWR,* vol. 1. • "Great appearances": George Washington, September 1797, in *DGW,* vol. 6. • "The charge": Alexander Hamilton, Printed Version of the "Reynolds Pamphlet," 1797, in *PAH,* vol. 21. • stop sending: George Washington to Philip Freneau, Mount Vernon, July 5, 1797, in *PGWR,* vol. 1; George Washington to James McHenry, Mount Vernon, August 14, 1797, in *PGWR,* vol. 1; James McHenry to George Washington, near Downingston, October 2, 1797, in *PGWR,* vol. 1; George Washington to Clement Biddle, Mount Vernon, September 15, 1797, in *PGWR,* vol. 1. • "Clear & very warm": George Washington, October 1797, in *DGW,* vol. 6. • "various acts": Nelligan, *Old Arlington,* 43. • less than a year: Martha Washington to Elizabeth Dandridge Henley, Mount Vernon, August 20, 1797, in Fields, ed., *"Worthy Partner,"* 307. • "upbraid": George Washington to Samuel Stanhope Smith, Mount Vernon, October 9, 1797, in *PGWR,* vol. 1. • family tradition: Zagarri, ed., *David Humphreys' "Life of General Washington" with George Washington's "Remarks,"* 6; Chernow, *Washington,* 9–12 and 18; George Washington to George Washington Parke Custis, Mount Vernon, July 23, 1797, in *PGWR,* vol. 1. • "many of": James Madison, Conversations with Washington, May 5–25, 1792, in *PGWP,* vol. 10. • "From his": George Washington to Samuel Stanhope Smith, Mount Vernon, May 24, 1797, in *PGWR,* vol. 1. • coddled: Martha Washington to Fanny Bassett, Mount Vernon, February 25, 1788, in Fields, ed., *"Worthy Partner,"* 206; Flexner, *George Washington: The Forge of Experience,* 261–69; Lee, "Memoir of George Washington Parke Custis," 34 and 38. For Washington's concerns about young Virginians being spoiled, see Zagarri, ed., *David*

Humphreys' *"Life of George Washington"* with *George Washington's "Remarks,"* 6. • "is bound": Editorial Note, Tobias Lear to George Washington, Philadelphia, April 3, 1791, in *PGWP,* vol. 8. • "a heart-rending": George Washington to David Stuart, Mount Vernon, January 22, 1798, in *PGWR,* vol. 2. • national university: George Washington to St. George Tucker, Mount Vernon, May 30, 1797, in *PGWR,* vol. 1; Arnebeck, *Through a Fiery Trial,* 411; Eugene E. Prussing, *The Estate of George Washington, Deceased* (Boston: Little, Brown, 1927), 173–90; George Washington to Edmund Randolph, Philadelphia, December 15, 1794, in *PGWP,* vol. 17. • "Cold & frosty": George Washington, October 1797, in *DGW,* vol. 6. • "authentic": George Washington to Alexander Hamilton, Mount Vernon, October 8, 1797, in *PGWR,* vol. 1. • "It will": George Washington to Timothy Pickering, Mount Vernon, December 11, 1797, in *PGWR,* vol. 1. • "delicate": George Washington to Lafayette, Mount Vernon, October 8, 1797, in *PGWR,* vol. 1. • "leaped for": A. A. Parker, *Recollections of General Lafayette on His Visit to the United States, in 1824 and 1825* (Keene, NH: Sentinel, 1879), 99–100. • hung the key: Staples, "A Day at Mount Vernon, in 1797," 74; A. Levasseur, *La-*

fayette in America in 1824 and 1825; or, Journal of a Voyage to the United States, trans. John D. Godman, vol. 1 (Philadelphia: Carey and Lea, 1829), 182. For the Bastille being torn down, see Unger, Lafayette, 240. • "is a tribute": Lafayette to George Washington, Paris, March 17, 1790, in PGWP, vol. 5. • peel: George Washington to Lafayette, Mount Vernon, July 25, 1785, in PGWCF, vol. 3; George Washington to William Pearce, Philadelphia, May 22, 1796, in WGW, 35:67; Niemcewicz, "Acute Observations: From Domestic Pursuits to Concern for the Nation," 71–72. • "rags": Philadelphia Gazette, February 11, 1797. • imprisoned her: Lasteyrie, Life of Madame de Lafayette, 161 and 264–322; Jason Lane, General and Madame de Lafayette: Partners in Liberty's Cause in the American and French Revolutions (Lanham, MD: Taylor, 2003), 205–11 and 219; Unger, Lafayette, 286–90; Laura Auricchio, The Marquis: Lafayette Reconsidered (New York: Vintage Books, 2014), 268–69. • "I cannot": Marquise de Lafayette to George Washington, Chavaniac near Brioude, March 12, 1793, in PGWP, vol. 12. • "I send you my": Lasteyrie, Life of Madame de Lafayette, 312–22. • "Treat him": Unger, Lafayette, 45–46 and 214. • "perfect love":

George Washington to Lafayette, West Point, September 30, 1779, in *PGWRW*, vol. 22. • named: Unger, *Lafayette*, 107–8. • "second father": Editorial Note, Felix Frestel to George Washington, Boston, August 31, 1795, in *PGWP*, vol. 18; Georges Washington Lafayette to George Washington, Boston, August 31, 1795, in *PGWP*, vol. 18. • third party: George Washington to George Cabot, Philadelphia, September 7, 1795, in *PGWP*, vol. 18; George Washington to Georges Washington Lafayette, Philadelphia, November 22, 1795, in *PGWP*, vol. 19. • "a thousand": Felix Frestel to George Washington, New York, December 25, 1795, in *PGWP*, vol. 19. • "to stand": George Washington to Georges Washington Lafayette, Philadelphia, November 22, 1795, in *PGWP*, vol. 19. • "The idea": Alexander Hamilton to George Washington, New York, November 26, 1795, in *PGWP*, vol. 19. • eat: Alexander Hamilton to George Washington, New York, December 24, 1795, in *PGWP*, vol. 19; Georges Washington Lafayette to George Washington, March 28, 1796, in *PGWP*, vol. 19. • understood: George Washington to Lafayette, Mount Vernon, October 8, 1797, in *PGWR*, vol. 1. • "public character": George Washington to Alexander Hamilton, Philadelphia, November 23, 1795, in *PGWP,* vol. 19. • "I have": Georges Washington Lafayette to George Washington, New York, October 22, 1797, in *PGWR,* vol. 1. • stop in Princeton: George Washington to Samuel Stanhope Smith, Mount Vernon, October 9, 1797, in *PGWR,* vol. 1; Georges Washington Lafayette and Felix Frestel to George Washington, New York, October 21, 1797, in *PGWR,* vol. 1. • wilderness: Eleanor Parke Custis to Elizabeth Bordley, Mount Vernon, November 23, 1797, in Brady, ed., *George Washington's Beautiful Nelly,* 43. • "an earlier": George Washington to Georges Washington Lafayette, Mount Vernon, December 5, 1797, in *PGWR,* vol. 1. • Liston: Henrietta Liston to James Jackson, 1796, in Perkins, "A Diplomat's Wife in Philadelphia," 605; Henrietta Liston to James Jackson, Norfolk, December 8, 1797, in Perkins, "A Diplomat's Wife in Philadelphia," 614; George Washington, November 1797, in *DGW,* vol. 6; George Washington, December 1797, in *DGW,* vol. 6; Eleanor Parke Custis to Elizabeth Bordley, Mount Vernon, November 23, 1797, in Brady, ed., *George Washington's Beautiful Nelly,* 43; George Washington to Bushrod Washington, Mount Vernon, November 3, 1797, in *PGWR,* vol. 1; Frederick Kitt to George Washington, Philadelphia,

January 15, 1798, in *PGWR*, vol. 2. • "exceedingly": George Washington to Bushrod Washington, Mount Vernon, October 23, 1797, in *PGWR*, vol. 1. • "apoplectic": Martha Washington to Elizabeth Willing Powel, Mount Vernon, December 17, 1797, in *PGWR*, vol. 1. • piazza: Flexner, *George Washington: Anguish and Farewell*, 391; Custis, *Recollections and Private Memoirs of Washington*, 171. • "It is time": George Washington to Oliver Wolcott Jr., Mount Vernon, December 17, 1797, in *PGWR*, vol. 1. • "Complete": John Marshall to George Washington, The Hague, September 15, 1797, in *PGWR*, vol. 1. For more background on the coup, see Doyle, *The Oxford History of the French Revolution*, 329–31; Hibbert, *The Days of the French Revolution*, 294–98. • laugh: George Washington to John Marshall, Mount Vernon, December 4, 1797, in *PGWR*, vol. 1. • "quit politics": George Washington to William Vans Murray, Mount Vernon, December 3, 1797, in *PGWR*, vol. 1. • "I shall": George Washington to James Anderson, Mount Vernon, December 21, 1797, in *PGWR*, vol. 1. • "doubt": James Craik to George Washington, December 1, 1797, in *PGWR*, vol. 1. For the deal, see Carroll and Ashworth, *George Washington*, 7:485–86. • "experienced": Richard Parkinson to George Washington, Doncaster, August 28, 1797, in *PGWR*, vol. 1. • Scotsman: Pogue, *Founding Spirits*, 111–16. • "trifles": George Washington to James Anderson, Mount Vernon, December 21, 1797, in *PGWR*, vol. 1. • "Now & then": George Washington to George Washington Parke Custis, Mount Vernon, January 7, 1798, in *PGWR*, vol. 2. • "misspend": George Washington to David Stuart, Mount Vernon, January 22, 1798, in *PGWR*, vol. 2. • "opulent": Zagarri, ed., *David Humphreys' "Life of General Washington" with George Washington's "Remarks,"* 6. • "in cannon": John Nicholas to George Washington, Charlottesville, November 18, 1797, in *PGWR*, vol. 1. For Washington not knowing Nicholas's profession, see George Washington to Bushrod Washington, Mount Vernon, March 8, 1798, in *PGWR*, vol. 2. • "unclaimed": John Nicholas to George Washington, Charlottesville, November 18, 1797, in *PGWR*, vol. 1. For background on Nicholas, see Manning J. Dauer, "The Two John Nicholases: Their Relationship to Washington and Jefferson," *American Historical Review* 45, no. 2 (January 1940): 342–48; V. Dennis Golladay, "Jefferson's 'Malignant Neighbor,' John Nicholas, Jr.," *Virginia*

Magazine of History and Biography 86, no. 3 (July 1978): 306–19. • "an old": John Nicholas to George Washington, Charlottesville, November 18, 1797, in *PGWR,* vol. 1. • "I know not": George Washington to John Nicholas, Mount Vernon, November 30, 1797, in *PGWR,* vol. 1. • attacks: John Langhorne to George Washington, Warren, Albemarle County, September 25, 1797, in *PGWR,* vol. 1. • "If they": George Washington to John Nicholas, Mount Vernon, November 30, 1797, in *PGWR,* vol. 1. • "entertaining": John Nicholas to George Washington, Charlottesville, December 9, 1797, in *PGWR,* vol. 1.

Chapter Four: Secret Letters
Prune Street: Thomas Law, Diary for 1798, Thomas Law Papers, LOC; Arnebeck, *Through a Fiery Trial,* 455, 467, and 469–70. For background on Law, see Bordewich, *Washington,* 171–74; Allen C. Clark, *Greenleaf and Law in the Federal City* (Washington, DC: W. F. Roberts, 1901), 223–44. • "prize": Thomas Law, "A Family Picture," October 11, 1832, Thomas Law Papers, LOC. For the marriage and background on Betsey, see Clark, *Greenleaf and Law in the Federal City,* 236–37; Arnebeck, *Through a Fiery Trial,* 347; Custis, *Recollections and Private*

Memoirs of Washington, 37. For Law wishing for Washington's esteem, see Thomas Law to Dear Brother, Mount Vernon, December 15, 1799, in Thomas Law, "Thomas Law's Description of the Last Illness and Death of George Washington," *Mount Vernon Ladies' Association of the Union: Annual Report, 1972* (1973): 30. • dinner party: Abigail Adams to Mary Smith Cranch, Philadelphia, February 21, 1798, in *APAFC,* vol. 12; Abigail Adams to Thomas Boylston Adams, Philadelphia, March 18, 1798, in *APAFC,* vol. 12; Thomas Jefferson to Thomas Willing, February 23, 1798, in *PTJ,* vol. 30; Custis, *Recollections and Private Memoirs of Washington,* 364–66. • "What would": *Philadelphia Aurora General Advertiser,* February 23, 1798. • "ignobly": Thomas Law, Diary for 1798, Thomas Law Papers, LOC. • "ardent": Hoyt, "Self-Portrait: Eliza Custis, 1808," 95. For Law struggling to soothe, see Thomas Law, "A Family Picture," October 11, 1832, Thomas Law Papers, LOC. • "It would mortify": Clark, *Greenleaf and Law in the Federal City,* 242–43. For more evidence of Betsey's irritation, see William Cranch to Abigail Adams, Washington, March 12, 1798, in *APAFC,* vol. 12. • cabinet secretaries: Abigail Adams to William Smith, Philadelphia, February 28, 1798, in *APAFC,* vol. 12; Thomas Jefferson to James Madison, March 2, 1798, in *PTJ,* vol. 30. • inquiry: George Washington to William Augustine Washington, Mount Vernon, February 27, 1798, in *PGWR,* vol. 2; Editorial Note, William Augustine Washington to George Washington, Haywood, March 23, 1798, in *PGWR,* vol. 2; Martha Washington to Elizabeth Willing Powel, Mount Vernon, December 17, 1797, in *PGWR,* vol. 1. • "paid very": George Washington to Isaac Heard, Philadelphia, May 2, 1792, in *PGWP,* vol. 10. • "inscriptions": George Washington to William Augustine Washington, Mount Vernon, February 27, 1798, in *PGWR,* vol. 2. • family Bible: Washington Family Bible Page, MV, online; George Washington, February 1798, in *DGW,* vol. 6; *Baltimore Telegraphe and Daily Advertiser,* February 17, 1798; Eleanor Parke Custis to Elizabeth Bordley, Mount Vernon, March 20, 1798, in Brady, ed., *George Washington's Beautiful Nelly,* 46–47. • "under the": John Nicholas to George Washington, Charlottesville, February 22, 1798, in *PGWR,* vol. 2. • helped draft: John Nicholas to George Washington, Charlottesville, February 22, 1798, in *PGWR,* vol. 2. • "after several": George Washington, Comments on Monroe's *A View of the Conduct of the Executive of the United States,* 1798, in *PGWR,* vol. 2. • Bache to publish: DeConde, *Entangling Alliance,* 383–87. • mailed: Timothy Pickering to George Washington, Philadelphia, January 20, 1798, in *PGWR,* vol. 2. • "embarrassment": James Monroe, *A View of the Conduct of the Executive, in the Foreign Affairs of the United States* (Philadelphia: Benjamin Franklin Bache, 1797), iii–lxvi. • "None but": George Washington, Comments on Monroe's *A View of the Conduct of the Executive of the United States,* 1798, in *PGWR,* vol. 2. • response built: George Washington to Timothy Pickering, Mount Vernon, February 6, 1798, in *PGWR,* vol. 2; Editorial Note, George Washington, Comments on Monroe's *A View of the Conduct of the Executive of the United States,* 1798, in *PGWR,* vol. 2. • "self-importance": George Washington, Comments on Monroe's *A View of the Conduct of the Executive of the United States,* 1798, in *PGWR,* vol. 2. • "death warrant": Timothy Pickering to George Washington, Philadelphia, January 20, 1798, in *PGWR,* vol. 2. • "overturn": John Nicholas to George Washington, Charlottesville, February 22, 1798, in *PGWR,* vol. 2. • "Nothing short": George Washington to John Nicholas, Mount Vernon, March 8, 1798, in *PGWR,* vol. 2. • sixty degrees: George Washington, March 1798, in *DGW,* vol. 6. • "[Nicholas] seems": George Washington to Bushrod Washington, Mount Vernon, March 8, 1798, in *PGWR,* vol. 2. For background on Bushrod, see Wayland, *The Washingtons and Their Homes,* 285–87. • "Misrepresentation": George Washington to Alexander White, Mount Vernon, March 1, 1798, in *PGWR,* vol. 2. • "surprise": George Washington to Alexander White, Mount Vernon, March 1, 1798, in *PGWR,* vol. 2. • fuss: William Cranch to Abigail Adams, Washington, March 12, 1798, in *APAFC,* vol. 12. • "high-toned": George Washington to David Stuart, New York, July 26, 1789, in *PGWP,* vol. 3. • financial support: Arnebeck, *Through a Fiery Trial,* 463–70; Alexander White to George Washington, Washington, January 8, 1798, in *PGWR,* vol. 2; Alexander White to George Washington, February 1, 1798, in *PGWR,* vol. 2; William C. di Giacomantonio, "All the President's Men: George Washington's Federal City Commissioners," *Washington History* 3, no. 1 (Spring/Summer 1991): 65–70. • "an uncommon": Alexander White to George Washington, Philadelphia, February 20, 1798, in *PGWR,* vol. 2. • "he had a":

Alexander White to George Washington, Philadelphia, March 10, 1798, in *PGWR,* vol. 2. • "reverse": George Washington to Alexander White, Mount Vernon, March 25, 1798, in *PGWR,* vol. 2. • monitoring: George Washington to Alexander White, Mount Vernon, March 1, 1798, in *PGWR,* vol. 2. • not satisfied: Oliver Wolcott Jr. to George Washington, Philadelphia, January 12, 1798, in *PGWR,* vol. 2; James McHenry to George Washington, Philadelphia, February 1, 1798, in *PGWR,* vol. 2; Timothy Pickering to George Washington, Philadelphia, March 10, 1798, in *PGWR,* vol. 2; George Washington to Oliver Wolcott Jr., Mount Vernon, January 22, 1798, in *PGWR,* vol. 2; George Washington to James McHenry, Mount Vernon, January 28, 1798, in *PGWR,* vol. 2; Abigail Adams to John Quincy Adams, Philadelphia, February 10, 1798, in *APAFC,* vol. 12; DeConde, *The Quasi-War,* 49 and 63–64. • "Are our": George Washington to James McHenry, Mount Vernon, March 4, 1798, in *PGWR,* vol. 2. • "We can only": DeConde, *The Quasi-War,* 66. • "some knowledge": Alexander White to George Washington, Philadelphia, March 17, 1798, in *PGWR,* vol. 2. • "It is": Abigail Adams to Mary Smith Cranch, March 20, 1798, in *APAFC,* vol. 12. • million: Abigail

Adams to Elizabeth Smith Shaw Peabody, Philadelphia, February 13, 1798, in *APAFC,* vol. 12. • "piratical": Abigail Adams to John Quincy Adams, Philadelphia, February 10, 1798, in *APAFC,* vol. 12. For the widened latitude, see DeConde, *The Quasi-War,* 53. • seeking war: Page Smith, *John Adams* (New York: Doubleday, 1962), 2:957–58. • "How different": Smith, *John Adams,* 2:958. • happily celebrated: Abigail Adams to John Adams, Quincy, March 1, 1797, in *APAFC,* vol. 12. • "Placing": Abigail Adams to William Smith, Philadelphia, February 28, 1798, in *APAFC,* vol. 12. • "The President of": Abigail Adams to Mary Smith Cranch, Philadelphia, February 15, 1798, in *APAFC,* vol. 12. • "The task": Abigail Adams to Mary Smith Cranch, Philadelphia, June 23, 1797, in *APAFC,* vol. 12. • begged: McCullough, *John Adams,* 479–82. • "cake": Abigail Adams to Mary Smith Cranch, Philadelphia, June 23, 1797, in *APAFC,* vol. 12. • uproar: Abigail Adams to Mary Smith Cranch, Philadelphia, June 3, 1797, in *APAFC,* vol. 12. • "Mr. Washington": John Adams to John Quincy Adams, East Chester, November 3, 1797, in *APAFC,* vol. 12. • "If my": George Washington to John Adams, February 20, 1797, quoted in Abigail Adams to John Quincy Adams, Quincy, March 3,

1797, in *APAFC,* vol. 12. • most sensitive: Abigail Adams to John Quincy Adams, East Chester, November 3, 1797, in *APAFC,* vol. 12. • repent: Abigail Adams to Mary Smith Cranch, April 4, 1798, in *APAFC,* vol. 12. • "No, not": Elkins and McKitrick, *The Age of Federalism,* 569–75; DeConde, *The Quasi-War,* 46–52 and 66–73. • "were struck": Abigail Adams to Mary Smith Cranch, April 4, 1798, in *APAFC,* vol. 12. • "real Americans": Abigail Adams to John Quincy Adams, Philadelphia, April 21, 1798, in *APAFC,* vol. 12. For the cockades, see Abigail Adams to Mary Smith Cranch, Philadelphia, April 13, 1798, in *APAFC,* vol. 12. • sent addresses: Abigail Adams to Mary Smith Cranch, Philadelphia, April 22, 1798, in *APAFC,* vol. 12. • "with a degree": Abigail Adams to John Quincy Adams, Philadelphia, April 13, 1798, in *APAFC,* vol. 12. • "it has been": Abigail Adams to Thomas Boylston Adams, Philadelphia, May 1, 1798, in *APAFC,* vol. 13. • "That was": Abigail Adams to Mary Smith Cranch, April 26, 1798, in *APAFC,* vol. 12. • treated Washington: Abigail Adams to William Smith, March 20, 1798, in *APAFC,* vol. 12. • "sedition bill": Abigail Adams to Mary Smith Cranch, April 26, 1798, in *APAFC,* vol. 12. • "richly": Abigail Adams to William

Smith, Philadelphia, November 21, 1797, in *APAFC,* vol. 12. • "old": Abigail Adams to Mary Smith Cranch, Philadelphia, April 28, 1798, in *APAFC,* vol. 12. • "to arms": McCullough, *John Adams,* 501. • "I never": Abigail Adams to Mary Smith Cranch, Philadelphia, May 20, 1798, in Stewart Mitchell, *New Letters of Abigail Adams, 1788–1801* (Boston: Houghton Mifflin, 1947), 178. • buff: Chernow, *Alexander Hamilton,* 17, 51, 501–2, 508, 548–49, 554–55, and 562–64; John Jay to Alexander Hamilton, Albany, April 19, 1798, in *PAH,* vol. 21; Alexander Hamilton, Uniform of the Army of the United States, December 1799, in *PAH,* vol. 24. • "There may": Alexander Hamilton to John Jay, New York, April 24, 1798, in *PAH,* vol. 21. • "invited to": Alexander Hamilton to George Washington, New York, June 2, 1798, in *PGWR,* vol. 2. • living quarters: Chernow, *Alexander Hamilton,* 91. • "I always": Alexander Hamilton to Philip Schuyler, Headquarters, New Windsor, February 18, 1781, in *PAH,* vol. 2. • "ill humor": Alexander Hamilton to James McHenry, New Windsor, February 18, 1781, in *PAH,* vol. 2. For Hamilton taking to the field, see Chernow, *Alexander Hamilton,* 159 and 162–65. • "The General is": Alexander Hamilton to Philip Schuyler, Headquarters, New Windsor, February 18, 1781, in *PAH,* vol. 2. • Newburgh: Chernow, *Alexander Hamilton,* 176–80; Larson, *The Return of George Washington,* 13–19. • "the crisis": Richard H. Kohn, "The Washington Administration's Decision to Crush the Whiskey Rebellion," *Journal of American History* 59, no. 3 (December 1972): 571. For urging Washington to accept the presidency, see Alexander Hamilton to George Washington, New York, September 1788, in *PGWP,* vol. 1. • serve a third: Alexander Hamilton to George Washington, New York, July 5, 1796, in *PAH,* vol. 20. • "habitual": Alexander Hamilton, "Letter from Alexander Hamilton, Concerning the Public Conduct and Character of John Adams, Esq. President of the United States," October 24, 1800, in *PAH,* vol. 25. For more about Hamilton's search for an alternative to Adams, see Chernow, *Alexander Hamilton,* 510–11; Pasley, *The First Presidential Contest,* 204–8. • be well: Chernow, *Alexander Hamilton,* 547. • "Mr. Adams never": Alexander Hamilton, "Letter from Alexander Hamilton, Concerning the Public Conduct and Character of John Adams, Esq. President of the United States," October 24, 1800, in *PAH*, vol. 25. For more about this "channel," see DeConde, *The Quasi-War*, 18–19, 22–23, and 64–65; Timothy Pickering to Alexander Hamilton, Philadelphia, March 25, 1798, in *PAH*, vol. 21. • "I am sure": James McHenry to Alexander Hamilton, Philadelphia, January 26, 1798, in *PAH*, vol. 21. • Mac: Karen E. Robbins, *James McHenry, Forgotten Federalist* (Athens: University of Georgia Press, 2013), 9 and 41. For Hamilton's view of McHenry, see Alexander Hamilton to George Washington, Philadelphia, July 29, 1798, in *PGWR*, vol. 2. • "A mitigated": Alexander Hamilton to James McHenry, New York, early 1798, in *PAH*, vol. 21. For "fortify," see Alexander Hamilton, "The Stand No. VI," New York, April 19, 1798, in *PAH*, vol. 21. • "many of": Alexander Hamilton, "The Stand No. I," New York, March 30, 1798, in *PAH*, vol. 21. • "On religious": Alexander Hamilton to James McHenry, New York, early 1798, in *PAH*, vol. 21. • "twenty gods": Wood, *Empire of Liberty*, 585–86. • "Of all": George Washington to the People of the United States, United States, September 17, 1796, in *Claypoole's American Daily Advertiser*, September 19, 1796. For Hamilton's authorship of the line, see Alexander Hamilton, "Original Major

Draft for an Address Called 'Copy Considerably Amended,' " in Paltsits, ed., *Washington's Farewell Address,* 192. • "[The address] seems": "Phocion No. X," *Gazette of the United States,* October 27, 1796. For Hamilton being "Phocion," see Chernow, *Alexander Hamilton,* 511–12. • "high priest": Alexander Hamilton, "The Stand No. VII," New York, April 21, 1798, in *PAH,* vol. 21. • militias: Alexander Hamilton, "The Stand No. VI," New York, April 19, 1798, in *PAH,* vol. 21; DeConde, *The Quasi-War,* 90–91. • "Experienced": Alexander Hamilton, "The Stand No. I," New York, March 30, 1798, in *PAH,* vol. 21. • deputy: Alexander Hamilton to George Washington, New York, June 2, 1798, in *PGWR,* vol. 2. • "misspent": George Washington to George Washington Parke Custis, Mount Vernon, May 10, 1798, in *PGWR,* vol. 2. • no interest: George Washington Parke Custis to George Washington, Annapolis, April 2, 1798, in *PGWR,* vol. 2; George Washington to George Washington Parke Custis, Mount Vernon, April 15, 1798, in *PGWR,* vol. 2; George Washington to Bartholomew Dandridge, Mount Vernon, January 25, 1799, in *PGWR,* vol. 3. • "perfectly federal": Eleanor Parke Custis to Elizabeth Bordley, Hope Park, May 14, 1798, in Brady, ed., *George Washington's*

Beautiful Nelly, 52. • "democratic murderers": Eleanor Parke Custis to Elizabeth Bordley, Mount Vernon, November 23, 1797, in Brady, ed., *George Washington's Beautiful Nelly,* 41. • "whiskers": Eleanor Parke Custis to Elizabeth Bordley, Hope Park, May 14, 1798, in Brady, ed., *George Washington's Beautiful Nelly,* 52. • "corruption": George Washington to James Lloyd, Mount Vernon, April 15, 1798, in *PGWR,* vol. 2. • "leaders": George Washington to Timothy Pickering, Mount Vernon, April 16, 1798, in *PGWR,* vol. 2. • "some": George Washington to James McHenry, Mount Vernon, March 27, 1798, in *PGWR,* vol. 2. • "humiliation": Editorial Note, George Washington, May 1798, in *DGW,* vol. 6. • "No one": George Washington to John Adams, Mount Vernon, June 17, 1798, in *PGWR,* vol. 2. For Washington's reaction to Adams basking, see Julian Ursyn Niemcewicz, *Under Their Vine and Fig Tree: Travels Through America in 1797–1799, 1805 with Some Further Account of Life in New Jersey,* trans. Metchie J. E. Budka (Elizabeth, NJ: Grassman, 1965), 107. • last resort: George Washington to James McHenry, Mount Vernon, May 6, 1798, in *PGWR,* vol. 2. • new financial: Arnebeck, *Through a Fiery Trial,* 477–78. • Visiting:

George Washington, May 1798, in *DGW,* vol. 6. • "The late": Thomas Law to George Washington, May 4, 1798, in *PGWR,* vol. 2. • "jealousy": George Washington to Thomas Law, Mount Vernon, May 7, 1798, in *PGWR,* vol. 2.

Chapter Five: The Once and Future Commander in Chief

"Five and": George Washington to Sarah Cary Fairfax, Mount Vernon, May 16, 1798, in *PGWR,* vol. 2. • "the object": George Washington to Sarah Cary Fairfax, Camp at Fort Cumberland, September 12, 1758, in *PGWCL,* vol. 6. • return home: Wilson Miles Cary, *Sally Cary: A Long Hidden Romance of Washington's Life* (New York: De Vinne, 1916), 5 and 44; George Washington to George William Fairfax, State of New York, July 10, 1783, in *WGW,* 27:57; Henriques, *Realistic Visionary,* 76. • "wondered often": George Washington to Sarah Cary Fairfax, Mount Vernon, May 16, 1798, in *PGWR,* vol. 2. • "During this": George Washington to Sarah Cary Fairfax, Mount Vernon, May 16, 1798, in *PGWR,* vol. 2. For surveying Alexandria, see Flexner, *George Washington: The Forge of Experience,* 41. • "spend": George Washington to Sarah Cary Fairfax, Mount Vernon, May 16, 1798, in *PGWR,* vol. 2. • the wind: George Washington, May 1798, in *DGW,* vol. 6. • "often": George Washington to Sarah Cary Fairfax, Mount Vernon, May 16, 1798, in *PGWR,* vol. 2. • "ruins": George Washington to George William Fairfax, Mount Vernon, February 27, 1785, in *PGWCF,* vol. 2. • "I feel": George Washington to Sarah Cary Fairfax, Camp at Fort Cumberland, September 12, 1758, in *PGWCL,* vol. 6. • "None of which": George Washington to Sarah Cary Fairfax, Mount Vernon, May 16, 1798, in *PGWR,* vol. 2. • brother-in-law: George Washington to Bryan Fairfax, Mount Vernon, May 18, 1798, in *PGWR,* vol. 2. • "voluminous": George Washington to James McHenry, Mount Vernon, July 29, 1798, in *PGWR,* vol. 2. • revisions: Abbot, "An Uncommon Awareness of Self: The Papers of George Washington," 281–82; Preface, in *PGWCL,* vol. 1; Editorial Note, The Letter Book for the Braddock Campaign, in *PGWCL,* vol. 1. • "In order": George Washington to Sarah Cary Fairfax, Bullskin Plantation, April 30, 1755, in *PGWCL,* vol. 1. • His mother had: Flexner, *George Washington: The Forge of Experience,* 116–17; George Washington to Robert Orme, Mount Vernon, April 2, 1755, in *PGWCL,* vol. 1; Zagarri, ed., *David Humphreys' "Life of General Washington" with*

George Washington's "Remarks," 9–14. • "my inclinations": George Washington to William Fitzhugh, Belvoir, November 15, 1754, in *PGWCL,* vol. 1. For more about Washington's complaint, see Zagarri, ed., *David Humphreys' "Life of General Washington" with George Washington's "Remarks,"* 14; Freeman, *George Washington,* 1:385–91 and 439–45; Flexner, *George Washington: The Forge of Experience,* 95 and 122. • "volunteer": George Washington to Robert Orme, Mount Vernon, March 15, 1755, in *PGWCL,* vol. 1. • slowed: Ellis, *His Excellency,* 21; George Washington to Sarah Cary Fairfax, Fort Cumberland, May 14, 1755, in *PGWCL,* vol. 1. • "I hope": George Washington to John Augustine Washington, Winchester, May 28, 1755, in *PGWCL,* vol. 1. • "Am I": George Washington to Sarah Cary Fairfax, Fort Cumberland, June 7, 1755, in *PGWCL,* vol. 1. For the mission back east, see Flexner, *George Washington: The Forge of Experience,* 123. • "Honored Madam": George Washington to Mary Ball Washington, Fort Cumberland, June 7, 1755, in *PGWCL,* vol. 1. For the lack of letters, see Flexner, *George Washington: The Forge of Experience,* 125. • "excessively ill": George Washington to John Augustine

Washington, June 28, 1755–July 2, 1755, in *PGWCL*, vol. 1. For Washington's suggestion to Braddock, see Freeman, *George Washington*, 2:52–53. • wagons: George Washington, Memorandum, July 8–9, 1755, in *PGWCL*, vol. 1; Freeman, *George Washington*, 2:60–61. • "We were": George Washington to Robert Dinwiddie, Fort Cumberland, July 18, 1755, in *PGWCL*, vol. 1. • "As I have": George Washington to John Augustine Washington, Fort Cumberland, July 18, 1755, in *PGWCL*, vol. 1. • retreat: Zagarri, ed., *David Humphreys' "Life of General Washington" with George Washington's "Remarks,"* 16–19; George Washington to Mary Ball Washington, Fort Cumberland, July 18, 1755, in *PGWCL*, vol. 1. • "impervious": Zagarri, ed., *David Humphreys' "Life of General Washington" with George Washington's "Remarks,"* 18. • blame: George Washington to Robert Orme, Mount Vernon, July 28, 1755, in *PGWCL*, vol. 1; George Washington to Robert Dinwiddie, Fort Cumberland, July 18, 1755, in *PGWCL*, vol. 1. • "I have been": George Washington to John Augustine Washington, Mount Vernon, August 2, 1755, in *PGWCL*, vol. 1. • "the esteem": George Washington to Warner Lewis, Mount

Vernon, August 14, 1755, in *PGWCL,* vol. 1. • castigated: Sarah Cary Fairfax, Ann Spearing, and Elizabeth Dent to George Washington, Belvoir, July 26, 1755, in *PGWCL,* vol. 1. • "reputation": George Washington to Warner Lewis, Mount Vernon, August 14, 1755, in *PGWCL,* vol. 1. • "dishonor": George Washington to Mary Ball Washington, Mount Vernon, August 14, 1755, in *PGWCL,* vol. 1. • "I think": George Washington to Warner Lewis, Mount Vernon, August 14, 1755, in *PGWCL,* vol. 1. For the original, see George Washington Papers, LOC. • acceded: Freeman, *George Washington,* 2:106–13. • "Colonel of": Robert Dinwiddie to George Washington, Commission, Williamsburg, August 14, 1755, in *PGWCL,* vol. 2. • "say no": George Washington to Sarah Cary Fairfax, Camp at Rays Town, September 25, 1758, in *PGWCL,* vol. 6. • delegated: George Washington to Sarah Cary Fairfax, Mount Vernon, May 16, 1798, in *PGWR,* vol. 2. • "With respect": Martha Washington to Sarah Cary Fairfax, Mount Vernon, May 17, 1798, in Editorial Note, George Washington to Sarah Cary Fairfax, Mount Vernon, May 16, 1798, in *PGWR,* vol. 2. • "a fine": Martha Washington to Sarah Cary Fairfax, Mount Vernon, May 17, 1798, in Fields, ed., *"Worthy Partner,"*

315. • "Mrs. Washington": George Washington to Bryan Fairfax, Mount Vernon, May 18, 1798, in *PGWR,* vol. 2. For Washington concealing his own letter, see Flexner, *George Washington: Anguish and Farewell,* 355. • set off: George Washington, May 1798, in *DGW,* vol. 6. • "Here is": Niemcewicz, *Under Their Vine and Fig Tree,* 78, 85, and 93. For the girl's first steps and Washington's effect on children, see George Washington to Thomas Law, Mount Vernon, December 25, 1797, in *PGWR,* vol. 1; Eleanor Parke Custis Lewis to Elizabeth Bordley Gibson, February 23, 1823, MV. • "Oh well": Niemcewicz, *Under Their Vine and Fig Tree,* 84 and 86–87. For betting on billiards, see Chernow, *Washington,* 134. • enough rain: George Washington to Robert Lewis, Mount Vernon, June 4, 1798, in *PGWR,* vol. 2. • "intention": George Washington to James Anderson, Federal City, May 22, 1798, in *PGWR,* vol. 2. • "strict integrity": George Washington to James Anderson, Mount Vernon, June 11, 1798, in *PGWR,* vol. 2. • "Strange": George Washington to James Anderson, Federal City, May 22, 1798, in *PGWR,* vol. 2. • "suffocated": George Washington to James Anderson, Mount Vernon, June 11, 1798, in *PGWR,* vol. 2. • distillery: George Washington to

William Fitzhugh, Mount Vernon, May 30, 1798, in *PGWR,* vol. 2. • "relieved": George Washington to James Anderson, Federal City, May 22, 1798, in *PGWR,* vol. 2. • "Clouds gathering": George Washington, May 1798, in *DGW,* vol. 6. • puddles: Niemcewicz, *Under Their Vine and Fig Tree,* 87. • "At the": Alexander Hamilton to George Washington, New York, May 19, 1798, in *PGWR,* vol. 2. • "The state": George Washington to Alexander Hamilton, Mount Vernon, May 27, 1798, in *PGWR,* vol. 2. • "If I did": George Washington to Alexander Hamilton, Mount Vernon, May 27, 1798, in *PGWR,* vol. 2. • "You ought": Alexander Hamilton to George Washington, New York, May 19, 1798, in *PGWR,* vol. 2. • "There is no": George Washington to Alexander Hamilton, Mount Vernon, May 27, 1798, in *PGWR,* vol. 2. • "generals of juvenile": George Washington to James McHenry, Mount Vernon, July 4, 1798, in *PGWR,* vol. 2. • "a man more": George Washington to Alexander Hamilton, Mount Vernon, May 27, 1798, in *PGWR,* vol. 2. • "once before": George Washington to Alexander Hamilton, Mount Vernon, May 27, 1798, in *PGWR,* vol. 2. • "inconsistency": George Washington to Alexander Hamilton, Mount Vernon, August 28, 1788, in *PGWCF,* vol. 6. • "intermeddle": Freeman, *George Washington,* 6:84. • "A citizen": Alexander Hamilton to George Washington, New York, September 1788, in *PGWP,* vol. 1. • "present peaceful": George Washington to Alexander Hamilton, Mount Vernon, May 27, 1798, in *PGWR,* vol. 2. • "recollection": George Washington to Sarah Cary Fairfax, Mount Vernon, May 16, 1798, in *PGWR,* vol. 2. • "no business": George Washington to Sarah Cary Fairfax, Camp at Fort Cumberland, September 12, 1758, in *PGWCL,* vol. 6. • "crisis": George Washington to Alexander Hamilton, Mount Vernon, May 27, 1798, in *PGWR,* vol. 2. • "the esteem": George Washington to Warner Lewis, Mount Vernon, August 14, 1755, in *PGWCL,* vol. 1. • "It may well": George Washington to Alexander Hamilton, Mount Vernon, May 27, 1798, in *PGWR,* vol. 2. • "If you": Alexander Hamilton to George Washington, New York, June 2, 1798, in *PGWR,* vol. 2. • "[The general] is": Niemcewicz, *Under Their Vine and Fig Tree,* xxiii–xxiv, 71–72, 84, and 86–87. • twelve: George Washington, June 1798, in *DGW,* vol. 6. • "a member": Niemcewicz, *Under Their Vine and Fig Tree,* 85, 96, 103, and 105. • "[The general] has": Niemcewicz, *Under Their Vine and Fig Tree,* 97, 101–2, and 107. • "formidable": John

Marshall to George Washington, Paris, March 8–10, 1798, in *PGWR,* vol. 2. For this being the letter Niemcewicz heard, see Editorial Note, John Marshall to George Washington, Paris, March 8–10, 1798, in *PGWR,* vol. 2. • "speak with so": Niemcewicz, *Under Their Vine and Fig Tree,* 107. • "for the last": Niemcewicz, *Under Their Vine and Fig Tree,* 108. • down King: *Claypoole's American Daily Advertiser,* July 19, 1798; George Washington, July 1798, in *DGW,* vol. 6; Carroll and Ashworth, *George Washington,* 7:508. • "turn": George Washington to John Adams, Mount Vernon, July 4, 1798, in *PGWR,* vol. 2. • an invitation: George Washington to John Adams, Mount Vernon, June 17, 1798, in *PGWR,* vol. 2. • "I must": John Adams to George Washington, Philadelphia, June 22, 1798, in *PGWR,* vol. 2. • "delicate": George Washington to James McHenry, Mount Vernon, July 4, 1798, in *PGWR,* vol. 2. • explicit: James McHenry to George Washington, Philadelphia, June 26, 1798, in *PGWR,* vol. 2. • "restless act": George Washington to James McHenry, Mount Vernon, July 4, 1798, in *PGWR,* vol. 2. • "entire confidence": George Washington to John Adams, Mount Vernon, July 4, 1798, in *PGWR,* vol. 2. • "Viewing": George Washington to James McHenry, Mount

Vernon, July 4, 1798, in *PGWR,* vol. 2. • his pleasure: *Claypoole's American Daily Advertiser,* July 19, 1798. • "Many considerations": George Washington to George Washington Parke Custis, Mount Vernon, June 13, 1798, in *PGWR,* vol. 2. • that summer: George Washington to Bryan Fairfax, Mount Vernon, May 18, 1798, in *PGWR,* vol. 2; Bryan Fairfax to George Washington, London, August 21–23, 1798, in *PGWR,* vol. 2; Bryan Fairfax to George Washington, York, September 7, 1798, in *PGWR,* vol. 2. • "description": George William Fairfax to George Washington, June 23, 1785, in *PGWCF,* vol. 3. • "the happiest": George Washington to George William Fairfax, Mount Vernon, February 27, 1785, in *PGWCF,* vol. 2. • "produced many": George William Fairfax to George Washington, June 23, 1785, in *PGWCF,* vol. 3. • "memento": George Washington to Sarah Cary Fairfax, Mount Vernon, May 16, 1798, in *PGWR,* vol. 2. • preserved: Henriques, *Realistic Visionary,* 79. • "the world": George Washington to Sarah Cary Fairfax, Camp at Fort Cumberland, September 12, 1758, in *PGWCL,* vol. 6. For the detail of the chest, see Custis, *Recollections and Private Memoirs of Washington,* 484 and 528.

parading: *Gazette of the United States,* July 5, 1798. • "young men": John D. R. Platt, *The Home and Office of Benjamin Franklin Bache (America's First Modern Newsman): 322 Market Street, Philadelphia, PA* (Washington, DC: National Park Service, 1970), 102–3. • "prostitute": Jeffrey L. Pasley, *The Tyranny of the Printers: Newspaper Politics in the Early American Republic* (Charlottesville: University of Virginia Press, 2001), 82, 88–89, and 100. • "his country": Tench Coxe to Margaret Bache, September 13, 1798, in Tench Coxe Papers, HSP. • "awe": Benjamin Franklin Bache, *Truth Will Out: The Foul Charges of the Tories Against the Editor of the Aurora Repelled by Positive Proof and Plain Truth and His Base Calumniators Put to Shame,* 1. • "GEORGE": *Philadelphia Aurora General Advertiser,* July 4, 1798. • sedition bill: James Tagg, *Benjamin Franklin Bache and the Philadelphia Aurora* (Philadelphia: University of Pennsylvania Press, 1991), 371–75. • "Anything in": Benjamin Franklin Bache to Dear Sir, June 8, 1798, Castle-Bache Collection, APS. • "prosecution": Tagg, *Benjamin Franklin Bache and the Philadelphia Aurora,* 340–43, 377–88, and 395. For more details, see Pasley, *The*

Tyranny of the Printers, 98–99; James Morton Smith, "The 'Aurora' and the Alien and Sedition Laws: The Editorship of Benjamin Franklin Bache," *Pennsylvania Magazine of History and Biography* 77, no. 1 (January 1953): 10–21; DeConde, *The Quasi-War,* 56–59; Elkins and McKitrick, *The Age of Federalism,* 575–79. • "mercantile": *Philadelphia Aurora General Advertiser,* July 10, 1798. • "himself at": Arthur Scherr, "Inventing the Patriot President: Bache's 'Aurora' and John Adams," *Pennsylvania Magazine of History and Biography* 119, no. 4 (October 1995): 377, 379, 380, 381, and 384–85. • "If ever": Tagg, "Benjamin Franklin Bache's Attack on George Washington," 224. • Constitution: Henry Tazewell to Thomas Jefferson, Philadelphia, July 5, 1798, in *PTJ,* vol. 30; James McHenry to George Washington, Philadelphia, July 3, 1798, in *PGWR,* vol. 2. • "He retired": *Philadelphia Aurora General Advertiser,* July 13, 1798. • "He would": [Benjamin Franklin Bache], *Remarks Occasioned by the Late Conduct of Mr. Washington as President of the United States* (Philadelphia: Benjamin Franklin Bache, 1797), 5–11. For Bache's authorship, see Tagg, "Benjamin Franklin Bache's Attack on George Washington," 224–25. • new army: Richard H. Kohn, *Eagle and Sword: The Federalists and the Creation of the Military Establishment in America, 1783–1802* (New York: Free Press, 1975), 226, 229, 229n, and 231. • "standing army": *Philadelphia Aurora General Advertiser,* May 11, 1798. • "The cloud": [Bache], *Remarks Occasioned by the Late Conduct of Mr. Washington as President of the United States,* 3. • "Truth": Bache, *Truth Will Out,* 1. • mail daily: George Washington to Timothy Pickering, Mount Vernon, July 11, 1798, in *PGWR,* vol. 2; Flexner, *George Washington: Anguish and Farewell,* 398. • "I have been": George Washington to Tobias Lear, Mount Vernon, July 4, 1798, in *PGWR,* vol. 2. • "I never": George Washington to Tobias Lear, Mount Vernon, June 26, 1798, in *PGWR,* vol. 2. For Lear misappropriating the money, see Brighton, *The Checkered Career of Tobias Lear,* 150–52. • newspapers delivered: George Washington to Henry Knox, Mount Vernon, August 9, 1798, in *PGWR,* vol. 2. • "The crisis": James McHenry to George Washington, Philadelphia, July 3, 1798, in *PGWR,* vol. 2. • "without any": George Washington to John Adams, Mount Vernon, September 25, 1798, in *PGWR,* vol. 3. • "sorrow": George Washington to John

Adams, Mount Vernon, September 25, 1798, in *PGWR,* vol. 3. • "regret": George Washington to Timothy Pickering, Mount Vernon, July 11, 1798, in *PGWR,* vol. 2. • "sensations": George Washington to Henry Knox, Mount Vernon, August 9, 1798, in *PGWR,* vol. 2. • McHenry presented: James McHenry to John Adams, Mount Vernon, July 12, 1798, in Jared Sparks, *The Writings of George Washington* (Boston: Russell, Shattuck, and Williams, 1836), 11:533–34. • "To you": John Adams to George Washington, Philadelphia, July 7, 1798, in *PGWR,* vol. 2. • said no: Elkins and McKitrick, *The Age of Federalism,* 630. • "talents were": George Washington to Alexander Hamilton, Mount Vernon, August 9, 1798, in *PGWR,* vol. 2. • secretary to: Robbins, *James McHenry, Forgotten Federalist,* 37–51; George Washington to James McHenry, September 14, 1798, in *PGWR,* vol. 2. • "Take the": George Washington to James McHenry, Mount Vernon, September 16, 1798, in *PGWR,* vol. 3. • "[would] be": George Washington to James McHenry, Mount Vernon, September 16, 1798, in *PGWR,* vol. 3. • government's friends: Alexander Hamilton to George Washington, July 8, 1798, in *PGWR,* vol. 2. • next morning: James McHenry to John Adams, Mount

Vernon, July 12, 1798, in Sparks, *The Writings of George Washington,* 11:533–34. • "conditional": George Washington to James McHenry, Mount Vernon, September 16, 1798, in *PGWR,* vol. 3. • list of candidates: John Adams to James McHenry, Philadelphia, July 6, 1798, in Sparks, *The Writings of George Washington,* 11:531–32; James McHenry to John Adams, Mount Vernon, July 12, 1798, in Sparks, *The Writings of George Washington,* 11:533–34. • "It may be": Alexander Hamilton to George Washington, July 8, 1798, in *PGWR,* vol. 2. • "intrigue": John Adams to Benjamin Rush, Quincy, August 23, 1805, in Biddle, ed., *Old Family Letters,* 76–77. • to be Republicans!: John Adams to James McHenry, Philadelphia, July 6, 1798, in Sparks, *The Writings of George Washington,* 11:531–32; George Washington, Suggestions for Military Appointments, Mount Vernon, July 14, 1798, in *PGWR,* vol. 2; Timothy Pickering to George Washington, Trenton, September 13, 1798, in *PGWR,* vol. 2. • "All violent": George Washington to William Richardson Davie, Mount Vernon, October 24, 1798, in *PGWR,* vol. 3. • "What pity": George Washington to Charles Carroll, Mount Vernon, August 2, 1798, in *PGWR,* vol. 2. • "occasion": George Washington to James Mc-Henry, Mount Vernon, July 5, 1798, in *PGWR,* vol. 2. For background on Craik, see Knox, "The Medical History of George Washington, His Physicians, Friends and Advisers," 183–85. • "chief": Timothy Pickering to George Washington, Philadelphia, July 6, 1798, in *PGWR,* vol. 2. • three major: George Washington to Alexander Hamilton, Mount Vernon, July 14, 1798, in *PGWR,* vol. 2. • "disbanded": George Washington to Henry Knox, Mount Vernon, August 9, 1798, in *PGWR,* vol. 2. • "If we": George Washington to John Adams, Mount Vernon, September 25, 1798, in *PGWR,* vol. 3. • "public estimation": George Washington to Henry Knox, Mount Vernon, July 16, 1798, in *PGWR,* vol. 2. • abdicated: Chernow, *Washington,* 719–21, 727–28, and 786. • "abilities": George Washington to John Adams, Mount Vernon, September 25, 1798, in *PGWR,* vol. 3. • "much advanced": George Washington to Timothy Pickering, Mount Vernon, July 11, 1798, in *PGWR,* vol. 2. • levity: Chernow, *Washington,* 203–5. • "With respect": George Washington to John Adams, Mount Vernon, September 25, 1798, in *PGWR,* vol. 3. • Pinckney versus Hamilton: George Washington to Timothy Pickering, Mount Vernon, July 11, 1798, in

PGWR, vol. 2. • "did not possess": Elkins and McKitrick, *The Age of Federalism*, 391. • tear: Thomas Jefferson to George Washington, Philadelphia, May 23, 1792, in *PGWP*, vol. 10. • "be so": George Washington to Timothy Pickering, Mount Vernon, July 11, 1798, in *PGWR*, vol. 2. For the Spanish colonies, see DeConde, *The Quasi-War*, 113–16. • "confidential": Timothy Pickering to George Washington, Philadelphia, July 6, 1798, in *PGWR*, vol. 2. • "whence alone": George Washington to Henry Knox, Mount Vernon, August 9, 1798, in *PGWR*, vol. 2. For a view of McHenry's role, see John Adams to James McHenry, Quincy, September 13, 1798, in Charles Francis Adams, *The Works of John Adams, Second President of the United States* (Boston: Little, Brown, 1853), 8:593–94. • "[It] is": George Washington to Alexander Hamilton, Mount Vernon, July 14, 1798, in *PGWR*, vol. 2. • consult more: George Washington to Henry Knox, Mount Vernon, August 9, 1798, in *PGWR*, vol. 2; George Washington to John Adams, Mount Vernon, September 25, 1798, in *PGWR*, vol. 3; George Washington, July 1798, in *DGW*, vol. 6. • chain of command: George Washington, Suggestions for Military Appointments, Mount Vernon, July 14, 1798, in *PGWR*, vol. 2; George Washington to Henry Knox, Mount Vernon, July 16, 1798, in *PGWR,* vol. 2; George Washington to Henry Knox, Mount Vernon, August 9, 1798, in *PGWR,* vol. 2; George Washington to John Adams, Mount Vernon, September 25, 1798, in *PGWR,* vol. 3. • "wish": George Washington to Alexander Hamilton, Mount Vernon, July 14, 1798, in *PGWR,* vol. 2. • "most confidential": George Washington to John Adams, Mount Vernon, September 25, 1798, in *PGWR,* vol. 3. • "in opposition": George Washington to Timothy Pickering, Mount Vernon, July 11, 1798, in *PGWR,* vol. 2. • "Encumber[ing]": George Washington to John Adams, Mount Vernon, September 25, 1798, in *PGWR,* vol. 3. • "suggested": George Washington, Suggestions for Military Appointments, Mount Vernon, July 14, 1798, in *PGWR,* vol. 2. • "best qualified": James McHenry to John Adams, Mount Vernon, July 12, 1798, in Sparks, *The Writings of George Washington,* 11:533–34. For Washington's insistence on making this point clear, see George Washington to James McHenry, Mount Vernon, September 16, 1798, in *PGWR,* vol. 3; Bernard C. Steiner, *The Life and Correspondence of James McHenry: Secretary of War Under Washington and Adams* (Cleveland: Burrows Brothers, 1907), 312. • breakfast: James

McHenry to George Washington, Philadelphia, July 18, 1798, in *PGWR,* vol. 2; Abigail Adams to Catherine Nuth Johnson, Philadelphia, June 26, 1798, in *APAFC,* vol. 13; Abigail Adams to Mary Smith Cranch, Philadelphia, July 17, 1798, in *APAFC,* vol. 13; Abigail Adams to Elizabeth Smith Shaw Peabody, Philadelphia, June 22, 1798, in *APAFC,* vol. 13; Abigail Adams to Mary Smith Cranch, Philadelphia, June 23, 1798, in *APAFC,* vol. 13. • "purer air": Abigail Adams to Elizabeth Smith Shaw Peabody, Philadelphia, June 22, 1798, in *APAFC,* vol. 13. • adjourned: Abigail Adams to Mary Smith Cranch, Philadelphia, July 13, 1798, in *APAFC,* vol. 13; Elkins and McKitrick, *The Age of Federalism,* 595–96. • "many bellied": Ferling, *John Adams,* 340 and 355. • circumstances: Smith, *John Adams,* 2:972–73; Kohn, *Eagle and Sword,* 231. • "Whom shall": Pickering and Upham, *The Life of Timothy Pickering,* 3:462–63; Timothy Pickering to George Washington, Trenton, September 13, 1798, in *PGWR,* vol. 2. • "conceited": John Adams to Abigail Adams, Philadelphia, January 9, 1797, in *APAFC,* vol. 11. • "the very": Abigail Adams to John Adams, Quincy, January 28, 1797, in *APAFC,* vol. 11. • adultery: Abigail Adams to Thomas Boylston Adams, Philadelphia,

January 3, 1798, in *APAFC,* vol. 12; John Adams to Benjamin Rush, Quincy, November 11, 1806, in Biddle, ed., *Old Family Letters,* 118. • "[would] become": Abigail Adams to William Smith, Philadelphia, July 7, 1798, in *APAFC,* vol. 13. • "The knowledge": Abigail Adams to Mary Smith Cranch, July 3, 1798, in *APAFC,* vol. 13. For Adams suspecting Washington would accept, see John Adams to Oliver Wolcott Jr., Quincy, September 24, 1798, in Adams, *The Works of John Adams, Second President of the United States,* 8:601n–4n. • "Feeling": George Washington to John Adams, Mount Vernon, July 13, 1798, in *PGWR,* vol. 2. • "pleased": James McHenry to George Washington, Philadelphia, July 18, 1798, in *PGWR,* vol. 2. • publish them: *Annals of the Congress of the United States,* Senate, 5th Cong., 2nd session, 621–23. • "General Washington made": James McHenry to George Washington, Trenton, September 19, 1798, in *PGWR,* vol. 3. • So said: John Adams to James McHenry, Quincy, August 29, 1798, in Adams, *The Works of John Adams, Second President of the United States,* 8:587–89. • "In this house": Freeman, *George Washington,* 4:395. • "opinion": John Adams to James McHenry, Philadelphia, July 6, 1798, in Sparks, *The Writings of*

George Washington, 11:531–32. • "Colonel Hamilton": James McHenry to George Washington, Trenton, September 19, 1798, in *PGWR,* vol. 3. • "extraordinary pains": John Adams to James McHenry, Quincy, September 13, 1798, in Adams, *The Works of John Adams, Second President of the United States,* 8:593–94. For Adams's view of McHenry, see Abigail Adams to Thomas Boylston Adams, Quincy, June 12, 1800, Adams Family Papers, reel 398, MHS. • "popular": John Adams to Oliver Wolcott Jr., Quincy, September 24, 1798, in Adams, *The Works of John Adams, Second President of the United States,* 8:601n–4n. • even "rank": John Adams to Benjamin Rush, Quincy, August 23, 1805, in Biddle, ed., *Old Family Letters,* 74. • "puppyhood": John Adams to Abigail Adams, Philadelphia, January 9, 1797, in *APAFC,* vol. 11. • "not a native": John Adams to Oliver Wolcott Jr., Quincy, September 24, 1798, in Adams, *The Works of John Adams, Second President of the United States,* 8:601n–4n. For the alien acts, see DeConde, *The Quasi-War,* 99–100. • one arrangement: John Adams to James McHenry, Quincy, August 14, 1798, in Adams, *The Works of John Adams, Second President of the United States,* 8:580. • compromise: James McHenry to George

Washington, Trenton, September 19, 1798, in *PGWR*, vol. 3; John Adams to Oliver Wolcott Jr., Quincy, September 24, 1798, in Adams, *The Works of John Adams, Second President of the United States*, 8:601n–4n. • administrative officer: Kohn, *Eagle and Sword*, 233–34; James McHenry to George Washington, Trenton, September 19, 1798, in *PGWR*, vol. 3. • "a bankrupt": Abigail Adams to William Smith, Philadelphia, July 23, 1798, in *APAFC*, vol. 13. • conspiracy: *Annals of the Congress of the United States*, Senate, 5th Cong., 2nd session, 624; James McHenry to George Washington, Trenton, September 19, 1798, in *PGWR*, vol. 3; Abigail Adams to Mary Smith Cranch, East Chester, July 29, 1798, in *APAFC*, vol. 13. • "dupe": John Adams to James McHenry, Quincy, August 29, 1798, in Adams, *The Works of John Adams, Second President of the United States*, 8:587–89. • "If I should": John Adams to Oliver Wolcott Jr., Quincy, September 24, 1798, in Adams, *The Works of John Adams, Second President of the United States*, 8:601n–4n. For the correction to the quotation, see Chernow, *Alexander Hamilton*, 559. • "I opened": Henry Knox to George Washington, Boston, July 29, 1798, in *PGWR*, vol. 2. • bookseller: For background on Knox, see Mark Puls, *Henry Knox: Visionary General of the American Revolution* (New York: St. Martin's, 2008). • "esteem": Henry Knox to George Washington, Boston, July 29, 1798, in *PGWR,* vol. 2. For the rebuke during the Whiskey Rebellion, see Puls, *Henry Knox,* 217–20; Henry Knox to Alexander Hamilton, Philadelphia, October 8, 1794, in *PAH,* vol. 17. • "I find": Henry Knox to George Washington, Boston, July 29, 1798, in *PGWR,* vol. 2. • "There has": Henry Knox to George Washington, Boston, July 29, 1798, in *PGWR,* vol. 2.

Chapter Seven: Second-in-Command
Distance delayed: James McHenry to George Washington, Trenton, September 19, 1798, in *PGWR,* vol. 3; Kohn, *Eagle and Sword,* 241–42. For the example of the time elapsed between Washington asking the president's permission to hire a secretary and receiving an answer, see George Washington to James McHenry, July 29, 1798, in *PGWR,* vol. 2; James McHenry to George Washington, War Department, August 6, 1798, in *PGWR,* vol. 2; James McHenry to John Adams, War Department, August 4, 1798, Adams Family Papers, reel 390, MHS; John Adams to James McHenry, Quincy, August 14, 1798, in Adams, *The*

Works of John Adams, Second President of the United States, 8:580; James McHenry to John Adams, War Department, August 20 [22], 1798, Adams Family Papers, reel 390, MHS; James McHenry to George Washington, Trenton, August 25, 1798, in *PGWR,* vol. 2. • "When I": Robbins, *James McHenry, Forgotten Federalist,* 45. • "I expected": George Washington to James McHenry, Mount Vernon, July 5, 1798, in *PGWR,* vol. 2. • "I am thrown": George Washington to James McHenry, Mount Vernon, July 29, 1798, in *PGWR,* vol. 2. • "ignorant": George Washington to James McHenry, Mount Vernon, August 10, 1798, in *PGWR,* vol. 2. • Silver Grays: George Washington to James McHenry, Mount Vernon, July 27, 1798, in *PGWR,* vol. 2. • "You will perhaps": Eleanor Parke Custis to James McHenry, Mount Vernon, July 26, 1798, Sol Feinstone Collection, APS. • "If you could": James McHenry to George Washington, Philadelphia, June 26, 1798, in *PGWR,* vol. 2. • few clerks: Robbins, *James McHenry, Forgotten Federalist,* 16–36, 158, and 186; James McHenry to George Washington, War Department, August 8, 1798, in *PGWR,* vol. 2; Powell, *Bring Out Your Dead,* 9, 27, and 48; James McHenry to John Adams, Philadelphia, August 4, 1798, Adams Family Papers, reel 390, MHS. • "old bilious": James McHenry to George Washington, War Department, August 8, 1798, in *PGWR,* vol. 2. • recommendations: James McHenry to Alexander Hamilton, Philadelphia, April 14, 1797, in *PAH,* vol. 21; DeConde, *The Quasi-War,* 22–23. • "Ham": Robbins, *James McHenry, Forgotten Federalist,* 41. • "I observe": Alexander Hamilton to James McHenry, Philadelphia, July 30, 1798, in *PAH,* vol. 22. • Insulting: Robbins, *James McHenry, Forgotten Federalist,* 204–5; Alexander Hamilton to George Washington, Philadelphia, July 29, 1798, in *PGWR,* vol. 2. • "I find": James McHenry to John Adams, War Department, August 4, 1798, Adams Family Papers, reel 390, MHS. • solution: James McHenry to Alexander Hamilton, War Department, July 25, 1798, in *PAH,* vol. 22; Alexander Hamilton to James McHenry, Philadelphia, July 30, 1798, in *PAH,* vol. 22. • "If these": James McHenry to John Adams, War Department, August 4, 1798, Adams Family Papers, reel 390, MHS. • "If it": John Adams to James McHenry, Quincy, August 14, 1798, in Adams, *The Works of John Adams, Second President of the United States,* 8:580. For the receipt and reaction to the letter, see

James McHenry to George Washington, Trenton, September 19, 1798, in *PGWR,* vol. 3. • Thunder: George Washington, August 1798, in *DGW,* vol. 6. • fever: George Washington to Bushrod Washington, Mount Vernon, August 27, 1798, in *PGWR,* vol. 2. • "I endeavored": George Washington to James McHenry, September 3, 1798, in *PGWR,* vol. 2. • break: George Washington, August 1798, in *DGW,* vol. 6. • "The question": George Washington to George Washington Parke Custis, Mount Vernon, July 24, 1798, in *PGWR,* vol. 2. • "moped": George Washington to David Stuart, Mount Vernon, August 13, 1798, in *PGWR,* vol. 2. • "little jealousies": George Washington to Henry Knox, Mount Vernon, August 9, 1798, in *PGWR,* vol. 2. • "used every": Charles Carter Jr. to George Washington, Culpeper, July 25, 1798, in *PGWR,* vol. 2. • "informer": Bushrod Washington to George Washington, Richmond, August 7, 1798, in *PGWR,* vol. 2. • "If he": George Washington to Bushrod Washington, Mount Vernon, August 12, 1798, in *PGWR,* vol. 2. • "McHenry is": Alexander Hamilton to George Washington, Philadelphia, July 29, 1798, in *PGWR,* vol. 2. • "short": George Washington to James McHenry, Mount Vernon, September 14, 1798, in *PGWR,* vol. 2. • "I would":

George Washington to James McHenry, Mount Vernon, August 10, 1798, in *PGWR,* vol. 2. • "heavy fog": George Washington, August 1798, in *DGW,* vol. 6. • "My *present*": George Washington to William Fitzhugh, Mount Vernon, August 5, 1798, in *PGWR,* vol. 2. For Washington's weight, see Flexner, *George Washington: Anguish and Farewell,* 403n. • dismounted: George Washington to John Tayloe, Mount Vernon, July 21, 1798, in *PGWR,* vol. 2. • "mistaken idea": George Washington to James McHenry, Mount Vernon, July 28, 1798, in *PGWR,* vol. 2. • "Should you": Alice DeLancey Izard to George Washington, Charleston, June 25, 1798, in *PGWR,* vol. 2. • "nothing can": George Washington to Charles Carroll, Mount Vernon, August 2, 1798, in *PGWR,* vol. 2. • "If real": George Washington to David Stuart, Mount Vernon, December 30, 1798, in *PGWR,* vol. 3. For the fear of upsetting Martha, see George Washington to James McHenry, Chester, December 14, 1798, in *PGWR,* vol. 3. • "No foreigner": George Washington to Alexander Hamilton, Mount Vernon, August 9, 1798, in *PGWR,* vol. 2. For the request Hamilton forwarded, see Editorial Note, George Washington to Alexander Hamilton, Mount Vernon, August 9, 1798, in *PGWR,* vol. 2. •

could wait: George Washington to Alexander Hamilton, Mount Vernon, August 9, 1798, in *PGWR,* vol. 2. • "I am assailed": George Washington to James McHenry, Mount Vernon, July 29, 1798, in *PGWR,* vol. 2. • more than a day: George Washington to Alexander Spotswood, Mount Vernon, March 25, 1799, in *PGWR,* vol. 3. • "leisure hours": George Washington to James McHenry, Mount Vernon, July 29, 1798, in *PGWR,* vol. 2. • "inattention": George Washington to James Mease McRea, Mount Vernon, August 4, 1798, in *PGWR,* vol. 2. • Craik: George Washington, August 1798, in *DGW,* vol. 6; George Washington to Bushrod Washington, Mount Vernon, August 27, 1798, in *PGWR,* vol. 2; George Washington to James McHenry, Mount Vernon, September 3, 1798, in *PGWR,* vol. 2; George Washington to James McHenry, Mount Vernon, July 5, 1798, in *PGWR,* vol. 2; George Washington, Suggestions for Military Appointments, Mount Vernon, July 14, 1798, in *PGWR,* vol. 2; *Annals of the Congress of the United States,* Senate, 5th Cong., 2nd session, 623; Carroll and Ashworth, *George Washington,* 7:527 and 638–39; Rudolph Marx, "A Medical Profile of George Washington," *American Heritage* 6, no. 5 (August 1955), online; Knox, "The

Medical History of George Washington, His Physicians, Friends and Advisers," 179; Chernow, *Washington,* 23. • "A thousand": George Washington to Alexander Hamilton, Mount Vernon, August 9, 1798, in *PGWR,* vol. 2. • "possess": George Washington to James McHenry, Mount Vernon, July 29, 1798, in *PGWR,* vol. 2. • disturbing reports: James McHenry to George Washington, Trenton, August 25, 1798, in *PGWR,* vol. 2. For the likelihood that Washington heard rumors of the change before McHenry's letter, see Timothy Pickering to Alexander Hamilton, Trenton, August 21, 1798, in *PAH,* vol. 22. • "After what": James McHenry to John Adams, Trenton, August 20 [22], 1798, Adams Family Papers, reel 390, MHS. For the reason the author has corrected the date in the text, see James McHenry to George Washington, Trenton, September 19, 1798, in *PGWR,* vol. 3. • "You speak": John Adams to James McHenry, Quincy, August 29, 1798, in Adams, *The Works of John Adams, Second President of the United States,* 8:587–89. For "your most obedient," see John Adams to James McHenry, Quincy, August 29, 1798, Adams Family Papers, reel 390, MHS. • "My mind": Alexander Hamilton to James McHenry, New York, September 8, 1798, in

Alexander Hamilton Papers, LOC. • "I cannot blame": James McHenry to Alexander Hamilton, Trenton, September 10, 1798, in Alexander Hamilton Papers, LOC. • "Considering": Oliver Wolcott Jr. to John Adams, Trenton, September 17, 1798, in George Gibbs, *Memoirs of the Administrations of Washington and John Adams: Edited from the Papers of Oliver Wolcott, Treasury Secretary* (New York, 1846), 2:93–99. For "your most obedient," see Oliver Wolcott Jr. to John Adams, Trenton, September 17, 1798, Adams Family Papers, reel 391, MHS. • "The subject": Draft, George Washington to John Adams, Mount Vernon, September 25, 1798, in George Washington Papers, LOC. • "rough draft": George Washington to James McHenry, Mount Vernon, September 26, 1798, in *PGWR,* vol. 3. • "Lengthy": Draft, George Washington to John Adams, Mount Vernon, September 25, 1798, George Washington Papers, LOC. • "[I] retain": George Washington to James McHenry, Mount Vernon, October 1, 1798, in *PGWR,* vol. 3. • "the bark": George Washington to James McHenry, Mount Vernon, September 3, 1798, in *PGWR,* vol. 2. For Washington's attitude toward medicine, see George Washington to Landon Carter, Mount Vernon, October 5, 1798, in *PGWR,* vol. 3; Custis, *Recollections and Private Memoirs of Washington,* 162; George Washington to Tobias Lear, Mount Vernon, August 2, 1798, in *PGWR,* vol. 2. • "nearly a": George Washington to Alexander Spotswood, Mount Vernon, September 14, 1798, in *PGWR,* vol. 2. For the joke, see Editorial Note, George Washington to Alexander Spotswood, Mount Vernon, September 14, 1798, in *PGWR,* vol. 2. • inspecting land: George Washington, September 1798, in *DGW,* vol. 6. • "as high": George Washington to Arthur Young, Philadelphia, December 5, 1791, in *PGWP,* vol. 9. For the comparisons to Philadelphia, see Arnebeck, *Through a Fiery Trial,* 490–91. • balustrade: Arnebeck, *Through a Fiery Trial,* 497. • "camp out": Niemcewicz, *Under Their Vine and Fig Tree,* 86. • "earlier": George Washington to Alexander White, Mount Vernon, September 12, 1798, in *PGWR,* vol. 2. For the decision where to build, see Editorial Note, Alexander White to George Washington, Washington, September 8, 1798, in *PGWR,* vol. 2. • "[The] negroes": George Washington to Alexander Spotswood, Mount Vernon, September 14, 1798, in *PGWR,* vol. 2. • "long letters": George Washington to James Anderson, Mount Vernon, September 16, 1798, in *PGWR,* vol. 3. • Wash had: Editorial Note, George Washington to John McDowell, Mount Vernon, September 2, 1798, in *PGWR*, vol. 2. • "It is for": George Washington to James McHenry, Mount Vernon, September 14, 1798, in *PGWR*, vol. 2. • "Illuminati": Editorial Note, G. W. Snyder to George Washington, Frederick Town, August 22, 1798, in *PGWR*, vol. 2. • "will leave": George Washington to James McHenry, Mount Vernon, September 30, 1798, in *PGWR*, vol. 3. • "The temper": George Washington to Bushrod Washington, Mount Vernon, August 27, 1798, in *PGWR*, vol. 2. For Washington's previous approach to congressional elections, see George Washington to John Francis Mercer, Mount Vernon, September 26, 1792, in *PGWP*, vol. 11. • "Every man": John Marshall to James K. Paulding, Richmond, April 14, 1835, in *The Papers of John Marshall*, vol. 12, ed. Charles F. Hobson (Chapel Hill: University of North Carolina Press, 2006), 480–82. • *"private"*: George Washington to James McHenry, Mount Vernon, October 1, 1798, in *PGWR*, vol. 3. • forwarded: Editorial Note, James McHenry to George Washington, Trenton, September 10, 1798, in *PGWR*, vol. 2; James McHenry to George Washington, Trenton, September 19, 1798, in *PGWR*, vol. 3. • "There is": John Adams to George Washington, Quincy, October 9, 1798, in *PGWR,* vol. 3. • almost grateful: George Washington to John Adams, Mount Vernon, October 21, 1798, in *PGWR,* vol. 3. • image: James McHenry to George Washington, Philadelphia, August 13, 1798, in *PGWR,* vol. 2; Editorial Note, James McHenry to George Washington, Philadelphia, August 13, 1798, in *PGWR,* vol. 2; Flexner, *George Washington: Anguish and Farewell,* 424–25. • "most gloomy": John Adams to James McHenry, Quincy, October 22, 1798, in Adams, *The Works of John Adams, Second President of the United States,* 8:612–13. • "confined": John Adams to George Washington, Quincy, October 9, 1798, in *PGWR,* vol. 3. For Abigail's sickness, see McCullough, *John Adams,* 508–14. • "no more": John Adams to Benjamin Rush, Quincy, November 11, 1807, in Biddle, ed., *Old Family Letters,* 172–73. • "consent": John Adams to Oliver Wolcott Jr., Quincy, September 24, 1798, in Adams, *The Works of John Adams, Second President of the United States,* 8:601n–4n. • Washington's nephew: Timothy Pickering to John Adams, Trenton, September 20, 1798, Adams Family Papers, reel 391, MHS. • "I know by": John Adams to Timothy Pickering, Quincy, September 26, 1798, in Adams, *The Works of John Adams, Second President of the United States,* 8:597. • Elbridge Gerry: John Adams to William Cunningham, Quincy, March 20, 1809, in John Adams and William Cunningham, *Correspondence Between the Hon. John Adams, Late President of the United States, and the Late William Cunningham, Esq.* (Boston: E. M. Cunningham, 1823), 100–8; Abigail Adams to Mary Smith Cranch, Philadelphia, June 13, 1798, in *APAFC,* vol. 13; Elkins and McKitrick, *The Age of Federalism,* 607–9; DeConde, *The Quasi-War,* 160–64. • "At present": John Adams to James McHenry, Quincy, October 22, 1798, in Adams, *The Works of John Adams, Second President of the United States,* 8:612–13. For the taxes, see McCullough, *John Adams,* 507; DeConde, *The Quasi-War,* 102. • "plan": John Adams to James Lloyd, Quincy, March 6, 1815, in Adams, *The Works of John Adams, Second President of the United States,* 10:134–36; Rufus King to Timothy Pickering, February 26, 1798, in Adams, *The Works of John Adams, Second President of the United States,* 8:585–86. For brief background on Miranda, see DeConde, *The Quasi-War,* 116–17. • "knew not": John Adams to James Lloyd, Quincy,

March 26, 1815, in Adams, *The Works of John Adams, Second President of the United States,* 10:139–43. • "It appeared": John Adams to James Lloyd, Quincy, March 27, 1815, in Adams, *The Works of John Adams, Second President of the United States,* 10:143–46. For Adams saying the United States and Spain were at peace and Miranda's troop request, see John Adams to Timothy Pickering, Quincy, October 3, 1798, in Adams, *The Works of John Adams, Second President of the United States,* 8:600; Francisco de Miranda to John Adams, London, March 24, 1798, in Adams, *The Works of John Adams, Second President of the United States,* 8:569–72. • recruiting: James McHenry to John Adams, War Department, October 15, 1798, Adams Family Papers, reel 391, MHS; James McHenry to John Adams, War Department, October 18, 1798, Adams Family Papers, reel 391, MHS; John Adams to James McHenry, Quincy, October 22, 1798, in Adams, *The Works of John Adams, Second President of the United States,* 8:612–13; McCullough, *John Adams,* 511–13; Elkins and McKitrick, *The Age of Federalism,* 607–9.

Chapter Eight: Bewitched

Alexandria: George Washington, November 1798, in *DGW,* vol. 6. • "servants": George Washington to James McHenry, Mount Vernon, November 4, 1798, in *PGWR,* vol. 3. For hiring Lear, see George Washington to Tobias Lear, Mount Vernon, August 30, 1798, in *PGWR,* vol. 2. • "disrespect": George Washington to Lawrence Lewis, Philadelphia, December 2, 1798, in *PGWR,* vol. 3. For more about the morning awkwardness, see Lawrence Lewis to George Washington, Mount Vernon, November 21, 1798, in *PGWR,* vol. 3; Flexner, *George Washington: Anguish and Farewell,* 413. • "five stallions": Richard Parkinson to George Washington, Liverpool, August 28, 1798, in *PGWR,* vol. 2. • "surprised": George Washington to James Anderson, Mount Vernon, November 3, 1798, in *PGWR,* vol. 3. • Lafayette: Lafayette to George Washington, Wittmold-Holstein, May 20, 1798, in *PGWR,* vol. 2; George Washington to Timothy Pickering, Mount Vernon, October 18, 1798, in *PGWR,* vol. 3; Lafayette to George Washington, Lehmkuhlen, December 27, 1797, in *PGWR,* vol. 1; George Washington to Lafayette, Mount Vernon, December 25, 1798, in *PGWR,* vol. 3. For the fear of meddling aliens, see George Washington to Alexander Spotswood Jr., Philadelphia, November 22, 1798, in *PGWR,* vol. 3. • "public theatre": George Washington to Bushrod Washington, Mount Vernon, August 12, 1798, in *PGWR,* vol. 2. For the riding horse, see William Fitzhugh to George Washington, Ravensworth, September 15, 1798, in *PGWR,* vol. 3; Editorial Note, William Fitzhugh to George Washington, Ravensworth, September 15, 1798, in *PGWR,* vol. 2; George Washington to James McHenry, Mount Vernon, January 6, 1799, in *PGWR,* vol. 3. • "just under": George Washington to John Greenwood, Philadelphia, December 14, 1798, in *PGWR,* vol. 3. For more about the dental request, see George Washington to John Greenwood, Mount Vernon, November 5, 1798, in *PGWR,* vol. 3; George Washington to John Greenwood, Philadelphia, December 7, 1798, in *PGWR,* vol. 3. • horsemen: George Washington, November 1798, in *DGW,* vol. 6. • camps: James McHenry to George Washington, Philadelphia, November 9, 1798, in *PGWR,* vol. 3. • "apprehension": George Washington to Elizabeth Willing Powel, Philadelphia, November 17, 1798, in *PGWR,* vol. 3. • quarters: *Claypoole's American Daily Advertiser,* November 12, 1798; George Washing-

ton, November 1798, in *DGW*, vol. 6. •
delay: Thomas Jefferson to John Barnes,
Monticello, November 23, 1798, in *PTJ*,
vol. 30; Thomas Jefferson to James Madison, Monticello, November 17, 1798, in
PTJ, vol. 30. • "Spies": Thomas Jefferson to
Samuel Smith, Monticello, August 22,
1798, in *PTJ*, vol. 30. For details of Jefferson's paranoia, see Thomas Jefferson to
John Barnes, Monticello, August 31, 1798,
in *PTJ*, vol. 30; Thomas Jefferson to James
Madison, Philadelphia, April 5, 1798, in
PTJ, vol. 30; Malone, *Jefferson and the
Ordeal of Liberty*, 400 and 410. • "words":
Thomas Jefferson to James Madison, November 3, 1798, in *PTJ*, vol. 30. For news
of the persecution of the printers, see James
Thomson Callender to Thomas Jefferson,
Rasberryplain, September 22, 1798, in *PTJ*,
vol. 30; James Thomson Callender to
Thomas Jefferson, Rasberryplain, October
26, 1798, in *PTJ*, vol. 30; James Morton
Smith, "Sedition in the Old Dominion:
James T. Callender and the Prospect Before
Us," *Journal of Southern History* 20, no. 2
(May 1954): 158–59. • "I know not":
Thomas Jefferson to John Taylor, November
26, 1798, in *PTJ*, vol. 30. • "the greatest":
Thomas Jefferson to Samuel Smith, Monticello, August 22, 1798, in *PTJ*, vol. 30. • "It

was": Thomas Jefferson to John Taylor, Philadelphia, June 4, 1798, in *PTJ,* vol. 30. For the conspiracy, see Thomas Jefferson to Thomas Mann Randolph, Philadelphia, February 22, 1798, in *PTJ,* vol. 30; Thomas Jefferson to Stevens Thomson Mason, Monticello, October 11, 1798, in *PTJ,* vol. 30. • secede: Thomas Jefferson to John Taylor, Philadelphia, June 4, 1798, in *PTJ,* vol. 30; Thomas Jefferson to James Monroe, June 12, 1796, in *PTJ,* vol. 29. • "friendless": Thomas Jefferson, Fair Copy, Kentucky Resolutions of 1798, *PTJ,* vol. 30. For background, see Adrienne Koch and Harry Ammon, "The Virginia and Kentucky Resolutions: An Episode in Jefferson's and Madison's Defense of Civil Liberties," *William and Mary Quarterly* 5, no. 2 (April 1948): 145–76. • "no secrets": Thomas Jefferson to Wilson Cary Nicholas, Monticello, October 5, 1798, in *PTJ,* vol. 30. • similar resolution: Thomas Jefferson to James Madison, Monticello, November 17, 1798, in *PTJ,* vol. 30. • "hotheaded": James Madison to Thomas Jefferson, June 3, 1798, in *PTJ,* vol. 30. • "A mind": Larson, *The Return of George Washington,* 59. • "No business": George Washington to David Stuart, New York, July 26, 1789, in *PGWP,* vol. 3. • "many": George Washington, November

513

1798, in *DGW,* vol. 6. • "servants": George Washington, General Washington's Account of His Interview with Dr. Blackwell and Dr. Logan, November 13, 1798, George Washington Papers, LOC. • "Envoy Logan": George Washington to William Vans Murray, Mount Vernon, December 26, 1798, in *PGWR,* vol. 3. For background on the Logan mission, see Frederick B. Tolles, "Unofficial Ambassador: George Logan's Mission to France, 1798," *William and Mary Quarterly* 7, no. 1 (January 1950): 1–25. • "finally": George Washington, General Washington's Account of His Interview with Dr. Blackwell and Dr. Logan, November 13, 1798, George Washington Papers, LOC. • "by means": George Washington to William Vans Murray, Mount Vernon, December 26, 1798, in *PGWR,* vol. 3. • "unconstitutionality": George Washington to Alexander Spotswood Jr., Philadelphia, November 22, 1798, in *PGWR,* vol. 3. • "scarcely": George Washington to Alexander Addison, Philadelphia, December 6, 1798, in *PGWR,* vol. 3. • strict schedule: George Washington to Lawrence Lewis, Philadelphia, December 2, 1798, in *PGWR,* vol. 3; Brighton, *The Checkered Career of Tobias Lear,* 153; Editorial Note, George Washington, Alexander Hamilton, and Charles

Cotesworth Pinckney, Philadelphia, November 1798, Candidates for Army Appointments from Virginia, in *PGWR,* vol. 3; *Gazette of the United States,* November 13, 1798; James McHenry to George Washington, War Department, November 10, 1798, in *PGWR,* vol. 3; George Washington to James McHenry, Philadelphia, December 13, 1798, in *PAH,* vol. 22. • "Smaller matters": George Washington to Alexander Hamilton and Charles Cotesworth Pinckney, Philadelphia, November 10, 1798, in *PGWR,* vol. 3. • morning meeting: George Washington to Lawrence Lewis, Philadelphia, December 2, 1798, in *PGWR,* vol. 3; Brighton, *The Checkered Career of Tobias Lear,* 153. • "If . . . not": George Washington to William Thornton, Mount Vernon, December 20, 1798, in *PGWR,* vol. 3. • Robert Morris: George Washington, November 1798, in *DGW,* vol. 6. • "Virginia was": Albert Gallatin to Hannah Gallatin, Philadelphia, December 7, 1798, in Henry Adams, *The Life of Albert Gallatin* (Philadelphia: J. B. Lippincott, 1879), 223. • Aaron Burr: George Washington, November 1798, in *DGW,* vol. 6; John Adams to Benjamin Rush, Quincy, August 23, 1805, in Biddle, ed., *Old Family Letters,* 76–77; McCullough, *John Adams,* 515–16. For evidence that

Hamilton would have considered giving Burr a commission, see Alexander Hamilton to Oliver Wolcott Jr., New York, June 28, 1798, in *PAH,* vol. 21; Alexander Hamilton to James McHenry, New York, February 6, 1799, in *PAH,* vol. 22. • meals he shared: Chernow, *Washington,* 790. • "Did the": Elizabeth Willing Powel to George Washington, Philadelphia, March 11, 1797, in *PGWR,* vol. 1. • "the honor": George Washington to Elizabeth Willing Powel, Philadelphia, November 17, 1798, in *PGWR,* vol. 3. • "pleasure of": George Washington to Elizabeth Willing Powel, December 1, 1798, in *PGWR,* vol. 3. • "book of prints": Elizabeth Willing Powel to George Washington, Market Street, December 3, 1798, in *PGWR,* vol. 3. • "heart": Elizabeth Willing Powel to George Washington, Philadelphia, December 7, 1798, in *PGWR,* vol. 3. • annual message: Carroll and Ashworth, *George Washington,* 7:554. • "to a close": George Washington to Elizabeth Willing Powel, Philadelphia, December 9, 1798, in *PGWR,* vol. 3. For not dining out, see George Washington, December 1798, in *DGW,* vol. 6. • "handsome muslin": George Washington to Elizabeth Willing Powel, Eight Street, December 4, 1798, in *PGWR,* vol. 3. • Eliza worried: Elizabeth

Willing Powel to George Washington, Market Street, December 3, 1798, in *PGWR,* vol. 3. • "The difference": George Washington to Elizabeth Willing Powel, Eight Street, December 4, 1798, in *PGWR,* vol. 3. • sixty-five: Editorial Note, Elizabeth Willing Powel to George Washington, Philadelphia, December 7, 1798, in *PGWR,* vol. 3. • "Is there": George Washington to Elizabeth Willing Powel, Eight Street, December 4, 1798, in *PGWR,* vol. 3. • thread cases: Editorial Note, Elizabeth Willing Powel to George Washington, Philadelphia, December 7, 1798, in *PGWR,* vol. 3; George Washington, Ledger C, *The George Washington Financial Papers Project,* online; Elizabeth Willing Powel to Martha Washington, November 31, 1787, in Fields, ed., *"Worthy Partner,"* 199. For additional money spent on "gloves & muslin" for Martha Washington — expenses that Washington evidently did not view as "memento[es]" for her perhaps because Tobias Lear made the purchases at her own request — see Editorial Note, George Washington to James McHenry, Mount Vernon, January 6, 1799, in *PGWR,* vol. 3. • three inches: George Washington, December 1798, in *DGW,* vol. 6. • "extreme": George Washington to James McHenry, Susquehanna, December 16,

1798, in *PGWR,* vol. 3. • "erasures": George Washington to James McHenry, Philadelphia, December 13, 1798, in *PGWR,* vol. 3. • "In contemplating": George Washington to James McHenry, Philadelphia, December 13, 1798, in *PAH,* vol. 22. • "I am really": George Washington to James McHenry, Philadelphia, December 13, 1798, in *PGWR,* vol. 3. • travel expenses: George Washington to James McHenry, Mount Vernon, January 6, 1799, in *PGWR,* vol. 3. • "far": George Washington to the District of Columbia Commissioners, October 4, 1798, in *PGWR,* vol. 3. • "recourse": George Washington to Robert Lewis, Mount Vernon, January 23, 1799, in *PGWR,* vol. 3. For the search for cash sources, see George Washington to James Anderson, Mount Vernon, September 16, 1798, in *PGWR,* vol. 3; Robert Lewis to George Washington, Spring Hill, February 13, 1799, in *PGWR,* vol. 3; George Washington to James Welch, Mount Vernon, February 15, 1799, in *PGWR,* vol. 3. • full compensation: George Washington to John Adams, Mount Vernon, July 13, 1798, in *PGWR,* vol. 2; James McHenry to George Washington, Trenton, August 25, 1798, in *PGWR,* vol. 2; George Washington to James McHenry, Mount Vernon, January 6, 1799, in *PGWR,* vol. 3;

Chernow, *Washington,* 187–88 and 552; Freeman, *George Washington,* 6:194–95 and 225. • "I had rather": George Washington to James McHenry, Mount Vernon, January 6, 1799, in *PGWR,* vol. 3. For McHenry eventually sending another month's salary, see James McHenry to George Washington, War Department, January 10, 1799, in *PGWR,* vol. 3. • "You know": George Washington to James McHenry, Susquehanna, December 16, 1798, in *PGWR,* vol. 3. • "consent": George Washington to James McHenry, Chester, December 14, 1798, in *PGWR,* vol. 3. • "not seem": George Washington to David Stuart, Mount Vernon, December 30, 1798, in *PGWR,* vol. 3. • "glad of": George Washington to James McHenry, Mount Vernon, August 10, 1798, in *PGWR,* vol. 2. • "regret": Lawrence Lewis to George Washington, Mount Vernon, November 21, 1798, in *PGWR,* vol. 3. • "smallest": George Washington to Bartholomew Dandridge, Mount Vernon, January 25, 1799, in *PGWR,* vol. 3. • reservations: Flexner, *George Washington: Anguish and Farewell,* 419n. • "idleness": George Washington to Lawrence Lewis, Mount Vernon, September 20, 1799, in *PGWR,* vol. 4. • "intermeddle": Martha Washington to Fanny Bassett Washington,

Philadelphia, September 29, 1794, in Fields, ed., *"Worthy Partner,"* 276. • "I am too": George Washington to Lund Washington, Newburgh, August 13, 1783, MV, online. • Nelly celebrated: George Washington to Georges Washington Lafayette, Mount Vernon, December 25, 1798, in *PGWR,* vol. 3. • six letters: George Washington to Lafayette, Mount Vernon, December 25, 1798, in *PGWR,* vol. 3. • "perfectly clear": George Washington, December 1798, in *DGW,* vol. 6. • "No one": George Washington to Lafayette, Mount Vernon, December 25, 1798, in *PGWR,* vol. 3. • Christmas dinner: Carroll and Ashworth, *George Washington,* 7:559–60; Baker, *Washington After the Revolution,* 349. • "the leaders": George Washington to John Marshall, Mount Vernon, December 30, 1798, in *PGWR,* vol. 3. For Washington's receipt of the pamphlet and general approval of Addison's work, see George Washington to Alexander Addison, Philadelphia, December 6, 1798, in *PGWR,* vol. 3; George Washington to Alexander Addison, Mount Vernon, March 4, 1799, in *PGWR,* vol. 3. • "to make": Alexander Addison, *Liberty of Speech, and of the Press: A Charge to the Grand Juries of the County Courts of the Fifth Circuit of the State of Pennsylvania* (Washington, PA: John Colerick, 1798), 13–14. •

"When I": George Washington to John Quincy Adams, January 20, 1799, in *PGWR,* vol. 3. • "The whole": Richard Parkinson, *A Tour in America, in 1798, 1799, and 1800* (London, 1805), 1:5, 9, 52–54, and 63. • "poor": Parkinson, *A Tour in America,* 1:5–7 and 55–57. • "surprised": Parkinson, *A Tour in America,* 2:420, 425–26, 436, and 440.

Chapter Nine: Guardianship
"that the": George Washington to Eleanor Parke Custis, Philadelphia, March 21, 1796, in *PGWP,* vol. 19. • "Cupid": Eleanor Parke Custis to Elizabeth Bordley, Mount Vernon, February 3, 1799, in Brady, ed., *George Washington's Beautiful Nelly,* 58. • "was very": Ribblett, *Nelly Custis,* 44. • wooed her: George Washington to James McHenry, Mount Vernon, February 16, 1799, in *PGWR,* vol. 3. • "resemblance": Ribblett, *Nelly Custis,* 42; Custis, *Recollections and Private Memoirs of Washington,* 147. • enormous: Weld, *Travels Through the States of North America,* 86n; Rembrandt Peale, Notes for "Washington and His Portrait," circa 1857, MV. • Grandpapa's vigor: Brady, ed., *George Washington's Beautiful Nelly,* 12; Ribblett, *Nelly Custis,* 88–91. • "My prospects": Eleanor Parke Custis to Elizabeth

Bordley, Mount Vernon, February 3, 1799, in Brady, ed., *George Washington's Beautiful Nelly,* 59–60. • guardian: Ribblett, *Nelly Custis,* 45; Eleanor Parke Custis Lewis to Elizabeth Bordley Gibson, February 23, 1823, MV. • "There will be": George Washington to Lawrence Lewis, Mount Vernon, January 23, 1799, in *PGWR,* vol. 3. • "splendidly": Custis, *Recollections and Private Memoirs of Washington,* 450. • "silver stars": George Washington to James McHenry, Philadelphia, December 13, 1798, in *PAH,* vol. 22. • "best": George Washington to James McAlpin, Mount Vernon, January 27, 1799, in *PGWR,* vol. 3. • "connoisseurs": George Washington to James McHenry, Mount Vernon, January 27, 1799, in *PGWR,* vol. 3. • delivery date: George Washington to James McAlpin, Mount Vernon, January 27, 1799, in *PGWR,* vol. 3. • assume control: James Gunn to Alexander Hamilton, Philadelphia, December 19, 1798, in *PAH,* vol. 22. • "rich": Alexander Hamilton to James McHenry, New York, January 7, 1799, in *PAH,* vol. 22. • "But that": Alexander Hamilton to Elizabeth Hamilton, Philadelphia, December 10, 1798, in *PAH,* vol. 22. • tripling: Elkins and McKitrick, *The Age of Federalism,* 615–16. • "What additional": Theodore Sedgwick to Alexander Hamilton, Philadelphia, February 7, 1799, in *PAH*, vol. 22. • victim of its: George Washington to James McHenry, Philadelphia, December 13, 1798, in *PAH*, vol. 22. • insurance: DeConde, *The Quasi-War,* 124–30. • "Some late": George Washington to James McHenry, Philadelphia, December 13, 1798, in *PAH*, vol. 22. • Bonaparte: DeConde, *The Quasi-War,* 161; Doyle, *The Oxford History of the French Revolution,* 338–39. • "internal": Alexander Hamilton to Harrison Gray Otis, New York, December 27, 1798, in *PAH*, vol. 22. • "revision": Alexander Hamilton to Theodore Sedgwick, New York, February 2, 1799, in *PAH*, vol. 22. • "mass": Alexander Hamilton to Timothy Pickering, New York, June 7, 1798, in *PAH*, vol. 21. • "destroy": Alexander Hamilton to Theodore Sedgwick, New York, February 2, 1799, in *PAH*, vol. 22. • "purchase": William Heth to Alexander Hamilton, Petersburg, January 18, 1799, in *PAH*, vol. 22. • whiskey: Alexander Hamilton to Harrison Gray Otis, New York, December 27, 1798, in *PAH*, vol. 22. • "offensive operations": Alexander Hamilton to James Gunn, New York, December 22, 1798, in *PAH*, vol. 22. • "long": Alexander Hamilton to Harrison Gray Otis, New York, January 26, 1799, in *PAH*, vol. 22. For the connection between expanding the Union and preserving it, see Aaron N. Coleman, " 'A Second Bounaparty?' A Reexamination of Alexander Hamilton During the Franco-American Crisis, 1796–1801," *Journal of the Early Republic* 28, no. 2 (Summer 2008): 205–8; DeConde, *The Quasi-War,* 116; Alexander Hamilton, "The Stand No. IV," New York, April 12, 1798, in *PAH,* vol. 21. • "adventurer": Editorial Note, Francisco de Miranda to Alexander Hamilton, London, February 7, 1798, in *PAH,* vol. 21. For Miranda's letter to Hamilton, see Francisco de Miranda to Alexander Hamilton, London, April 6, 1798, in *PAH,* vol. 21. • logic: Alexander Hamilton to James McHenry, New York, early 1798, in *PAH,* vol. 21. • "If universal": Alexander Hamilton to Harrison Gray Otis, New York, January 26, 1799, in *PAH,* vol. 22. • "furnish": Alexander Hamilton to Rufus King, New York, August 22, 1798, in *PAH,* vol. 22. • "descend": John C. Hamilton, *Life of Alexander Hamilton: A History of the Republic of the United States As Traced in His Writings and Those of His Contemporaries* (Boston: Houghton, Osgood, 1879), 7:211–20. For the need for "secrecy," see John C. Hamilton's annotation on Alexander Hamilton to Francisco de Miranda, New York, August 22, 1798, Alexander

Hamilton Papers, LOC. • "inconvenient": James McHenry to Alexander Hamilton, War Department, January 22, 1799, in *PAH,* vol. 22. • "It may": Alexander Hamilton to George Washington, New York, February 16, 1799, in *PGWR,* vol. 3. • "I shall": John Adams to Abigail Adams, Philadelphia, February 22, 1799, in *APAFC,* vol. 13. For dancing, see John Adams to Abigail Adams, Philadelphia, February 22, 1799, Adams Family Papers, MHS, online; Ferling, *John Adams,* 203. • in his honor: Mary Smith Gray Otis to Abigail Adams, Philadelphia, January 20, 1799, in *APAFC,* vol. 13; William Smith Shaw to Abigail Adams, Philadelphia, January 21, 1799, in *APAFC,* vol. 13; John Adams to Abigail Adams, Philadelphia, February 9, 1799, in *APAFC,* vol. 13; Ferling, *John Adams,* 370. • "talkative": John Adams to Abigail Adams, January 1, 1799, in *APAFC,* vol. 13. • decline: Abigail Adams to John Adams, Quincy, February 20, 1799, in *APAFC,* vol. 13. • "poor boy": John Adams to Abigail Adams, Philadelphia, February 25, 1799, in *APAFC,* vol. 13. For background on Thomas, see Ferling, *John Adams,* 375. For the chatter, see John Adams to Abigail Adams, Philadelphia, November 11, 1794, in *APAFC,* vol. 10. • envied: John Adams to Abigail Adams,

Philadelphia, January 1, 1799, in *APAFC*, vol. 13. • "I do not": Abigail Adams to John Adams, Quincy, January 12, 1799, in *APAFC*, vol. 13. • more evidence: John Adams to Abigail Adams, Philadelphia, January 16, 1799, in *APAFC*, vol. 13; Ferling, *John Adams*, 375. • "stark mad": Elkins and McKitrick, *The Age of Federalism*, 616–17. • "wretch": John Adams to George Washington, Philadelphia, February 19, 1799, in *PGWR*, vol. 3. For Barlow's letter and background, see Joel Barlow to George Washington, Paris, October 2, 1798, in *PGWR*, vol. 3; DeConde, *The Quasi-War*, 155. • "Restoring peace": George Washington to John Adams, Mount Vernon, February 1, 1799, in *PGWR*, vol. 3. • "could I understand": John Adams to William Cunningham, Quincy, March 20, 1809, in Adams and Cunningham, *Correspondence Between the Hon. John Adams, Late President of the United States, and the Late William Cunningham, Esq.*, 100–8. • "Always": McCullough, *John Adams*, 523. • no need: John Adams to George Washington, Philadelphia, February 19, 1799, in *PGWR*, vol. 3. • wore white: Mary Custis Lee deButts, ed., *Growing Up in the 1850s: The Journal of Agnes Lee* (Chapel Hill: University of North Carolina Press, 1984), 80–81; Custis, *Recollections and Private Memoirs of Washington,* 450. • "trifling": George Washington to James McHenry, Mount Vernon, January 27, 1799, in *PGWR,* vol. 3. For Bushrod, see George Washington to James McAlpin, Mount Vernon, February 10, 1799, in *PGWR,* vol. 3; George Washington to James McHenry, Mount Vernon, February 10, 1799, in *PGWR,* vol. 3; Flexner, *George Washington: Anguish and Farewell,* 419–20. • gold thread: Editorial Note, George Washington to James McAlpin, Mount Vernon, February 10, 1799, in *PGWR,* vol. 3. • "Miss Custis": George Washington, February 1799, in *DGW,* vol. 6. For the slaves, see deButts, ed., *Growing Up in the 1850s,* 80–81. • "invading enemy": *Georgetown Centinel of Liberty,* February 19, 1799. • chances: George Washington to Edward Carrington, Mount Vernon, August 5, 1798, in *PGWR,* vol. 2. • "surprise": George Washington to Timothy Pickering, Mount Vernon, March 3, 1799, in *PGWR,* vol. 3. • motives: George Washington to John Adams, Mount Vernon, March 3, 1799, in *PGWR,* vol. 3. • "Had we": George Washington to Timothy Pickering, Mount Vernon, March 3, 1799, in *PGWR,* vol. 3. • "We were all": Timothy Pickering to George Washington, Philadelphia, February 21, 1799, in

PGWR, vol. 3. • "the course": George Washington to Timothy Pickering, Mount Vernon, March 3, 1799, in *PGWR,* vol. 3. • "the world": George Washington to James McHenry, Mount Vernon, March 25, 1799, in *PGWR,* vol. 3. • "the zeal": George Washington to Alexander Hamilton, Mount Vernon, February 25, 1799, in *PGWR,* vol. 3. • state senate: John Tayloe to George Washington, Mount Airy, February 10, 1799, in *PGWR* vol. 3. • "friends of": George Washington to John Tayloe, Mount Vernon, February 12, 1799, in *PGWR,* vol. 3. • "dissolve": George Washington to Patrick Henry, Mount Vernon, January 15, 1799, in *PGWR,* vol. 3. • nephew's relative rank: George Washington to James McHenry, Mount Vernon, January 28, 1799, in *PGWR,* vol. 3. • "The condition": George Washington to James McHenry, Mount Vernon, February 16, 1799, in *PGWR,* vol. 3. • "divert his": George Washington to David Stuart, Mount Vernon, December 30, 1798, in *PGWR,* vol. 3. For another iteration of Mars and Venus, see George Washington to Charles Cotesworth Pinckney, Mount Vernon, March 31, 1799, in *PGWR,* vol. 3. • "If I": George Washington to James McHenry, Mount Vernon, March 25, 1799, in *PGWR,* vol. 3. • rejected: George Washington Parke Custis to George Washington, Marlborough, June 17, 1798, in *PGWR,* vol. 2. • "housemaid": George Washington, Slave List, June 1799, in *PGWR,* vol. 4. For the fate of Caroline, who later appeared first on Wash's draft list of the dower slaves, see List of the Different Drafts of Negroes, Peter Family Papers, MV; Horn, *The Man Who Would Not Be Washington,* 72; Elizabeth Brown Pryor, *Reading the Man: A Portrait of Robert E. Lee Through His Private Letters* (New York: Viking, 2007), 138–39 and 525. • "cold": Custis, *Recollections and Private Memoirs of Washington,* 450–51. For Washington buying Lee, see Chernow, *Washington,* 118. • "Ah": Custis, *Recollections and Private Memoirs of Washington,* 451.

Chapter Ten: Testament
"Here": Thomas Boylston Adams to William Smith Shaw, Washington City, May 21, 1799, in *APAFC,* vol. 13. • "fine spacious": Thomas Boylston Adams to John Quincy Adams, Baltimore, June 3, 1799, in *APAFC,* vol. 13. For the unfillable void, see Thomas Boylston Adams to Abigail Adams, Philadelphia, June 9, 1799, in *APAFC,* vol. 13. • "Affairs": Thomas Boylston Adams to Abigail Adams, Philadelphia, June 9, 1799, in

APAFC, vol. 13. • cornerstone: Thomas Law to George Washington, April 25, 1799, in *PGWR,* vol. 4. For Thomas Boylston Adams receiving an update on the city's boarding-houses, see Thomas Boylston Adams to John Quincy Adams, Baltimore, June 3, 1799, in *APAFC,* vol. 13. • healthful: Thomas Boylston Adams to John Quincy Adams, Baltimore, June 3, 1799, in *APAFC,* vol. 13; Arnebeck, *Through a Fiery Trial,* 473 and 491. • "I was": Thomas Boylston Adams to Abigail Adams, Philadelphia, June 9, 1799, in *APAFC,* vol. 13. • reelection: John Adams to Abigail Adams, Philadelphia, February 22, 1799, in *APAFC,* vol. 13; John Adams to Abigail Adams, March 7, 1799, in *APAFC,* vol. 13. • "an ill-timed": Thomas Boylston Adams to John Adams, Quincy, March 1, 1799, in *APAFC,* vol. 13. For adding envoys, see DeConde, *The Quasi-War,* 184–85. • "flattering": Thomas Boylston Adams to John Quincy Adams, Baltimore, June 3, 1799, in *APAFC,* vol. 13. • "Excessive": Thomas Boylston Adams to William Smith Shaw, Philadelphia, June 8, 1799, in Charles Grenfill Washburn, "Letters of Thomas Boylston Adams to William Smith Shaw, 1799–1823," *Proceedings of the American Antiquarian Society* 27, no. 1 (April 1917): 88–90. • "frequently": George Washington to Alexander Spotswood, Mount Vernon, March 25, 1799, in *PGWR*, vol. 3. • revolting: James McHenry to George Washington, Philadelphia, March 30, 1799, in *PGWR*, vol. 3; James McHenry to George Washington, Philadelphia, March 31, 1799, in *PGWR*, vol. 3; George Washington to James McHenry, Mount Vernon, April 7, 1799, in *PGWR*, vol. 3. • "Six days": George Washington to James McHenry, Mount Vernon, April 23, 1799, in *PGWR*, vol. 4. • "Mercury at 52": George Washington, April 1799, in *DGW*, vol. 6. • "in much": George Washington to Roger West, Mount Vernon, April 23, 1799, in *PGWR*, vol. 4. • "standing": *Alexandria Times,* April 24, 1799; Roger West to George Washington, W. Grove, April 23, 1799, in *PGWR*, vol. 4; Editorial Note, Roger West to George Washington, W. Grove, April 23, 1799, in *PGWR*, vol. 4. • opponent: *Alexandria Times,* April 25, 1799; Enclosure, William B. Harrison to George Washington, April 24, 1799, in *PGWR*, vol. 4. • hundred votes: Edward Carrington to George Washington, Richmond, April 25, 1799, in *PGWR*, vol. 4. For background on Marshall's election, see Editorial Note, Congressional Election Campaign, in *The Papers of John Marshall,* 3:494–502. • "easily": George Washington to John Marshall, Mount Vernon, December 30, 1798, in *PGWR,* vol. 3. • closer vote: Bushrod Washington to George Washington, Walnut Farm, April 26, 1799, in *PGWR,* vol. 4; Thomas Jefferson, Memorandum of a Meeting of the Heads of the Executive Departments, March 9, 1792, in *PGWP,* vol. 10; Thomas Boyd, *Light-Horse Harry Lee* (New York: Charles Scribner's Sons, 1931), 13, 179–85, and 245–48; George Washington to Alexander Spotswood, Mount Vernon, October 4, 1795, in *PGWP,* vol. 19; George Washington to Henry Lee, Mount Vernon, April 2, 1797, in *PGWR,* vol. 1; George Washington to Henry Lee, Mount Vernon, September 8, 1797, in *PGWR,* vol. 1; Henry Lee to George Washington, Richmond, August 17, 1794, in *PGWP,* vol. 16; Thomas E. Templin, *Henry "Light Horse Harry" Lee: A Biography* (University of Kentucky Dissertation, 1975), 433–41; Henry Lee to George Washington, Richmond, January 29, 1799, in *PGWR,* vol. 3. • "some egregious": George Washington to John Trumbull, Mount Vernon, June 25, 1799, in *PGWR,* vol. 4. • "That we": George Washington to William Augustine Washington, Mount Vernon, May 20, 1799, in *PGWR,* vol. 4. • "Morning clear": George Washington, May 1799, in *DGW,* vol. 6. •

"dropped": George Washington to Lawrence Lewis, Mount Vernon, September 20, 1799, in *PGWR,* vol. 4. For Nelly's sadness, see Eleanor Parke Custis to Elizabeth Bordley, Mount Vernon, February 3, 1799, in Brady, ed., *George Washington's Beautiful Nelly,* 60; Eleanor Parke Custis Lewis to Elizabeth Bordley, Mount Vernon, November 4, 1799, in Brady, ed., *George Washington's Beautiful Nelly,* 62. • "leisure hours": George Washington, Last Will and Testament, July 9, 1799, in *PGWR,* vol. 4. • "would be": George Washington to James Anderson, Mount Vernon, September 20, 1799, in *PGWR,* vol. 4. • "Clear &": George Washington, May 1799, in *DGW,* vol. 6. • "to obtain": John Searson to George Washington, City of Washington, April 18, 1799, in *PGWR,* vol. 3. • "beauteous": John Searson, *Mount Vernon, a Poem* (Philadelphia, 1800), 10. • "use": George Washington, Last Will and Testament, July 9, 1799, in *PGWR,* vol. 4. • "More rain": George Washington, May 1799, in *DGW,* vol. 6. • "new scene": George Washington to William Herbert, Mount Vernon, June 25, 1799, in *PGWR,* vol. 4. • "This business": George Washington to William Herbert, Mount Vernon, September 1, 1799, in *PGWR,* vol. 4. • "small": William Thornton to George Washington, City of

Washington, May 31, 1799, in *PGWR,* vol. 4. • "No departure": George Washington to William Thornton, Federal City, June 1, 1799, in *PGWR,* vol. 4. • "all parts": George Washington, Last Will and Testament, July 9, 1799, in *PGWR,* vol. 4. • "a moment": George Washington to St. George Tucker, Mount Vernon, May 30, 1797, in *PGWR,* vol. 1. • congressional appropriations: George Washington, Last Will and Testament, July 9, 1799, in *PGWR,* vol. 4; George Washington, Extract from Will, December 15, 1794, in *PGWP,* vol. 17. • "limpingly": George Washington to Charles Carroll, Mount Vernon, July 21, 1799, in *PGWR,* vol. 4. • Liberty Hall: George Washington to Robert Brooke, Philadelphia, March 15, 1795, in *PGWP,* vol. 17; Washington Academy Trustees to George Washington, Washington Academy, April 12, 1798, in *PGWR,* vol. 2; George Washington, Last Will and Testament, July 9, 1799, in *PGWR,* vol. 4. • "Morning heavy": George Washington, July 1799, in *DGW,* vol. 6. • "excellent": Baker, *Washington After the Revolution,* 356. • "disappointment": James McHenry to George Washington, Philadelphia, June 28, 1799, in *PGWR,* vol. 4. For the coat saga, see George Washington to James McHenry, Mount Vernon, June 7, 1799, in *PGWR,* vol.

4; James McAlpin to George Washington, Philadelphia, June 27, 1799, in *PGWR,* vol. 4. • *"not merely":* John Trumbull to George Washington, London, March 24, 1799, in *PGWR,* vol. 3. • "practice": James McHenry to George Washington, Philadelphia, June 24, 1799, in *PGWR,* vol. 4. • "defensive": George Washington to John Trumbull, Mount Vernon, June 25, 1799, in *PGWR,* vol. 4. • "eventual": James McHenry to George Washington, War Department, May 2, 1799, in *PGWR,* vol. 4. • eligible name: George Washington to John Marshall, Edward Carrington, and William Heth, Mount Vernon, May 12, 1799, in *PGWR,* vol. 4. • Wash asking: Editorial Note, George Washington to James McHenry, Mount Vernon, June 7, 1799, in *PGWR,* vol. 4; George Washington to James McHenry, Mount Vernon, July 14, 1799, in *PGWR,* vol. 4. • "Not to": George Washington, Last Will and Testament, July 9, 1799, in *PGWR,* vol. 4. For the injunction to Wash, see Horn, *The Man Who Would Not Be Washington,* 81. • "Clear with": George Washington, July 1799, in *DGW,* vol. 6. • "hand and": George Washington, Last Will and Testament, July 9, 1799, in *PGWR,* vol. 4. For the total pages, see Prussing, *The Estate of George Washington, Deceased,* 42–70. • dread:

George Washington to Alexander Spotswood, Philadelphia, November 23, 1794, in *PGWP,* vol. 17. For the survey, see George Washington, Slave List, June 1799, in *PGWR,* vol. 4. • "unfortunate": Morgan, " 'To Get Quit of Negroes,' " 416 and 422. • "power": George Washington, Last Will and Testament, July 9, 1799, in *PGWR,* vol. 4. • "body servant": George Washington to Burwell Bassett Jr., Mount Vernon, August 11, 1799, in *PGWR,* vol. 4. • "a destiny": Morgan, " 'To Get Quit of Negroes,' " 423. For the concern about the executors, see Wiencek, *An Imperfect God,* 356. • twice: George Washington to Robert Lewis, Mount Vernon, August 17, 1799, in *PGWR,* vol. 4; George Washington to Robert Lewis, Mount Vernon, December 7, 1799, in *PGWR,* vol. 4. • "the most painful": George Washington, Last Will and Testament, July 9, 1799, in *PGWR,* vol. 4. For the number of slaves he owned, see George Washington, Slave List, June 1799, in *PGWR,* vol. 4. • "Morning a little": George Washington, July 1799, in *DGW,* vol. 6. • "marks": George Washington to Jonathan Trumbull Jr., Mount Vernon, July 21, 1799, in *PGWR,* vol. 4. • "some [other]": Jonathan Trumbull Jr. to George Washington, Lebanon, June 22, 1799, in *PGWR,* vol. 4. • "The line": George Washington to Jonathan Trumbull Jr., Mount Vernon, July 21, 1799, in *PGWR*, vol. 4. • "in terms": George Washington, Last Will and Testament, July 9, 1799, in *PGWR*, vol. 4. • "the seat": George Washington to Jonathan Trumbull Jr., Mount Vernon, July 21, 1799, in *PGWR*, vol. 4. • circulated: Jonathan Trumbull Jr. to Oliver Wolcott Jr., Lebanon, June 22, 1799, in Gibbs, *Memoirs of the Administrations of Washington and John Adams,* 2:243; Oliver Wolcott Jr. to Jonathan Trumbull Jr., Philadelphia, July 16, 1799, in Gibbs, *Memoirs of the Administrations of Washington and John Adams,* 2:245–46; Jonathan Trumbull Jr. to Timothy Pickering, Lebanon, June 22, 1799, in Timothy Pickering Papers, reel 24, MHS. • "all the": Timothy Pickering to William Vans Murray, Trenton, October 4, 1799, in Worthington Chauncey Ford, ed., *Letters of William Vans Murray to John Quincy Adams, 1797–1803* (Washington, DC, 1914), 600–1. • delaying: Clarfield, *Timothy Pickering and American Diplomacy,* 200–10; DeConde, *The Quasi-War,* 216–18; Timothy Pickering to John Adams, Department of State, August 23, 1799, Adams Family Papers, reel 396, MHS. • "what the": Timothy Pickering to John Adams, Trenton,

September 11, 1799, in Adams, *The Works of John Adams, Second President of the United States,* 9:23–25. For the coup and rumors, see DeConde, *The Quasi-War,* 217; Doyle, *The Oxford History of the French Revolution,* 371; Elkins and McKitrick, *The Age of Federalism,* 637–41. • "new facts": Timothy Pickering to John Adams, Trenton, September 24, 1799, in Adams, *The Works of John Adams, Second President of the United States,* 9:36–37. • "This great": Timothy Pickering to George Washington, Trenton, October 24, 1799, in *PGWR,* vol. 4. For Hamilton, see Timothy Pickering to George Washington, Trenton, October 9, 1799, in *PGWR,* vol. 4; Elkins and McKitrick, *The Age of Federalism,* 640–41. • "modest": Timothy Pickering, "Washington," September 21, 1825, in Timothy Pickering Papers, reel 46, MHS. • "splendor": Timothy Pickering to Dwight Foster, Philadelphia, January 8, 1801, in Timothy Pickering Papers, reel 14, MHS. • "vanity": Clarfield, *Timothy Pickering and American Diplomacy,* 208. • Internationally: Timothy Pickering to William Vans Murray, Trenton, October 25, 1799, in Ford, ed., *Letters of William Vans Murray to John Quincy Adams,* 610–12; Timothy Pickering to George

Washington, Trenton, October 24, 1799, in *PGWR*, vol. 4; Elkins and McKitrick, *The Age of Federalism*, 640–41. • "change the": Timothy Pickering to George Cabot, Trenton, October 22, 1799, in Henry Cabot Lodge, *Life and Letters of George Cabot* (Boston: Little, Brown, 1878), 248–49. For a similar letter, see Timothy Pickering to Fisher Ames, Trenton, October 24, 1799, in Timothy Pickering Papers, reel 12, MHS. • "I have flattered": George Cabot to Timothy Pickering, Brookline, October 31, 1799, in Lodge, *Life and Letters of George Cabot*, 249–50. • fever: George Washington, September 1799, in *DGW*, vol. 6; George Washington to Thomas Peter, Mount Vernon, September 7, 1799, in *PGWR*, vol. 4; George Washington to Lawrence Lewis, Mount Vernon, September 28, 1799, in *PGWR*, vol. 4; George Washington to William Vans Murray, Mount Vernon, October 27, 1799, in *PGWR*, vol. 4; George Washington, October 1799, in *DGW*, vol. 6; Eleanor Parke Custis Lewis to Elizabeth Bordley, Mount Vernon, November 4, 1799, in Brady, ed., *George Washington's Beautiful Nelly*, 61–63. • "The death": George Washington to Burgess Ball, Mount Vernon, September 22, 1799, in *PGWR*, vol. 4. • black seal: George Washington to Lawrence

Lewis, Mount Vernon, September 20, 1799, in *PGWR,* vol. 4. • "departed": George Washington to James McHenry, Mount Vernon, November 5, 1799, in *PGWR,* vol. 4. For the mail, see George Washington to Robert Lewis, Mount Vernon, August 23, 1799, in *PGWR,* vol. 4. • "no doubt of": George Washington to Alexander Hamilton, Mount Vernon, September 29, 1799, in *PGWR,* vol. 4. For Washington's advocacy for Harpers Ferry, see Merritt Roe Smith, "George Washington and the Establishment of the Harpers Ferry Armory," *Virginia Magazine of History and Biography* 81, no. 4 (October 1973): 415–36. • "surprised": George Washington to Timothy Pickering, Mount Vernon, November 3, 1799, in *PGWR,* vol. 4. • "I have, for": George Washington to James McHenry, Mount Vernon, November 17, 1799, in *PGWR,* vol. 4. • "No tongue": George Washington to Jonathan Trumbull Jr., Mount Vernon, August 30, 1799, in *PGWR,* vol. 4. • "very heavy": George Washington, November 1799, in *DGW,* vol. 6. • communion: Henriques, *Realistic Visionary,* 169–76; Richard Brookhiser, *Founding Father: Rediscovering George Washington* (New York: Free Press, 1996), 144–46; Mary V. Thompson, *"In the Hands of a Good Providence": Religion in the*

Life of George Washington (Charlottesville: University of Virginia Press, 2008), 77–79; George Washington to John Augustine Washington, Fort Cumberland, July 18, 1755, in *PGWCL,* vol. 1. • "short-lived": George Washington to Lafayette, Mount Vernon, December 8, 1784, in *PGWCF,* vol. 2. • "was owing": Custis, *Recollections and Private Memoirs of Washington,* 458–59. • "most precious": George Washington to James Anderson, Mount Vernon, September 16, 1799, in *PGWR,* vol. 4. • faux stone: George Washington to William Thornton, Mount Vernon, October 1, 1799, in *PGWR,* vol. 4; George Washington to Bryan Fairfax, Mount Vernon, November 30, 1799, in *PGWR,* vol. 4. • wiped: Custis, *Recollections and Private Memoirs of Washington,* 459.

Chapter Eleven: Washington Sinks
conceivable office: Thomas Jefferson to James Monroe, Philadelphia, May 21, 1798, in *PTJ,* vol. 30; Stevens Thomson Mason to James Monroe, Philadelphia, January 24, 1799, in *The Papers of James Monroe: Selected Correspondence and Papers, 1796–1802,* vol. 4, ed. Daniel Preston (Santa Barbara: Greenwood, 2012), 324. • "correct": John Guerrant Jr. to James Monroe, Goochland, October 14, 1799, in Preston, ed., *The*

Papers of James Monroe, 4:330. For Monroe's return to Virginia, see Harry Ammon, *James Monroe: The Quest for National Identity* (Charlottesville: University Press of Virginia, 1990), 163–73. • oppose the nomination: John Guerrant Jr. to James Monroe, Goochland, October 14, 1799, in Preston, ed., *The Papers of James Monroe,* 4:330. • "to exclude": *Richmond Examiner,* December 3, 1799, in *The Papers of James Monroe,* 4:334. • sensational: James Monroe to Elbridge Gerry, New York, July 13, 1797, in Preston, ed., *The Papers of James Monroe,* 4:161; James Monroe to Timothy Pickering, Philadelphia, July 19, 1797, in Preston, ed., *The Papers of James Monroe,* 4:165–66; James Monroe to Enoch Edwards, Albemarle, February 12, 1798, in Preston, ed., *The Papers of James Monroe,* 4:247; Ammon, *James Monroe,* 138–40. • evidence: James Madison to James Monroe, December 2, 1799, in *The Papers of James Madison: Congressional Series,* vol. 17, ed. William T. Hutchinson et al. (Charlottesville: University of Virginia Press, 1991), 285–86; James Monroe to James Madison, Albemarle, December 7, 1799, in Hutchinson et al., ed., *The Papers of James Madison: Congressional Series,* 17:287–92;

Enoch Edwards to James Monroe, Frankford, April 20, 1798, in Preston, ed., *The Papers of James Monroe,* 4:267–68; James Monroe to James Madison, Paris, July 5, 1796, in *The Papers of James Madison: Congressional Series,* vol. 16, 374–80; James Monroe to John Dawson, Albemarle, March 26, 1798, in Preston, ed., *The Papers of James Monroe,* 4:257–59. • "dance": James Monroe to Thomas Jefferson, Albemarle, March 26, 1798, in *PTJ,* vol. 30. • challenge: James Monroe to James Madison, Albemarle, December 7, 1799, in *The Papers of James Madison: Congressional Series,* 17:287–92; James Monroe, Response to John Adams Speech, June 1798, in Preston, ed., *The Papers of James Monroe,* 4:283–85. • "Your military": James Monroe, Essay to George Washington, 1798, in Preston, ed., *The Papers of James Monroe,* 4:301–4. For more on the essay, see William M. Ferraro, "George Washington and James Monroe: Military Compatriots, Political Adversaries, and Nationalist Visionaries," in Robert M. S. McDonald, *Sons of the Father: George Washington and His Protégés* (Charlottesville: University of Virginia, 2013), 110–11. • "The more": James Monroe to Thomas Jefferson, Richmond, June 1798, in

PTJ, vol. 30. • "The administration": James Monroe to Thomas Jefferson, Fredericksburg, May 4, 1798, in *PTJ,* vol. 30. • "sink": James Monroe, Notes on Measures for Opposing the Federalists, February 1799, in Preston, ed., *The Papers of James Monroe,* 4:327. • "large circle": George Washington, December 1799, in *DGW,* vol. 6. For "falling weather," see George Washington, January 1760, in *DGW,* vol. 1. • By ten: Tobias Lear, The Journal Account, Mount Vernon, December 15, 1799, in *PGWR,* vol. 4; George Washington to James Anderson, Mount Vernon, December 13, 1799, in *PGWR,* vol. 4. • winter quarters: George Washington, December 1799, in *DGW,* vol. 6; Enclosure, George Washington to James Anderson, Mount Vernon, December 10, 1799, in *PGWR,* vol. 4; George Washington, Agreement with William Pearce, Mount Vernon, September 23, 1793, in *PGWP,* vol. 14. • "Such a pen": George Washington to James Anderson, Mount Vernon, December 13, 1799, in *PGWR,* vol. 4. • no "ease": George Washington to James Anderson, Mount Vernon, December 10, 1799, in *PGWR,* vol. 4. • "interests": George Washington to William Thornton, Mount Vernon, December 8, 1799, in *PGWR,* vol. 4. • "infamous": George Washington to Alexander Hamilton, Mount Vernon, June 26, 1796, in *PAH,* vol. 20. For the number of newspapers, see Wood, *Empire of Liberty,* 479. • "destroy all": George Washington to Timothy Pickering, Mount Vernon, August 4, 1799, in *PGWR,* vol. 4. • "ill-founded": George Washington to the People of the United States, United States, September 17, 1796, in *Claypoole's American Daily Advertiser,* September 19, 1796. • "a more destructive": George Washington to William Vans Murray, Mount Vernon, October 26, 1799, in *PGWR,* vol. 4. • "mere chaos": George Washington to James Anderson, Mount Vernon, December 10, 1799, in *PGWR,* vol. 4. • regretted: George Washington to James Anderson, Mount Vernon, December 13, 1799, in *PGWR,* vol. 4. • "entire new": George Washington to James Anderson, Mount Vernon, December 10, 1799, in *PGWR,* vol. 4. • given birth: George Washington, November 1799, in *DGW,* vol. 6; George Washington to William Augustine Washington, Mount Vernon, October 29, 1799, in *PGWR,* vol. 4; George Washington to James Anderson, Mount Vernon, December 10, 1799, in *PGWR,* vol. 4; George Washington to Robert Lewis, Mount Vernon, December 7, 1799, in *PGWR,* vol. 4; Thomas Law to Dear Brother, Mount

Vernon, December 15, 1799, in Law, "Thomas Law's Description of the Last Illness and Death of George Washington," 30; Pogue, *Founding Spirits,* 119. • "so soon": George Washington to James Anderson, Mount Vernon, December 10, 1799, in *PGWR,* vol. 4. • "exhausted": George Washington to James Anderson, Mount Vernon, December 10, 1799, in *PGWR,* vol. 4. For the nineteen pages, see Editorial Note, Enclosure, George Washington to James Anderson, Mount Vernon, December 10, 1799, in *PGWR,* vol. 4. • "not to quit": Martha Washington to Elizabeth Willing Powel, Mount Vernon, December 17, 1797, in *PGWR,* vol. 1. • "cold rain": George Washington, December 1799, in *DGW,* vol. 6. • signature: Tobias Lear, The Journal Account, Mount Vernon, December 15, 1799, in *PGWR,* vol. 4. • "The establishment": George Washington to Alexander Hamilton, Mount Vernon, December 12, 1799, in *PGWR,* vol. 4. • "The weather was": Tobias Lear, The Journal Account, Mount Vernon, December 15, 1799, in *PGWR,* vol. 4. • "hanging": Tobias Lear, The Diary Account, Mount Vernon, December 14, 1799, in *PGWR,* vol. 4. • "take cold": Tobias Lear to Mary Lear, Mount Vernon, December 16, 1799, in Tobias Lear, "Letter from Tobias

Lear," *The Mount Vernon Ladies' Association of the Union: Annual Report, 1911* (May 1911): 52–54. • "great coat": Tobias Lear, The Diary Account, Mount Vernon, December 14, 1799, in *PGWR,* vol. 4. • three inches: George Washington, December 1799, in *DGW,* vol. 6; Tobias Lear, The Diary Account, Mount Vernon, December 14, 1799, in *PGWR,* vol. 4. • "became perfectly": George Washington, December 1799, in *DGW,* vol. 6. • those trees: Tobias Lear, The Diary Account, Mount Vernon, December 14, 1799, in *PGWR,* vol. 4. • parlor: Tobias Lear, The Diary Account, Mount Vernon, December 14, 1799, in *PGWR,* vol. 4; Eleanor Parke Custis Lewis to Mary Pinckney, Mount Vernon, January 12, 1800, MV. For the weak voice, see Chernow, *Washington,* 581. • "high": George Washington to James McHenry, Mount Vernon, August 11, 1799, in *PGWR,* vol. 4. For the rumor about Adams's letter, see James McHenry to George Washington, Philadelphia, November 10, 1799, in *PGWR,* vol. 4. For background about the sedition case, see James Morton Smith, "The 'Aurora' and the Alien and Sedition Laws: The Editorship of William Duane," *Pennsylvania Magazine of History and Biography* 77, no. 2 (April 1953): 123–55. •

"explanation": George Washington to James McHenry, Mount Vernon, November 17, 1799, in *PGWR,* vol. 4. • "blind": George Washington to Timothy Pickering, Mount Vernon, July 14, 1799, in *PGWR,* vol. 4. • "buy[ing]": William Vans Murray to George Washington, August 17, 1799, in *PGWR,* vol. 4. • "embarrassing": George Washington to William Vans Murray, Mount Vernon, October 26, 1799, in *PGWR,* vol. 4. • word of his ship: George Washington to Timothy Pickering, Mount Vernon, November 3, 1799, in *PGWR,* vol. 4. • Holland: Timothy Pickering to George Washington, Trenton, October 24, 1799, in *PGWR,* vol. 4; Editorial Note, James Madison to James Monroe, December 2, 1799, in *The Papers of James Madison: Congressional Series,* 17:285–86; Doyle, *The Oxford History of the French Revolution,* 372–73. • "What will be": George Washington to William Vans Murray, Mount Vernon, October 26, 1799, in *PGWR,* vol. 4. For the source of this speculation, see Flexner, *George Washington: Anguish and Farewell,* 430. • Lear read these: Tobias Lear, The Diary Account, Mount Vernon, December 14, 1799, in *PGWR,* vol. 4. • "The house were": *Virginia Argus,* December 10, 1799. • "Mr. [James] Madison": *Virginia Argus,* December 10, 1799. • thirteen: Tobias Lear, The Diary Account, Mount Vernon, December 14, 1799, in *PGWR,* vol. 4; Brighton, *The Checkered Career of Tobias Lear,* 16, 34, 110–16, and 147–59. • "broke out": Custis, *Recollections and Private Memoirs of Washington,* 416–18 and 418n. • "He appeared much": Tobias Lear, The Diary Account, Mount Vernon, December 14, 1799, in *PGWR,* vol. 4. For Lear and Jefferson, see Thomas Jefferson, Notes on Conversations with Tobias Lear and John Beckley, April 7, 1793, in *PTJ,* vol. 25. • "I found": Tobias Lear, The Diary Account, Mount Vernon, December 14, 1799, in *PGWR,* vol. 4. • skilled: Tobias Lear, The Journal Account, Mount Vernon, December 15, 1799, in *PGWR,* vol. 4. • "mixture of molasses": Tobias Lear, The Journal Account, Mount Vernon, December 15, 1799, in *PGWR,* vol. 4. • "no relief": Tobias Lear, The Diary Account, Mount Vernon, December 14, 1799, in *PGWR,* vol. 4. • "sage": Tobias Lear, The Journal Account, Mount Vernon, December 15, 1799, in *PGWR,* vol. 4. For Craik's arrival, also see Carroll and Ashworth, *George Washington,* 7:640–41. • "which produced": Tobias Lear, The Diary Account, Mount Vernon, December 14, 1799, in *PGWR,* vol. 4. • "ran slowly": Tobias Lear, The Journal Account,

Mount Vernon, December 15, 1799, in *PGWR*, vol. 4. • thirties: Howard A. Kelly and Walter L. Burrage, *American Medical Biographies* (Baltimore: Norman, Remington, 1920), 153, 257–58, and 312–13; J. Upshur Dennis, "The Last Portrait of Washington, and the Painter of It," *Century Magazine* 67, no. 4 (February 1904): 628. • "He needs": Gustavus Richard Brown to James Craik, January 2, 1800, in Dennis, "The Last Portrait of Washington, and the Painter of It," 628; Robert H. White, "Washington: His Last Illness and Medical Treatment," *Tennessee Historical Quarterly* 13, no. 1 (March 1954): 11. • thirty-two: Carroll and Ashworth, *George Washington,* 7:641. • Outside: Tobias Lear, The Journal Account, Mount Vernon, December 15, 1799, in *PGWR*, vol. 4. • "Inflammatory": Elisha Cullen Dick to Thomas Semmes, Alexandria, January 10, 1800, in J. A. Nydegger, "The Last Illness of George Washington," *Medical Record* 92 (December 29, 1917): 1128. For the modern medical diagnosis of acute epiglottitis, see Peter R. Henriques, "The Final Struggle Between George Washington and the Grim King: Washington's Attitude Toward Death and an Afterlife," *Virginia Magazine of History and Biography* 107, no. 1 (Winter 1999): 79–85; White

McKenzie Wallenborn, "George Washington's Terminal Illness: A Modern Medical Analysis of the Last Illness and Death of George Washington," in *The Papers of George Washington,* November 5, 1997, online. For older theories, see Walter A. Wells, "Last Illness and Death of Washington," *Virginia Medical Monthly* 53, no. 16 (January 1927): 629–42. • "a violent": Gustavus Richard Brown to James Craik, January 2, 1800, in Dennis, "The Last Portrait of Washington, and the Painter of It," 628; White, "Washington: His Last Illness and Medical Treatment," 11. • "a man whose": Elisha C. Dick, "Facts and Observations Relative to the Disease of Cynanche Trachealis, or Croup," *Philadelphia Medical and Physical Journal,* supplement 3 (May 1809): 247–53. For evidence that Dick proposed the tracheotomy after the fourth bleeding and not before, see Elisha Cullen Dick to Thomas Semmes, Alexandria, January 10, 1800, in Nydegger, "The Last Illness of George Washington," 1128. • "the disease was": Dick, "Facts and Observations Relative to the Disease of Cynanche Trachealis, or Croup," 245–47 and 252–53. • "The disorder": Tobias Lear, The Diary Account, Mount Vernon, December 14, 1799, in *PGWR,* vol. 4. • large bed: Martha Washington, The Will of Martha Washington of Mount Vernon, March 4, 1804, Circuit Court of Fairfax County, online; Prussing, *The Estate of George Washington, Deceased,* 416; Henriques, *Realistic Visionary,* 82. • "burn": Tobias Lear, The Journal Account, Mount Vernon, December 15, 1799, in *PGWR,* vol. 4. • "I find": Tobias Lear, The Diary Account, Mount Vernon, December 14, 1799, in *PGWR,* vol. 4. • "old vault": George Washington, Last Will and Testament, July 9, 1799, in *PGWR,* vol. 4. • "down the stream": George Washington to Marquise de Lafayette, Mount Vernon, April 4, 1784, in *PGWCF,* vol. 1. • "change": Tobias Lear to Mary Lear, Mount Vernon, December 16, 1799, in Lear, "Letter from Tobias Lear," 52–54. • "happier": Henriques, "The Final Struggle Between George Washington and the Grim King," 94. • "from whence": George Washington to Lafayette, Newburgh, April 5, 1783, in *WGW,* 26:298. • "the world": Henriques, "The Final Struggle Between George Washington and the Grim King," 91–94 and 96. For more about poets and history, see George Washington to Lafayette, Mount Vernon, May 28, 1788, in *PGWCF,* vol. 6. • "arrange and record": Tobias Lear, The Diary Account, Mount Vernon, December 14, 1799, in *PGWR*, vol. 4. • Christopher, Caroline: George Washington, Slave List, June 1799, in *PGWR*, vol. 4; "A List of Negroes Belonging to Martha Washington," Mount Vernon, March 5, 1801, Peter Family Papers, MV; Tobias Lear, The Diary Account, Mount Vernon, December 14, 1799, in *PGWR*, vol. 4. • "found in": George Washington to Roger West, Mount Vernon, September 19, 1799, in *PGWR*, vol. 4. • on his feet: Tobias Lear, The Journal Account, Mount Vernon, December 15, 1799, in *PGWR*, vol. 4; Tobias Lear, The Diary Account, Mount Vernon, December 14, 1799, in *PGWR*, vol. 4. • "I feel myself": Tobias Lear, The Diary Account, Mount Vernon, December 14, 1799, in *PGWR*, vol. 4. • "Doctor, I": Tobias Lear, The Journal Account, Mount Vernon, December 15, 1799, in *PGWR*, vol. 4. • "What hour": Tobias Lear, The Journal Account, Mount Vernon, December 15, 1799, in *PGWR*, vol. 4. • "Tis": Tobias Lear, The Diary Account, Mount Vernon, December 14, 1799, in *PGWR*, vol. 4. • Nothing more: Carroll and Ashworth, *George Washington*, 7:641. • Martha sat: Tobias Lear, The Diary Account, Mount Vernon, December 14, 1799, in *PGWR*, vol. 4. • "glide gently": George Washington to Marquise de Lafayette, Mount Vernon, April 4, 1784, in

PGWCF, vol. 1. • pulse: Tobias Lear, The Diary Account, Mount Vernon, December 14, 1799, in *PGWR,* vol. 4.

Chapter Twelve: Washington Rises

measurement: Tobias Lear, Diary, December 1799, HSP, online. • "frozen": William Thornton, Draft Account, in C. M. Harris, ed., *Papers of William Thornton, 1781–1802* (Charlottesville: University Press of Virginia, 1995), 528. • "No sorrow": William Thornton to Samuel Blodget, February 21, 1800, in Harris, ed., *Papers of William Thornton,* 538. • "presumptuous": William Thornton to Anthony Fothergill, City of Washington, October 10, 1797, in Harris, ed., *Papers of William Thornton,* 425–26. For the late entry, see Harris, ed., *Papers of William Thornton,* xlvii. • "grandeur": George Washington to Commissioners for the District of Columbia, Philadelphia, March 3, 1793, in *PGWP,* vol. 12. • Messengers: Tobias Lear, Diary, December 1799, HSP, online; William Buckner McGroarty, "The Death of Washington," *Virginia Magazine of History and Biography* 54, no. 2 (April 1946): 152–53. • "a stiffened": William Thornton, Draft Account, in Harris, ed., *Papers of William Thornton,* 528. For the timing, see Tobias Lear, Diary, December 1799, HSP, online.

• "Considering": Tobias Lear, Diary, December 1799, HSP, online. • crowd formed: *Georgetown Centinel of Liberty,* December 20, 1799; Tobias Lear, Diary, December 1799, HSP, online. • "It is": George Washington, Last Will and Testament, July 9, 1799, in *PGWR,* vol. 4. • procession: *Georgetown Centinel of Liberty,* December 20, 1799; Tobias Lear, Diary, December 1799, HSP, online. • sun set: *Georgetown Centinel of Liberty,* December 20, 1799; Tobias Lear, Diary, December 1799, HSP, online. • "open": Carroll and Ashworth, *George Washington,* 7:627. • "upon a larger": George Washington, Last Will and Testament, July 9, 1799, in *PGWR,* vol. 4. • "At the time": William Thornton to John Marshall, City of Washington, January 2, 1800, in Harris, ed., *Papers of William Thornton,* 526–27. • "last temporal": William Thornton to John Marshall, City of Washington, January 2, 1800, in Harris, ed., *Papers of William Thornton,* 527. • "An eminent": John Adams to William Stephens Smith, Philadelphia, March 3, 1800, Adams Family Papers, reel 120, MHS. • princes: Abigail Adams to Mary Smith Cranch, Philadelphia, February 27, 1800, in Mitchell, ed., *New Letters of Abigail Adams,* 234–36; Abigail Adams to

Mary Smith Cranch, Philadelphia, December 30, 1799, in Mitchell, ed., *New Letters of Abigail Adams,* 224–25; Gerald E. Kahler, *The Long Farewell: Americans Mourn the Death of George Washington* (Charlottesville: University of Virginia Press, 2008), 12. • personal secretary: John Adams to Martha Washington, Philadelphia, December 27, 1799, in Fields, ed., *"Worthy Partner,"* 327–28; Abigail Adams to Mary Smith Cranch, Philadelphia, December 18, 1799, in *Proceedings of the Massachusetts Historical Society,* 2nd series, 3 (April 1887): 275. • "mock funerals": John Adams to Benjamin Rush, Quincy, June 21, 1811, in Biddle, ed., *Old Family Letters,* 286–88; John Adams to Thomas Jefferson, Quincy, September 3, 1816, in *The Papers of Thomas Jefferson: Retirement Series,* vol. 10, ed. J. Jefferson Looney (Princeton: Princeton University Press, 2013), 359–61. • "muffled": Kahler, *The Long Farewell,* 31–33 and 50; *Claypoole's American Daily Advertiser,* December 27, 1799. For Harry Lee's speech and his debts being known to Adams, see Henry Lee III, *Funeral Oration* (Philadelphia, 1800), 16; James McHenry to George Washington, Trenton, September 19, 1798, in *PGWR,* vol. 3. • "expression": Abigail Adams to Elizabeth Cranch Norton, Philadelphia, December 28, 1799, Adams Family Papers, reel 396, MHS. • "millions": John Adams to Benjamin Rush, Quincy, June 12, 1812, in Biddle, ed., *Old Family Letters,* 396. • "his aversion": John Adams to John Trumbull, Quincy, July 27, 1805, Rosenbach. • "savior": Abigail Adams to Mary Smith Cranch, Philadelphia, January 28, 1800, in Mitchell, ed., *New Letters of Abigail Adams,* 228–31. For an example of the kind of eulogy that upset the Adamses, see Thomas Paine, *Eulogy on the Life of General Washington* (Newburyport: Edmund M. Blunt, 1800), 5–22. • "a man": Abigail Adams to Elizabeth Smith Shaw Peabody, Philadelphia, February 4, 1800, in Abigail Adams, *Abigail Adams: Letters,* ed. Edith Gelles (New York: Library of America, 2016), 676–79. • "a few steps": Robert P. Hay, "George Washington: American Moses," *American Quarterly* 21, no. 4 (Winter 1969): 786. • "injustice": John Adams to William Stephens Smith, Philadelphia, March 3, 1800, Adams Family Papers, reel 120, MHS. • military glory: John Adams to Uzal Ogden, Philadelphia, February 17, 1800, Adams Family Papers, reel 120, MHS. • costly: DeConde, *The Quasi-War,* 262–67. • Bonaparte: Edward J. Larson, *A Magnificent*

Catastrophe: The Tumultuous Election of 1800, America's First Presidential Campaign (New York: Free Press, 2007), 67; Kahler, *The Long Farewell,* 125; Thomas Jefferson to Uzal Ogden, Philadelphia, February 12, 1800, in *PTJ,* vol. 31. For "Corsican," see Thomas Boylston Adams to John Quincy Adams, Philadelphia, February 1, 1800, Adams Family Papers, reel 397, MHS. • "pretension": John Adams to *Boston Patriot,* 1809, Founders Online, National Archives, online. • "General Washington's death": James McHenry to John Adams, War Department, May 31, 1800, in *PAH,* vol. 24. For the report, see Editorial Note, James McHenry to John Adams, War Department, May 31, 1800, in *PAH,* vol. 24. • "bastard": James McHenry to John Adams, War Department, May 31, 1800, in *PAH,* vol. 24. For the reports of Hamilton campaigning and the New York election, see Kohn, *Eagle and Sword,* 264; Larson, *A Magnificent Catastrophe,* 95–96, 106, and 124–25. • persuaded Washington: John Adams to Benjamin Rush, Quincy, June 12, 1812, in Biddle, ed., *Old Family Letters,* 396; Kohn, *Eagle and Sword,* 266–67. • "take care": James McHenry to John Adams, War Department, May 31, 1800, in *PAH,* vol. 24. • "unpopular": Theodore Sedgwick to Alexander

Hamilton, Philadelphia, February 7, 1799, in *PAH,* vol. 22. For Pickering, see Smith, *John Adams,* 2:1029–30; Kohn, *Eagle and Sword,* 264–66; Abigail Adams to Catherine Johnson, Philadelphia, May 18, 1800, Adams Family Papers, reel 397, MHS. • relocating: Abigail Adams to John Quincy Adams, Philadelphia, May 15, 1800, in Adams, *Abigail Adams,* 687–90; Arnebeck, *Through a Fiery Trial,* 564–70; Bordweich, *Washington,* 242–43; John Ball Osborne, "The Removal of the Government to Washington," *Records of the Columbia Historical Society* 3 (1900): 136–51; McCullough, *John Adams,* 541. • rotated: Bordewich, *Washington,* 27. • "nexus": John Adams to Benjamin Rush, Quincy, December 28, 1807, in Biddle, ed., *Old Family Letters,* 174. • "raised": John Adams to Benjamin Rush, Quincy, August 14, 1811, in Biddle, ed., *Old Family Letters,* 345. • active a role: Bordewich, *Washington,* 210–11. • "uncomfortably": Abigail Adams to William Cranch, February 3, 1800, Adams Family Papers, reel 397, MHS. For the hotel, see Abigail Adams to Catherine Johnson, Philadelphia, May 18, 1800, Adams Family Papers, reel 397, MHS. • town houses: Arnebeck, *Through a Fiery Trial,* 538, 545, 549, and

579. • "sleep": John Adams to Abigail Adams, Washington, June 13, 1800, Adams Family Papers, MHS, online. • answer depended: Abigail Adams to Abigail Adams Smith, Washington, November 21, 1800, in Adams, *Abigail Adams,* 706–8. • "The president's house": Abigail Adams to Mary Smith Cranch, Washington, November 21, 1800, in Mitchell, ed., *New Letters of Abigail Adams,* 257. • "grand": Abigail Adams to Abigail Adams Smith, Washington, November 21, 1800, in Adams, *Abigail Adams,* 706–8. • "beautiful": Abigail Adams to Abigail Adams Smith, Washington, November 21, 1800, in Adams, *Abigail Adams,* 706–8. For the slaves, see Abigail Adams to Cotton Tufts, City of Washington, November 28, 1800, Adams Family Papers, reel 399, MHS. • "all that shall": John Adams to Abigail Adams, President's House, November 2, 1800, Adams Family Papers, MHS, online. • "ages": Abigail Adams to Mary Smith Cranch, Washington, November 21, 1800, in Mitchell, ed., *New Letters of Abigail Adams,* 259. • more wood: Abigail Adams to Abigail Adams Smith, Washington, November 21, 1800, in Adams, *Abigail Adams,* 706–8; Abigail Adams to Abigail Adams Smith, Washington, November 27, 1800, in Abigail Adams, *Letters of Mrs. Adams,* 4th

ed., ed. Charles Francis Adams (Boston: Wilkins, Carter, 1848), 384–85. • "a city in": Abigail Adams to Cotton Tufts, City of Washington, November 28, 1800, Adams Family Papers, reel 399, MHS. • "scattered": Abigail Adams to Abigail Adams Smith, Washington, November 21, 1800, in Adams, *Abigail Adams,* 706–8. • "In this": Arnebeck, *Through a Fiery Trial,* 573–74 and 591–604; Bordewich, *Washington,* 253–56. • "new part": Abigail Adams to Cotton Tufts, City of Washington, November 28, 1800, Adams Family Papers, reel 399, MHS. • next door: Constance McLaughlin Green, *Washington: Village and Capital, 1800–1878* (Princeton: Princeton University Press, 1962), 3–4; Dumas Malone, *Jefferson the President: First Term, 1801–1805* (Boston: Little, Brown, 1970), 46. • "My nearest": Abigail Adams to Abigail Adams Smith, Washington, November 27, 1800, in Adams, ed., *Letters of Mrs. Adams,* 384–85. • "I feel": Abigail Adams to Cotton Tufts, City of Washington, November 28, 1800, Adams Family Papers, reel 399, MHS. • "split": Abigail Adams to John Quincy Adams, Quincy, September 1, 1800, Adams Family Papers, reel 398, MHS. • "been firm": Abigail Adams to Benjamin Rush, Quincy, October 18, 1800, Adams Family

Papers, reel 399, MHS. • "Little General": Abigail Adams to John Quincy Adams, Quincy, September 1, 1800, Adams Family Papers, reel 398, MHS. • "gross lies": Abigail Adams to Mary Smith Cranch, Washington, November 21, 1800, in Mitchell, ed., *New Letters of Abigail Adams,* 258. For the book, see Alexander Hamilton, "Letter from Alexander Hamilton, Concerning the Public Conduct and Character of John Adams, Esq., President of the United States," October 24, 1800, in *PAH,* vol. 25. • extreme: Abigail Adams to John Quincy Adams, Quincy, September 1, 1800, Adams Family Papers, reel 398, MHS. • South Carolina: Larson, *A Magnificent Catastrophe,* 239–41; DeConde, *The Quasi-War,* 288; Abigail Adams to Thomas Boylston Adams, Washington, December 13, 1800, in Adams, *Abigail Adams,* 710–12; Ferling, *John Adams,* 402 and 405–6. • "private troubles": Abigail Adams to Thomas Boylston Adams, Washington, December 25, 1800, in Adams, *Abigail Adams,* 715–18. • become a farmer: Abigail Adams to Thomas Boylston Adams, Washington, December 13, 1800, in Adams, *Abigail Adams,* 710–12. • "pressing invitation": Abigail Adams to Mary Smith Cranch, Washington, December 21, 1800, in Adams, *Abigail Adams,* 712–15. • "Major

Custis": Abigail Adams to Abigail Adams Smith, Washington, November 21, 1800, in Adams, *Abigail Adams,* 706–8. • "handsomer": Abigail Adams to Thomas Boylston Adams, Washington, December 25, 1800, in Adams, *Abigail Adams,* 715–18. • "The house has": Abigail Adams to Mary Smith Cranch, Washington, December 21, 1800, in Adams, *Abigail Adams,* 712–15. • "painful sensations": George Washington, Last Will and Testament, July 9, 1799, in *PGWR,* vol. 4. For the will being published, see Fritz Hirschfeld, *George Washington and Slavery: A Documentary Portrayal* (Columbia: University of Missouri Press, 1997), 213. • "She did not": Abigail Adams to Mary Smith Cranch, Washington, December 21, 1800, in Adams, *Abigail Adams,* 712–15. • visibly: Nicholls, "Lady Henrietta Liston's Journal of Washington's 'Resignation,' Retirement, and Death," 519–20. • "beautiful": Abigail Adams to Mary Smith Cranch, Richmond Hill, June 28, 1789, in *APAFC,* vol. 8. For the teeth, see Brady, *Martha Washington,* 27 and 177; Benjamin Fendall to George Washington, Cedar-Hill, August 10, 1799, in *PGWR,* vol. 4. • "shed": Abigail Adams to Mary Smith Cranch, Philadelphia, January 7, 1800, in Mitchell, ed., *New Letters of Abigail Adams,* 227. • "Taught": Martha

Washington to John Adams, Mount Vernon, December 31, 1799, in Fields, ed., *"Worthy Partner,"* 332. • "penned": Abigail Adams to Hannah Smith, Philadelphia, January 17, 1800, in Smith-Carter Family Papers, reel 4, MHS. • pyramid: Rubil Morales-Vázquez, "Imagining Washington: Monuments and Nation Building in the Early Capital," *Washington History* 12, no. 1 (Spring/Summer 2000): 22–24; Harris, ed., *Papers of William Thornton,* 522–24. • "At the very": Abigail Adams to Thomas Boylston Adams, Washington, December 25, 1800, in Adams, *Abigail Adams,* 715–18. • state delegations: Larson, *A Magnificent Catastrophe,* 242–44; Abigail Adams to Cotton Tufts, Washington, December 27, 1800, Adams Family Papers, reel 399, MHS; John Adams to Elbridge Gerry, Washington, December 30, 1800, in Adams, *The Works of John Adams, Second President of the United States,* 9:577–78. • "impiety": Thomas Jefferson to Samuel Miller, Philadelphia, February 25, 1800, in *PTJ,* vol. 31. For gossip and other details about Jefferson's reaction to Washington's death, see McCullough, *John Adams,* 534; Thomas Jefferson to William Jackson, March 1, 1800, in *PTJ,* vol. 31; Malone, *Jefferson and the Ordeal of Liberty,* 442–44. • "firm believer": Jonathan Mitchell Sewall, "An Eulogy on the Late General Washington," in *Eulogies and Orations on the Life and Death of General George Washington, First President of the United States of America* (Boston: Manning and Loring, 1800), 37. • "unbeliever": R. W. G. Vail, ed., "A Dinner at Mount Vernon: From the Unpublished Journal of Joshua Brookes (1773–1859)," *New-York Historical Society Quarterly* 31, no. 2 (April 1947): 82. For more about the implicit comparisons, see Kahler, *The Long Farewell,* 62; Thomas Jefferson, Notes on a Conversation with Benjamin Rush, February 1, 1800, in *PTJ,* vol. 31; Henriques, "The Final Struggle Between George Washington and the Grim King," 96. • "intimately": Thomas Jefferson to Walter Jones, Monticello, January 2, 1814, in *The Papers of Thomas Jefferson: Retirement Series,* vol. 7, ed. J. Jefferson Looney (Princeton: Princeton University Press, 2010), 100–3. • "greatest man": Vail, ed., "A Dinner at Mount Vernon," 81–82. • "naturally distrustful": Thomas Jefferson to Walter Jones, Monticello, January 2, 1814, in Looney, ed., *The Papers of Thomas Jefferson: Retirement Series,* 7:100–3. • "no idea": Vail, ed., "A Dinner at Mount Vernon," 81–82. • "lie": Thomas Jefferson to James Monroe, June

12, 1796, in *PTJ,* vol. 29. • "vessel": Thomas Jefferson to Benjamin Rush, Washington, December 14, 1800, in *PTJ,* vol. 32. For the connection to Washington's death, see Malone, *Jefferson and the Ordeal of Liberty,* 443. • "a mausoleum": Thomas Jefferson to Thomas Mann Randolph, Washington, January 1, 1801, in *PTJ,* vol. 32. • "yield": Thomas Jefferson to Mary Jefferson Eppes, Washington, January 4, 1801, in *PTJ,* vol. 32. For Jefferson's doubts as to what would happen before the trip, see Thomas Jefferson to Caesar A. Rodney, Washington, December 21, 1800, in *PTJ,* vol. 32. • journey: Thomas Jefferson to Mary Jefferson Eppes, Washington, January 4, 1801, in *PTJ,* vol. 32; Malone, *Jefferson and the Ordeal of Liberty,* 491; Thomas Jefferson, 1801, in *Jefferson's Memorandum Books,* 2:1032. • "dear Patcy": George Washington to Martha Washington, Philadelphia, June 18, 1775, in Fields, ed., *"Worthy Partner,"* 159–60. • burn: Fields, ed., *"Worthy Partner,"* 464–65. • exempt: Timothy Pickering to Martha Washington, Department of State, April 7, 1800, in Fields, ed., *"Worthy Partner,"* 373. • "Nor could": Lafayette to Martha Washington, La Grange, February 28, 1800, Peter Family Papers, MV. • "the numerous": Alexander Hamilton to Martha Washington,

New York, January 12, 1800, in *PAH,* vol. 24. • "lost a": Elizabeth Willing Powel to Martha Washington, Philadelphia, December 24, 1799, in Fields, ed., *"Worthy Partner,"* 325–26. • "little book": M. L. Weems to Martha Washington, Dumfries, March 8, 1800, in Fields, ed., *"Worthy Partner,"* 360. • "Should it": M. L. Weems to Martha Washington, February 22, 1800, in M. L. Weems, *A History of the Life and Death, Virtues and Exploits, of General George Washington, Faithfully Taken from Authentic Documents,* 2nd ed. (Philadelphia: John Bioren, 1800). • "Grateful": Martha Washington to Catherine Livingston Garretson, Mount Vernon, March 15, 1800, in Fields, ed., *"Worthy Partner,"* 364. • "old man": Brady, *Martha Washington,* 115. • "the still": Martha Washington to Mercy Otis Warren, New York, December 26, 1789, in Fields, ed., *"Worthy Partner,"* 223. • "much too": Martha Washington to John Dandridge, Mount Vernon, April 20, 1789, in Fields, ed., *"Worthy Partner,"* 213. • "never": Thomas Law to Dear Brother, Mount Vernon, December 15, 1799, in Law, "Thomas Law's Description of the Last Illness and Death of George Washington," 30. • garret: Thomas Pim Cope, "Mount Vernon During Martha Washington's Last Days," in Lee, ed. *Expe-*

riencing Mount Vernon, 96–97; Ellen McCallister, "This Melancholy Scene," *The Mount Vernon Ladies' Association of the Union: Annual Report, 1981* (1982): 13–14; Prussing, *The Estate of George Washington, Deceased,* 415. • "expect to be": Martha Washington to Mary Stillson Lear, Mount Vernon, November 11, 1800, in Fields, ed., *"Worthy Partner,"* 394. • "There was now": John Cotton Smith to Judge Daggett, Washington, January 6, 1802, in William W. Andrews, *The Correspondence and Miscellanies of the Hon. John Cotton Smith* (New York: Harper and Brothers, 1847), 61. • some things: Martha Washington to Martha Washington Dandridge, Mount Vernon, February 12, 1801, in Fields, ed., *"Worthy Partner,"* 396; Eleanor Parke Custis Lewis to Mary Pinckney, Mount Vernon, May 9, 1801, MV; Cope, "Mount Vernon During Martha Washington's Last Days," 100. • hospitality: Custis, *Recollections and Private Memoirs of Washington,* 512–13. • "occurrence": Andrews, *The Correspondence and Miscellanies of the Hon. John Cotton Smith,* 224–25. For hoping Pinckney would win the presidency, see Eleanor Parke Custis Lewis to Mary Pinckney, Mount Vernon, November 9, 1800, MV. • "What [else]": Abigail Adams to Mary Smith Cranch, Washington, December 21, 1800, Adams, *Abigail Adams,* 712–15. • "power": George Washington, Last Will and Testament, July 9, 1799, in *PGWR,* vol. 4. • "The blacks": Martha Washington to Fanny Bassett Washington, Philadelphia, May 25, 1795, in Fields, ed., *"Worthy Partner,"* 287. For the argument that Martha would not have emancipated her slaves, see Martha Washington, Codicil, The Will of Martha Washington of Mount Vernon, March 4, 1804, Circuit Court of Fairfax County, online; Ellis, *His Excellency,* 260; Wiencek, *An Imperfect God,* 358. • "as a parent": Abigail Adams to Mary Smith Cranch, Washington, December 21, 1800, in Adams, *Abigail Adams,* 712–15. • "he must have": Andrews, *The Correspondence and Miscellanies of the Hon. John Cotton Smith,* 224–25. • "one of the": William Parker Cutler and Julia Perkins Cutler, *Life, Journals and Correspondence of Rev. Manasseh Cutler* (Cincinnati: Robert Clarke, 1888), 2:56. • "Democrats": George Washington to Jonathan Trumbull Jr., Mount Vernon, July 21, 1799, in *PGWR,* vol. 4; George Washington to James McHenry, Mount Vernon, September 30, 1798, in *PGWR,* vol. 3; Wood, *Empire of Liberty,* 718. • "triumph": Eleanor Parke Custis Lewis to

Mary Pinckney, Mount Vernon, May 9, 1801, MV.

Epilogue: We Are All

on foot: Larson, *A Magnificent Catastrophe,* 271–72; Malone, *Jefferson the President: First Term,* 3–4 and 17; Margaret Bayard Smith to Susan B. Smith, March 4, 1801, in Margaret Bayard Smith, *The First Forty Years of Washington Society,* ed. Gaillard Hunt (New York: Charles Scribner's Sons, 1906), 25–26. • "I have": Thomas Jefferson, First Inaugural Address, March 4, 1801, in *PTJ,* vol. 33. • "We have": Thomas Jefferson, First Inaugural Address, March 4, 1801, in *PTJ,* vol. 33. For no Federalists voting for Jefferson, see Larson, *A Magnificent Catastrophe,* 268. • lowercase: Malone, *Jefferson the President: First Term,* 20. • "speculators": For the words quoted in this sentence, the author has used the plural, even though some of the terms appeared only in the singular earlier. • "Remember": Custis, *Recollections and Private Memoirs of Washington,* 440 and 513–14. • Lear: Brighton, *The Checkered Career of Tobias Lear,* 169–82 and 329–31; Editorial Note, The Missing George Washington Diary, in *The Papers of John Marshall,* vol. 6, ed. Charles F. Hobson

(Chapel Hill: University of North Carolina Press, 1990), 192–94; Tobias Lear to John Marshall, Boston Harbor, August 13, 1803, in Hobson, ed., *The Papers of John Marshall,* 6:194–96; Henry Lee IV, *Observations on the Writings of Thomas Jefferson, with Particular Reference to the Attack They Contain on the Memory of the Late Gen. Henry Lee,* 2nd ed. (Philadelphia, 1839), 91–92. • "fully": *Richmond Recorder,* April 6, 1803. For the reaction Nicholas expected and the reaction he received, see Golladay, "Jefferson's 'Malignant Neighbor,' John Nicholas, Jr.," 316–17. • four grandchildren: Ribblett, *Nelly Custis,* 56–59 and 91; Horn, *The Man Who Would Not Be Washington,* 37–38 and 72; List of the Different Drafts of Negroes, Peter Family Papers, MV. • burn: Nelligan, *Old Arlington,* 135–37; Green, *Washington,* 61–64; Ted Pulliam, "Alexandria Surrenders — August 1814," *Alexandria Gazette Packet,* August 28, 2014. For "Major Custis," see Robert E. Lee to Charles Carter Lee, Washington, May 2, 1836, Robert E. Lee Papers, University of Virginia. • "capital error": Kenneth R. Bowling, "Thank You, General Ross: How Washington Won the Battle to Keep the Federal Government in 1814," *Washington History* 29, no. 2 (Fall 2017): 44. For Pickering's politics at the time, see Clarfield, *Timothy Pickering and the American Republic,* 219–28 and 249–60. • Hamilton: Timothy Pickering, "Hamilton," June 2, 1827, in Timothy Pickering Papers, reel 46, MHS; Timothy Pickering to Dwight Foster, Philadelphia, January 8, 1801, in Timothy Pickering Papers, reel 14, MHS; *Annals of the Congress of the United States,* House, 13th Cong., 3rd session, 395–96; Green, *Washington,* 67; Clark, *Greenleaf and Law in the Federal City,* 285–89; Bordewich, *Washington,* 260. • Lafayette: Unger, *Lafayette,* 349–57; Achenbach, *The Grand Idea,* 241–45, 249–52, 261–62, and 281–82; Horn, *The Man Who Would Not Be Washington,* 19–20, 50–51, and 81. • retrocession: Horn, *The Man Who Would Not Be Washington,* 54 and 60–61. • "cast into": Abigail Adams to Thomas Boylston Adams, Washington, December 25, 1800, in Adams, *Abigail Adams,* 715–18. For a biographer making a similar point to Abigail's, see Marcus Cunliffe, *George Washington: Man and Monument* (Boston: Little, Brown, 1958), 3–5 and 22–24.

BIBLIOGRAPHY

The author used archival collections from the American Philosophical Society, Fairfax County Circuit Court, Fred W. Smith National Library for the Study of George Washington at Mount Vernon, Historical Society of Pennsylvania, Library of Congress, Maryland Historical Society, Massachusetts Historical Society, New York Public Library, Rosenbach of Philadelphia, University of Virginia, and Virginia Historical Society. What follows is a list of published documents cited. It does not include period newspapers, which the reader will find referenced in the notes.

Abbot, W. W. "An Uncommon Awareness of Self: The Papers of George Washington." In Higginbotham, ed., *George Washington Reconsidered,* 275–86.

Achenbach, Joel. *The Grand Idea: George Washington's Potomac and the Race to the*

West. New York: Simon & Schuster, 2004.

Adams, Abigail. *Abigail Adams: Letters.* Edited by Edith Gelles. New York: Library of America, 2016.

———. *Letters of Mrs. Adams.* 4th ed. Edited by Charles Francis Adams. Boston: Wilkins, Carter, 1848.

Adams, Charles Francis. *The Works of John Adams, Second President of the United States.* Vols. 8, 9, and 10. Boston: Little, Brown, 1853–1856.

Adams, Henry. *The Life of Albert Gallatin.* Philadelphia: J. B. Lippincott, 1879.

Adams, John. *The Adams Papers: Diary and Autobiography of John Adams.* Vol. 3. Edited by L. H. Butterfield. Cambridge: Harvard University Press, 1961.

———. *The Adams Papers: Papers of John Adams.* Vol. 17. Edited by Gregg L. Lint et al. Cambridge: Belknap, 2014.

Adams, John, and William Cunningham. *Correspondence Between the Hon. John Adams, Late President of the United States, and the Late William Cunningham, Esq.* Boston: E. M. Cunningham, 1823.

Adams Family. *The Adams Papers: Adams Family Correspondence.* Edited by L. H. Butterfield et al. 13 vols. Cambridge: Harvard University Press, 1963–.

Addison, Alexander. *Liberty of Speech, and of the Press: A Charge to the Grand Juries of the County Courts of the Fifth Circuit of the State of Pennsylvania.* Washington, PA: John Colerick, 1798.

Allen, William C. *History of the United States Capitol: A Chronicle of Design, Construction, and Politics.* Washington, DC: Government Printing Office, 2001.

Ammon, Harry. *James Monroe: The Quest for National Identity.* Charlottesville: University Press of Virginia, 1990.

Andrews, William W. *The Correspondence and Miscellanies of the Hon. John Cotton Smith.* New York: Harper and Brothers, 1847.

Annals of the Congress of the United States.

Arnebeck, Bob. *Through a Fiery Trial: Building Washington, 1790–1800.* Lanham, MD: Madison, 1991.

Auricchio, Laura. *The Marquis: Lafayette Reconsidered.* New York: Vintage Books, 2014.

[Bache, Benjamin Franklin]. *Remarks Occasioned by the Late Conduct of Mr. Washington as President of the United States.* Philadelphia: Benjamin Franklin Bache, 1797.

Bache, Benjamin Franklin. *Truth Will Out:*

The Foul Charges of the Tories Against the Editor of the Aurora Repelled by Positive Proof and Plain Truth and His Base Calumniators Put to Shame.

Bacon-Foster, Corra. "Early Chapters in the Development of the Potomac Route to the West." *Records of the Columbia Historical Society* 15 (1912): 96–322.

Baker, William Spohn. *Washington After the Revolution, 1784–1799.* Philadelphia, 1897.

Biddle, Alexander, ed. *Old Family Letters: Copied from the Originals for Alexander Biddle.* Philadelphia: J. B. Lippincott, 1892.

Bordewich, Fergus M. *Washington: The Making of the American Capital.* New York: Amistad, 2008.

Bowling, Kenneth R. "Thank You, General Ross: How Washington Won the Battle to Keep the Federal Government in 1814." *Washington History* 29, no. 2 (Fall 2017): 42–49.

Boyd, Thomas. *Light-Horse Harry Lee.* New York: Charles Scribner's Sons, 1931.

Brady, Patricia, ed. *George Washington's Beautiful Nelly: The Letters of Eleanor Parke Custis Lewis to Elizabeth Bordley Gibson, 1794–1851.* Columbia: University of

South Carolina Press, 2006.

Brady, Patricia. *Martha Washington: An American Life.* New York: Viking, 2005.

Brighton, Ray. *The Checkered Career of Tobias Lear.* Portsmouth: Portsmouth Marine Society, 1985.

Brookhiser, Richard. *Founding Father: Rediscovering George Washington.* New York: Free Press, 1996.

Burns, Eric. *Infamous Scribblers: The Founding Fathers and the Rowdy Beginnings of American Journalism.* New York: Public Affairs, 2006.

Carroll, John Alexander, and Mary Wells Ashworth. *George Washington.* Vol. 7. New York: Charles Scribner's Sons, 1957.

Cary, Wilson Miles. *Sally Cary: A Long Hidden Romance of Washington's Life.* New York: De Vinne, 1916.

Chernow, Ron. *Alexander Hamilton.* New York: Penguin Books, 2004.

———. *Washington: A Life.* New York: Penguin Books, 2010.

Clarfield, Gerard H. *Timothy Pickering and American Diplomacy, 1795–1800.* Columbia: University of Missouri Press, 1969.

———. *Timothy Pickering and the American Republic.* Pittsburgh: University of Pittsburgh Press, 1980.

Clark, Allen C. *Greenleaf and Law in the Federal City.* Washington, DC: W. F. Roberts, 1901.

Coleman, Aaron N. " 'A Second Bounaparty?' A Reexamination of Alexander Hamilton During the Franco-American Crisis, 1796–1801." *Journal of the Early Republic* 28, no. 2 (Summer 2008): 183–214.

Cope, Thomas Pim. "Mount Vernon During Martha Washington's Last Days." In Lee, ed., *Experiencing Mount Vernon,* 95–102.

Cunliffe, Marcus. *George Washington: Man and Monument.* Boston: Little, Brown, 1958.

Custis, George Washington Parke. *Recollections and Private Memoirs of Washington.* New York: Derby & Jackson, 1860. Repr., Bridgewater, VA: American Foundation Publications, 1999.

Cutler, William Parker, and Julia Perkins Cutler. *Life, Journals and Correspondence of Rev. Manasseh Cutler.* Vol. 2. Cincinnati: Robert Clarke, 1888.

Dalzell, Robert F., Jr., and Lee Baldwin Dalzell. *George Washington's Mount Vernon: At Home in Revolutionary America.* New York: Oxford University Press, 1998.

Dauer, Manning J. "The Two John Nicholases: Their Relationship to Washington and Jefferson." *American Historical Review* 45, no. 2 (January 1940): 338–53.

deButts, Mary Custis Lee, ed. *Growing Up in the 1850s: The Journal of Agnes Lee.* Chapel Hill: University of North Carolina Press, 1984.

DeConde, Alexander. *Entangling Alliance: Politics and Diplomacy Under George Washington.* Durham: Duke University Press, 1958.

———. *The Quasi-War: The Politics and Diplomacy of the Undeclared War with France, 1797–1801.* New York: Charles Scribner's Sons, 1966.

Dennis, J. Upshur. "The Last Portrait of Washington, and the Painter of It." *Century Magazine* 67, no. 4 (February 1904): 627–29.

di Giacomantonio, William C. "All the President's Men: George Washington's Federal City Commissioners." *Washington History* 3, no. 1 (Spring/Summer 1991): 52–75.

Dick, Elisha C. "Facts and Observations Relative to the Disease of Cynanche Trachealis, or Croup." *Philadelphia Medical and Physical Journal,* supplement 3 (May

1809): 242–56.

Doyle, William. *The Oxford History of the French Revolution.* New York: Oxford University Press, 1989.

Dunbar, Erica Armstrong. *Never Caught: The Washingtons' Relentless Pursuit of Their Runaway Slave, Ona Judge.* New York: Atria, 2017.

Elkins, Stanley, and Eric McKitrick. *The Age of Federalism.* New York: Oxford University Press, 1993.

Ellis, Joseph J. *American Sphinx: The Character of Thomas Jefferson.* New York: Vintage Books, 1996.

———. *Founding Brothers: The Revolutionary Generation.* New York: Vintage Books, 2000.

———. *His Excellency: George Washington.* New York: Vintage Books, 2005.

———. *Passionate Sage: The Character and Legacy of John Adams.* New York: Norton, 2001.

Ferling, John. *The Ascent of George Washington: The Hidden Political Genius of an American Icon.* New York: Bloomsbury, 2009.

———. *John Adams: A Life.* New York: Oxford University Press, 1992.

Ferraro, William M. "George Washington

and James Monroe: Military Compatriots, Political Adversaries, and Nationalist Visionaries." In Robert M. S. McDonald, ed., *Sons of the Father: George Washington and His Protégés* (Charlottesville: University of Virginia Press, 2013), 99–120.

Fields, Joseph E., ed. *"Worthy Partner": The Papers of Martha Washington.* Westport, CT: Greenwood, 1994.

Flexner, James Thomas. *George Washington: Anguish and Farewell, 1793–1799.* Boston: Little, Brown, 1972.

————. *George Washington: The Forge of Experience, 1732–1775.* Boston: Little, Brown, 1965.

————. *George Washington and the New Nation, 1783–1793.* Boston: Little, Brown, 1970.

Ford, Worthington Chauncey, ed. *Letters of William Vans Murray to John Quincy Adams, 1797–1803.* Washington, DC, 1914.

Founders Online. National Archives. Online.

Fowler, William M., Jr. *American Crisis: George Washington and the Dangerous Two Years After Yorktown, 1781–1783.* New York: Walker, 2011.

Freeman, Douglas Southall. *George Washington: A Biography.* 6 vols. New York:

Charles Scribner's Sons, 1948–1954.

———. *R. E. Lee*. Vol. 1. New York: Charles Scribner's Sons, 1934. Repr., Safety Harbor, FL: Simon Publications, 2001.

Gibbs, George. *Memoirs of the Administrations of Washington and John Adams: Edited from the Papers of Oliver Wolcott, Treasury Secretary*. Vol. 2. New York, 1846.

Golladay, V. Dennis. "Jefferson's 'Malignant Neighbor,' John Nicholas, Jr." *Virginia Magazine of History and Biography* 86, no. 3 (July 1978): 306–19.

Green, Constance McLaughlin. *Washington: Village and Capital, 1800–1878*. Princeton: Princeton University Press, 1962.

Greiff, Constance M. *Independence: The Creation of a National Park*. Philadelphia: University of Pennsylvania Press, 1987.

Hamilton, Alexander. *The Papers of Alexander Hamilton*. Edited by Harold C. Syrett et al. 27 vols. New York: Columbia University Press, 1961–1987.

Hamilton, John C. *Life of Alexander Hamilton: A History of the Republic of the United States As Traced in His Writings and Those of His Contemporaries*. Vol. 7. Boston: Houghton, Osgood, 1879.

Harris, C. M., ed. *Papers of William Thornton, 1781–1802*. Charlottesville: University

Press of Virginia, 1995.

Hay, Robert P. "George Washington: American Moses." *American Quarterly* 21, no. 4 (Winter 1969): 780–91.

Henriques, Peter R. "The Final Struggle Between George Washington and the Grim King: Washington's Attitude Toward Death and an Afterlife." *Virginia Magazine of History and Biography* 107, no. 1 (Winter 1999): 73–97.

———. *Realistic Visionary: A Portrait of George Washington.* Charlottesville: University of Virginia Press, 2006.

Hibbert, Christopher. *The Days of the French Revolution.* New York: Harper Perennial, 2002.

Higginbotham, Don, ed. *George Washington Reconsidered.* Charlottesville: University Press of Virginia, 2001.

Hirschfeld, Fritz. *George Washington and Slavery: A Documentary Portrayal.* Columbia: University of Missouri Press, 1997.

Hogeland, William. *The Whiskey Rebellion: George Washington, Alexander Hamilton, and the Frontier Rebels Who Challenged America's Newfound Sovereignty.* New York: Simon & Schuster, 2006.

Horn, Jonathan. *The Man Who Would Not Be Washington: Robert E. Lee's Civil War* and His Decision That Changed American History. New York: Scribner, 2015.

Hoyt, William D. "Self-Portrait: Eliza Custis, 1808." Virginia Magazine of History and Biography 53, no. 2 (April 1945): 89–100.

Jefferson, Thomas. Jefferson's Memorandum Books. Vol. 2. Edited by James A. Bear Jr. and Lucia C. Stanton. Princeton: Princeton University Press, 1997.

———. "Letters from Thomas Jefferson to Judge William Johnson." South Carolina Historical and Genealogical Magazine 1, no. 1 (January 1900): 3–12.

———. The Papers of Thomas Jefferson. Edited by Julian P. Boyd et al. 43 vols. Princeton: Princeton University Press, 1950–.

———. The Papers of Thomas Jefferson: Retirement Series. Vols. 7, 10, and 12. Edited by J. Jefferson Looney. Princeton: Princeton University Press, 2010–2015.

Kahler, Gerald E. The Long Farewell: Americans Mourn the Death of George Washington. Charlottesville: University of Virginia Press, 2008.

Kelly, Howard A., and Walter L. Burrage. American Medical Biographies. Baltimore: Norman, Remington, 1920.

Knox, J. H. Mason, Jr. "The Medical History of George Washington, His Physicians, Friends and Advisers." *Bulletin of the Institute of the History of Medicine* 1, no. 5 (June 1933): 174–91.

Koch, Adrienne, and Harry Ammon. "The Virginia and Kentucky Resolutions: An Episode in Jefferson's and Madison's Defense of Civil Liberties." *William and Mary Quarterly* 5, no. 2 (April 1948): 145–76.

Kohn, Richard H. *Eagle and Sword: The Federalists and the Creation of the Military Establishment in America, 1783–1802.* New York: Free Press, 1975.

———. "The Inside History of the Newburgh Conspiracy: America and the Coup d'Etat." *William and Mary Quarterly* 27, no. 2 (April 1970): 187–220.

———. "The Washington Administration's Decision to Crush the Whiskey Rebellion." *Journal of American History* 59, no. 3 (December 1972): 567–84.

Lane, Jason. *General and Madame de Lafayette: Partners in Liberty's Cause in the American and French Revolutions.* Lanham, MD: Taylor, 2003.

Larson, Edward J. *A Magnificent Catastrophe: The Tumultuous Election of 1800, America's First Presidential Campaign.*

New York: Free Press, 2007.

⸻. *The Return of George Washington: Uniting the States, 1783–1789*. New York: William Morrow, 2014.

Lasteyrie, Mme de. *Life of Madame de Lafayette*. Translated by Louis de Lasteyrie. London: Barthes and Lowell, 1872.

Latrobe, Benjamin Henry. "Washington Has Something Uncommonly Majestic and Commanding in His Walk, His Address, His Figure and His Countenance." In Lee, ed., *Experiencing Mount Vernon*, 56–66.

Law, Thomas. "Thomas Law's Description of the Last Illness and Death of George Washington." *Mount Vernon Ladies' Association of the Union: Annual Report, 1972* (1973): 28–31.

Lawler, Edward, Jr. "The President's House in Philadelphia: The Rediscovery of a Lost Landmark." *Pennsylvania Magazine of History and Biography* 126, no. 1 (January 2002): 5–95.

Lear, Tobias. "Letter from Tobias Lear." *Mount Vernon Ladies' Association of the Union: Annual Report, 1911* (May 1911): 52–54.

Lee, Henry, III. *Funeral Oration*. Philadelphia, 1800.

Lee, Henry, IV. *Observations on the Writings*

of *Thomas Jefferson, with Particular Reference to the Attack They Contain on the Memory of the Late Gen. Henry Lee.* 2nd ed. Philadelphia, 1839.

Lee, Jean B., ed. *Experiencing Mount Vernon: Eyewitness Accounts, 1784–1865.* Charlottesville: University of Virginia Press, 2006.

Lee, Mary Custis. "Memoir of George Washington Parke Custis." In Custis, *Recollections and Private Memoirs of Washington,* 7–72.

Lengel, Edward G. *First Entrepreneur: How George Washington Built His — and the Nation's — Prosperity.* Boston: Da Capo, 2016.

Levasseur, A. *Lafayette in America in 1824 and 1825; or, Journal of a Voyage to the United States.* Translated by John D. Godman. Vol. 1. Philadelphia: Carey and Lea, 1829.

Lodge, Henry Cabot. *Life and Letters of George Cabot.* Boston: Little, Brown, 1878.

Longmore, Paul K. *The Invention of George Washington.* Charlottesville: University of Virginia Press, 1999.

Louis-Philippe. *Diary of My Travels in America.* Translated by Stephen Becker. New

York: Delacorte, 1977.

Madison, James. *The Papers of James Madison: Congressional Series*. Vols. 16 and 17. Edited by William T. Hutchinson et al. Charlottesville: University of Virginia Press, 1989–1991.

Malone, Dumas. *Jefferson and the Ordeal of Liberty.* Boston: Little, Brown, 1962.

————. *Jefferson the President: First Term, 1801–1805.* Boston: Little, Brown, 1970.

————. *Jefferson the Virginian.* Boston: Little, Brown, 1948.

Manca, Joseph. *George Washington's Eye: Landscape, Architecture, and Design at Mount Vernon.* Baltimore: Johns Hopkins University Press, 2012.

Marshall, John. *The Papers of John Marshall.* Vol. 3. Edited by William C. Stinchcombe and Charles T. Cullen. Chapel Hill: University of North Carolina Press, 1979.

————. *The Papers of John Marshall.* Vols. 6 and 12. Edited by Charles F. Hobson. Chapel Hill: University of North Carolina Press, 1990–2006.

Marx, Rudolph. "A Medical Profile of George Washington." *American Heritage* 6, no. 5 (August 1955), online.

Maxey, David W. *A Portrait of Elizabeth Willing Powel, 1743–1830.* Philadelphia: American Philosophical Society, 2006.

McCallister, Ellen. "This Melancholy Scene." *Mount Vernon Ladies' Association of the Union: Annual Report, 1981* (1982): 13–15.

McCullough, David. *John Adams.* New York: Simon & Schuster, 2001.

McGroarty, William Buckner. "The Death of Washington." *Virginia Magazine of History and Biography* 54, no. 2 (April 1946): 152–56.

Meacham, Jon. *Thomas Jefferson: The Art of Power.* New York: Random House, 2013.

Middlekauff, Robert. *The Glorious Cause: The American Revolution, 1763–1789.* New York: Oxford University Press, 2005.

Mitchell, Stewart, ed. *New Letters of Abigail Adams, 1788–1801.* Boston: Houghton Mifflin, 1947.

Monroe, James. *The Papers of James Monroe: Selected Correspondence and Papers, 1796–1802.* Vol. 4. Edited by Daniel Preston. Santa Barbara: Greenwood, 2012.

———. *A View of the Conduct of the Executive, in the Foreign Affairs of the United States.* Philadelphia: Benjamin Franklin Bache, 1797.

Morales-Vázquez, Rubil. "Imagining Washington: Monuments and Nation Building in the Early Capital." *Washington History* 12, no. 1 (Spring/ Summer 2000): 12–29.

Morgan, Philip D. " 'To Get Quit of Negroes': George Washington and Slavery." *Journal of American Studies* 39, no. 3 (December 2005): 403–29.

Morse, Jedidiah. *The American Geography, or A View of the Present Situation of the United States.* Elizabethtown, NJ, 1789.

Myer, Donald Beekman. *Bridges and the City of Washington.* Washington, DC: United States Commission of Fine Arts, 1974.

Nelligan, Murray H. *Old Arlington: The Story of the Lee Mansion National Memorial.* Columbia University Dissertation, 1953.

Nicholls, James C. "Lady Henrietta Liston's Journal of Washington's 'Resignation,' Retirement, and Death." *Pennsylvania Magazine of History and Biography* 95, no. 4 (October 1971): 511–20.

Niemcewicz, Julian Ursyn. "Acute Observations: From Domestic Pursuits to Concern for the Nation." In Lee, ed., *Experiencing Mount Vernon,* 69–87.

———. *Under Their Vine and Fig Tree: Travels Through America in 1797–1799, 1805 with Some Further Account of Life in New Jersey.* Translated by Metchie J. E. Budka.

Elizabeth, NJ: Grassman, 1965.

Nydegger, J. A. "The Last Illness of George Washington." *Medical Record* 92 (December 29, 1917): 1128.

Osborne, John Ball. "The Removal of the Government to Washington." *Records of the Columbia Historical Society* 3 (1900): 136–60.

Paine, Thomas. *Eulogy on the Life of General Washington.* Newburyport: Edmund M. Blunt, 1800.

Paltsits, Victor Hugo, ed. *Washington's Farewell Address.* New York: New York Public Library, 1935.

Parker, A. A. *Recollections of General Lafayette on His Visit to the United States, in 1824 and 1825.* Keene, NH: Sentinel, 1879.

Parkinson, Richard. *A Tour in America, in 1798, 1799, and 1800.* 2 vols. London, 1805.

Pasley, Jeffrey L. *The First Presidential Contest: 1796 and the Founding of American Democracy.* Lawrence: University Press of Kansas, 2013.

———. *The Tyranny of the Printers: Newspaper Politics in the Early American Republic.* Charlottesville: University of Virginia Press, 2001.

Perkins, Bradford. "A Diplomat's Wife in Philadelphia: Letters of Henrietta Liston, 1796–1800." *William and Mary Quarterly* 11, no. 4 (October 1954): 592–632.

Pickering, Octavius, and Charles W. Upham. *The Life of Timothy Pickering.* Vol. 3. Boston: Little, Brown, 1873.

Pickering, Timothy. *Letters Addressed to the People of the United States of America, on the Conduct of the Past and Present Administrations of the American Government, Towards Great Britain and France.* London, 1811.

———. "Report of the Secretary of State Respecting the Depredations on the Commerce of the United States, Since the First of October, 1796." In *American State Papers: Foreign Relations* (Washington, DC: Gales and Seaton, 1832), 2:28–65.

Platt, John D. R. *The Home and Office of Benjamin Franklin Bache (America's First Modern Newsman): 322 Market Street, Philadelphia, PA.* Washington, DC: National Park Service, 1970.

Pogue, Dennis J. *Founding Spirits: George Washington and the Beginnings of the American Whiskey Industry.* Buena Vista, VA: Harbour Books, 2011.

Powell, J. H. *Bring Out Your Dead: The Great*

Plague of Yellow Fever in Philadelphia in 1793. Philadelphia: University of Pennsylvania Press, 1993.

Prussing, Eugene E. *The Estate of George Washington, Deceased.* Boston: Little, Brown, 1927.

Pryor, Elizabeth Brown. *Reading the Man: A Portrait of Robert E. Lee Through His Private Letters.* New York: Viking, 2007.

Pulliam, Ted. "Alexandria Surrenders — August 1814." *Alexandria Gazette Packet,* August 28, 2014.

Puls, Mark. *Henry Knox: Visionary General of the American Revolution.* New York: St. Martin's, 2008.

Randolph, Edmund. *A Vindication of Edmund Randolph.* Philadelphia, 1795. Repr., Richmond: Charles H. Wynne, 1855.

Rappleye, Charles. *Robert Morris: Financier of the American Revolution.* New York: Simon & Schuster, 2010.

Ribblett, David L. *Nelly Custis: Child of Mount Vernon.* Mount Vernon: Mount Vernon Ladies' Association, 1993.

Riley, Edward M. "The Independence Hall Group." *Transactions of the American Philosophical Society* 43, no. 1 (1953): 7–42.

———. "Philadelphia, the Nation's Capital,

1790–1800." *Pennsylvania History* 20, no. 4 (October 1953): 357–79.

Robbins, Karen E. *James McHenry, Forgotten Federalist.* Athens: University of Georgia Press, 2013.

Scharf, J. Thomas, and Thompson Westcott. *History of Philadelphia, 1609–1884.* Vol. 1. Philadelphia: L. H. Everts, 1884.

Scherr, Arthur. "Inventing the Patriot President: Bache's 'Aurora' and John Adams." *Pennsylvania Magazine of History and Biography* 119, no. 4 (October 1995): 369–99.

Schwartz, Barry. *George Washington: The Making of an American Symbol.* New York: Free Press, 1987.

Searson, John. *Mount Vernon, a Poem.* Philadelphia, 1800.

Sewall, Jonathan Mitchell. "An Eulogy on the Late General Washington." In *Eulogies and Orations on the Life and Death of General George Washington, First President of the United States of America* (Boston: Manning and Loring, 1800), 30–43.

Smith, James Morton. "The 'Aurora' and the Alien and Sedition Laws: The Editorship of Benjamin Franklin Bache." *Pennsylvania Magazine of History and Biography* 77, no. 1 (January 1953): 3–23.

————. "The 'Aurora' and the Alien and Sedition Laws: The Editorship of William Duane." *Pennsylvania Magazine of History and Biography* 77, no. 2 (April 1953): 123–55.

————. "Sedition in the Old Dominion: James T. Callender and the Prospect Before Us." *Journal of Southern History* 20, no. 2 (May 1954): 157–82.

Smith, Jean Edward. *John Marshall: Definer of a Nation.* New York: Henry Holt, 1996.

Smith, Margaret Bayard. *The First Forty Years of Washington Society.* Edited by Gaillard Hunt. New York: Charles Scribner's Sons, 1906.

Smith, Merritt Roe. "George Washington and the Establishment of the Harpers Ferry Armory." *Virginia Magazine of History and Biography* 81, no. 4 (October 1973): 415–36.

Smith, Page. *John Adams.* Vol. 2. New York: Doubleday, 1962.

Sparks, Jared. *The Life of George Washington.* Vol. 2. Boston: Ferdinand Andrews, 1839.

————. *The Writings of George Washington.* Vol. 11. Boston: Russell, Shattuck, and Williams, 1836.

Staples, Hamilton B. "A Day at Mount

Vernon, in 1797." In *Proceedings of the American Antiquarian Society* (Worcester: Charles Hamilton, 1879), 70–79.

Steiner, Bernard C. *The Life and Correspondence of James McHenry: Secretary of War Under Washington and Adams.* Cleveland: Burrows Brothers, 1907.

Tagg, James. *Benjamin Franklin Bache and the Philadelphia Aurora.* Philadelphia: University of Pennsylvania Press, 1991.

―――. "Benjamin Franklin Bache's Attack on George Washington." *Pennsylvania Magazine of History and Biography* 100, no. 2 (April 1976): 191–230.

Templin, Thomas E. *Henry "Light Horse Harry" Lee: A Biography.* University of Kentucky Dissertation, 1975.

Thompson, Mary V. " 'I Never See That Man Laugh to Show His Teeth': Relationships Between Whites and Blacks at George Washington's Mount Vernon." Mount Vernon Ladies' Association, 1995. Online.

―――. *"In the Hands of a Good Providence": Religion in the Life of George Washington.* Charlottesville: University of Virginia Press, 2008.

―――. " 'They Appear to Live Comfortable Together': Private Life of the Mount

Vernon Slaves." Lecture, Mount Vernon, November 3, 1994.

Tolles, Frederick B. "Unofficial Ambassador: George Logan's Mission to France, 1798." *William and Mary Quarterly* 7, no. 1 (January 1950): 1–25.

Torrence, Clayton. "Arlington and Mount Vernon, 1856." *Virginia Magazine of History and Biography* 57, no. 2 (April 1949): 140–75.

Twining, Thomas. *Travels in America 100 Years Ago: Being Notes and Reminiscences.* New York: Harper and Brothers, 1893.

Twohig, Dorothy. " 'That Species of Property': Washington's Role in the Controversy over Slavery." In Higginbotham, ed., *George Washington Reconsidered,* 114–38.

Unger, Harlow Giles. *Lafayette.* New York: John Wiley & Sons, 2002.

United States Bureau of the Census. *Population of the 33 Urban Places: 1800* (1998).

Vail, R. W. G., ed. "A Dinner at Mount Vernon: From the Unpublished Journal of Joshua Brookes (1773–1859)." *New-York Historical Society Quarterly* 31, no. 2 (April 1947): 72–86.

Wainwright, Nicholas B. "The Powel Portrait of Washington by Joseph Wright."

Pennsylvania Magazine of History and Biography 96, no. 4 (October 1972): 419–23.

Wallenborn, White McKenzie. "George Washington's Terminal Illness: A Modern Medical Analysis of the Last Illness and Death of George Washington." In *The Papers of George Washington* (November 5, 1997), online.

Wansey, Henry. *An Excursion to the United States of North America, in the Summer of 1794.* 2nd ed. Salisbury, England: J. Easton, 1798.

Washburn, Charles Grenfill. "Letters of Thomas Boylston Adams to William Smith Shaw, 1799–1823." *Proceedings of the American Antiquarian Society* 27, no. 1 (April 1917): 83–176.

Washington, George. *The Diaries of George Washington.* Edited by Donald Jackson et al. 6 vols. Charlottesville: University Press of Virginia, 1976–1979.

———. *The George Washington Financial Papers Project.* Edited by Jennifer E. Stertzer et al. Charlottesville: Washington Papers, 2017. Online.

———. *The Papers of George Washington: Colonial Series.* Edited by W. W. Abbot et al. 10 vols. Charlottesville: University Press of Virginia, 1983–1995.

————. *The Papers of George Washington: Confederation Series.* Edited by W. W. Abbot et al. 6 vols. Charlottesville: University Press of Virginia, 1992–1997.

————. *The Papers of George Washington: Presidential Series.* Edited by W. W. Abbot et al. 19 vols. Charlottesville: University of Virginia Press, 1987–.

————. *The Papers of George Washington: Retirement Series.* Edited by W. W. Abbot et al. 4 vols. Charlottesville: University Press of Virginia, 1998–1999.

————. *The Papers of George Washington: Revolutionary War Series.* Edited by W. W. Abbot et al. 26 vols. Charlottesville: University of Virginia Press, 1985–.

————. *The Writings of George Washington from the Original Manuscript Sources, 1749–1799.* Edited by John C. Fitzpatrick. 39 vols. Washington, DC: Government Printing Office, 1931–1944.

Watson, Elkanah. "Two of the Richest Days of My Life." In Lee, ed., *Experiencing Mount Vernon,* 20–25.

Wayland, John W. *The Washingtons and Their Homes.* Baltimore: Clearfield, 1944. Repr., Baltimore: Genealogical Publishing, 1998.

Weems, M. L. *A History of the Life and*

Death, Virtues and Exploits, of General George Washington, Faithfully Taken from Authentic Documents. 2nd ed. Philadelphia: John Bioren, 1800.

Weinberger, Bernhard Wolf. *An Introduction to the History of Dentistry in America: Washington's Need for Medical and Dental Care; Houdon's Life Mask Versus His Portraitures.* Vol. 2. St. Louis: C. V. Mosby, 1948.

Weld, Isaac, Jr. *Travels Through the States of North America and the Provinces of Lower Canada, During the Years 1795, 1796, and 1797.* 4th ed. London: John Stockdale, 1800.

Wells, Walter A. "Last Illness and Death of Washington." *Virginia Medical Monthly* 53, no. 16 (January 1927): 629–42.

White, Robert H. "Washington: His Last Illness and Medical Treatment." *Tennessee Historical Quarterly* 13, no. 1 (March 1954): 3–11.

Wiencek, Henry. *An Imperfect God: George Washington, His Slaves, and the Creation of America.* New York: Farrar, Straus and Giroux, 2003.

Winik, Jay. *The Great Upheaval: America and the Birth of the Modern World, 1788–1800.* New York: Harper, 2007.

Wood, Gordon S. *Empire of Liberty: A History of the Early Republic, 1789–1815.* New York: Oxford University Press, 2009.

Zagarri, Rosemarie, ed. *David Humphreys' "Life of General Washington" with George Washington's "Remarks."* Athens: University of Georgia Press, 1991.

ILLUSTRATION CREDITS

Insert

1. Courtesy of the Prints & Photographs Division, Library of Congress
2. Courtesy of the Philadelphia History Museum at the Atwater Kent, Historical Society of Pennsylvania Collection, Bridgeman Images
3. Courtesy of the Library Company of Philadelphia
4. Courtesy of Mount Vernon Ladies' Association
5. Courtesy of the Prints & Photographs Division, Library of Congress
6. Courtesy of Mount Vernon Ladies' Association
7. Courtesy of the National Portrait Gallery, Smithsonian Institution
8. Courtesy of the National Gallery of Art
9. Courtesy of the Corcoran Collection, National Gallery of Art
10. Courtesy of the National Gallery of Art

11. Courtesy of the National Gallery of Art
12. Courtesy of the New-York Historical Society
13. Courtesy of the National Gallery of Art
14. Courtesy of the Prints & Photographs Division, Library of Congress
15. Courtesy of the National Portrait Gallery, Smithsonian Institution
16. Courtesy of the Pennsylvania Academy of the Fine Arts, Philadelphia; Henry D. Gilpin Fund
17. Courtesy of the National Portrait Gallery, Smithsonian Institution
18. From the author's collection
19. Courtesy of the Prints & Photographs Division, Library of Congress
20. Courtesy of the Library Company of Philadelphia
21. Courtesy of the Prints & Photographs Division, Library of Congress
22. From the author's collection

ABOUT THE AUTHOR

Jonathan Horn is a former White House presidential speechwriter and the author of *The Man Who Would Not Be Washington,* which was a *Washington Post* bestseller. He has appeared on CNN, Fox News, MSNBC, and *PBS NewsHour* and has written for the *Washington Post,* the *New York Times'* Disunion series, *Politico Magazine,* the *Daily Beast,* the *Weekly Standard,* and other outlets. A graduate of Yale University, he lives in Bethesda, Maryland, with his wife, daughter, and dog.